Buddhist Modernities

The transformations Buddhism has been undergoing in the modern age have inspired much research over the last decade. The main focus of attention has been the phenomenon known as Buddhist modernism, which is defined as a conscious attempt to adjust Buddhist teachings and practices in conformity with the modern norms of rationality, science, or gender equality. This book advances research on Buddhist modernism by attempting to clarify the highly diverse ways in which Buddhist faith, thought, and practice have developed in the modern age, both in Buddhist heartlands in Asia and in the West. It presents a collection of case studies that, taken together, demonstrate how Buddhist traditions interact with modern phenomena such as colonialism and militarism, the market economy, global interconnectedness, the institutionalization of gender equality, and recent historical events such as de-industrialization and the socio-cultural crisis in post-Soviet Buddhist areas. This volume shows how the (re)invention of traditions constitutes an important pathway in the development of Buddhist modernities and emphasizes the pluralistic diversity of these forms in different settings.

Hanna Havnevik is professor of Religious Studies at the Department of Culture Studies and Oriental Languages, University of Oslo, Norway.

Ute Hüsken is professor of South Asia Studies at the Department of Culture Studies and Oriental Languages at Oslo University, Norway.

Mark Teeuwen is professor of Japanese Studies at the University of Oslo, Norway.

Vladimir Tikhonov is professor of Korean and East Asian Studies at the University of Oslo, Norway.

Koen Wellens is associate professor of Chinese Studies at the Department of Culture Studies and Oriental Languages at Oslo University, Norway.

Routledge Studies in Religion

For a full list of titles in this series, please visit www.routledge.com

46 Scripturalizing the Human
The Written as the Political
Edited by Vincent L. Wimbush

47 Translating Religion
What is Lost and Gained?
Edited by Michael P. Dejonge and Christiane Tietz

48 Refractions of the Scriptural
Critical Orientation as Transgression
Edited by Vincent L. Wimbush

49 Innovative Catholicism and the Human Condition
Jane Anderson

50 Religion and Ecological Crisis
The "Lynn White Thesis" at Fifty
Edited by Todd LeVasseur and Anna Peterson

51 Secular Cosmopolitanism, Hospitality, and Religious Pluralism
Andrew Fiala

52 Religion, Migration, and Mobility
The Brazilian Experience
Edited by Cristina Maria de Castro and Andrew Dawson

53 Hans Mol and the Sociology of Religion
Adam J. Powell with original essays by Hans Mol

54 Buddhist Modernities
Re-Inventing Tradition in the Globalizing Modern World
*Edited by Hanna Havnevik, Ute Hüsken, Mark Teeuwen,
Vladimir Tikhonov and Koen Wellens*

Buddhist Modernities
Re-Inventing Tradition in the
Globalizing Modern World

**Edited by Hanna Havnevik,
Ute Hüsken, Mark Teeuwen,
Vladimir Tikhonov and
Koen Wellens**

LONDON AND NEW YORK

First published 2017 by Routledge

2 Park Square, Milton Park, Abingdon, Oxfordshire OX14 4RN
52 Vanderbilt Avenue, New York, NY 10017

Routledge is an imprint of the Taylor & Francis Group, an informa business

First issued in paperback 2019

Copyright © 2017 Taylor & Francis

The right of Hanna Havnevik, Ute Hüsken, Mark Teeuwen, Vladimir
Tikhonov and Koen Wellens to be identified as the authors of the editorial
material, and of the authors for their individual chapters, has been asserted
in accordance with sections 77 and 78 of the Copyright, Designs and
Patents Act 1988.

All rights reserved. No part of this book may be reprinted or reproduced or
utilised in any form or by any electronic, mechanical, or other means, now
known or hereafter invented, including photocopying and recording, or in
any information storage or retrieval system, without permission in writing
from the publishers.

Notice:
Product or corporate names may be trademarks or registered trademarks, and
are used only for identification and explanation without intent to infringe.

Library of Congress Cataloging-in-Publication Data
Names: Havnevik, Hanna, 1957– editor.
Title: Buddhist modernities : re-inventing tradition in the globalizing
    modern world / edited by Hanna Havnevik, Ute Hüsken, Mark Teeuwen,
    Vladimir Tikhonov, and Koen Wellens.
Description: New York : Routledge, 2017. | Series: Routledge studies in
    religion ; 54 | Includes bibliographical references and index.
Identifiers: LCCN 2016047550 | ISBN 9781138687844 (hardback : alk. paper) |
    ISBN 9781315542140 (ebook)
Subjects: LCSH: Buddhist modernism—Case studies.
Classification: LCC BQ316 .B86 2017 | DDC 294.309/03—dc23
LC record available at https://lccn.loc.gov/2016047550

ISBN: 978-1-138-68784-4 (hbk)
ISBN: 978-0-367-87891-7 (pbk)

Typeset in Times New Roman
by Apex CoVantage, LLC

Contents

List of Contributors	ix
Acknowledgements	xiii

1 Buddhist Modernities: Modernism and Its Limits   1

MARK TEEUWEN

PART 1
Early Meetings with Modernity   13

2 The Scope and Limits of Secular Buddhism: Watanabe Kaikyoku and the Japanese New Buddhist "Discovery of Society"   15

JAMES MARK SHIELDS

3 Buddhism and the Capitalist Transformation of Modern Japan: Sada Kaiseki (1818–1882), Uchiyama Gudō (1874–1911), and Itō Shōshin (1876–1963)   33

FABIO RAMBELLI

4 Parsing Buddhist Modernity in Republican China: Ten Contrasting Terms   51

JUSTIN R. RITZINGER

5 Seeking the Colonizer's Favours for a Buddhist Vision: The Korean Buddhist Nationalist Paek Yongsŏng's (1864–1940) Imje Sŏn Movement   66

HWANSOO KIM

vi *Contents*

PART 2
Revivals and Neo-Traditionalist Inventions 89

6 Buddhism in Contemporary Kalmykia: "Pure" Monasticism
versus Challenges of Post-Soviet Modernity 91
VALERIYA GAZIZOVA

7 Buddhist Modernity and New-Age Spirituality in
Contemporary Mongolia 115
HANNA HAVNEVIK

8 Yumaism: A New Syncretic Religion among the
Sikkimese Limbus 133
LINDA GUSTAVSSON

PART 3
Contemporary Sangha-State Relations 149

9 Failed Secularization, New Nationalism, and Governmentality:
The Rise of Buddhism in Post-Mao China 151
KOEN WELLENS

10 Militarized Masculinity with Buddhist Characteristics:
Buddhist Chaplains and Their Role in the South Korean
Army 165
VLADIMIR TIKHONOV

11 Re-Enchantment Restricted: Popular Buddhism and
Politics in Vietnam Today 183
AIKE P. ROTS

12 "Buddhism Has Made Asia Mild": The Modernist
Construction of Buddhism as Pacifism 204
ISELIN FRYDENLUND

PART 4
Institutional Modernity 223

13 Family, Gender, and Modernity in Japanese Shin Buddhism 225
JESSICA STARLING

Contents vii

14 **Theravāda Nuns in the United States: Modernization and Traditionalization** 243
UTE HÜSKEN

15 **Some Reflections on Thích Nhất Hạnh's Monastic Code for the Twenty-First Century** 259
JENS W. BORGLAND

16 **Modernizing American Zen through Scandal: Is "The Way" Really the Way?** 282
STUART LACHS

Index 297

Contributors

Jens W. Borgland is 2016 Postdoctoral Fellow, The Robert H. N. Ho Family Foundation Program in Buddhist Studies, at the Department of Religious Studies, McMaster University. His research interests focus on Indian Buddhist monastic law and Buddhist monastic law codes, especially the Mūlasarvāstivāda vinaya tradition, as well as Buddhist manuscripts in Sanskrit and Tibetan. His current research project is titled "A First Edition, Translation and Study of the Sanskrit text of the Naiḥsargika Section of Guṇaprabha's Vinayasūtravṛttyabhidhānasvāvyākhyāna—his auto-commentary on the Vinayasūtra".

Iselin Frydenlund is senior researcher at the Peace Research Institute Oslo, PRIO and postdoctoral fellow at the Norwegian School of Theology, MF. She is a religious studies scholar, working on Theravada Buddhism, politics and violence, and has written extensively about Buddhism and the civil war in Sri Lanka. She has also been engaged in intra-Buddhist dialogue projects together with Buddhist monastic institutions in Sri Lanka, Thailand and Myanmar. She is currently working on legal regulation of religion in Myanmar and is co-editing a book on Buddhist-Muslim relations in South and Southeast Asia.

Valeriya Gazizova received her PhD in Mongol Studies from the University of Oslo, the Department of Culture Studies and Oriental Languages, in 2015. Her main field is Mongol religions and culture, particularly the history of Buddhism and folk religion in Kalmykia in modern times. Another area of her research is folk ritual healing and shamanism among the Mongolian and Turkic peoples of Russia. She is currently writing a book on religious revitalization and change and its role in identity formation in post-Soviet Kalmykia, based on her PhD dissertation *A Study of Contemporary Kalmyk Religion.*

Linda Gustavsson's Master's thesis "Religion and Identity Politics in the Indian Himalayas: Religious Change and Identity Construction among the Limboos of Sikkim" (2013) is based on fieldwork in Sikkim. She has worked as research assistant at the Department of Culture Studies and Oriental Languages, University of Oslo, and is currently applying for funding for a PhD project on religious change in Sikkim.

x *Contributors*

Hanna Havnevik is professor of Religious Studies at the Department of Culture Studies and Oriental Languages, University of Oslo. She specialises in Tibetan Buddhism, and her research interests cover popular religion, Tibetan religious history, Tibetan biographical literature and gender relations in Tibetan societies. She has conducted fieldwork in Buddhist communities in Tibet, the Himalayas and Mongolia. Havnevik is the author of *Tibetan Buddhist Nuns: History, Cultural Norms and Social Reality* (1989) and "The Life of Jetsun Lochen Rinpoche (1865–1951) as Told in Her Autobiography" (doctoral dissertation, 1999), and she is the co-editor of *Women in Tibet* (2005) and *From Bhakti to Bon* (2015).

Ute Hüsken is professor of South Asia Studies at the Department for Culture Studies and Oriental Languages at Oslo University. She was trained as an Indian and Tibetan studies scholar and as a cultural anthropologist. She was a long-time member of the "Dynamics of Ritual" collaborative research centre at the University of Heidelberg, and is a co-editor of the Oxford Ritual Studies Series (Oxford University Press). Her main publications include *Die Vorschriften für die buddhistische Nonnengemeinde im Vinaya-Piṭaka der Theravādin* (1997), *When Rituals Go Wrong. Mistakes, Failure, and the Dynamics of Ritual* (2007), and *Viṣṇu's Children: Prenatal Life-Cycle Rituals in South India* (2009).

Hwansoo Kim is an associate professor at Duke University. His research primarily concerns Korean and Japanese Buddhism from the late nineteenth to the mid-twentieth centuries in the context of colonialism, imperialism, and modernity. He is the author of *Empire of the Dharma: Korean and Japanese Buddhism, 1877–1912* (2013), and is now working on his second book, tentatively titled *A Transnational History of Colonial Korean Buddhism (1910–1945)*.

Stuart Lachs is an independent researcher living in New York City. His research interests are Chan/Zen Buddhism and the sociology of religion. He is active in the Columbia University Buddhist Studies Workshop, the Princeton University Buddhist Studies Workshop and the Oslo Buddhist Studies Forum. Apart from open-access online publications, he has published the papers "The Zen Master and Dharma Transmission: A Seductive Mythology", in *Minority Religions and Fraud: In Good Faith* (2014), and "Denial of Ritual in Zen Writing", in *The Ambivalence of Denial* (2016). He is also a Zen practitioner, practicing since 1967.

Fabio Rambelli is professor of Japanese religions and ISF endowed chair in Shinto Studies, University of California Santa Barbara. His research focuses primarily on the intellectual history of Shinto and the cultural analysis of the Buddhist tradition in Japan. He is the author of *Buddhist Materiality: A Cultural History of Objects in Japanese Buddhism* (2008) and *Zen Anarchism: The Egalitarian Dharma of Uchiyama Gudō* (2013).

Justin R. Ritzinger is assistant professor of Religious Studies at the University of Miami. His work focuses on the re-imagining of Chinese Buddhism primarily in the first half of the twentieth century. His publications include

Contributors xi

"Original Buddhism and Its Discontents: Chinese Buddhist Exchange Monks and the Search for the Pure Dharma in Ceylon", "The Awakening of Faith in Anarchism: A Forgotten Chapter in the Chinese Buddhist Encounter with Modernity", "Dependent Co-evolution: Kropotkin's Theory of Mutual Aid and Its Appropriation by Chinese Buddhists", and "If We Build It, He Will Come: Hope, Eschatology and the Modern Reinvention of Maitreya in China". He is the author of a forthcoming monograph, entitled *Anarchy in the Pure Land: Reinventing the Cult of Maitreya in Modern Chinese Buddhism*.

Aike P. Rots is associate professor at the University of Oslo. Most of his research has been concerned with religion in contemporary Japan, but he has long had an interest in Vietnam and followed developments there as well. His research interests include: relations between religion, political ideology and identity construction; processes of secularization and sacralization; theories of place-making and (sacred) space; and conceptualizations of nature and the environment. He is the author of several articles and book chapters, as well as the monograph *Shinto, Nature and Ideology in Contemporary Japan: Making Sacred Forests* (Bloomsbury, forthcoming).

James Mark Shields is associate professor of Comparative Humanities and Asian Thought at Bucknell University (Lewisburg, PA). He conducts research on modern Buddhist thought, Japanese philosophy, and comparative ethics. In addition to several dozen published articles, chapters and translations, he is author of *Critical Buddhism: Engaging with Modern Japanese Buddhist Thought* (2011) and is currently completing a book manuscript on progressive and radical Buddhism in Japan.

Jessica Starling is assistant professor of religious studies at Lewis & Clark College. Her research concerns the role of women in the Japanese True Pure Land Buddhist School (Jōdo Shinshū). Her book manuscript, *Guardians of the Buddha's Home: Domestic Religion in the Contemporary Jōdo Shinshū* (forthcoming from University of Hawai'i Press) employs ethnographic methods to examine the uses of Buddhist doctrine in personal narratives, the negotiation of gender and family roles, and the material dimensions of Buddhist worship at contemporary Japanese temples. Her articles have appeared in the *Eastern Buddhist*, the *Japanese Journal of Religious Studies, Religion Compass*, and the *Journal of Global Buddhism*.

Mark Teeuwen is professor of Japanese studies at the University of Oslo. He has written broadly on the history of Japanese religion, with a focus on Shinto and its interactions with esoteric Buddhism. Among his recent publications are *A New History of Shinto* (2010) and *A Social History of the Ise Shrines: Divine Capital* (2017), both co-authored with John Breen. He is currently co-editing a special volume on "The Formations of the Secular in Japan" for *Japan Review* (with Aike P. Rots).

xii *Contributors*

Vladimir Tikhonov (Korean name Pak Noja) is a full professor at Oslo University. His main field is the history of ideas in early modern Korea, particularly Social Darwinist influences in the formative period of Korean nationalism in the 1880s-1910s. Another major area of his research is the history of Korean Buddhism in modern times, particularly in connection with nationalism and militarist violence. Recently, he has co-edited (with Torkel Brekke) *Buddhism and Violence: Militarism and Buddhism in Modern Asia* (2012), and published *Modern Korea and its Others: Perceptions of the Neighbouring Countries and Korean Modernity* (2015).

Koen Wellens is associate professor at the Department for Culture Studies and Oriental Languages at Oslo University, where he teaches classes on religion in modern China. His disciplinary background is social anthropology. His publications include the book *Religious Revival in the Tibetan Borderlands: The Premi of Southwest China* (2010) and several articles on religious policy in the People's Republic of China, such as "Negotiable Rights? China's Ethnic Minorities and the Right to Freedom of Religion" (2009).

Acknowledgements

This book is an outcome of the international workshop on Buddhist modernities convened in December 2013 at Oslo University. We would like to offer our deep thanks to our department—Department of Culture Studies and Oriental Languages (IKOS, a department of the Faculty of Humanities)—for the financial support that made our workshop possible. A special note of thanks goes to Nguyen Nhung Lu, our enthusiastic, miraculously diligent and meticulous workshop secretary, who did everything possible and impossible to ensure that the gathering could proceed smoothly and productively. We would like also to thank all the workshop participants, both those who eventually contributed their presentations to our book and those who, for a variety of reasons, could not do so.

After the workshop, the preparations for the book publication were continuously supported by a generous grant from the Department of Culture Studies and Oriental Languages. Much of the editorial work was graciously taken over by Stig Oppedal. We are deeply grateful to him for the dedicated, scrupulous job he so brilliantly did. It was largely thanks to his efforts that our book could in the end take its present shape.

We also owe gratitude to Routledge for having agreed to publish a book with obviously somewhat limited commercial perspectives. We will always remember Andrew Weckenmann, Allie Simmons and all the other colleagues at Routledge with thankfulness for their boundless patience with us. Concomitantly, our profound thanks go to the three anonymous reviewers whose detailed and constructive criticisms and suggestions contributed to improving the texts by our contributors. As a result of our interaction with the reviewers and Routledge editors, the chapter sequence was changed as well, improving the logical structure of the book as a whole.

All in all, we hope that this book will become one more stepping-stone on the way towards deeper understanding of the diversity of ways in which Buddhism has been adjusting itself to the conditions of the modern world. We expect it to be useful for a number of students of Buddhism, both inside and outside of the academia.

May 27, 2016
The Editors

1 Buddhist Modernities
Modernism and Its Limits

Mark Teeuwen

In a 1973 article, the Indologist Heinz Bechert proposed to distinguish between three forms of Buddhism, reflecting different stages of development: canonical, traditional, and modern Buddhism.[1] Bechert was among the first Western scholars to use such terms as modern Buddhism, modernistic Buddhism, and Buddhist modernism. In doing so, he was finally giving some credence to Buddhist leaders in various corners of Asia who had begun to use similar terms already a century earlier.[2]

Bechert saw the origins of Buddhist modernism in 1870s Sri Lanka (Ceylon), when Buddhists began to challenge Christian missionaries to public debates. Buddhist modernists reacted to Christian deprecation of Buddhism as, at best, primitive idolatry, and they argued that Buddhist doctrine was both rational and consistent with Western science. They sought to make Buddhism relevant to social and political issues within the colonial context by idealizing the Buddhist kingdoms and the "democratic" Sangha of pre-colonial times. Their brand of Buddhism was in many ways a radically new form of Buddhist doctrine, designed by activists who were determined to find a place for their tradition in the modern conceptual landscape that was being imposed by the British. In that landscape, politics, science, and religion were mapped out as separate domains, each with its own rules. Modernist Buddhists felt that they either had to re-mould their tradition in such a way that it fitted this map, or end up in the dustbin of superstition, another new term that served to distinguish "good" from "bad" religion.

Bechert makes it clear that it was no easy matter to modernize Buddhism in this manner. Modernist Buddhists faced scepticism not only from the missionaries and the colonial authorities but also from "traditionalist" Buddhists. The hierarchical structures of Sri Lanka's Sangha, combined with what Bechert (1973: 92) calls "monastic landlordism", did not help in making the Buddhist establishment receptive to the political aims of modernists. Institutional realities ensured that new ideas remained marginal. At the same time, the disestablishment of Sri Lankan Buddhism, which was freed of state control but retained its economic clout, created a space for experiments, including modernism. A similar phenomenon, Bechert argues, occurred in British Burma, but not in other places. In Thailand and Cambodia, for example, the state retained control over monastic

2   Mark Teeuwen

appointments and monastic wealth, narrowing (for the time being) the space for modernist impulses to gain momentum. These and other circumstances created significant differences between Theravāda countries when it comes to the ways in which Buddhism reacted to the advent of modernity.

Bechert's pioneering studies of Buddhism and modernity presented a complicated picture that was later filled out by Gombrich and Obeyesekere (1988), Lopez (1995), and other scholars (see McMahan 2008: 7–8). An institutionalized Buddhist establishment closely linked to the pre-modern state struggled to adapt to a new political, social, and conceptual order. Modernism was only one strategy to reposition Buddhism in a modern context; traditionalism was another attractive alternative. "Traditionalism", like modernism, could mean many things, including revalorizing ritual, lineage-based authority, and ethnic (or racial) values. It should be noted that those reactions, too, were modern ways of dealing with a modern crisis. Both modernists and traditionalists created modern Buddhist discourses. In fact, many modernists, too, appealed to tradition: they often presented their reformed Buddhism as a return to canonical Buddhism and supported their views with (selective) re-readings of the canon. Modernism tended to take on a typical utopian structure, seeking to overcome a corrupt present by returning to a golden past in a bright future. The main difference between modernists and traditionalists was that the former tended to look for authority primarily in the canon, while the latter sought to uphold the institutionalized authority of the Sangha and its current leaders.

Bechert stresses differences between national settings, and these are of course highly significant. Yet many aspects of his account are immediately recognizable for those who study Buddhist modernism beyond Sri Lanka or even the Theravāda sphere. In Japan, for example, Buddhism was marginalized when a modern nation-state was created in 1868, and this inspired Buddhists to engage in diverse experiments, some modernist and others traditionalist in nature. Reformers had some success in projecting a new image of Buddhism, but that success was limited by institutional structures, which proved remarkably resilient and resisted rapid reform even in the face of radical social changes. In contrast to Sri Lanka, temples in Japan lost most of their lands. This forced many temples to close, while among those that survived, performing funerals for lay patrons remained the main source of income. A temple economy based on funerals and memorial services was not easily reconciled with modernist ideals, because it relied on notions of ritual karma transfer and ancestral protection of the household. In the late nineteenth century, Buddhists in Japan campaigned for official recognition as Japan's state religion—or, if this was seen as disadvantageous in a world dominated by Christian powers, for special treatment as Japan's prevalent and most "useful" religion (Maxey 2014: 222). This could not be done without finding a place for Buddhism within the modern framework of politics, science, and religion. As in Sri Lanka, this created a host of contradictions: between universalism and nationalism; between secular usefulness in this world and religious practice directed towards the other world; and, not least, between modernist discourse and traditional institutional structures. Such contradictions have made some scholars

Buddhist Modernities 3

of Japanese modern Buddhism "sceptical about whether Japanese Buddhism has ever modernized" (Hayashi 2006: 205).

Contradictions, however, are arguably in themselves a prominent characteristic of modernity. In the nineteenth and early twentieth centuries, modernity revolved around the nation-state and its attempts to find ways to establish state authority over, beyond, or in conjunction with religious authority. This coincided with the transition to capitalist, fossil-fuel-based production and trade, increasing globalization, social upheaval (migration, urbanization, industrialization, new forms of social organization), and, not least, new forms of identity politics involving national, ethnic, racial, class, and religious identities. On all these levels, modernity unleashed tremendous pressures towards rationalization and standardization, but also opened up for new forms of pluralism. Most nation-states adopted a model that isolated religion from politics as a private domain of subjective, optional belief.[3] This forced the institutions that were now labelled "religion" to reorganize and compete with each other for "believers", within a framework that was at odds with the institutional logic that had formed Buddhism as it existed in society. Like other religions, Buddhism increasingly found that it had to adapt itself to a pluralist "religious marketplace" at the margins of the state.

This required different kinds of modernism than those of the nineteenth century—although, as we shall see, there is also a great deal of continuity. In *The Making of Buddhist Modernism*, David L. McMahan (2008: 13) argues that meetings between modernizing Asian Buddhists and new Western followers and practitioners have created a hybrid brand of Buddhist thought, marked by "individualism, egalitarianism, liberalism, democratic ideals, and the impulse to social reform". Such Buddhist modernism has given a new boost to practices that had been pioneered already by late-nineteenth-century modernists, such as meditation and the reading of Buddhist texts by laypeople outside of monastic transmission lineages. In present-day Buddhist modernism, the earlier discourse of Buddhism's compatibility with scientific rationalism lingers, but it is increasingly overshadowed by a form of Romantic expressionism that emphasizes individual experiences of the sacred and the spiritual. Where earlier modernists sought to be modern by being scientific, philosophically up-to-date, and patriotic, many modernists of the late twentieth century and our own century have rather stressed creativity, spontaneity, mystery, and sensitivity to nature and the interconnectedness of all life (2008: 12). The former distanced themselves from "fanciful" mythology and "magical" ritual, while the latter tend to re-mythologize and actively create new rituals designed to have a psychological effect.

The emergence of new Buddhist groups beyond traditional forms of religious authority has generated counter-reactions, both from institutions that (used to) represent such authority and from lay groups that seek for more authentic, demanding forms of practice. McMahan describes such reactions as instances of re-traditionalization, and emphasizes that these are as modern as the modernist instances of de-traditionalization that triggered them. He points out that we are witnessing a "postmodern" plurality of very different forms of Buddhist modernism (2008: 244), with some stressing doctrinal rationality or scientific

4 *Mark Teeuwen*

effectiveness, and others re-enchantment and holistic spirituality. This plurality includes both do-it-yourself groups of laypeople practising chanting or mindfulness, and new groups of traditional (or traditionalist) forest-dwelling monks seeking to revive a dying tradition of strict asceticism.

The empirical data underlying McMahan's study are largely from North America, but nevertheless, he sees the Buddhist modernism that he describes as a global phenomenon, as influential in Asia as it is in the West. There is, however, an important difference that distinguishes Buddhism in its old heartlands from North American Buddhism: the existence of old, well-entrenched Buddhist institutions with a long history of relations with state and society, with cultural authority, and with considerable financial needs and interests. In a country where Buddhism is central to national identity, and where the Sangha is a part of most people's lives, the dynamics of Buddhism's modernization are by necessity different from a country where Buddhism is a new phenomenon. In places where history has tied the interests of Buddhist sects to patriarchal ancestor worship, the national army, or a landowner class, the challenges of modernity will be met in very different ways. Likewise, even in places where Buddhism lacks institutional continuity (such as Mongolia and Kalmykia), it will cater to needs that are very different from those that produce Buddhist modernism of the North American type, as described by McMahan.

It is this opening that this volume seeks to fill. It would be unfair to accuse scholars like Lopez and McMahan of universalizing a particular brand of Buddhist modernism that gained global currency in the late twentieth century. Yet modernist tendencies in global Buddhism have perhaps been overemphasized or presented as overly uniform, obscuring the plurality that McMahan calls "postmodern".[4] By bringing together short essays on the ways Buddhist actors have dealt with modernity (in whatever form and shape), this volume brings out the great variety of ways in which different "Buddhisms" have reacted to the many variants of modernity that they have faced in the recent past or are facing today. What these brief glimpses make clear is that Buddhist responses to their local brands of modernity display many similarities but are always conditioned by local circumstances.

The volume contains four sections, organized by themes rather than nationally defined Buddhist traditions. The first section, "Early Meetings with Modernity", presents case studies of various Buddhists figures who sought to come to terms with modernity in East Asian contexts (pre-war Japan, Republican China, colonial Korea), ranging from socialists to nationalists, and from lay intellectuals and monastic drop-outs to figures of authority within the Sangha. The nation-state, competition with and influence from Christianity, and the fight against "superstition" emerge as consistent themes in all these cases, although in many different configurations.

The second section, "Revivals and Neo-traditionalist Inventions", looks at two ex-communist regions where Buddhism is re-establishing itself (Kalmykia and Mongolia), and the related case of the recent invention of a modern ethnic religion in Sikkim. In all these instances, institutions must be either invented or revived after a long period of total collapse. In all cases, notions of national or ethnic identity are of central importance, but so are other aspects of modernity, such as urbanization, competition in the religious marketplace, and influence from global Buddhist modernism and New Age movements.

The third section, "Contemporary Sangha-state Relations", focuses on different instances of modern-day entanglements of Buddhism with the state. The first two essays discuss negotiations between the state and Buddhism in China and South Korea, showing that in both these countries, the state seeks to co-opt Buddhism but also makes sure to keep it at arm's length. The third essay presents the example of a modernist monk who engaged in such negotiations with the state (Vietnam), and lost. The final essay discusses the emergence of the modern notion of a pacifist Buddhism and discusses the complications of this notion in the context of armed conflict in contemporary Sri Lanka.

The fourth and final section, "Institutional Modernity", contains four case studies where modernity has put pressure on Buddhist institutions to adapt. The focus in this section is on issues of gender equality and democratic accountability. Presenting cases from Japan and the West, the essays in this section show how modern concerns collide with institutional structures from another age, at times forcing through modernist reforms, but at other times failing to find a way forward. Again, this section shows that modernism does not rule the ground alone and that even in places where Buddhism is new, traditional structures and ideas continue to define what kinds of modernization are desirable, or even possible.

Part 1: Early Meetings with Modernity

James Mark Shields focuses on a group of Japanese "middle-class intellectuals who tried to create what they called a "New Buddhism" in roughly the first decade of the twentieth century. The New Buddhism Fellowship that they founded was dominated by educators and writers, although it also included some priests. They defined their movement in opposition to what they called old Buddhism, which they saw as decadent, superstitious, pessimistic, and fanciful. In their manifesto, they pledged to "foster sound faith, knowledge, and moral principles in order to bring about fundamental improvements to society". Shields points out that this group was indebted to both Unitarian and socialist thought. While embracing a modernist vision of religion as rational, personal faith, they resisted the equally modern marginalization of religion as a private, depoliticized affair, and saw its essence in social activism—while remaining critical of the "vulgar materialism" of more radical socialists. This movement serves as a striking example of yet another attempt to give new relevance to Buddhism in a modern conceptual setting.

Fabio Rambelli introduces three Japanese Buddhist priests, two with a Shinshū background (Sada Kaiseki and Itō Shōshin) and one Sōtō Zen (Uchiyama Gudō), who reacted in striking ways to the wave of modernization that

6   *Mark Teeuwen*

transformed Japan in the years between 1868 and 1945. Within the new scheme of things, Buddhism was largely relegated to the private realm of spirituality and "the mind", but these thinkers, each in their own way, attempted to paint on a larger canvass. Sada advocated Buddhist theories of science and economy, engaging actively in very public and political campaigns. Uchiyama embraced anarchist communism and was hanged for his political activism. Itō, finally, moved from an early interest in socialism to "Mikadoism", arguing that Buddhism could foster selfless loyalty to the imperial state. Rambelli uses these three examples to point at the basic issues that Buddhists faced during this period: the question of to what degree Buddhism can continue to function as an "autonomous discourse" within a modern setting, and the question of how it should relate to the nation-state. The very different answers offered by Sada, Uchiyama, and Itō reflect the plurality of Buddhist modernity.

Justin R. Ritzinger offers a bird's-eye view of the modernization of Buddhism in Republican China (1911–1949) by proposing five sets of contrasting concepts that are particularly helpful in analyzing the terrain: establishment/upstart, religion/superstition, nationalism/internationalism, lay/monastic, and this-worldly/other-worldly. The republican period brought not only new problems but also new possibilities. Buddhism managed to reconfigure itself as a "religion", and thus as a possible ally of the state against "superstition". Drawing partly on Japanese examples, Buddhists sought to find a place for their tradition in the "project of national salvation": strengthening the state by unifying and invigorating the Chinese people. Competition with Christianity, the prototype of "religion", pushed Buddhism to adopt features of that category that had been marginal or non-existent before. Buddhism made itself available as a new lay Buddhist identity, and lay groups became so active that they encroached on monastic authority. At the same time, Chinese Buddhism remained "shaped and informed by tradition", resulting in a plurality of forms that span the spectrum from the "modern" to the "traditional".

Hwansoo Kim introduces the life and activities of a Korean monk, Paek Yongsŏng, during the Japanese occupation of his country (1910–1945). Paek's ambitions to unite Korean Buddhism under Imje Sŏn (J. Rinzai Zen, Ch. Linji Chan) were unsuccessful, and he remained an outsider to the Buddhist establishment. This has inspired present-day Korean Buddhists to "canonize" Paek as "an unbending nationalist" in opposition to the colonial government. Kim demonstrates that Paek's main struggles were against Korean rivals and the low social status of Buddhist monks in general and reveals that he at times did not hesitate to ally himself with Japanese figures of influence who appeared sympathetic to his cause. Paek's story is as illustrative of twenty-first-century identity politics within South Korean Buddhism as it is of the messy struggle for survival in colonial times.

Part 2: Revivals and Neo-Traditionalist Inventions

Valeriya Gazizova outlines the revival of Buddhism in the Autonomous Republic of Kalmykia in Russia, from 1988 until today. Kalmykia is a perfect showcase for the dilemmas sketched above. Buddhism has enjoyed active support from the republic and its president as a hallmark of original Kalmyk culture. It has not proved easy, however, to build up Buddhism again after its eradication from Kalmykia in the 1930s, and the catastrophe of the exile of Kalmyks from their lands between 1943 and 1957. Gazizova describes how a traditionalist obsession with purity (based around Gelugpa monasteries with fully ordained, celibate monks) clashes with a social reality where few aspire to, or have the means to, pursue such a career. A purist centre fades into a more flexible periphery, where non-celibate "lamas" offer services to lay villagers. Emerging Kalmykian Buddhism displays a unique yet recognizable blend of modernism and traditionalism, shaped by ethnic nationalism, political ambition, individuals' search for meaning and healing, and, not least, the demands of the bureaucracy and the market.

Mongolia shares many traits with Kalmykia, not least a history of communist repression of religion that ended in 1990. **Hanna Havnevik** follows the main trends that shaped Buddhism's restoration and revitalization in the decades since 1990. Again, we encounter a plurality of Buddhisms, ranging from attempts to re-establish an orthodox, "pure" Gelugpa monastic tradition with the help of Tibetan expertise and support from the Dalai Lama. The Gelugpa tradition represents itself as modern in the sense that it shuns "superstition" and presents itself as scientifically and philosophically sound. It is challenged, though, by other new kinds of temples and Buddhist enterprises that cater more directly to the needs of laypeople. Some emphasize meditation and social work, while others offer rituals of healing, divination, and even "summoning money." Havnevik notes the important role of women, who prefer to work as active "semi-renouncers" and run "business temples", showing little taste for the Gelugpa role of celibate nuns. As in Kalmykia, reimported Buddhism has adopted a stunning plurality of guises, dictated as much by social demand, economic dynamics, and a search for national identity as by concerns of orthodoxy.

Linda Gustavsson analyzes Yumaism (Yuma Samyo), a "new religion" in Sikkim that does not identify itself as Buddhist, but is of interest in this context because it shares many traits with "modern Buddhism" as described by McMahan in general, and because it draws on modernist tendencies in Tibetan Buddhism in particular. Yumaism was "invented" recently as the indigenous religion of the Limbu Scheduled Tribe in Sikkim. Gustavsson shows how Yumaism seeks to present itself as traditional and modern at the same time, by preserving a tenuous link with village ritual while transferring authority to new (urban) actors and redefining Yuma worship in such modernist, "Protestant" terms, as an internalized practice of spiritual self-improvement rather than a localized form of communal ritual. The development of Limbu village practice into an urban religion is in many ways similar to how village Buddhism developed into modern Buddhism throughout the region. At the same time, Gustavsson underlines the importance of the local context. In this case, the forms taken by Yumaism are determined not only by modernist and indigenist ideals, but also by state policies vis-à-vis Scheduled Tribes.

8 *Mark Teeuwen*

Part 3: Contemporary Sangha-State Relations

Koen Wellens looks at recent developments in the relation of Buddhism with the state in China. Here, forced secularization (culminating in the Cultural Revolution) gave way to a policy of tolerating religion in 1978. Since the 1980s, however, the Communist Party has been accommodating to a reality that belies the official ideology, which assumes that science and prosperity will eradicate people's need for religion. Rather than passively wait for religion to fade away, the party has made ambiguous but real approaches to Buddhism, which it sees as a possible ally in the battle against both alleged "evil" sects (e.g. Falungong) and foreign religions (Christianity and Islam). If there has to be religion in China's future, the party prefers "harmonious" Buddhism over other competitors. As in Kalmykia and Mongolia, Buddhism's resurgence in China has been aided by a perception of the religion as a part of the nation's cultural heritage, and while Buddhism is far from becoming a "state religion", it enjoys both goodwill and certain privileges from the authorities.

Vladimir Tikhonov sheds light on the "mutually beneficial symbiosis" that exists between selected religions, including one Buddhist sect, and the state in South Korea, by way of the military. These religions are granted the opportunity to provide chaplains to the army. In a country with a compulsory two- to three-year military service and a competitive religious marketplace, the army is an important site of proselytization. In return, chaplains support the values of the army and concentrate on helping recruits to adapt to the discipline of barracks life. Tikhonov has interviewed acting and retired Buddhist chaplains to find out how they see the role of Buddhism in a military context. While this setting is particularly poignant, Tikhonov points out that there is nothing unique to the use of practices like mindfulness meditation to discipline members of corporate organizations. In large organizations and corporations, Buddhists have found a new market for traditional methods of "overcoming the self". This, Tikhonov argues, constitutes a central aspect of the modern re-invention of Buddhism.

Aike P. Rots investigates the ambiguous relationship between Buddhism and the state in contemporary Vietnam. Vietnam is described both as a society where religion is booming, or at least becoming more visible, and as a country that actively represses religion, in spite of its public face as a state with religious freedom. Rots presents two case studies that show how both of these characterizations can be true at the same time. He takes us first to the booming (and bustling) port city of Da Nang, where politicians not only allow a broad range of religious institutions and practices to flourish, but actively seek to gain legitimacy from participating in local religious life. Then he analyzes the modernist Buddhist movement of Thích Nhất Hạnh and its problematic relations with the Vietnamese state. First celebrated as a star of Vietnamese "Zen", Hạnh and his movement were harassed out of the country after 2008; Rots argues that the reason was his public questioning of the official rhetoric of religious freedom in Vietnam.

Iselin Frydenlund investigates the rise of the idea that Buddhism is a pacifist religion that rejects war as a matter of principle. While *ahiṃsa* (no-harm) is an important theme found in classical Buddhist treatises and the Jātakas, Frydenlund points out that injunctions against violence apply to a particular domain of salvific practice, without condemning violence in the domain of the king and the warrior caste. The development from *ahiṃsa* to pacifism was a central aspect of the modernization of Buddhism that emerged in a complicated dialogue between Western constructions of Buddhism (both sceptical and romantic) and Buddhist reformers in Sri Lanka, notably the father of Buddhist modernism, Dharmapala. Buddhist peacefulness served to contrast tolerant Buddhism with belligerent Christianity and Islam. At the same time, space remained for a Buddhist just-war ideology that was held forth by many Buddhists in Sri Lanka in the fight against "Tamil terrorism". After the Second World War, Gandhi, the Dalai Lama, and Japanese Buddhist groups like Soka Gakkai have contributed further to solidifying the notion of a pacifist Buddhism. Today, pacifism functions as a powerful trademark of Buddhism that gives the religion an edge in a global religious market.

Part 4: Institutional Modernity

Jessica Starling draws our attention to recent debates about the position of "temple wives" within Japanese Shinshū Buddhism. This sect has a long tradition of a married priesthood, with priests and their wives running temples together and passing the temple on to their son or adopted son-in-law. In the 1980s, temple wives campaigned to improve their status from that of domestic helpers to more equal partners in the running of the temple. In their campaigns, they drew on modernist ideas that were not always easily combined, notably the notion of faith as individual, privatized faith, which tends to lead to an emphasis on passive conformity, and the ideal of faith-based social activism, which focuses on changing reality rather than the mind. Although the campaign had some success in changing sect bylaws, Starling shows that the social reality of temple life resists radical change. Her chapter serves as a reminder that modernist ideas, even if they win broad acceptance, often come into conflict with local personal relationships premised on obligation and complementary gender roles.

Ute Hüsken discusses the revival of the monastic order of nuns in the Theravāda tradition, centuries after the transmission of the ordination was broken. Without fully ordained nuns, it is impossible to ordain new nuns if one follows the letter of the law, and opposition to nuns' ordinations remains vigorous in some circles. Yet new ways to deal with this problem have been pioneered in many places, from Sri Lanka and Thailand to the United States. Hüsken argues that critics who see the revival of nuns' ordinations as a Western imposition fail to recognize the active role of Asian monks and nuns of various kinds, both in Asia and in the United States. Is the resurrection of such an order at this point in time a "modernist" phenomenon, reflecting modern concerns with gender equality? While the answer to this question appears obvious, Hüsken points out that this modernization is very concerned to appear as a return to tradition, first and foremost by attaching supreme importance to the classical Vinaya and stressing that the revival is a

10   *Mark Teeuwen*

restoration rather than an innovation. In this way, Hüsken reminds us that modernism and traditionalism overlap and that one can take the guise of the other.

Jens W. Borgland zooms in on a concrete example of modernization in the form of a new *Prātimokṣa* law code, introduced by Thích Nhất Hạnh (who also features in Rots's chapter) for use in his monasteries in France and the United States. In the light of the canonical nature of the *Prātimokṣa*, which has been regarded as the unchangeable words of the Buddha, this is a drastic step, and the fact that this has now proved possible is in itself a testimony to modernity's power to challenge traditional authority. On the other hand, Borgland argues that Hạnh's revised *Prātimokṣa* is not as radical a break with the past as it may seem. There is a long tradition of "updating" or circumventing monastic law without changing the *Prātimokṣa* itself, by way of local ordinances and the use of "legalizers"—laypeople who do for monastics what monastics are banned from doing themselves. Hạnh's revised *Prātimokṣa* might be regarded as a particularly thorough and content-wise not very radical local ordinance that is unconventional only in its form.

Stuart Lachs analyzes how modern American Zen passed from a first phase of "partial modernization" to a subsequent phase of adaptation to modern Western values. Lachs uses the career of Joshu Sasaki *rōshi* and the organization he founded as a case study. Sasaki's Zen was modernist in many ways; it concentrated on the "classical" modernist pursuit of teaching meditation to lay practitioners of both sexes. In other ways, however, Sasaki did not adhere to modern Western values such as democracy, openness, accountability, and gender equality. Lachs described how the internal logic of institutionalized Zen opened up for various kinds of abuse (notably sexual abuse against female practitioners). Eventually, however, the scandal broke, leading to disillusionment, decline, self-reflection, and eventually a reorganization that has brought many Zen institutions more in line with the rest of society. This case shows that "modernity" is a moving target, and that yesterday's modernism can easily become today's traditionalism.

Notes

1. Bechert first launched the term Buddhist modernism in his trilogy *Buddhismus, Staat, und Gesellschaft in den Ländern des Theravāda-Buddhismus* (1966–1973).
2. In my own area of specialization, Japan, terms like *gendai bukkyō* and *kindai bukkyō* (lit. "contemporary Buddhism" and "modern Buddhism") have been used from the 1910s onwards; as Shields's essay in this volume shows, "new Buddhism" goes back even further.
3. There are, of course, many exceptions, including the communist countries that feature in this volume, which (at times) sought to destroy religion as a competitor of state authority. As we shall see, however, even these regimes have gravitated towards variants of the model here described.
4. Others, notably Peter L. Berger (2014), would regard this very plurality as a hallmark of modernity rather than as a sign that modernity is being superseded.

References

Bechert, Heinz. 1966–1973. *Buddhismus, Staat, und Gesellschaft in den Ländern des Theravāda-Buddhismus*. 3 vols. Frankfurt: Alfred Metzner Verlag.

───. 1973. "Sangha, State, Society, 'Nation': Persistence of Traditions in 'Post-Traditional' Buddhist Societies." *Daedalus* 102 (1): 85–95.

Berger, Peter L. 2014. *The Many Altars of Modernity: Toward a Paradigm for Religion in a Pluralist Age*. Boston: De Gruyter.

Gombrich, Richard, and Gananath Obeyesekere. 1988. *Buddhism Transformed: Religious Change in Sri Lanka*. Princeton, NJ: Princeton University Press.

Hayashi, Makoto. 2006. "Religion in the Modern Period." In *Nanzan Guide to Japanese Religions*, edited by Paul L. Swanson and Clark Chilson, 202–219. Honolulu: University of Hawai'i Press.

Lopez, Donald S., Jr., ed. 1995. *Curators of the Buddha: The Study of Buddhism under Colonialism*. Chicago: University of Chicago Press.

Maxey, Trent E. 2014. *The "Greatest Problem": Religion and State Formation in Meiji Japan*. Cambridge, MA: Harvard University Asia Center.

McMahan, David L. 2008. *The Making of Buddhist Modernism*. Oxford: Oxford University Press.

Part 1

Early Meetings with Modernity

2 The Scope and Limits of Secular Buddhism

Watanabe Kaikyoku and the Japanese New Buddhist "Discovery of Society"

James Mark Shields

Introduction: Rethinking Buddhist "Modernism"

The term *modernism* is notoriously difficult to pin down. In attempting to do so, one often gets caught in a frustrating tautology, such as "anything relating to modern thought, culture, or practice"—which, of course, begs the question as to the definition of the terms *modern* and *modernity*. As an adjective used to describe one's own particular location in time, usually vis-à-vis a perceived break with the immediate past, cognates of the term "modern" have existed in European languages since the early Renaissance, when critics referred to the work of Giotto di Bondone (1267–1337) as being "modern" due to his revolutionary use of three-dimensional space and incipient "realism". It is of note that the Japanese term closest to "modern"—*kindai*—appears at roughly the same time, in the work of Kamo no Chōmei (1153–1216), who wrote of the "modern" poetry of his day (Kamo 1998: 70–79). Although the precise nuances of the term in its early use will remain obscure, it represents, at the very least, a minimal sense of historical consciousness, if not an incipient concept of "progress"—that is, an understanding that human beings can bring about significant cultural changes, through their own agency as individuals and communities, and that these changes can be both beneficial and unsettling, often at one and the same time.[1] How such a worldview relates (or conflicts) with more "traditional" understandings of knowledge, power, and authority is, of course, the primary story of the past few centuries, and it is indeed at least as much "story" as "history".

In the West, a number of scholarly works of the past few decades have sought to elucidate "Buddhist modernism" as a general category of thought and practice. Of these, Heinz Bechert (*Buddhismus, Statt und Gesellschaft*, 1966–1968) and Donald Lopez (*Prisoners of Shangri-La*, 1998; *A Modern Buddhist Bible*, 2002) have done the most to define Buddhist modernism. In his foreword to Paul Carus's *Gospel of Buddhism* (1894), a *locus classicus* of Buddhist modernism, Lopez provides a brief summary of the essential features of what he calls "modern Buddhism", which has become a standard for other scholars in the field:

> Modern Buddhism seeks to distance itself from those forms of Buddhism that immediately precede it and even those that are contemporary with it. Its proponents viewed ancient Buddhism, especially the enlightenment of the

16 James Mark Shields

Buddha 2,500 years ago, as the most authentic moment in the long history of Buddhism. It is also the form of Buddhism, they would argue, that is most compatible with the ideals of the European Enlightenment, ideals such as reason, empiricism, science, universalism, individualism, tolerance, freedom, and the rejection of religious orthodoxy. It stresses equality over hierarchy, the universal over the local, and often exalts the individual over the community.

(Lopez 2004: 8)

Lopez's understanding of modern Buddhism clearly resonates in the writings and activism of the figures discussed in this chapter—though it is, in fact, more reflective of the "early" period of Japanese Buddhist modernism, characterized by the figures of the so-called Buddhist Enlightenment, then of the "middle" and "late" periods as represented by more "progressive" movements such as the New Buddhist Fellowship and Youth League for Revitalizing Buddhism. This is especially true of Lopez's final feature: the exaltation of the individual over the community. Here Juliane Schober's more recent remarks are pertinent:

Many theorists writing on modernity and civil society presume that the western model of religion in modern, civil society applies equally to non-western cultures and their religious traditions. Yet modernizing reforms of religion do not inevitably engender individualism, a Protestant ethic, the development of capitalism, and the relegation of religion to the private sphere.

(Schober 2011: 148)

In fact, religious modernism in Asia (and perhaps elsewhere) often leads to what Bruce Lincoln would call a "maximalist" understanding of culture, in which religion is "the central domain of culture, [and] deeply involved in ethical and aesthetic practices constitutive of the community", as opposed to the "minimalist" approach, whereby religion is restricted, in Weberian fashion, "to the private sphere and metaphysical concerns" (Lincoln 2006: 59; see also Schober 2011: 72).[2] Furthermore, this is true of both "reactionary" and "progressive" modernisms. In general, we might say that while Lopez's summary applies to some extent to *all* forms of Buddhist modernism, it remains heavily inflected with assumptions that are more specifically germane to Buddhist modernism constructed by *Western* Buddhists—and we must thus be cautious in applying it to so-called indigenous forms of Buddhist modernism (while acknowledging that all forms of Buddhist modernism are to some extent "hybrid"), such as those arising out of the Southeast Asian and Japanese (and more recently, Chinese, Vietnamese, and Tibetan) contexts.

Heinz Bechert, who seems to have established the concept of Buddhist modernism in his *Buddhismus, Staat und Gesellschaft* (1966–1968), points to the following key features:

1) a demythologization of doctrine and cosmology;
2) a de-emphasis on ritual, and a focus on meditation;

Scope and Limits of Secular Buddhism 17

3) a commitment to reason and science;
4) a commitment to social reform and democracy;
5) a connection to nationalist and anti-colonialist movements.

(Bechert 1966–1968: 1, 255)

While broadly consistent with Lopez's themes, the emphasis on social reform is one that, in the context of Japan, would eventually connect some forms to Buddhist modernism to progressive and radical social movements, effectively creating a division between Buddhist modernists committed to large-scale social and political reform and those more inclined towards individual renewal by way of meditation, spiritual renewal, and "culture". In addition, while Bechert's acknowledgment of the link between some forms of Buddhist modernism and nationalist independence movements is directed primarily towards the case of Ceylon/Sri Lanka, it also has resonance with the situation of late Meiji Japan, during which a great many intellectuals—both secular and religious, "progressive" and "reactionary"—felt encroaching Western colonialism as a palpable, existential threat. Finally, while most of the modernists and progressives in the present study share a commitment to "reason and science", tensions arise when it comes to the issue of "materialism"— both philosophical and historical/dialectical. These tensions, which appear most openly in the work of Buddhist socialists, are explored below.[3]

The Birth of "New Buddhism"

Founded in 1899, the New Buddhist Fellowship (hereafter NBF) consisted of roughly a dozen young scholars and activists—we might alternatively call them *enthusiasts*—a number of whom had studied under late-Meiji Buddhist Enlightenment figures Murakami Senshō (1851–1929) and Inoue Enryō (1858–1919).[4] Principal among them were three former members of the Furukawa Rosen's (1871–1899) recently defunct Keiikai or Warp and Woof Society: Sakaino Kōyō (1871–1933), Sugimura Sojinkan (1872–1945), and Watanabe Kaikyoku.[5] Other founding members were Takashima Beihō (1875–1949), Tanaka Jiroku (1869–?), Andō Hiroshi (1869–1942), and Katō Genchi (1873–1965).[6] Born with the dawn of the new century, in the wake of the first Sino-Japanese War of 1894–1895 and amidst the conflux of new social forces and contradictions brought on by industrial capitalism,[7] and continuing for sixteen years amidst the first sparks of the ultranationalist and militarist ideologies that would explode in the early Shōwa period, the New Buddhists were representative of Japanese Buddhist modernism in what can be called an "intermediary" period. In several important respects, they are the first true Buddhist "modernists" in Japan, if not the world.

Like the short-lived Warp and Woof Society and the like-minded progressive Buddhists of the 1890s, the New Buddhists were harshly critical of the "old Buddhism", which they believed had been complicit in the conservative forces that had thus far inhibited "progress" in Japan—particularly in the areas of education, politics, and ethics. Like many of their more conservative peers, they also promoted abstinence, non-smoking, and an end to prostitution. While

18   *James Mark Shields*

the fellowship was overtly lay-oriented, several of the New Buddhists had been ordained as Buddhist priests, and most had some sort of Buddhist educational background—especially via the Nishi Honganji branch of the Shin (True Pure Land) sect, one of the largest and most powerful institutions in Japanese Buddhism. Indeed, the prototypical New Buddhist was born into a Shin sect temple family, educated at the sect's Futsū Kyōkō/Bungakuryō, and spent time as a student and/or instructor at Inoue Enryō's Tetsugakkan. While their occupations varied, many worked as journalists, educators, or writers. In short, while they hardly represented an elite stratum of society, they can certainly be characterized as a movement of middle-class intellectuals.

In July 1900, a magazine—initially more of a "bulletin"—called *New Buddhism* (*Shin Bukkyō*) was launched as the fledgling movement's mouthpiece. The first edition begins with the group's "manifesto". By turns inflammatory, sentimental, and self-consciously poetic—showing, in short, all the qualities and faults of youthful idealism—this brief piece opens with an apocalyptic call to arms: "Humanity," it begins (SB 1 (1) [July 1900]: 3), "is in a state of decline. Society has been corrupted to its roots, and the rushing water of a great springtide threatens to drown us all, as at the time of the Great Flood. Moreover, religions, which are supposed to give light to darkness and provide solace, have been losing strength year by year." In short, given the benighted state of Japanese society at the turn of the twentieth century, the New Buddhists were compelled to establish their organization. This is quickly followed by a scathing attack on "old Buddhism" (*kyū bukkyō*) as being little more than a rotting corpse, its adherents weeping "tears of joy" over their palatial buildings and fine brocades:

> These people know how to worship wooden statues and sutras, how to stand before monks at a temple, and how to listen to the sermons. Earnestly holding to the embedded prejudices of their respective sect, they are mutually well versed in worthless matters. They can skilfully mouth the chants, and know how to take the prayer beads and sutras in their hands. Have they not already abandoned the life of faith? If these things make up what is called "Buddhism", then it is an "old Buddhism" that is on the verge of death.
>
> (SB 1 (1) [July 1900]: 3)

Here the New Buddhists are clearly adopting the discourse of Buddhist "decadence" (*daraku*) that arose with neo-Confucians of the Edo period and was eventually adopted by secularists and Shinto nativists alike in the early years of Meiji. This discourse also played a significant role in the mid-Meiji Buddhist Enlightenment—particularly the writings of Inoue Enryō and Nakanishi Ushirō. Along with Buddhism, however, traditional forms of Shinto reverence and folk worship also come under attack in the New Buddhist manifesto: prayers and petitions for health, wealth, and recovery from illness, whether directed to Inari, Fudō Myōō, the Dragon King, or one of the Seven Gods of Fortune (*shichi fukujin*), are criticized as being "superstitious". Though Enryō's "magical Buddhism" appears to be the primary locus of critique, other terms used to describe

Scope and Limits of Secular Buddhism 19

the "old Buddhism" are "pessimistic" (*enseiteki*), for its denial of this-worldly happiness, and "imaginary" (*kūsōteki*), for its elaborate cosmology. In short (SB 1 (1) [July 1900]: 3), "the new Buddhism that we advocate will include none of these attitudes or practices. New Buddhists are naturally opposed to old Buddhists—or perhaps, we might rather say that we pray that they will be saved from their illusions."

At the end of the manifesto, we find the New Buddhist Fellowship's *Statement of General Principles* (*kōryō*), summarized in the following six points:

1. We regard a sound Buddhist faith as our fundamental principle.
2. We will work hard to foster sound faith, knowledge, and moral principles in order to bring about fundamental improvements to society.
3. We advocate the free investigation of Buddhism in addition to other religions.
4. We resolve to destroy superstition.
5. We do not accept the necessity of preserving traditional religious institutions and rituals.
6. We believe the government should refrain from favouring religious groups or interfering in religious matters.

(SB 1 (1) [July 1900]: 6)

As the final point above shows, unlike some other reformers of the day, the New Buddhists were not looking for government support of Buddhism—in fact, they were highly critical of *any* government involvement in religious matters.[8] This was based on their analysis of Buddhism during the late Edo and early Meiji periods, which, in their estimation, had become corrupted by state support. At a methodological level, this rejection of state-supported religion allows the New Buddhists to engage with political issues while avoiding the trend towards what Carol Glück has called the Meiji "denaturing of politics" vis-à-vis the rhetoric of harmony. Indeed, although they did support a pan-sectarian Buddhism, the New Buddhists were, from the beginning, palpably uninterested in "harmony", as their pointed and frequently aggressive style indicates.[9]

New Buddhism covered a wide range of issues, including research on Buddhist origins, historical studies of religion, original poems, translations of articles on Western religions, and discussions of the Russo-Japanese War and the problem of religious missionaries in China and Korea. Despite the increasing dangers posed by increasing government censorship, the New Buddhists engaged in mild forms of social activism, by protesting, for example, the government's actions during the Tetsugakkan Affair of 1902 and the publication of the Ministry of Education's Order Number One (*kunrei ichigō*) in 1906.[10] They also expressed criticism of neo-Confucianism, *bushidō*, the Boshin Imperial Rescript (*Boshin shōsho*) of 1908,[11] as well as the state-sponsored Hōtoku and National Morality (*kokumin dōtoku*) movements.[12] Some members openly expressed a feeling of "war weariness" at the time of the Russo-Japanese War—though none went so far as to publicly oppose the war. As a result of these activities, their magazine was forcibly shut down several times during its brief existence.[13]

20   *James Mark Shields*

In addition to the journal, the New Buddhists held regular public meetings (*kōkai enzetsukai*)—no less than 173 between May 1891 and June 1915—during which various speakers declaimed to a wide range of topics.[14] As might be expected, their forthright critique of "old"—that is, institutional—Buddhism led to denunciation from the late-Meiji Buddhist establishment and forced the group to work semi-secretly (Yoshida [1959] 1992: 369). But as Davis (1992: 168) notes, while some New Buddhists "tried to move towards the workers, like other 'bourgeois intellectuals', their sympathies usually stopped short of direct political action". This point is reiterated by Takahashi (2011: 74–75), who concludes: "Although the New Buddhists were neither 'antigovernment' nor 'antinationalist', their actions confirm a certain 'rebellious spirit' [*hankotsu seishin*] underlying their relations to authority." In what follows, I will examine some general features of the thought of New Buddhists, as expressed in the pages of *New Buddhism*, before turning to the life and work of Watanabe Kaikyoku. In addition to providing some background on his activities, I will focus especially on his arguments and ideas regarding "socially active Buddhism" (*shakaiteki bukkyō*).

Repayment of Debt as Social Obligation/Activism

It bears noting here that the "freedom" espoused by the New Buddhists, in terms of being able to express their own unvarnished thoughts on a wide range of issues, was taken quite seriously. As a result, there is no single "New Buddhist" viewpoint on the various issues, whether religious or secular, discussed in the pages of the journal. And yet, one of the principal foundations of New Buddhist thought—shared to some extent with the so-called Meiji Buddhist Enlightenment[15]—was a reinterpretation of the traditional East Asian Buddhist understanding of compassion as a form of "repaying debt" (*hōon*). A brief consideration of this topic will help to clarify the NBF interpretation of "society"—and by extension, modernity—in terms of classical East Asian/Buddhist conceptions.

In a chapter on the relationship between this way of thinking about debt and secular logic, Ikeda Eishun has traced the genealogy of *hōon shisō*, noting the particular problems of this doctrine when used in a Buddhist context. Ikeda argues that the Meiji Buddhist interpretation of *hōon*, which is directed towards the people, is based on a foundation borrowed from secular thought. In particular, the New Buddhists understood that, by merging the doctrine of the Four Debts (*shion*) with other teachings such as the Ten Good (Lay) Precepts (*jūzenkai*), the Precept to Assist Sentient Beings (*nyōeki ujōkai*), and the Three Cumulative Pure Precepts (*sanju jōkai*), they could raise its logical value and provide a certain measure of intentionality.[16]

In making the case that Buddhists—and Japanese people more generally—owed a debt of gratitude to "all sentient beings" (*shuyō-on*), somewhat loosely interpreted to mean *society*, the New Buddhists attempted to combine traditional Buddhist teachings and Confucian concepts of debt and gratitude with the emerging constitutional language of the day (see Gluck 1985: 233–242). In turn, it was the role of the sovereign or state to preserve the political order (*kengi*). It is important to note that the direction of "repayment of debt" here is specifically to "society" and not to "the nation" or "state"—as was frequently suggested by Meiji Buddhist reformers and restorationists.[17] As such, they distinguished themselves from conservative factions, both religious and political, that emphasized the necessity of returning gratitude via complete submission to the emperor, state, or "national body" (*kokutai*), but also (albeit more subtly) from more moderate liberals who pushed for a form of modern Buddhism that could offer "practical benefits" to the nation/state. Thus, following Winston Davis (1992: 179), the New Buddhists were at the forefront of what may be called "the Buddhist discovery of society". While this is true of the movement as a whole, the figure who arguably best represents the NBF turn towards society is the Jōdo priest and scholar Watanabe Kaikyoku.

Watanabe Kaikyoku: Buddhist Social Work and Mutual Aid

Watanabe Kaikyoku was born in Tawaramachi, in the Asakusa area of Tokyo, in January 1872, just as the *Haibutsu kishaku* persecution of Buddhism was coming to an end.[18] In 1885, at the age of thirteen, he entered the priesthood at the Jōdo temple Genkakuji in Koishikawa, under the tutelage of Hashiyama Kaitei. In 1887, at the age of fifteen, Watanabe became a student in the Jōdo (Pure Land) sect head temple school in Tokyo. Two years later, he began a six-year course of specialized study, for which his 1895 graduation thesis garnered top honours among all Jōdo sect schools in the Kantō region. At this time, at the age of twenty-three, he also became editor-in-chief of the sect's journal *Jōdo kyōhō*, which would go on to become, along with *Bukkyō*, an important mouthpiece for Buddhist reform in the late Meiji and Taishō periods. In 1898, Watanabe took up a position as the sixteenth chief priest of Saikōji temple in Tokyo. In 1899, along with Sakaino Kōyō, Takashima Beihō, and a few other like-minded young Buddhist activists and scholars, he established the New Buddhist Fellowship.

The formative event in Watanabe's early life was no doubt his appointment as the Jōdo sect's first-ever foreign exchange student. Though initially appointed to this post soon after his graduation in 1896, it was four more years before Watanabe would finally travel to Germany to study Buddhism (including Sanskrit and Pali) and comparative religions under the direction of Swiss Indologist Ernst Leumann (1859–1931) at Straßburg University. He would remain in Germany for the next ten years. It was during his time in Germany that Watanabe became convinced that the bearer of social change must be the religious believer—and, by extension, faith itself. At the same time, Watanabe continued to wrestle with the question of how, precisely, Buddhists might best involve themselves in social work (Kikuchi 2007: 5). While these issues were central to the work of other New Buddhists, Watanabe's insights are distinctive because, though a founding member of the fellowship, he was, like D. T. Suzuki, a New Buddhist *in absentia*—or perhaps, a "foreign correspondent".

Before leaving for Europe in 1900, Watanabe had already produced seven articles: three dealt with Tibetan Buddhism, and the other four with Brahmanism and

22 James Mark Shields

the relation between Buddhism and Indian religions (Kikuchi 2007: 5). Beginning in 1900, he began to contribute articles and opinion pieces to the newly founded *New Buddhism*. Upon his return to Japan, he continued his studies, even as his commitment to social activism deepened. Throughout his entire life, Watanabe held to his conviction—which seems to have developed during his decade in Germany—that all his social commitments and activities needed to be grounded in the doctrines of Mahāyāna Buddhism. In contrast to quite a few priests and scholars alike, he not only saw no contradiction between undertaking serious scholarship and engaging in social activism, but was convinced that the two fields were interdependent. Thus, his lifelong commitment to Buddhist studies can be best understood as a necessary foundation for his Buddhist social activism. His *Nichi sōkan rōzakan* (Daily Thoughts and Impressions), published in *Jōdo kyōhō* in 1901, impresses upon Japanese Buddhists the importance of scholarship and shows that in Germany it was natural for religionists to engage in social activism.

Upon his return to Japan in 1910, Watanabe reclaimed his old positions as editor-in-chief of *Jōdo kyōhō* and chief priest of Saikōji and took up additional positions as occasional lecturer at Shūkyō (now Taishō) and Tōyō universities. He also soon began to put his thoughts developed in Europe on Buddhist social activism into practice. In 1911, he established the Jōdoshū Rōdō Kyōsaikai (Jōdo Sect Labour and Mutual Aid Society) in Hiranomachi, Fukugawa-ku, Tokyo, and later in the same year became principal of Shibanaka School, a position he would retain until his death.[19] In 1919, at the age of forty-seven, Watanabe became director of the Mahāyāna Academy (Mahayana Gakuen), which had been established that same year by one of his former pupils, Hasegawa Ryōshin (1890–1966). He died in 1933, at the age of sixty-one.[20]

In a piece entitled "The Essence of Philanthropic Work", published in the December 1911 edition of *New Buddhism*, Watanabe provides some hints towards his social understanding of Buddhist practice. He begins by noting that "now is no longer the age for religions of heaven or the Pure Land. Today, our religion must be of the soil, *geta* [wooden clogs], and cold rice" (SB 12 (12) [December 1911]: 1387). From this plea for a religion focused on earthly matters, Watanabe quickly turns to a critique of the effects of industrial "progress" on humanity, particularly on the many who become "scraps" (*kuzu*) left behind by the capitalist-industrial system. If we cannot resolve the question of how to make use of the scraps, he argues, society itself is in danger (we might read this as a "warning" about the danger of socialist revolution). While charitable work might seem like a valid response to the problem, Watanabe argues that the contemporary attitude in Japan towards philanthropy, as well as the way it is generally carried out, is mistaken and wrong-headed. The problem is that many people in Japan take a "nouveau riche" attitude towards the poor and believe that they can solve the problem by simply throwing money their way. Watanabe argues, however, that this overly "materialistic" approach is condescending and wasteful and simply creates a separation between the giver and receiver. He contrasts this way of practising charity with the traditional Indian Buddhist conception of almsgiving as a form of reverence, and concludes that the future spirit of charity in Japan must rest on a

Scope and Limits of Secular Buddhism 23

"spirit of mutual love for humanity" (*jinrui sōai no seishin*) as well as the notion of "repaying debts" (*hōon shisō*) (SB 12 (12) [December 1911]: 1387). Together, these will provide a sense of dignity to the receiver as well as the giver.

Though he does not go into doctrinal specifics, here as elsewhere Watanabe makes reference to the fundamental Mahāyāna Buddhist concepts of altruism, universal Buddhahood, and the bodhisattvic spirit. He concludes this piece with an injunction for solid and penetrating research into the "symptoms" of social problems like poverty, suggesting labour insurance and retirement savings as possible ways to head off such problems before they manifest themselves. Here, too, he is employing traditional Buddhist ideas of investigating the causes of suffering in order to eliminate them, although his logic is social and economic rather than cognitive or psychological. On the whole, while the tone of this piece is not particularly radical, by continually questioning the value of charity, advocating further analysis into the causes and roots of poverty, and positing the need for a new way of thinking about these matters, Watanabe hints at the possibility that fundamental change may be required to fix a system that allows for so many "scraps" to fall under the banquet table of progress. While vague, his final words bear out this potentially radical edge (SB 12 (12) [December 1911]: 1389): "Religion today must make strenuous efforts and do whatever it takes to establish a sound basis for actual society."

In short, Watanabe's model of Buddhist social activism is based on two general principles (Kikuchi 2007: 7): first, a modernistic interpretation of the traditional Buddhist concept of one's "debt to all sentient beings" (*shujūon*) by which the "act of repaying kindness" (*hōongyō*) is understood to be nothing other than social activism; and second, a proposal to give renewed emphasis to the Buddhist precepts (*kairitsu*). It is this latter aspect that diverges from the work of Watanabe's NBF peers—most of whom firmly had rejected the traditional Buddhist institutional framework and associated practices as relics of "degenerate", "old Buddhism". As such, Watanabe presents a hybrid face, in line with both the general spirit of late-Meiji New Buddhism *and* the work of the earlier generation of *kairitsu* (precept) masters like Fukuda Gyōkai (1806–1888)—who, it turns out, was a teacher and mentor of the young Watanabe when he was a Jōdo sect acolyte (Maeda 2011: 77–86). Along the same lines, Watanabe's modernistic interpretation of the precepts is prescient of later forms of Socially Engaged Buddhism such as that of Vietnamese Zen teacher and activist Thích Nhất Hạnh (b. 1926), who has similarly sought to bridge modern and liberal social activism with (radically re-imagined) Buddhist practices and structural forms.

Although he appears—perhaps due to his commitment to the priesthood—to have been less inclined than some of his NBF peers to associate with secular leftists, I contend that, of all the New Buddhists, Watanabe was the first to truly cross the "threshold of modernity", in the sense of not merely recognizing the importance of social reform, but demonstrating a fundamental awareness of social and historical contingency and the resultant conclusion that human beings have both the capacity and the responsibility to remake society. As Justin Ritzinger has put it: "This threshold is the point at which it is recognized that the order of society

24   *James Mark Shields*

is not ordained but rather the product of social and historical forces, an understanding of which opens up the possibility of the reflexive reshaping of society through the exercise of human agency. Across the threshold, society becomes its own project."[21]

While Sakaino Kōyō, borrowing from Murakami Senshō, set the seeds for New Buddhist reform by insisting on the necessity of a "historical" Buddhism (*rekishiteki bukkyō*)—that is, one that both insists on a sound historical understanding of Buddhism and emphasizes its continued historical development (SB 3 (9) [September 1902]: 597)—Watanabe took this further by proposing a "social" or "societal" Buddhism (*shakaiteki bukkyō*),[22] that is, a Buddhism in which social concerns are informed and to a large degree directed by a deep recognition of the social and historical forces that condition our existence. For Watanabe, however, the Buddhist institution clearly had a role to play in this process of remaking society—to eliminate the traditional *sangha* entirely would be to throw out the Buddhist baby with the modernist bathwater. One way to understand this is to imagine the reformed *sangha* as a model and guide for the more socially conscious form of lay Buddhism promoted by the NBF.

Of Unitarians and Socialists

Of course, it would be too much to claim that Watanabe, or the NBF, was developing these modernistic ideas in a vacuum. They were clearly and unashamedly inspired by a number of overlapping cultural, intellectual, religious, social, and political currents of the tumultuous late-Meiji period. Two of these currents, in particular, bear noting. The first is Unitarianism, and the second (though not always distinct from the first) was the emerging socialist movement.

As early as the mid-1880s, a number of progressive Buddhists—particularly those outside of the traditional institutions—became attracted to Unitarianism as a liberal, reformist, and self-consciously modern template for religious practice. This connection would reach a peak in the mid-1890s and carry through the early years of the NBF, before gradually falling off (Thelle 1987: 181–193). Although the accommodation between Buddhist modernists and Unitarians was clearly pragmatic in nature, this does not take away from the fact that many of these figures were sincerely attracted to the progressive vision offered by this unorthodox Christian movement, whose followers sought a form of faith that could be justified by reason, that is, a "rational religion".[23] Like the New Buddhists, Unitarians were critical of the ritualistic and "superstitious" aspects of their own religious heritage, rejecting a number of fundamental Christian doctrines, such as the Trinity, original sin, atonement, and afterlife judgment, as well as more specifically sectarian doctrines like the Real Presence and predestination. Unitarian "ambassador" Arthur May Knapp (1841–1921), commissioned to travel to Japan in 1888 in order to encourage the fledgling association there, made note of a number "points of contact" between Unitarianism and Buddhism, including an emphasis on change, the human, and reason rather than on creation, the divine, and tradition. While sympathetic to Buddhism and appreciative of Buddhist interest in

Unitarianism, Knapp, as with so many other Christian missionaries (and Edo-period Confucians), ultimately found Buddhism "pessimistic" and "passive" (Thelle 1987: 187). Despite the hesitancy among some Unitarian missionaries, however, stronger connections were being made through networks "on the ground".

One little-known figure who provides an early bridge between not only Unitarianism and New Buddhism, but also the fledgling socialist movement, was Saji Jitsunen (1856–1920). Saji's primary task as a member of the Unitarian Association was to teach religion, ethics, philosophy, and sociology at the Unitarian theological school. A Sunday lecture series he organized became increasingly popular and drew a number of well-known speakers from the Buddhist and Shinto worlds. More interesting, however, and more significant for our purposes here, are the names of several other figures invited by Saji to speak at the Sunday lecture series, namely radicals such as Abe Isoo (1865–1949) and Murai Tomoyoshi (1861–1944). In fact, by the late 1890s, Saji had come into contact with the leftist currents sweeping into Japan and was particularly attracted to the vision offered by socialism. In 1899, he opened up the Unity Hall for the Society for the Study of Socialism (Shakaishugi Kenkyūkai), a study group founded in 1898 by Abe, Murai, Katayama Sen, Kōtoku Shūsui (1871–1911), Kinoshita Naoe (1869–1937), and Kawakami Kiyoshi (1873–1949). The group, which also included Saji himself, as well as the young journalist and future New Buddhist Sugimura Sojinkan, established a mandate to "investigate the theory of socialism and whether or not it can be applied in Japan" (Nozaki 2007: 38).[24] Reading a broad swath of Western progressive thinkers, including Saint-Simon (1760–1825), Charles Fourier (1772–1837), Pierre-Joseph Proudhon (1809–1865), Peter Kropotkin (1842–1921), Henry George (1839–1897), and Marx and Engels, the group would evolve first into the Shakaishugi Kyōkai in January 1900 and then—in reaction to increasing pressure from the state—into Japan's first, albeit short-lived, socialist party, the Shakai Minshutō, in 1901.[25] Although this relationship between Saji and the leading members of the socialist movement was soon disbanded for financial reasons, the impact of socialist and radical thought on Saji's writing is evident. Thus, with the possible exception of Tarui Tōkichi (1850–1922), Saji can lay claim to being the first "Buddhist socialist" of modern Japan.[26]

But what, exactly, does Saji's "Buddhist socialism" consist of? First, as already noted, Saji was clearly a "new Buddhist" in the sense that, like most Buddhist modernists before and after him, he was quick to denounce traditional, monastic, institutional Buddhism for being, among other things, conservative, parasitic, and superstitious. He was also, like Inoue Enryō and the NBF, committed to a form of Buddhism/religion that was grounded in reason—Thelle (1987: 191) goes so far as to call his work a form of "radical rationalism". At the same time, he holds to a number of basic Buddhist ideals, particularly in relation to ethics. Indeed, as with most Buddhist progressives to come—but in distinction from earlier modernist reformers—the emphasis of his work is squarely on social ethics and, as an extension of such, economic and political justice. In fact, it is precisely these matters, rather than some "deeper" level of spirituality or existential religious transformation, that become the fundamental core of Buddhist or

26   *James Mark Shields*

religious "truth". Thus, in Saji's work, a contrast is made not only between "old" and "new" Buddhism, but between "religious religion", concerned with matters of faith and ritual, and "ethical religion", which would wipe away these excrescences to lay bare the core of "religion", a core that is, ironically, "non-religious" (Takashima 1903: 210). Pressing social problems—including, especially, the problem of poverty—could be addressed only by the various religions setting aside their differences, that is, their dogmas and rituals, and joining together in direct socio-political engagement. Thus, in Saji we see the beginnings of what we might call a "denaturing" of religion, as traditionally and even modernistically conceived, so that religion and progressive social activism fuse into a single category.

And yet, despite strong links with a number of socialists, Christian, Unitarian, and otherwise, the leading members of the New Buddhist Fellowship were reluctant to throw their hat entirely into the ring for socialist revolution—mainly due to their reluctance to adopt a purely "materialist" perspective—a hesitation that finds clearest expression in a critique of their socialist peers. In a 1908 piece entitled "The Risk of Advocating for Material Civilization", Sakaino Kōyō argues that, despite the fact that the New Buddhists and socialists belong to the same "species" (*dōsei*, lit. "same sex"), New Buddhists cannot accept the "interpretation of practical human life" of their socialist friends, who, he argues, tend to "parrot the songs of French socialists and Russian nihilists" (SB 9 (3) [March 1908]: 551). The insinuation is clear: the problem of socialism in Japan—and perhaps particularly for Buddhists—is that it relies too heavily on a (Western?) materialist understanding of human flourishing, and thus cannot provide a critical brush sufficiently broad to deal with the breadth of problems facing modern Japan. Unsurprisingly, a similar critique of one-sidedness is raised against philosophical and literary "naturalism".[27] Of course, accusations of "crude materialism" are frequently based on simplified or inaccurate readings of Marx, particularly with regard to the issues of "poverty" and "alienation", but Sakaino's hesitation, one shared by most of the New Buddhists, is plausibly justified on the basis of "orthodox Marxist" interpretations of socialism, which tend towards economism and reductionist materialism. It is important to note here that the resistance to socialist materialism is rooted less in traditional "religious" concerns than in a broad commitment to liberal, "humanistic" values and a concomitant fear of dehumanization and totalitarianism.

The Legacy of the New Buddhist Fellowship

As noted at the outset of this essay, the New Buddhist movement—even if we confine it to the fellowship and journal that bore that banner—was a complex and diverse phenomenon, which resists a simple attempt at definition or explanation. And yet, as we have seen, there are certain basic ideas, ideals, and trends that characterize at least the work of the primary contributors to the NBF. First, they were explicitly and self-consciously "modernist", generally embracing the moniker "new" (*shin* 新) over "true" (*shin* 真) and emphasizing at all turns the need to bring Buddhism "in line" with contemporary thought, particularly modern science, philosophy, and ethics.

Moreover, from the above analysis of the work of some the primary members of the fellowship, it becomes clear that they were, above all, "humanists". According to Tzvetan Todorov (2002: 232), the "three pillars" of humanist morality are "the recognition of equal dignity for all members of the species; the elevation of the particular human being other than me as the ultimate goal of my actions; finally, the preference for the act freely chosen over one performed under constraint".[28] *Mutatis mutandis*, echoes of each of these three pillars can be found within the basic principles found in the NBF manifesto. At the same time, they were adamant about the need for religion in modern life and were generally critical of "vulgar materialism", even while firmly embracing "common sense" and "this-worldliness". Finally, the New Buddhists envisioned "Buddhism" as a general mode of life and thought, applicable in theory to all people and certainly not confined to monastics or Buddhist institutions.

Even more interesting, however, is the NBF's collective insistence on social and political concerns as being absolutely fundamental to (New) Buddhism. In their reinterpretation of the meaning of "repaying debt", they push this concept towards a socialist (or anarchist) imperative of social activism on the part of the poor/oppressed. Though hesitant, as we have seen, to embrace a fully materialist metaphysics, they were highly critical of inward-looking forms of "new" Buddhism such as Kiyozawa Manshi's *seishinshugi* (Spiritualism or Spiritual Activism), which they viewed as insufficiently attuned to social and political concerns.[29] On the other hand, a major criticism faced by the New Buddhists— and one raised by several members themselves in the pages of *New Buddhism*— was that they let social and political concerns overtake "spiritual" ones, and thus effectively removed themselves from mainstream Buddhist tradition. Along similar lines, critics such as Buddhist Enlightenment scholar and lay-activist Ōuchi Seiran questioned whether they could even call themselves "Buddhist" at all, given that they had failed to produce a "new faith".[30] This suspicion was no doubt exacerbated by the close connections between a number of New Buddhists and the fledgling socialist movement, including Kōtoku Shūsui (1871–1911) and Sakai Toshihiko (1871–1933)—connections that played no small role in the demise of the NBF in the years immediately following the High Treason Incident of 1911. And yet, while founding NBF member and "foreign correspondent" Watanabe Kaikyoku accepted all of the above premises for Buddhist reform, he held back from the radical laicizing inclinations of most of his NBF peers, and thus, arguably, had a more credible reply to critics who questioned whether "Buddhism"—even "New Buddhism"—could survive if completely detached from institutional structure and practices. For Watanabe, a radical re-imagining of the primary functions of a Buddhist priest and temple, that is, a reconfiguration of Buddhist practice along *social* lines, was a more plausible and laudable goal for "New Buddhism".

28 James Mark Shields

Notes

1. Also see, in this regard, Kawabata's (2007: 523) remarks on Murasaki Shikibu's *Tale of Genji* as a "modern" text.
2. I have my own issues with Lincoln's terms, which I shall leave aside here, except to say that these, too, are shaped by distinctively Weberian/Western assumptions about religion and society.
3. The most recent and also most comprehensive study of Buddhist modernism is David McMahan's *The Making of Buddhist Modernism* (2008). McMahan analyzes Buddhist modernism via the work of contemporary philosopher Charles Taylor, particularly the latter's three interwoven "discourses of modernity": Western monotheism, rationalism and scientific naturalism, and romantic expressivism (10). We see strains of all three of these Taylorian discourses in the New Buddhism in Japan, though I will not employ them here as heuristics. The fracturing of Buddhist modernism in Taishō and early Shōwa can, to a large extent, be understood in terms of the tensions implicit in the attempt to embrace both scientific naturalism and romantic expressivism—more specifically, the "conflict" between materialism and idealism as frameworks for understanding the Buddhadharma.
4. Apparently, Sakaino borrowed two hundred yen from Murakami to help start the NBF journal in 1900 (Yoshinaga 2011b: 35); see Takahashi (2011: 57–58) for more on the deep affiliations between the NBF and Inoue's Tetsugakkan/Tōyō University, from or at which all seven founding members either graduated or worked at one point.
5. See Takashima (1993: 193–199) for a first-hand reflection on the founding of the NBF.
6. These seven would be joined in the following years by *tanka* poet and novelist Ito Sachio (1864–1913), Tōru Dōgen (n.d.), Katō Totsudō (1870–1949), Suzuki Teitarō (Daisetsu) (1870–1966), Hayashi Takejirō (1871–1941), Tsuge Shūho (1871–1944), Tsuchiya Senkyō (1872–1956), Kawamura Tōjirō, Shimizu Tomojirō (n.d.), Hiroi Shintarō (n.d.), Wada Kakuji (1879–1962), Inoue Shūten (1880–1945), and Nishiyori Ichiroku (also a founding member of Warp and Woof).
7. The year 1900 saw the implementation of the Public Order and Police Law (*Chian keisatsu hō*), quickly deployed to proscribe the Social Democratic Party (Shakai Minshutō), Japan's first socialist party, soon after its formation in May 1901 (though not, as is often reported, on the exact day). The same law, or its later variant, the Public Order Preservation Law (*Chian iji hō*) of 1925, would later be used against the New Buddhists throughout the last years of Meiji and early Taishō, as well as against Seno'o Girō's Youth League for Revitalizing Buddhism in early Shōwa.
8. As Klautau (2008: 290) notes, Okamoto Ryūnosuke's (1852–1912) *Seikyō chūsei ron* (On the correct roles of church and state), published in 1899, exemplifies the plea among many within the Buddhist establishment for a "public recognition" of Buddhism as a state religion (*kokkyō*). This idea was supported by the resolution drafted at the national Buddhism convention held on 8 May 1899 at Chion-in temple in Kyoto, and by the work of Okamoto's younger contemporary Tsuji Zennosuke (1877–1955), though with important modifications. See Kashiwahara (1990: 141–144) and Tsuji (1900: 84).
9. In his preface to a recent comprehensive report on New Buddhism, Yoshinaga Shin'ichi (2011a: 1) confesses to being initially put off by the "surliness" (*buaisō na*) and pomposity (*dōdō taru*) of the New Buddhist manifesto. As a scholar who has worked extensively on the Critical Buddhist movement, I personally find their tone both familiar and refreshing in the context of modern Japanese scholarship.
10. For the NBF take on the Tetsugakkan Affair, see SB 4 (3) [March 1903]: 729–730: "Preoccupied with loyalty and patriotism (*chūkun aikoku*), the Ministry of Education is increasing its persecution of scholars for their freedom of thought."

Scope and Limits of Secular Buddhism 29

11. One of the practical effects of the Boshin Rescript was the formation of local organizations, called *boshinkai*, "dedicated to the promotion of morality and economics" (Gluck 1985: 198). As with the contemporaneous Hōtoku movement, the Meiji government was utilizing all possible avenues of "moral reform" to forestall the emergence of socialism in the countryside. See Gluck (1985: 197–199) for a list of other "moral reform associations" (*kyōfūkai*) and "youth associations" (*seinendan*) to emerge in the years between 1905 and 1912.

12. The rural Hōtoku societies, initially formed by progressive landlords in the early Meiji period, found government favour in their attempt to promote the "harmony of morality and economics". From 1903, they began to receive official support from the Home Ministry and, in 1906, were organized under an umbrella organization, the *Hōtokutai*. "Invoking the example of the Tokugawa agricultural moralist, Ninomiya Sontoku, they encouraged technical improvements and the repayment of virtue (*hōtoku*) through honesty, diligence, and communal cooperation" (Gluck 1985: 190).

13. Specifically, sales of SB 11 (9) [September 1910] and SB 14 (10) [October 1913] were prohibited by government censors.

14. See Takahashi (2011: 50). Takahashi notes that the while Sakaino, Beihō, and Katō Totsudō were regular speakers, other active participants to the journal, including Sugimura, Watanabe, and Suzuki, were less involved—probably due to the fact that they were often travelling (for the latter two, abroad).

15. Ikeda (1976: 18–31) argues that the teaching of the "four debts" (*shion setsu*) in particular provided the primary foundation for Meiji Buddhist reform movements; see also Kashiwahara (1990: 4).

16. And yet there were other contributors to the NBF journal who maintained serious doubt as to whether the doctrine of the Four Debts could deal with the rapid diversification of modern Japanese society and whether it could withstand logical criticism from outside. Perhaps the best representation of such a view was Sōtō Zen priest and scholar Nukariya Kaiten's (1867–1934) "Hōonshugi dōtokusetsu no nanten" (Problems with basing moral instruction on the concept of debt), published in *New Buddhism* in February 1906; see SB 7 (2) [February 1906]: 197–201.

17. E.g. the Hōkoku Gikai (Assembly to Repay [One's Debt to] the Nation) founded by Pure Land Buddhists in 1895. See Ives (2009: 22).

18. The following brief biography of Watanabe has been adapted from several sources, especially Maeda (2011).

19. Hasegawa, a student of both Watanabe and Buddhist social activist Yabuki Keiki (1879–1939), established the Mahayana Gakuen after returning from overseas study in Germany and the United States in 1919. See Kikuchi (2007: 3).

20. Although I focus here on Watanabe's contributions to the NBF, without a doubt his most important legacy to Buddhist scholarship was his co-editorship, with Takakusu Junjirō, of the Taishō Buddhist Canon (*Taishō shinshū daizōkyō*), published between 1924 and 1929.

21. Ritzinger (2014: 4). Ritzinger borrows this notion from Faubion (1993: 113–117) and Eisenstadt (2000: 1–3), who in turn rely heavily on the work of Max Weber.

22. I have not been able to discern whether Watanabe was in fact the first to employ this term, but he is clearly the scholar who did most towards developing the idea. "With his lifelong commitment to developing forms of social practice on the basis of Mahāyāna Buddhist doctrine, Jōdo sect priest Watanabe had a significant influence on the establishment of social activism in Japan" (Murota 2006: 127); also see Ōtani (2008: 6 n. 16).

23. Though this takes us well beyond the scope of this chapter, it is interesting to note that the modern (post-1885) history of Unitarianism includes a strong formative influence from the writings of Ralph Waldo Emerson, who, like many Transcendentalists, was open to and appreciative of Indian and Buddhist thought. Thus, the Unitarianism

30 James Mark Shields

being brought to Japan at this period was already itself rooted in a hybrid form of universalism.

24. For more on the Shakaishugi Kenkyūkai and Shakai Minshutō, see Ōta, *Meiji shakaishugi shiryō sōsho, 1.*

25. See Takeuchi (1967: 728), who argues, somewhat unfairly in my view, that the fact that these early Japanese progressives were reacting to external pressures makes their socialism "premature"—in other words, they were intellectually not quite "ready" for the more radical implications of socialist doctrine.

26. In May 1901, not long after this link between the socialists and Unitarians was broken (as noted, for financial reasons), the New Buddhist Fellowship began to hold some of its meetings in Unity Hall, a practice they continued until January 1912; see Yoshinaga (2011b: 37); for more on Saji's kindness towards the New Buddhists, see Takashima (1993: 204).

27. For more on the NBF critique of naturalism, see e.g. Tanaka's "Shizenshugi to wa nani zo" (SB 9 (3) [March 1908]: 555–562); Sakaino's "Shizenshugi no koto" (SB 9 (6) [June 1908]: 589–597); Tōru Dōgen's "Shizenshugi to shūkyō" (SB 9 (7) [July 1908]: 610–612).

28. See also Aso (2009) on the "slippage" between humanism and fascism.

29. For more on the New Buddhist critique of *seishinshugi*, see Fukushima (2003) and Yasutomi (2003: 108–109).

30. Of course, such criticisms raise numerous questions about the implications of complex but largely under-theorized terms such as "religion", "politics", "faith", and "practice".

References

Aso, Noriko. 2009. "Mediating the Masses: Yanagi Sōetsu and Fascism." In *The Culture of Japanese Fascism*, edited by Alan Tansman, 138–154. Durham, NC: Duke University Press.

Bechert, Heinz. 1966–1968. *Buddhismus, Staat und Gesellschaft in den Ländern des Theravāda-Buddhismus.* 3 vols. Vol. 1. Berlin: Alfred Metzner. Vols. 2–3. Wiesbaden: O. Harrassowitz.

Davis, Winston. 1992. *Japanese Religion and Society: Paradigms of Structure and Change.* Albany, NY: SUNY Press.

Eisenstadt, Shmuel N. 2000. "Multiple Modernities." *Daedalus* 129 (1): 1–29.

Faubion, James D. 1993. *Modern Greek Lessons: A Primer in Historical Constructivism.* Princeton, NJ: Princeton University Press.

Fukushima, Eiju. 2003. *Shisōshi to shite no "Seishinshugi"* ["Seishinshugi" in relation to the history of thought]. Kyoto: Hōzōkan.

Gluck, Carol. 1985. *Japan's Modern Myths: Ideology in the Late Meiji Period.* Princeton, NJ: Princeton University Press.

Ikeda, Eishun. 1976. *Meiji no shin bukkyō undō* [The Meiji New Buddhist movement]. Tokyo: Yoshikawa Kōbunkan.

Ives, Christopher. 2009. *Imperial-Way Zen: Ichikawa Hakugen's Critique and Lingering Questions for Buddhist Ethics.* Honolulu: University of Hawai'i Press.

Kamo, no Chōmei. 1998. *Hōjōki: Visions of a Torn World.* Translated by Yasuhiko Moriguchi and David Jenkins. Berkeley, CA: Stone Bridge Press.

Kashiwahara, Yūsen. 1990. *Nihon bukkyōshi: kindai* [Japanese Buddhist history: Modernity]. Tokyo: Yoshikawa Kōbunkan.

Kawabata, Yasunari. 2007. "Japan, the Beautiful, and Myself." In *The Columbia Anthology of Modern Japanese Literature.* Vol. 2, edited by Thomas Rimer and Van Gessel, 729–739. New York: Columbia University Press.

Scope and Limits of Secular Buddhism 31

Kikuchi, Yui. 2007. "Shukyōteki jissen to fukushi no rinen: Watanabe Kaikyoku no jiseki to chūshin toshite" [Ideas of religious practice and welfare: With a focus on the work and achievements of Watanabe Kaikyoku]. Web article. Accessed 1 August 2009. http://shukyo-shakaikoken.up.seesaa.net/image/kikuchiEFBC94.pdf.

Klautau, Orion. 2008. "Against the Ghosts of Recent Past: Meiji Scholarship and the Discourse on Edo-Period Buddhist Decadence." *Japanese Journal of Religious Studies* 35 (2): 263–303.

Lincoln, Bruce. 2006. *Holy Terrors: Thinking about Religion after September 11.* 2nd ed. Chicago: University of Chicago Press.

Lopez, Donald S., Jr. 2004. "Foreword." In: *The Gospel of Buddha: According to Old Records,* edited by Paul Carus, vii–ix. LaSalle, IL: Open Court Publications.

Maeda, Kasuo. 2011. *Shiun no hito, Watanabe Kaikyoku: Kochū ni tsuki o motomete* [Kaikyoku Watanabe, sovereign priest]. Tokyo: Pot Publishing.

McMahan, David L. 2008. *The Making of Buddhist Modernism.* New York: Oxford University Press.

Murota, Yasuo. 2006. *Jinbutsu de yomu kindai Nihon shakai fukushi no ayumi* [Understanding modern Japanese social welfare movements via people]. Tokyo: Minerva Shobō.

Nozaki, Kōichi. 2007. "Hirai Kinza to Yuniterian." In *Hirai Kinza ni okeru Meiji bukkyō no kokusaika ni kan suru: shūkyōshi, bunkashi kenkyū* [Hirai Kinza and the globalization of Japanese Buddhism of the Meiji period: A cultural and religio-historical study], 31–42. Web article. Accessed 8 April 2016. http://www.maizuru-ct.ac.jp/human/yosinaga/hirai_report.pdf.

Ōta, Masao, ed. 1973. *Meiji shakaishugi shiryō sōsho, 1: shakaishugi kyōkaishi (1900–1904)* [Meiji socialism document library 1: History of the socialist organization]. Tokyo: Shinsensha.

Ōtani, Eiichi. 2008. "Nakajima Shige no shakaiteki kirisutokyō to Seno'o Girō no shakaiteki bukkyō" [Nakajima Shige's socially activist Christianity and Seno'o Girō's socially activist Buddhism]. Paper delivered at the 67th Meeting of the Japanese Society of Religious Studies.

Ritzinger, Justin. 2014. "The Awakening of Faith in Anarchism: A Forgotten Chapter in the Chinese Buddhist Encounter with Modernity." In: *Against Harmony? Radical and Revolutionary Buddhism(s) in Thought and Practice,* edited by Patrice Ladwig and James Mark Shields, special issue, *Politics, Religion and Ideology* 15 (2): 224–243.

Schober, Juliane. 2011. *Modern Buddhist Conjunctures in Myanmar: Cultural Narratives, Colonial Legacies, and Civil Society.* Honolulu: University of Hawai'i Press.

Takahashi, Hara. 2011. "Shin bukkyō-to to wa dare ka?" [Who were the New Buddhists?]. In *Kindai Nihon ni okeru chishikijin shūkyō undō no gensetsu kūkan: "Shin Bukkyō" no shisōshi, bunkashiteki kenkyū* [The discursive space of an intellectual religious movement in modern Japan: A study of the journal *New Buddhism* from the viewpoint of the history of culture and thought], 47–79. Web article. Accessed 8 April 2016. http://www.maizuru-ct.ac.jp/human/yosinaga/shinbukkyo_report.pdf.

Takashima, En (Beihō), ed. 1903. *Shōrai no shukyō* [The future religion]. Tokyo: Shin Bukkyōto Dōshikai.

―――. 1993. *Takashima Beihō jijoden* [Autobiography of Takashima Beihō]. Tokyo: Ōzorasha.

Takeuchi, Yoshitomo. 1967. "The Role of Marxism in Japan." *Developing Economies* 5 (4): 727–735.

Thelle, Notto R. 1987. *Buddhism and Christianity in Japan: From Conflict to Dialogue.* Honolulu: University of Hawai'i Press.

32   James Mark Shields

Todorov, Tzvetan. 2002. *The Imperfect Garden: The Legacy of Humanism*. Princeton, NJ: Princeton University Press.

Tsuji, Zennosuke. 1900. " 'Seikyō chūseiron' o hyōsu" [A comment on the "correct theory of religion and state"]. *Shigaku zasshi* 11 (4): 74–89.

Yasutomi, Shin'ya. 2003. "The Way of Introspection: Kiyozawa Manshi's Methodology." *The Eastern Buddhist* 35 (1–2): 102–113.

Yoshida, Kyūichi. (1959) 1992. *Nihon kindai bukkyōshi kenkyū* [A study of modern Japanese Buddhist history]. Tokyo: Yoshikawa Kōbunkan.

Yoshinaga, Shin'ichi. 2011a. "Hajime ni" [Preface]. In *Kindai Nihon ni okeru chishikijin shūkyō undō no gensetsu kūkan: "Shin Bukkyō" no shisōshi, bunkashiteki kenkyū* [The discursive space of an intellectual religious movement in modern Japan: A study of the journal *New Buddhism* from the viewpoint of the history of culture and thought], 1–6. Web article. Accessed 8 April 2016. http://www.maizuru-ct.ac.jp/human/yosinaga/shin bukkyo_report.pdf.

————. 2011b. *"Shin bukkyō* to wa nani mono ka? 'jiyū tōkyū' to 'kenzen naru shinkō'" [What is *New Buddhism*?: Free investigation and sound faith]. In *Kindai Nihon ni okeru chishikijin shūkyō undō no gensetsu kūkan: "Shin Bukkyō" no shisōshi, bunkashiteki kenkyū* [The discursive space of an intellectual religious movement in modern Japan: A study of the journal *New Buddhism* from the viewpoint of the history of culture and thought], 27–43. Web article. Accessed 8 April 2016. http://www.maizuru-ct.ac.jp/human/yosinaga/shinbukkyo_report.pdf.

3 Buddhism and the Capitalist Transformation of Modern Japan

Sada Kaiseki (1818–1882),
Uchiyama Gudō (1874–1911), and
Itō Shōshin (1876–1963)

Fabio Rambelli*

This essay discusses different and conflicting attitudes towards the capitalist transformation that characterizes Japan's modernization between the mid-nineteenth and mid-twentieth centuries as shown by three exemplary figures of modern Japanese Buddhism, namely Sada Kaiseki, Uchiyama Gudō, and Itō Shōshin.

Sada Kaiseki (1818–1882) developed a full-fledged programme of resistance against early Meiji modernization, based on the revitalization and updating of Buddhist teachings about geography and astronomy, on the development of an original economic programme, and on public and political activism. Sada was aware that the features of modernity as related to the modernization process in which the Meiji government had embarked could be highly detrimental to Japanese culture and society as a whole and tried to come up with alternative measures.

Uchiyama Gudō (1874–1911) fully embraced socialism, especially in its radical form of anarchist communism. For him, Western modern capitalism was already a given social fact that had to be countered by activism aimed at the establishment of socialism. In his writings, he proposed a clear, albeit acerbic blueprint for the realization of a socialist "paradise" of equality and freedom, in which international anarchist themes intersected with Buddhist visions and elements from Edo-period social activism.

In contrast, Itō Shōshin (1876–1963) appears to have embraced several contradictory aspects of modernity. First, he became involved in progressive ideas stressing mutual aid as opposed to forms of social Darwinism including capitalism—a vision of mutual aid that had strong ties to the international socialist and anarchist movements—and tried to reinterpret it in terms of new modes of Buddhist thought, practice, and lifestyle adjusted to modernity. Later, he reconfigured his ideas of selflessness and mutual generosity to adapt them to the new totalitarian imperial system of Japan (in itself a by-product of modernity), by arguing that these ideas could be realized only under the supreme and quasi-transcendent guide of the emperor of Japan.

Beyond their respective differences, these three authors share the fact that they were free-thinking Buddhist intellectuals, not organic to any religious institution. This type of Buddhist intellectual was peculiar to the first stages of Japanese modernity, from the mid-nineteenth to mid-twentieth centuries, and faded away

34   Fabio Rambelli

during World War II; with them, Buddhist political intervention also disappeared from the Japanese public discourse.

Through a critical examination of these three authors, this essay aims at outlining some of the major challenges and conundrums that confronted the Buddhist world in Japan during its transition to a modern capitalist society.

General Considerations

There are many discussions about the nature and distinctive features of modernity, and attempts both political and intellectual to "go beyond" modernity, either forwards into a new and different society or backwards into an idealized vision of the past. All of these discussions share the fact that they already take place within an established and pervasive dimension we call "modernity"—so pervasive that it is difficult even to look outside of it, both in space and time, to find and understand different cultural models. An enormous literature exists on Japan's modernization, which began in the Meiji period (1868–1911); most authors emphasize well-known aspects, such as efforts aimed at catching up with advanced Western powers and the top-down imposition of capitalist economy. In all these accounts of Japanese processes of modernization, Japanese leaders tried to emulate the social, political, and economic structures of leading Western countries in order to be able to compete with them on an equal basis. However, the transplant into Japanese soil of what were perceived as dominant cultural models in advanced Western societies was not the only aspect of the Meiji cultural revolution. Many other cultural aspects and phenomena also began to circulate in Japan, including political doctrines such as socialism and anarchism, avant-garde art, and alternative lifestyles. Buddhism also had to come to terms with all this.

Ideally, this essay can be envisioned as a fragment in a larger project related to mapping what have been called "multiple modernities" or "vernacular modernities", in which different countries and cultural contexts develop multiple understandings of what modernity means and the different paths to achieve it, also on the basis of vernacularization of Western discourses. S. N. Eisenstadt was perhaps the first author to use the term "multiple modernities" in a 1999 essay. In it, Eisenstadt wrote that "the appropriation of different themes and institutional patterns of the original Western modern civilization in non-Western European societies did not entail their acceptance in their original form" but rather "the continuous selection, reinterpretation and reformulation of such themes". As a result, non-Western societies developed "different interpretations and far-reaching reformulations of the initial cultural program of modernity, its basic conceptions and premises" (Eisenstadt 2003: 2, 526, 550).

On the other hand, the concept of "vernacular modernity" was first introduced by Stuart Hall in a 1993 lecture to refer to the distinctive nature of African American contribution to American culture:

> the experience of blacks in the new world, their historical trajectory into and through the complex histories of colonization, conquest, and enslavement, is

The Capitalist Transformation 35

distinct and unique and it empowers people to speak in a distinctive voice. But it is not a voice outside of and excluded from the production of modernity in the twentieth century. It is another kind of modernity. It is a vernacular modernity, it is the modernity of the blues, the modernity of gospel music, it is the modernity of hybrid black music in its enormous variety throughout the New World.

(Hall 1995: 11)

In this essay, I suggest that it is particularly productive to think about Buddhist interactions with multiple processes of modernization in Japan as cases of vernacular attempts to cope with modernity.

We should probably keep in mind that, whenever phenomena of social transformation occur on this enormous scale, most people, including intellectuals, policy-makers, and religious specialists, simply try to come to terms with such transformations and adjust their lives (and, perhaps, their thought as well) to the new times. This seems to be true also in the case of the religious transformations that took place during the Meiji period as a result of state policies and more general social processes, especially the forced separation of Shinto from Buddhism (*shinbutsu bunri*), which often resulted in anti-Buddhist persecutions (known as *haibutsu kishaku*) in 1868–1872. These religious changes were not simply motivated by the desire to restrain the power of Buddhist institutions and ideas; rather, they aimed to eliminate traditional forms of religiosity and folk cultures. However, a significant (albeit little studied) aspect of Meiji history is the scarcity of mass popular activity against such religious transformations. There may have been unrest and malcontent, passive resistance, even a few riots, but nothing really so serious as to prevent state agencies and other groups to carry out their own agenda. In this respect, what really strikes the interpreter today is the willingness of even the highest Buddhist clerical elites to give up their prerogatives, prestige, and honour, and accept the dictates from state agencies in charge of religious affairs. Many monastics simply disrobed themselves and abandoned their temples; others became Shinto priests almost overnight, and others stayed and accepted the new order and the subordinate role of Buddhism in it.[1]

Nonetheless, a number of people did try to make sense of what was happening and to formulate a new role for Buddhism. Sada Kaiseki, Uchiyama Gudō, and Itō Shōshin are particularly interesting, each in his own way, because of their struggles with a modernity in formation, in which old social and cultural models were no longer viable or even desirable, and there was the need to create and introduce new formations and to experiment with them. Sada, Uchiyama, and Itō questioned the role of Buddhism in this new cultural ordering of things that was being formed. They addressed a number of similar questions with strikingly different answers.

The first issue that they had to confront was the nature and significance of Buddhism. More specifically, was there a specific arena (either intellectual or social) that is proper to Buddhism? Shimaji Mokurai and others redefined Buddhism as the sole religion of Japan, reducing Shinto to traditional customs, and therefore,

36 Fabio Rambelli

as a religion, they put Buddhism in charge of general matters pertaining to the human "heart" (*kokoro*); other leading Buddhist intellectuals, such as Kiyozawa Manshi and Inoue Enryō, redefined Buddhism as, respectively, a form of spirituality or a philosophical system. These priests and intellectuals were giving Buddhism a new role, somehow at the margins of the core of what the Japanese of the time understood as modernity, namely new forms of science, new understanding of nature, and new social and political organizations.

Another issue that affected Buddhism at the time was the capitalist transformation of Japan.[2] Despite the momentous importance of this transformation, there are few studies on Buddhist reactions to it, beyond relatively facile references to Western individualism, social Darwinism, and greed. Recently, Slavoj Zizek has attempted to define the role of Buddhism in contemporary Western societies. He has argued that what he calls "Western Buddhism" is in fact the ideology of global, advanced capitalism. This so-called Western Buddhism "enables you to fully participate in the frantic pace of the capitalist game while sustaining the perception that you are not really in it; . . . and that what really matters to you is the peace of the Inner Self to which you know you can always withdraw" (Zizek 2001: 2). In short, "The 'Western Buddhist' meditative stance is arguably the most efficient way for us to fully participate in capitalist dynamics while retaining the appearance of mental sanity" (Zizek 2001: 1).[3] However, it appears that Buddhism's stance towards capitalism is not limited to the contemporary West; one could argue that, since a very early stage, Buddhism already contained and promoted a quasi- or proto-capitalist attitude. Contrary to received assumptions, Buddhism has never been a world-denying religion, unconcerned with, or clearly inimical to, economic activities. Buddhist institutions in East Asia have always functioned also as large economic hubs: they required a significant amount of labour, both skilled and unskilled; they purchased a vast array of different materials, goods, and services; they reclaimed and developed non-cultivated lands; they functioned as centres for industry (mills, presses), finance, commerce (market places), travel, professional guilds, and entertainment and performing arts.

In Meiji and Taishō Japan, Buddhist institutions had to change their economic attitudes. In addition to losing most traditional sources of economic support, they had to come up with ways to deal with the newly developing industrial capitalism. Meiji official policies aimed at "enriching the country and strengthening the army" (*fukoku kyōhei*) saw the support of Buddhist institutions and thinkers as a way to re-legitimize Buddhism after the early Meiji persecutions. This brought many Buddhists to accept various aspects of modernization, including the capitalist transformation of Japan. Shimaji Mokurai (1838–1911), for instance, personally endorsed the slogan of *fukoku kyōhei*, writing that public wealth is inseparable from military might since it requires economic development and the large production of natural products and industrial commodities (along Western, capitalist lines). Shimaji also adopted some common themes of capitalist discourse, such as the idea that individual effort will certainly result in economic

The Capitalist Transformation 37

profit, that enrichment is a natural human desire, that affluence is typical of the human condition (in contrast to scarcity and subsistence, which is closer to animal life), and that technological development will free humans from natural conditionings and limitations (Mokurai, quoted in Yoshida 1969: 35, 37).

We should not forget, however, that Japan already had a flourishing proto-capitalist economy, of which Buddhist temples were important agents, and perhaps the transition to modernity was not as radical and dramatic as many authors seem to suggest. In fact, the modernization process had already begun in the late Tokugawa period, with authors such as Ōkuni Takamasa (1792–1871; on Ōkuni Takamasa, see Breen 1996, 1997). Yoshida Kyūichi argued that Buddhism, in its desire to serve the country (*kokueki*), did not understand the logic and the spirit of the process of primitive accumulation that underlay the capitalist transformation of Japan (Yoshida 1964: 222–223, 1970: 57). Later, Yoshida continues, Buddhist intellectuals failed to understand the problems of the working class, and thus they also failed in proposing a viable socialist model. This was due to Buddhists' emphasis on harmonization (*chōwa*) and their desire to avoid both excessive exploitation by the capitalists and autonomous workers' initiatives such as strikes: in other words, they tried to restrain factory supervisors while at the same time educating docile workers. This attitude is particularly evident in the proselytizing activity endeavoured by several Buddhist organizations in factories in the Taishō and early Shōwa periods, which stressed concepts such as "enriching the country" (*fukoku*), compassion (*jihi*), and wisdom as guides in economic activities (Yoshida 1964: 421–424, 1970: 139–140). On the other hand, Buddhist institutions began to address some of the negative consequences on society caused by the rising Japanese capitalism by engaging in charitable activities (*jizen katsudō*).

Either way, through these reformulations, Buddhist organizations could continue their own activities (managing sectarian organizations and temples, performing funeral and other rituals, etc.) relatively undisturbed by the new cultural context, and they were more or less free to actively participate in this context or not and to choose how to participate and to what extent. In a sense, reformulations of Buddhism as proposed by Mokurai or Inoue were ways to "change everything so that nothing would change". In time, these new ways of seeing Buddhism came to constitute a sort of default, standard interpretation of the nature and significance of Buddhism. We could argue that Sada Kaiseki, Uchiyama Gudō, and Itō Shōshin, with their strikingly different ideas, positioned themselves at the margins of this default vision. Sada Kaiseki stressed that Buddhism, as a total cultural system, was not only about the heart/spirit or about concepts, but also and especially about everything else (the spirit playing only a minor role, if any, in his intellectual system). Indeed, Buddhism for him had strong material components, even visceral aspects: in his essays on society, which were deeply infused with his own understanding of Buddhism, Sada even discussed mixed marriages and international cuisine. Itō Shōshin, in contrast, had shifting ideas about the issue of the nature and role of Buddhism. At least in the modern Japanese context, Buddhism

38 *Fabio Rambelli*

was for Itō, rather than a way of life, a system of ethical behaviour and, above all, an important conceptual and philosophical system; however, Buddhism was ultimately not independent from the imperial state and the emperor's worship, for which it was supposed to provide intellectual support and justification. Finally, Uchiyama Gudō proposed yet another vision: Buddhism could help socialism transform the individuals and ultimately society as a whole, by abolishing the state and, above all, the emperor, the ultimate figure of the capitalist state's power and oppression.

Sada Kaiseki: Innovative Alternatives to Modernization

Sada Kaiseki was born in 1818 in present-day Yachiyo City, Kumamoto Prefecture (Kyūshū); he studied in Kyoto at the Honganji Higher Education Institute (*daigakurin*). He died in 1882 in Takada, present-day Niigata Prefecture, during one of his frequent lecture tours. Sada was one of the leading Buddhist public intellectuals of the time (on Sada Kaiseki, see Tanikawa 2002; Rambelli 2011). He founded and edited several newspapers and magazines, wrote articles and books, and gave well-attended lectures on several topics throughout Japan. He also submitted numerous policy statements and proposals (*kenpakusho*) to the government in which he criticized the Meiji state policies on several topics, ranging from strictly religious themes to international relations and economic issues. His intellectual activity ranged from geography and astronomy to economics and cultural politics. In all of these areas, Sada tried to formulate original and autonomous intellectual positions by recombining traditional knowledge and new Western ideas in ways that were not completely subservient to contemporaneous Euro-American discourses. Active at the time of formulation of fundamental modernization policies that would determine many future developments in Japan, Sada Kaiseki is a fascinating case of a Buddhist intellectual who did not hesitate to strongly criticize the Meiji government and to organize citizens' movements to counter its policies.

During his formative years in Kyoto, Sada studied Buddhist astronomy, in particular the then-popular theory, initially formulated by Fumon Entsū (1755–1834), known as *bonreki* (lit. "Indic calendrical sciences"). In a few years, Sada became one of the leading figures of the movement for the diffusion of Indic astronomy (known as *bonreki undō*), which he developed in an original way. *Bonreki* was a Buddhist response to the penetration of Western astronomy and geography in Japan. Western astronomy was deeply troubling to Buddhist intellectuals, who saw in the explicit negation of Buddhist traditional cosmology a threat against the very foundation of the Buddhist worldview. They argued that, once the structure of the Buddhist cosmos is put into question, doubts will arise concerning the existence of hells and heavens, so that also soteriology, the very essence of Buddhism, will eventually collapse. *Bonreki* is normally understood as an essentially reactionary, nationalistic, and Buddhist fundamentalist response to modernization and the impact of Western culture in Japan. However, it is possible to argue that the *bonreki* movement, especially in its later developments led by Sada, encompassed

The Capitalist Transformation 39

innovative and intellectually challenging elements, especially in its attempts to adapt Western science to the Buddhist worldview.

Sada chose to minimize mystical formulations and developed instead *bonreki*'s scientific approach. He emphasized that all astronomical theories, including modern Western ones, are essentially hypotheses based on interpretations of experience, which is in itself limited and potentially fallacious; he also proposed rational objections to Western hypotheses on the basis of his own observations and experience. In this way, he was able to suggest a possible coexistence (*kyōwa*) of different and alternative cosmologies (Sada [1877] 1980–1986: 392).

Over the years, Sada also developed his own economic theory, which became the main focus of his intellectual and political activities. Its most systematic statement is contained in a book, *Saibai keizairon* (Introduction to Cultivation-mode Economics, 1878–1879), and further developed in newspaper and magazine articles until his death. Sada defined economy (*keizai*) as the "unhindered circulation of commodities and money among the people" (Sada [1878–1879] 1967: 314). He envisioned economics as a system of relations and communications pervading society, in which human beings were related to the natural world, and producers and consumers were related to one another, allowing goods to flow freely throughout the social space. For Sada, agriculture was the basis of the Japanese economy, and as the very title *Saibai keizairon* makes clear, the basic model of his economic theory is agricultural cultivation (*saibai*), which is applied to all aspects of production in an attempt to outline a sustainable and community-based economic life. Emphasis on agriculture was a common theme of Edo-period intellectual discourse, shared by Confucians and Nativists, but also by new religious movements such as Ōmotokyō with its early rejection of modernization and capitalistic economy. However, Sada's stance was original in several respects, such as his emphasis on the duty of business to provide benefits for the totality of the people and not only for the entrepreneurs, his attention to traditional technologies and local products, and the importance he gave to expenditure, a significant contrast to the Confucian emphasis on "thrift" (*kensetsu*). Another interesting aspect of Sada's economic theory, especially in light of subsequent developments in Japanese society, is the importance he attributed to leisure or recreation (*asobi*)—both pleasurable activities (*yūraku*) and free time.

Essentially, Sada's economic theory is based on four interrelated ideas: the rejection of imported goods and the valorization of Japanese traditional technology and sensibility; the emphasis on consumption (demand-driven economy), in contrast to the government's policies privileging production (offer-driven model) based on heavy industries; the importance of leisure and conspicuous consumption of voluptuary goods and services; and, finally, the leading economic role of the urban higher classes, who are entrusted with improving the general economic condition of the populace at large.

Sada was against globalization and believed that economic issues should be solved exclusively within Japan. He argued that Japan and the Western countries (which he tended to consider as one, large system, rather than different and competing entities—an understanding that, within the context of the economic

40   *Fabio Rambelli*

conjuncture of the early Meiji state, was not totally incorrect) were very different in culture, environment, and national character; since their economic systems were also very different, Japan had everything to lose from its inclusion within a global commercial network dominated by Western powers. Sada tried to put into practice his ideas by organizing an aggressive campaign to boycott foreign goods, imported not only from the West but also from China, an effort in which he engaged himself until the very end.[4]

Concerning his metaphysical orientation, Sada was a philosophical materialist. As an expert in Buddhist cosmology and cosmogony, he subscribed to the classical Buddhist theories according to which the universe is in a constant and unceasing cycle of creation, growth, degeneration, and destruction, followed by a new creation, growth, degeneration, and destruction, and so on and so forth, without beginning or end. Moreover, all entities and beings in the universe are the result of the combination of material atoms (*mijin*), in an eternal movement of aggregation and disaggregation. The first atoms in such movement existed originally and spontaneously in nature, and are thus not the result of creation by intelligent design (see Sada [1879] 1980–1986). Also because of this outlook on reality, Sada was averse to spiritualistic or idealistic visions of the state and the body politic, mediated both from Shinto Nativism and German idealism, which formed the "spiritual" core of the Meiji state in striking contrast to its open support of scientific rationality.

In terms of political praxis in general, Sada was profoundly critical of Meiji government policies towards modernization, which he saw as a thoughtless and grotesque adoption of alien ways and fashions from the West—calendar, clothes, hairstyles, material objects, intellectual systems, sensibilities—which would ultimately have disastrous consequences for the Japanese people and their culture. Sada was in principle not against progress, the improvement of material and spiritual civilization, perhaps not even against modernization per se—the process known in Japan at the time as *bunmei kaika* ("civilization and development"). However, he argued that there is no single path to progress and, in particular, that the Western way to development was definitely not appropriate to Japan.

Uchiyama Gudō and the Vision of a Buddhist Anarchist Society

Uchiyama Gudō was born in May 1874 in Ojiya, present-day Niigata Prefecture, in the family of an impoverished wood artisan.[5] Almost nothing is known of Uchiyama's life between his elementary school years and his later affiliation with the Sōtō Zen establishment. After receiving middle-school level education and religious training at temples in Kanagawa Prefecture, Uchiyama became interested in the arising socialist movement around 1903 and began to read the most influential socialist publication in Japan, the *Heimin shinbun* ("The People's Newspaper"), founded by Kōtoku Shūsui (1871–1911) and others in 1903.[6] In 1904, he became the resident priest of Rinsenji, a small mountain temple in Ōhiradai near Hakone.

The Capitalist Transformation 41

At the time, it had only some forty families of parishioners (*danka*), most of whom were affected by deep poverty and engaged in subsistence economy. He met with Kōtoku and other radical intellectuals in 1905 and began to participate in their activities. In 1908, Uchiyama started a clandestine printing activity in the back of the main hall of his temple. Because of his affiliation with this group of anarchists, he became involved in an alleged plot to assassinate the emperor, which became the pretext for the so-called High Treason Incident (*taigyaku jiken*). All leading anarchists, including Kōtoku and Uchiyama, were arrested and accused of high treason; after what is now considered a rigged trial, orchestrated by the Japanese government to get rid of the radical left, several of them were sentenced to death, and Uchiyama was hanged on 24 January 1911.[7]

Uchiyama did not write much; still, his authorial activity is remarkable, if we only consider that he had a middle-school education and that he printed his own pamphlets himself. In addition to personal letters addressed to friends and fellow radicals and a few contributions to the *Heimin shinbun*, he wrote and published in his clandestine press *Museifu kyōsan kakumei* ("Anarchist-Communist Revolution", 1908), a passionate and incendiary pamphlet on labour exploitation, state authoritarianism, and liberation politics, in which Uchiyama famously criticized the contemporary imperial system and denied the divine nature of the emperor. In addition, two incomplete manuscripts remain, dating to the last months of his life and most likely written in prison, namely *Heibon no jikaku* ("Common Consciousness") and the so-called *Gokuchū shuki* ("Prison Manuscript"), where Uchiyama attempted a more systematic treatment of his religious and political ideals. Uchiyama also published two short Japanese translations of articles from the international anarchist movement.

As *Museifu kyōsan kakumei*'s subtitle "Why is life so hard for tenant farmers?" suggests, Uchiyama conceived this text as a sermon directed to tenant farmers, primarily his own parishioners. Accordingly, it is written in a simple language and orchestrates simple ideas in a forceful style. The main points of the text are as follows: (i) the land is a natural resource and as such should not belong to any individual, but instead should be commonly owned and cultivated; (ii) individuals should live off their own work, which is based on their tastes and capacities, and one's surplus should be used to counterbalance other people's deficiencies; (iii) accumulation of private capital should be avoided, and all wealth should be shared; (iv) the state government is an instrument of oppression of the workers and should be eliminated, with taxation and military conscription being especially odious; (v) the head of the government, the emperor, is not the descendant of gods, as the state propaganda maintains, but rather the descendant of "murderers and thieves" from a "remote corner of Kyushu"; (vi) war is caused by the states and not by their citizens, so that abolishing the state will bring an end to the cause for war all over the world; (vii) anarcho-communism is the solution, beginning by forming labour unions and expanding their impact from a village to the state to the entire world, at which point the ideal of anarcho-communism, that is, freedom and a comfortable life for all, will be realized; and (viii) such a revolutionary

42   Fabio Rambelli

movement requires self-sacrifice and readiness to use violence. Interestingly, explicit Buddhist themes and doctrines are absent.[8]

Heibon no jikaku is an incomplete manuscript that was returned to Uchiyama's relatives after his execution; it is possible that Uchiyama wrote it in prison before execution. In the text, Uchiyama sets out to define the necessary state of mind (consciousness) that would lead individuals and communities to realization of an ideal anarchist society.[9] He argues that the acquisition of consciousness will transform the way in which people see themselves, their place in society, and the way they live. The family, as the smallest and most intimate human group, is the centre of the programme of revolutionary transformation; therefore, the head of the household should lead family members to awaken their own consciousness. Particularly important is the egalitarian example that the head sets for the other members, especially his children (by raising them in the habit of acting in their own way), as the future free individuals of the anarchic paradise; and the elders, the hardest people to educate to the new social model. Uchiyama also treats women as equal to men and as equally autonomous and free individuals.

In the workplace, Uchiyama stresses the need to establish trade unions and turn factories into collective properties belonging to the workers. He is more sceptical about the acquisition of consciousness among farmers, perhaps on the basis of his own experiences with tenant farmers at his temple, whom he describes as generally conservative and influenced by feudal mores and thus devoid of spirit of initiative. In addition to the fact that capitalists and landowners should turn their properties into communal assets, Uchiyama proposes the establishment of workers' relief funds (insurance) and free and universal education and health care. Significant is also the emphasis on workers' welfare outside of work time, with the proposed creation of "clubs" (recreational facilities) where members can pursue their interests, deepen their education and knowledge, and refine their artistic tastes. Particularly important is free public education for working-class children, which will give them the opportunity to develop their work skills and attitudes so that they can become active and autonomous workers.

Uchiyama decided to employ socialism, especially anarchism, in order to bridge Buddhist spirituality and social revolutionary activism; in this sense, Buddhism and anarchism were for Uchiyama mutually reinforcing, rather than being conflicting and mutually exclusive (Morinaga 1984: 148–149). Uchiyama's anarchist Buddhism sought not only to improve living conditions, but also and especially to create a communist society of free individuals and communities—a new condition he expressed with the soteriological and eschatological image of paradise (*tengoku*), a term that occurs several times in *Heibon no jikaku*. The choice of this terminology is significant because in Japanese *tengoku* refers explicitly to the Christian paradise and not to the Buddhist realms of bliss, normally expressed by terms such as *gokuraku* ("land of supreme bliss") or *jōdo* ("pure land"). We can understand Uchiyama's use of this Christian image in various ways. In the first place, Christianity in Meiji Japan was closely related to the development of the socialist movement, and some Christian themes may have influenced the overall terminology of liberational discourses. Second, international socialist and anarchist movements already employed many Christian eschatological images, including the secularist appropriation of Jesus as a fighter for the liberation of the oppressed. Finally, the Buddhist notion of a Pure Land had come to be associated with a postmortem realm of the dead and was hardly appealing for a thriving revolutionary attempt at changing the present society.

In stark contrast to Sada Kaiseki, Uchiyama's analysis of contemporaneous Japanese society was mediated by a socialist perspective that took for granted the existence of an already established and thriving capitalist mode of production. For him, modern Western capitalism was not something to avoid, but a real and present enemy that had to be countered by activism aimed at the establishment of socialism. Uchiyama was strongly critical of social injustice caused by wealth disparity, which he explained as the result of a wrongful process of primitive accumulation. As a solution, he proposed various ways for people to acquire consciousness: the proletariat should unite and engage in collective action, such as strikes, refusal to pay taxes, objection to conscription, creation of associations for mutual aid, and so forth, while the capitalists should acknowledge their faults and redistribute their wealth among the collectivity. The acquisition of consciousness, a common theme in the literature of the international socialist movement, acquires a different resonance when discussed by a practising Zen monk, as a process analogous to that leading one to awakening.

It is interesting to note here that Uchiyama's blueprint for realizing a future anarcho-communist society owed a lot to his reading of anarchist texts and his conversations with people belonging to Kōtoku Shūsui's entourage. But perhaps even more than that, Uchiyama's writings were the result of his own personal engagement with international anarchist thought and his own beliefs as a Buddhist, while participating in a shared Japanese discourse about social justice. However, Uchiyama does not appear to have influenced the next generation of Buddhist socialists such as Senoo Girō, and not even his former comrades Ishikawa Sanshirō (1876–1956) and Ōsugi Sakae (1885–1923).[10]

Itō Shōshin: The Cosmic Mission of Modern Japan

Itō Shōshin was born in 1876 in present-day Kuwana, Mie Prefecture, in a family of farmers, as Itō Kiyokurō. At thirteen, he took the ordination and received his Buddhist name Shōshin. He studied at Buddhist schools and attended Shinshū University (now Ōtani University), then located in Tokyo, under Kiyozawa Manshi. In 1904, when he was caring for his ill father, he had a religious experience that marked his entire life and subsequent career: he had a revelation of what he came to call "selfless love" (*mugaai*). In 1905, he created in present-day Hekinan City, Aichi Prefecture, an organization that he called Mugaen ("Garden of Selflessness") to practise and spread the content of his enlightenment; it attracted the attention and sympathy of leading members of the socialist movement. However, only a few months later, Itō shut it down for reasons that are not entirely clear. A few years later, he restarted it but with a different orientation. At the same time,

44   Fabio Rambelli

Itō also began a busy career as a public intellectual and proselytizer and engaged himself in numerous editorial activities (journals, publishing houses, books), conference tours, radio lectures, and academic endeavours.

At the time of establishing his Mugaen organization, Itō was briefly in touch with members of the rising Japanese socialist movement, such as Tokutomi Roka, Kōtoku Shūsui, Sakai Toshihiko, Kawakami Hajime, and Uchiyama Gudō. However, he quickly turned away from it. Subsequently, Itō gradually began to combine his ideas about selfless love as a universal cosmic principle with the more radical tendencies of emperor worship or Mikadoism, in forms that became more and more extreme. After the end of World War II, Itō stayed on the margins of the public discourse and did not publish much, but apparently never renounced his wartime positions. In fact, he argued that out of Japan's lost war came a new impulse for the realization of selfless love through pacifism. Let us now look at Itō's thought in some detail.

What he defined as "selfless love" (*mugaai*) is the fundamental essence of nature and the universe. As Itō explains,

> when each single entity within the universe entrusts its own whole life completely to the love of every other individual entity, and at the same time it loves with all its capacity all other individual entities, this spirit and this activity is the product of the activity of selfless love. . . . Each individual entity gives up any attempt to build up its own life project, but instead, by practising selflessness (*muga*), it entrusts its whole destiny, whatever that may be, to the love by the others; at the same time, it devotes all its forces and capacities to the love of others, without searching for any personal profit or advantage.
>
> (Itō 1956: 63)

Here, the expression "each single entity" refers not only to human beings, but to any entity in the whole universe, from astral bodies down to subatomic particles; for Itō, selfless love, as the essence of the entire universe, operates within and among everything in it. Next, Itō argues that the realization of this absolute truth enables one to overcome all suffering and distress, because everything that happens is a manifestation of this universal love-power; furthermore, every single entity in the universe aspires to experience and manifest selfless love. Finally, each of us will also eventually experience selfless love and put it into practice in all aspects of our life (Itō 1956: 62). Although the term selfless love is the result of an explicit combination of a Buddhist concept (*muga*, "selflessness") with a Christian one (*ai*, "love"), Itō emphasized that "selfless love", as the absolute truth of the universe, was independent of any established religion or philosophical system.

Initially, Itō thought that selfless love ought to be practised individually and through social action; this was the time of his brief rapprochement with the Japanese socialist movement. Itō's idea of selfless love did contain elements of communal sharing and mutual aid that characterized the early socialist movement in

Japan. However, Itō began to attempt to connect his idea of selfless love to the "spirit of the creation of Japan" (*kenkoku seishin*) as expressed in the ancient myths of *Kojiki* and *Nihon shoki*; in this way, it would be possible to transform the Japanese nation in terms of selfless love (*Nippon kokka sono mono no mugaai-ka*). As a result, Japan would win the Pacific War, create the East Asian Co-prosperity Sphere, and succeed in establishing a New World Order under the enlightened guide of the emperor as the embodiment of the supreme will of the Japanese gods and their moral values (especially, self-sacrifice and devotion to the collectivity).

In order to connect his own idea of selflessness with the imperial project of modern Japan, Itō turned his attention to what he variously calls Japanese spirit (*Nippon seishin*), Japanese thought (*Nippon shisō*), or Japanese philosophy (*Nippon tetsugaku*), which he identifies with the Way of the Gods (*kannagara no michi*) of Shinto-based radical nationalism. Itō claimed that the Japanese spirit is universal in its essence and underlies all religions: all religions and philosophies in fact aspire to attain the central values of the Way of the Kami, namely, harmony and selflessness. Indeed, Itō argues that the time has come for the unification of all world religions and philosophies (*mankyō kyōwa*), and that the great, historical mission of Japan (*Nippon no daishimei*), as the final unfolding of the Yamato spirit and the ultimate realization of the Way of the Kami, is the establishment of a new world order based on the ideals of cooperation and harmony (*daikyōwa sekai*); this new world order can be instituted by following the dictates of the Imperial Rescript on Education (*Kyōiku chokugo*), a fairly innocuous text that became the sacred book of the Japanese emperor's cult (Itō 1937a).[11]

His interest for the right-wing interpretations of Japanese myths brought Itō to question the validity of Buddhism in contemporary Japan. He concluded that Buddhism had serious flaws as it departed significantly from the imperial ideology (*kōdō*) and the fundamental aspects of Japanese national essence (*kokutai*). Indeed, Itō strove for several years to determine how Buddhism, despite these flaws and limitations, might still be useful for the Japanese in the new age of imperial rule and emperor's worship. Itō also concluded that only the elements of Buddhism that could be harmonized with the Japanese spirit had to be preserved; everything else, remnants from India and China, should be eliminated without regret.[12]

After the war, Itō became a pacifist. One of the last articles he published deals with the geopolitical security of postwar Japan; in it, Itō argued in favour of disarmament and support for the new Peace Constitution of postwar Japan (Itō 1951). However, Itō remained unrepentant of his support of wartime Japan's imperialist policies. He wrote that, although Japan's crushing defeat prevented the realization of this plan as he had conceived of it, the promulgation of Japan's new constitution could still become the foundation for world peace; this was indeed the result of Japan's transformation in light of selfless love (Itō 1956: 65). Thus, Itō argued somewhat fancifully that the postwar achievements of Japan were the results of his own ideals. This is a common position among right-wing thinkers in Japan today, for whom the war was an enormous sacrifice that was carried out in order to

46   *Fabio Rambelli*

create a prosperous country, never mind that future prosperity was not the primary reason for which the war was fought.

As we can see, Itō's intellectual career embodies several of the challenges and contradictions faced by Buddhist intellectuals during the high time of Japanese imperialism and emperor's worship. Itō was not satisfied with traditional, premodern teachings, and came up with his own formulation of an absolute truth, which he called "selfless love", and which explicitly combined elements from Buddhism and Christianity, with a strong awareness of new religious movements and spiritualism; this latter awareness was in itself an indication of dissatisfaction towards established Buddhism, a dissatisfaction that became explicit already in 1904 when he publicly announced his separation from the Jōdo Shinshū sect.

Itō attempted to connect his own spiritual experience of selfless love to social activity and politics: first by connecting it with the socialist movement and later with the *kokutai* imperial ideology; only at the end of his life did he espouse pacifism. Underlying all this was also Itō's sense, shared by many Japanese at the time, of the need for a new world order, no longer based on the principles sanctioned by Western imperialism. This new world order centred on Japan and its emperor ought to be more spiritual (as opposed to Western emphasis on materialistic concerns) and collective-national (rather than individualistic or supernational-socialist), and it had as its ultimate goal the realization of a supreme form of harmony (as opposed to hierarchy) and world peace. In Itō's view, harmony was the overcoming of individual differences, also in terms of thought and beliefs; that's why Itō (together with many authors at the time) insisted upon the unification of the world's religions and philosophies. It is possible to argue that Itō attempted to articulate a response to Western imperialism by rejecting both its capitalist policies and its socialist alternatives in a vision of totalitarian and spiritual harmony under the sacred leadership of the Japanese emperor, whom he envisioned as an absolute and divine Führer. In this sense, Itō, much like Uchiyama, was pursuing a personal solution to issues that were largely couched in a broader international context, from within a shared Japanese discourse (in this case, right-wing ideology).

Final Considerations

The struggle to redefine Buddhism, in order to adapt it to the new circumstances brought about by modernity, resulted in a neutral, default position that came to constitute the mainstream, and in many ways, still sets the tone of our contemporary understanding of Buddhism in Japan: a form of spirituality, which is generally expressed through the performance of rituals, and which is ultimately unrelated to politics, social movements, and economics. (Also because of this, Engaged Buddhism has never been a strong component of contemporary Japanese Buddhism.) Of course, this default position was largely based on the acceptance of modes of understanding coming from the West—in particular, the Euro-American North Atlantic regions that were largely indebted to post-Reformation ideas of religion

The Capitalist Transformation   47

as characterized by spiritual and ethical beliefs rooted in personal experience and expressed in rational, philosophical terms.

Around this default understanding, other positions and views also developed and were influential in some circles for some time. Some authors, such as Sada Kaiseki, rejected state-driven modernization in favour of continuity with premodern understandings and practices. Others accepted the challenge of modernity, but came up with alternative and more engaged ways to be modern, as it were. The socialist-anarchist movement, in particular with Uchiyama Gudō, claimed that to be a Buddhist means to be a socialist: Buddhism for him became the general framework within which a different discourse and practice of modernity could unfold—one that was against the kind of modernization favoured by the state and the ruling block, but emphasized, instead, mutual aid, cooperation, and sharing labour and resources. Itō Shōshin, after an initial contact with the socialist movement, subsequently distanced himself from it by drifting to the opposite pole, namely radical nationalist Mikadoism; for Itō, in this new phase of thought and activity, the modern Japanese nation-state centred on the absolute and divine figure of the emperor was the ultimate framework that would give Buddhism (albeit a Buddhism that had been purged of its deleterious Indian and Chinese influences) its supreme meaning—a meaning that was still subordinate to the essence of the Japanese national polity or *kokutai*.

A major issue for Buddhist intellectuals concerned Buddhism's role in the modern cultural order. More specifically, they debated whether Buddhism is an autonomous discourse capable of defining and controlling other discourses, or whether it is instead dependent upon other discourses and is thus defined by them. Sada strongly argued for the former position, Itō embraced the latter, and Uchiyama situated himself in between. Sada believed that Buddhism had to define and determine all other discourses, from geography and astronomy to the economy, social order, and even leisure; to him, being a Buddhist meant to have a general (but by no means simplistic or even fundamentalistic) vision of society deeply supported by and infused with Buddhist ideals. Uchiyama, instead, saw in Buddhism some fundamental elements in a socialist transformation of society, but he also knew that Buddhism had been (and was being) used as an ideological tool to justify exploitation and social injustice. In contrast, Itō tried to infuse Buddhism with a number of heterogeneous elements, and ultimately argued that the new Japanese imperial system forced Japanese Buddhists to come to terms with the fact that the Japanese emperor was the supreme divinity and thus surpassed even Śākyamuni and his teachings; Itō's own question was how to be a Buddhist when Buddhism had been relativized and rendered obsolete by Japanese imperial worship.

Another major issue concerned Buddhism's relation to the new, modern nation-state. It has been argued that the modern nation-state is perhaps the most important formation to emerge in modernity, and which indeed characterizes it. Seeing Buddhism as autonomous from the state, as Sada did, is a position that relativizes the totalizing tendencies of the latter; in contrast, seeing Buddhism as subservient to the state and, above all, to the emperor, as in Itō's case, radically redefines the role of Buddhism in society. It is true that Buddhism, throughout

48　*Fabio Rambelli*

its history, has had a conflicting relationship with the state and political authority, and interpreters argued for both Buddhism's separation from, and ultimate superiority with regards to, the state, and the state's right to control and supervise Buddhism. However, modernity radically changed the nature of the issue because of the formidable power (both in terms of suasion and coercion) of the modern state.

In any case, it is perhaps worth noting that these questions are themselves the products of modernity, and at the same time its symptoms. It would appear that, whenever people begin asking these kinds of questions, they are already living in modernity.

Notes

* I wish to express my gratitude to Mark Teeuwen, Vladimir Tikhonov, James Mark Shields, Sabine Frühstück, Luke Roberts, Dominic Steavu, Richard Payne, Micah Auerbach, and Stefania Travagnin for their insightful comments and suggestions at various stages in the preparation of this essay.
1. See Grapard (1984, 1992), Ketelaar (1990), and Rambelli (2012: esp. 68–76).
2. The Iwakura Mission of 1868–1869 was very influential in shaping the early phases of Japanese understanding of Western capitalism. See Tanaka (2003: esp. 85–110).
3. For a more recent discussion of this subject, see also Zizek (2014).
4. The last two years of Sada's life were dedicated to creating and organizing in various parts of Japan popular associations for the boycott of foreign products; he died during a lecture tour to sponsor such a society.
5. On Uchiyama Gudō, see Rambelli (2013).
6. Kōtoku Shūsui was one of the fathers of the Japanese socialist and anarchist movements in the early twentieth century. See Notehelfer (1971) and Tierney (2015).
7. Among the twenty-four people who were initially handed down a death sentence, there were three other Buddhists, in addition to Uchiyama: Takagi Kenmyō, Sasaki Dōgen, and Mineya Setsudō. Uchiyama was the only one who was actually executed; the others had the death penalty commuted to life sentences and all died in prison (Takagi committed suicide).
8. For a full translation of this text, see Rambelli (2013: 45–51).
9. Complete English translation in Rambelli (2013: 53–65).
10. On Senoo Girō, see Shields (2012); on Ishikawa Sanshirō, see Willems (2012); on Ōsugi Sakae, see Stanley (1982) and Ōsugi (1992).
11. On the production of the *Kyōiku Chokugo*, see Gluck (1985: esp. 120–127).
12. A systematic discussion of this subject can be found in his book *Shinsei bukkyōgaku* (The Right Study of Buddhism) (Itō 1942) and, in more succinct form, in the booklet *Ikita Amida-sama wa doko ni gozaru ka* (Itō 1937b).

References

Breen, John. 1996. "Accommodating the Alien: Ōkuni Takamasa and the Religion of the Lord of Heaven." In *Religion in Japan: Arrows to Heaven and Earth*, edited by Peter Kornicki and Mark McMullen, 179–197. Cambridge: Cambridge University Press.
———. 1997. "Shinto and Buddhism in Late Edo Japan: The Case of Ōkuni Takamasa and His School." *Current Issues in the Social Sciences and the Humanities* 14: 133–148.
Eisenstadt, S. H. 2003. *Comparative Civilizations and Multiple Modernities*. 2 vols. Leiden: Brill.
Gluck, Carol. 1985. *Japan's Modern Myths: Ideology in the Late Meiji Period*. Princeton, NJ: Princeton University Press.

The Capitalist Transformation 49

Grapard, Allan G. 1984. "Japan's Ignored Cultural Revolution: The Separation of Shinto and Buddhist Divinities in Meiji (*shimbutsu bunri*) and a Case Study: Tōnomine." *History of Religions* 23 (3): 240–265.

———. 1992. *Protocol of the Gods: A Study of the Kasuga Cult in Japanese History.* Berkeley, CA: University of California Press.

Hall, Stuart. 1995. "Negotiating Caribbean Identities." *New Left Review* 209 (January–February): 3–14. Accessed 7 March 2016. http://www.icm.arts.cornell.edu/stuart_hall_readings_2014/Hall%20-%20Negotiating%20Caribbean%20Identities.pdf.

Itō, Shinjō. 1937a. *Shūkyō Nippon no daijikaku.* Aichi: Mugaen hakkō.

———. 1937b. *Ikita Amida-sama wa doko ni gozaru ka.* Aichi: Mugaen hakkō.

———. 1942. *Shinsei bukkyōgaku.* Tokyo: Dōshi dōkōsha.

———. 1951. "Nippon no anzen hoshō no mondai: Ichi bukkyōto no jiji zuisō." *Sekai bukkyō* 6 (4): 19–21.

———. 1956. "Waga mugaai seikatsu shinjō." *Daisekai* 11 (7): 61–65.

Ketelaar, James E. 1990. *Of Heretics and Martyrs in Meiji Japan: Buddhism and Its Persecution.* Princeton, NJ: Princeton University Press.

Morinaga, Eizaburō. 1984. *Uchiyama Gudō.* Tokyo: Ronsōsha.

Notehelfer, F. G. 1971. *Kōtoku Shūsui: Portrait of a Japanese Radical.* Cambridge: Cambridge University Press.

Ōsugi, Sakae. 1992. *The Autobiography of Ōsugi Sakae.* Berkeley, CA: University of California Press.

Rambelli, Fabio. 2011. "Sada Kaiseki: An Alternative Discourse on Buddhism, Modernity, and Nationalism in the Early Meiji Period." In *Religion and Politics in Japan: Red Sun, White Lotus,* edited by Roy Starrs, 104–142. New York: Palgrave Macmillan.

———. 2012. "Iconoclasm and Religious Violence in Japan." In *Buddhism and Iconoclasm in East Asia: A History,* edited by Fabio Rambelli and Eric Reinders, 47–88. London: Bloomsbury.

———. 2013. *Zen Anarchism: The Egalitarian Dharma of Uchiyama Gudō.* Berkeley, CA: Institute of Buddhist Studies.

Sada, Kaiseki. (1877) 1980–1986. "Shijitsu tōshōgi ki shohen." In *Meiji bukkyō shisō shiryō shūsei.* Vol. 5, edited by Meiji bukkyō shisō shiryō shūsei henshū iinkai, 373–393. Kyoto: Dōhōsha.

———. (1878–1879) 1967. "Saibai keizairon." In *Meiji bunka zenshū.* Vol. 23, edited by Meiji Bunka Kenkyūkai, 307–410. Tokyo: Nihon hyōronsha.

———. (1879) 1980–1986. "Bukkyō sōseiki." In *Meiji bukkyō shisō shiryō shūsei.* Vol. 7, edited by Meiji bukkyō shisō shiryō shūsei henshū iinkai, 22–37. Kyoto: Dōhōsha.

Shields, James Mark. 2012. "A Blueprint for Buddhist Revolution: The Radical Buddhism of Seno'o Girō (1889–1961) and the Youth League for Revitalizing Buddhism." *Japanese Journal of Religious Studies* 39 (2): 331–351.

Stanley, Thomas A. 1982. *Ōsugi Sakae, Anarchist in Taishō Japan: The Creativity of the Ego.* Cambridge, MA: Council on East Asian Studies, Harvard University and Harvard University Press.

Tanaka, Akira. 2003. *Meiji Ishin to seiyō bunmei.* Tokyo: Iwanami shoten.

Tanikawa, Yutaka. 2002. " 'Kijin' Sada Kaiseki no kindai." *Jinbun gakuhō* 87 (December): 57–102.

Tierney, Robert Thomas. 2015. *Monster of the Twentieth Century: Kōtoku Shūsui and Japan's First Anti-Imperialist Movement.* Berkeley, CA: University of California Press.

Willems, Nadine. 2012. "Ishikawa Sanshiro's Vision of the Natural Order: The Agrarian Foundations of Early 20th-Century Japanese Anarchism." PhD diss., Oxford University.

50 *Fabio Rambelli*

Yoshida, Kyūichi. 1964. *Nihon kindai shakaishi kenkyū*. Tokyo: Yoshikawa Kōbunkan.

———, ed. 1969. *Meiji shūkyō bungakushū*. Vol. 1 [Meiji bungaku zenshū vol. 87]. Tokyo: Chikuma shobō.

———. 1970. *Nihon no kindai shakai to bukkyō*. Tokyo: Hyōronsha.

Zizek, Slavoj. 2001. "From Western Marxism to Western Buddhism." *Cabinet* 2 (Spring). Accessed 7 March 2016. http://www.cabinetmagazine.org/issues/2/western.php.

———. 2014. *Event*. London: Penguin Books.

4 Parsing Buddhist Modernity in Republican China

Ten Contrasting Terms

Justin R. Ritzinger[*]

Prologue

The republican period of Chinese history (1911–1949) was a time of tumultuous transformation when the pillars of the old world had crumbled and dreams of a new world abounded. The Manchu Qing dynasty that had governed China since 1644 collapsed in 1911, due to internal unrest and imperial predation. The republic that followed was frequently marked by war and political instability, but also a florescence of society and culture. Whereas early historiography looked to the former and saw "China in Disintegration" (Sheridan 1975), many scholars today have turned to the latter and found an "Age of Openness" (Dikötter 2008), a time in which new classes and social forces engaged with the currents of global culture to a remarkable degree and dared to dream of remaking China in ways large and small.[1]

For Buddhism, too, it was a time of both peril and possibility. The tradition faced a resource-hungry state, a new discursive and legal regime, and intellectual challenges from science and iconoclastic ideologies, as well as competition from missionary Christianity and home-grown salvationist movements. Yet the state's modernizing agendas created opportunities for alliance as well as occasions for conflict, new legal frameworks allowed claims to be made against the state, changes created new constituencies and sources of patronage, and contact with novel ideas inspired as well as challenged.[2]

In this chapter, I will paint a rough picture of the way Buddhists navigated this period and how their tradition was transformed in the process. I will do so through five pairs of contrasting terms. These terms are not simple dichotomies in which one term represents modernity and the other its opposite. Rather, they are landmarks that defined the geography that Buddhists of the period navigated. In some cases, one of the terms was clearly the "right answer": to be labelled "superstition" rather than "religion" would have been catastrophic. But in most, the two terms represent opposite points on a continuum or even two options to be balanced and combined: "nationalism" and "internationalism" were by no means mutually exclusive.

The account to be given here is necessarily limited by several factors. First, there is the sheer diversity of the country. By necessity, I focus on the elite male

52   *Justin R. Ritzinger*

figures and movements of the Buddhist heartland that have been best studied. Second, the republic was a period of rapid change that calls out for a diachronic approach. For the sake of clarity and concision, however, my account is synchronic. Third, the study of republican-era Chinese Buddhism is only just beginning to receive its full due. For contemporary scholars, as for Buddhists of the time, the insufficiency of the old verities is all too clear, and the new understandings that will replace them are still being constructed. This chapter is a snapshot of a field in accelerating motion.

Establishment and Upstart

It has been a convention in the study of republican-era Chinese Buddhism to think of the monastic and lay elite as divided into "conservatives" (*baoshou pai* 保守派) and "reformers" (*gaige pai* 改革派). This reflects classical modernization theory in which individuals and movements may be classed by whether they reject or embrace the inevitable changes wrought by modernity. The insufficiency of these terms has long been apparent to many scholars, however. Raoul Birnbaum has argued, for instance, that the vision of Buddhist teaching and practice promoted by "conservative" figures such as the Pure Land master Yinguang 印光 (1862–1940) actually represents a departure from tradition better termed "fundamentalism" (Birnbaum 2003a: 127). Similarly, I have shown that the paradigmatic "reformer" Taixu 太虛 (1890–1947) was not the secularizing iconoclast he has sometimes been made out to have been (Ritzinger 2010). While the disagreements and competition between various individuals and factions were real, the battle lines and alliances were less stable and clear-cut than the ideological binary of "conservative" and "reformer" would suggest.

With the terms "establishment" and "upstart", I want to suggest a different angle from which to view these figures. Rather than ideas and ideology, this pair refers to the bases of power and charisma that elite figures drew upon as they attempted to promote their particular agendas. "Establishment" refers to those institutions and practices that were already well established and important at the beginning of the period. These included abbotships of large public monasteries, Dharma transmission, patronage (given or received), and periods of sealed retreat (*biguan* 閉關), as well as reputation for spiritual attainment, scriptural learning, and personal probity. "Upstart", by contrast, refers to those novel institutions and practices by which a monastic or lay figure could make a reputation. These included the national Buddhist associations, Buddhist seminaries or academies, modern learning, lay societies, public lecture tours, and modern media (the periodical press, the semi-commercial book market, and radio). These constituted new niches in the religious ecosystem where upstarts might thrive.

The power and charisma of most major figures in this period relied on some combination of established and upstart institutions and practices. If we were to somehow quantify this, we would find a continuum with a few individuals at one or the other end of the spectrum, but most arrayed somewhere in the middle. The great Chan master Xuyun 虛雲 (1864?–1959), for instance, would fall near the establishment end. Revered for his spiritual attainments, he spent much of his career practising in seclusion, studying as an itinerant monk, and restoring great public monasteries that had fallen into disrepair or decadence with the patronage of elites (Xu Yun 1988). Although transcripts of his Dharma talks and various occasional writings appeared in Buddhist periodicals in the republic, the number is comparatively small. Works he authored were published there forty-eight times.[3] Although he would become involved in founding the Chinese Buddhist Association after the communist revolution, this was recognition of his charisma (and its apolitical character) rather than its source.

Among monks, Taixu falls towards the upstart end of the spectrum but perhaps not so far as might be expected. Taixu built his career on the periodical press with an amazing 1,729 publications.[4] His journal *Haichaoyin* 海潮音, in which a majority of them appeared, was the longest lived periodical of the republic and a centrepiece of his movement. Also central to his movement were his seminaries, most importantly the Wuchang Buddhist Academy (Wuchang foxue yuan 武昌佛學院), the Minnan Buddhist Academy (Minnan foxue yuan 閩南佛學院), and the Sino-Tibetan Doctrinal Institute (Hanzang jiaoli yuan 漢藏教理院), and the various lay societies in which he played a role, such as the Hankou Right Faith Society (Zhengxin hui 正信會). Part of his appeal to the young monks who studied in his seminaries and the urban elites who joined lay societies with ties to him lay in his engagement with modern learning. In both the range of issues he addressed and the manner in which he did so, he was very much a precursor to the "monk as public intellectual" role occupied today by figures such as the Dalai Lama. Yet he was in other respects an establishment figure. He was trained at the best public monasteries of the Jiangnan region and spent almost three years in secluded retreat. Although he lacked a base of support in a large public monastery in his early career, he later served as abbot of Xuedou Monastery in Zhejiang through the patronage of Chiang Kai-shek. Conversely, he was shut out of the leadership of the national Buddhist association by establishment figures such as Yuanying 圓瑛 (1878–1953) until after the Japanese defeat in World War II.

Other monastic luminaries fell in between. Yinguang 印光 (1861–1940), for example, is best remembered for his exemplary Pure Land piety and his transformation of the Lingyan shan 靈巖山 Monastery. Yet much of his fame is owed to the world of modern publishing. *The Writings of Master Yinguang* (Yinguang fashi wenchao 印光法師文鈔) was a leading Buddhist bestseller, reprinted several times over the period. A second collection, *The Wise Words of Master Yinguang* (Yingguang fashi jiayan lu 印光法師嘉言錄), also went through several printings. This was a key reason why so many laity of the day, influential and ordinary, sought to take refuge with him and new lay organizations sought his mentorship. Yinguang, in turn, actively cultivated his following among the new lay elite (Tarocco 2007: 61–64; Kiely 2010: 199–203).

While major monastic figures tended to draw primarily or at least partially on establishment sources of power and charisma, a few prominent lay figures made their name almost entirely as upstarts. Ouyang Jingwu 歐陽竟無 (1871–1943) owed his prominence to modern textual scholarship and education, on which basis

54   *Justin R. Ritzinger*

he actively rejected established roles and institutions (to be discussed below). Others cut a less radical figure. Wang Yiting 王一停 (1867–1938), although a leader in the new World Buddhist Householder Grove (Shijie fojiao jushi lin 世界佛教居士林) who had made his fortune in modern commerce, derived his prominence in part to his ability to act as a traditional lay patron who might offer financial support and intercede with the authorities on behalf of the monastic community (Katz 2014: 117–151).

Religion and Superstition

The collapse of the imperial polity and the rise of the secular nation-state was a watershed event that upended the religious ecosystem of China. Prior to the modern period, the state had been a religiously constituted entity overseeing a plural orthodoxy defined by Confucian socio-ethical norms. Traditions that upheld those norms were considered orthodox (*zheng* 正), and those that were seen to deviate from them were classed as heterodox (*xie* 邪) and subject to sporadic suppression. In contrast, the republic was to be secular in nature, legitimated not by heaven but the people. Religion was to be protected according to international norms, but separate from and subordinate to the state. Yet the category "religion" (*zongjiao* 宗教) was a novel one, and it was not immediately clear in the early years of the republic which of China's spiritual traditions should be included.

There was a clear prototype, however: Christianity. To be a "religion", in the minds of many reforming elites, was thus to be organized, useful, and "pure". The ideological project of secularization thus had as its unintended consequence a process of "religionization", as various religious groups attempted to remake themselves in this image. Distinctions were still drawn between good and bad religiosity, but the criteria and the labels had changed. "Orthodoxy" and "heterodoxy" were replaced by "religion" and "superstition", categories distinguished not by morality but rationality. In the minds of many modernizing elites, religion would have to be stripped of irrational superstition in order to have a place in modern China. Whether there would be anything left was a matter of disagreement (Nedostup 2009; Goossaert and Palmer 2011; Katz 2014).

This new framework had powerful repercussions. The new constitution guaranteed "freedom of religious belief" but not freedom of religious practice, much less freedom of superstitious practice. Even the freedom of religious belief was protected only "within the limits of the law". Religious groups and institutions thus occupied what Rebecca Nedostup has termed the "grey zone", a state of strategically ambiguous legality which allowed the secular state to intervene in the religious sphere it had ostensibly renounced. Practices could thus be defined as superstitious and banned, and temple properties could be confiscated to be put in the service of the "greater good" (Nedostup 2009: 106–108).

Of all of China's indigenous religious traditions, Buddhism proved the most able to rise to the challenge presented by this new discursive and legal terrain. In order to make themselves "legible" to the state and protect their interests in the new order, Buddhists required an organized church-like body to represent them. The

Buddhist Modernity in Republican China   55

end of the Qing dynasty and the first days of the republic saw the birth of several organizations devoted to specific projects or representing limited constituencies, but the first broadly representative body to be established was the 1912 General Buddhist Association of China (Zhonghua fojiao zonghui 中華佛教總會). It ceased operation in 1918 but paved the way for the more enduring Chinese Buddhist Association (Zhongguo fojiao hui 中國佛教會) founded in 1929 under the Nationalist regime. This new organization was recognized by the state and folded into its state corporatist model of governance, trading a measure of autonomy for legal legitimacy and a degree of authority over the religion. Its legal status and the extension of its presence to the district level in many areas of the country gave it a measure of real power and effectiveness in defending Buddhist interests and property (Welch 1968: 23–50; Nedostup 2009: 47–53; Goossaert and Palmer 2011: 73–79).

In establishing church-like bodies to represent them in the newly distinguished sphere of "religion", Buddhist monastics were no doubt aided by the traditional perception that they stood outside the ordinary social world (*fangwai* 方外). But this same perception caused them difficulty on the second criterion of "religion": utility. The parasitic character of monastics had been a staple of anti-clerical discourse in the late imperial period. Hence, it was important to demonstrate that Buddhism was an asset to society and to the project of building a modern China. Social welfare work of various kinds was pursued by a variety of figures and organizations. Lay groups were especially active in this regard. The World Buddhist Householder Grove and the Pure Karma Society (Jingye she 淨業社), as well as the Right Faith Society in Hankou, were active in areas such as education, disaster relief, and aid to the poor (Welch 1968: 78–79; Jessup 2010: 29–48). Monastics were also involved in social work, but their role was often less direct. Monasteries would establish charitable ventures such as orphanages, clinics, and primary schools, but staffed them primarily with laity rather than monks, who were generally not trained for such work (Welch 1968: 121–131).

The final implicit criterion delineating an acceptable "religion" from an unacceptable "superstition" was "purity". Goossaert glosses this as being "spiritual and ethical", but I would like to stretch it here to include being rational, or intellectually pure, as well. The reconceptualization and reorganization of Buddhism as a "religion" entailed a new concern for standards and boundaries among elite lay and monastic leaders. True Buddhism would have to be separated from the crass, vulgar, and unorthodox. As a result, many Buddhist leaders praised the pure spiritual character of their tradition and its lofty ethic of compassion and self-sacrifice while inveighing against misguided superstition and commercialized ritual for hire.

The concern for intellectual purity was manifest in a number of different areas. "Orthodoxy" became an important byword. Rhetorically, it contrasted nicely with "superstition", since in Chinese the former meant literally "right faith" (*zhengxin* 正信), while the latter meant "deluded faith" (*mixin* 迷信). This also fed the period's renewed interest in the canon. Individuals like Ouyang Jingwu sought the true Dharma through scholastic research in long-neglected sutras and

56 *Justin R. Ritzinger*

treatises, particularly of the Yogācāra tradition (Aviv 2013; Chen 2013), while Ding Fubao and others endeavoured to make the "turbid sea" of the scriptures navigable for ordinary people (Scott 2014). Finally, it was an important driver of the engagement with science. A number of Buddhists—notably Wang Xiaoxu 王小徐 (1875–1948), You Zhibiao 尤智表 (1901–?), and Taixu—engaged widely with the scientific ideas and discoveries of their day, attempting to show that Buddhism was fully compatible with science or even subsumed it as a kind of "higher empiricism". In so doing, they sought to establish Buddhist teaching as impeccably rational according to the highest benchmark of the day, thereby sharply distinguishing it from superstition (Chen and Deng 2003: 473–498; Ritzinger 2013; Hammerstrom 2015).

Nationalism and Internationalism

The formation of the nation-state and the discourse of "religion" also ensured the centrality of "nationalism" and "internationalism" to the transformation of Buddhism in republican China. National salvation was the overriding task of the day for politically aware Chinese. The continuing weakness of the republic led many to seek a comprehensive transformation of society and culture that would unify and invigorate the Chinese people in the service of national strength and development. Yet even as they were preoccupied with the fate of the nation, Chinese of the period were deeply engaged with the broader world, travelling and studying abroad, participating in international organizations, and keeping abreast of the latest developments in world affairs. The impact of international exchange was deepest in treaty ports such as Shanghai but stretched far beyond them. Buddhists were caught up in this sense of national crisis and deepening international ties along with everyone else. At the same time, they were also influenced by new ideas about the role a "religion" should play in a nation and a new conceptualization of "Chinese Buddhism" as one instantiation of a "world religion".

For some in this period, Buddhism served as a kind of badge of "cultural loyalism". At a time when May Fourth radicals were arguing that Chinese culture had to be jettisoned entirely in order to save the nation, embracing Buddhism was, amongst other things, "choosing to be Chinese" (Welch 1968: 261). That Buddhism, which had been marked by its foreign origins since its transmission, had come to be seen as part of the Chinese cultural tradition (whether to be accepted or rejected) was itself no small change, but many went further. It was widely believed that "religion" played an important role in a nation's character and served to unify the populace. Taixu and others argued that a reformed Buddhism could serve this role for China, acting as a counter to imperialism and Christianity and the foundation for a new civic morality (Lai 2013: 196). As Gregory Adam Scott has noted, this represents a kind of inversion of the typical paradigm of religious nationalism. Rather than being an injection of religious images and idioms into nationalist discourse, we see an infusion of nationalism into the project of Buddhist reform. Religious reform was in part to serve national salvation (Scott 2011).

Buddhist Modernity in Republican China 57

This is key to understanding many Buddhist interactions with the state in this period. It is remarkable that at a time when the state often menaced temple property and encroached on religious freedom, Buddhists did not react with antagonism but aligned themselves with the state's goals and occasionally even sought out its intervention. The national Buddhist associations claimed a special relationship with the state, endorsing its reform goals and adopting the discourse of anti-superstition (Goossaert and Palmer 2011: 76–77). Likewise, Shanghai's Pure Karma Society and World Buddhist Householder Grove reoriented themselves towards charity in response to the new Nationalist regime in the Nanjing decade (1927–1937), supplementing the cash-strapped local authorities' efforts in areas such as education even at the expense of the Buddhist character of their endeavours (Jessup 2010: 29–48). Even in the extreme case of participation in the war against the Japanese, Buddhists put themselves in the service of the state in the hopes of saving the nation (Xue Yu 2005). Yet, as Rongdao Lai points out, this embrace of the cause of national salvation constitutes a paradoxical form of resistance to the secularizing state. Such Buddhist activism amounts to a deliberate transgression of the boundaries within which the state wished to confine it (Lai 2013: 229–230).

At the same time, Buddhists of the republic were deeply involved in international exchange. Modern communications and transportation opened up new possibilities, while the idea of Buddhism as a "world religion" redefined the proper scope of Buddhist community and activity. Chinese Buddhists in this period developed a renewed interest in Buddhist teachings beyond their borders. From early on, the apparent success of Japan and its Buddhism in modernizing drew attention, as did the presence of Japanese missionaries on Chinese soil (Welch 1968: 160–173). Yang Wenhui's ties with Nanjio Bunyu led to the retrieval of lost texts from Japan and opened the way for the introduction of Japanese Buddhology (Welch 1968: 2–10). Taixu travelled there in 1918 and again in 1925 (Jiang 1998: 490–495; Goodell 2012: 109–120) as did a number of individuals attracted by the esoteric teachings of Shingon (Chen 2008: 388–394). In the 1920s, however, interest in Japanese esotericism was eclipsed by a fascination with Tibetan forms, as the Panchen Lama and others began to offer teachings and empowerments in China and a few individuals such as Fazun and Nenghai journeyed to Tibet to study (Welch 1968: 175–179; Tuttle 2005: 74–102, 2008; Chen 2008: 394–411; Scott 2011: 69–73). In the 1930s, reevaluation of "Hinayana" in light of Orientalist scholarship also led to interest in the Buddhism of Southeast Asia and especially Ceylon (Welch 1968: 179–183; Ritzinger 2014). In addition, under the influence of Christianity and the world religions paradigm, many Buddhists began to think more globally. Taixu, of course, is famous for his ambitions in this regard, dreaming of proselytizing the West and founding a series of "world" organizations that never lived up to their names (Welch 1968: 55–64; Pittman 2001: 106–130), but he was not alone as the "World" Buddhist Householder Grove in Shanghai attests. Rather, Taixu is simply the most obvious sign of a broader expansion of horizons and ambitions.

58 *Justin R. Ritzinger*

Occasionally, Buddhist internationalism was put in the service of the nation. Gray Tuttle has demonstrated the critical role Buddhists played in the Nationalists' engagements with the Tibetans. When nationalist and racial arguments failed, they turned to Buddhism as the foundation of exchange. State patronage of lamas and Chinese Buddhist initiatives focused on Tibet, such as Taixu's Sino-Tibetan Institute, provided a tenuous but critical link between Tibet and the Republic of China at a time when the former Qing territory had slipped away (Tuttle 2005). During World War II, Buddhist internationalism again came to the service of the nation, when Taixu was sent by the government on a Goodwill Tour of South and Southeast Asia in order to counter Japanese propaganda which portrayed the Nationalist regime as anti-Buddhist (Pittman 2001: 139–143). Here again we see not so much an instrumentalization of Buddhism, but Buddhists willingly putting themselves in the service of the nation and in the process demonstrating the value of their pan-Asian tradition.

Lay and Monastic

The republican period also saw important shifts in the internal structure of the Buddhist community. The laity took on a new sense of identity and a new prominence within the religion. While this fell well short of the kind of generalized rejection of clerical authority often said to be a feature of religious modernization, the laity did occasionally encroach on traditional monastic prerogatives. Such encroachment coupled with critiques from outside the Buddhist community created a sense of crisis among monastics, who called for reinventing the institution or returning to older models that they felt had become lost.

In the late imperial period, "lay Buddhist" identity was amorphous at best. Most religious non-professionals drew from a variety of traditions' ideas, techniques, and services with little sense of exclusive commitment to any of them. As Christian-derived notions of "religion" took root in the republic, a more defined, though still not always exclusive, lay Buddhist identity began to take shape among urban elites. This new identity was developed and articulated in a new institutional space, the Householder Grove (Jushi lin 居士林). Such organizations are said to have existed in major cities across China, but the World Buddhist Householder Grove and its sister association, the Pure Karma Society, are the most important and the best studied. Unlike the devotional societies of the imperial period, these associations were founded by the laity on their own initiative and undertook a variety of activities, including not only self-cultivation but scriptural study, publishing, and charity. The basis of association was not a shared activity, but a shared identity. This identity was, moreover, self-consciously articulated in contrast to monasticism. The Householder Grove was established in the heart of the modern metropolis to extend the Dharma where monastics could not easily reach. As Brooks Jessup has shown, these organizations created a quasi-monastic space that served many of the functions of a temple, while blending with the urban environment and more importantly the lifestyle of its inhabitants. Yet they did not reject monastics or monastic guidance. They sought

Buddhist Modernity in Republican China 59

out prominent monks such as Yinguang to serve as "guiding teachers" (*daoshi* 導師) and give lectures and invited a few monks to take up residence as in-house ritualists (Jessup 2010: 5–28).

More disruptive to traditional roles was Ouyang Jingwu. A formidable scholar and the head of an important institution of Buddhist learning, the China Inner Studies Institute (Zhina neixue yuan 支那內學院), he claimed the right to define orthodoxy, from which he excluded much of the Chinese Buddhist tradition. Moreover, he made sophisticated, textually grounded arguments that a properly qualified layman could teach monks and even be considered part of the jewel of the *sangha*, blurring if not completely erasing the distinction. Such radical claims brought criticism from monks across the spectrum from Yinguang to Yinshun 印順 (1906–2004), though other monks, especially among the young, were in fact eager to learn from him. At the outset of the republic, Ouyang had actually attempted not only to assert doctrinal authority but actual organizational power, when he and five other layman proposed a Chinese Buddhist Association (Zhongguo fojiao hui 中國佛教會) to Sun Yat-sen, which would have put the monastic community under lay leadership for the first time (Aviv 2011: 47–53).

While this extreme scenario did not come to pass, it is interesting to note that the laity, specifically the elite householders of Shanghai, did play an important role in the founding of a new Chinese Buddhist Association that was recognized by the Nationalists in 1929. As a result, they occupied 30 per cent of the leadership positions, and the association itself was headquartered in the Pure Karma Society's complex, the Garden of Awakening (Jue yuan 覺園). Both practically and symbolically, the laity enjoyed new power and prestige (Jessup 2010: 32–33).

In contrast, many monastics felt the *sangha* to be in a state of crisis. Criticism from without was vociferous. Anti-clericalism had long been a strain in elite discourse in China, but in the late Qing and the republic it grew stronger and took on new forms and new proponents. Christian missionaries with a few exceptions, for instance, held monks in contempt as ignorant, immoral, and useless (Welch 1968: 222–227). Such foreign disdain had significant impact in a country questioning the value of its traditions in light of its weakness in the face of imperialism. To these voices were added those of many Chinese intellectuals who had embraced secularist ideologies. In their view, monks were but unproductive purveyors of superstition who could play no role in the building of a modern China. Such criticisms were echoed in the concerns of the monastic community itself. Many monks felt that the *sangha* was deeply troubled and required reform, though the diagnoses of its ills and the prescriptions proposed for its recovery naturally varied.

One commonly cited cause of decline was laxity in monastic discipline. Many Buddhists felt that the purity that had characterized the *sangha* in former days had been lost. This position was found not only among so-called conservatives but reformers as well. Taixu frequently complained of the corruption of the *sangha*, and his student Fafang declared that the decline of discipline was so advanced that the precepts had nearly disappeared, so that there was hardly a

60   *Justin R. Ritzinger*

pure monk to be found. This was a position shared with the era's foremost Vinaya master, Hongyi 弘一 (1880–1942), who declared in 1935 that there were, in fact, no *bhikṣus* in China. A valid transmission required a quorum of five pure monks, and there had been no such quorum in a thousand years. The monks of China were thus *bhikṣus* in name only. One solution proposed was to seek the pure Original Buddhism said to still exist in Ceylon, and several of Taixu's students were sent in the 1930s and '40s to live according to what was thought to be the pristine Vinaya (Ritzinger 2014). Hongyi, in contrast, looked to the indigenous Buddhist tradition. Immersing himself in the canonical literature, he wrote extensively, advocating a return to the teachings of the Nanshan 南山 school propounded by Daoxuan 道宣 (596–667) (Birnbaum 2003b, 2007; Chen and Deng 2003: 463–465).

Another issue was a perceived incompatibility of the existing monastic system with modernity. Redressing this problem through a comprehensive reorganization of the *sangha* was a central, and unfulfilled, aim of Taixu's career. In the early days of the republic, he advocated "three great revolutions" (*san da geming* 三大革命), two of which were aimed at the organization and property of the *sangha*. In 1915, during a period of sealed retreat, he wrote his most famous work on the subject "On the Reorganization of the Sangha System" (Zhengli sengqie zhidu lun 整理僧伽制度論). He would revise the vision articulated in this essay several times throughout his career, but the key characteristics remained consistent. Taixu hoped for a monastic community that would be strengthened by hierarchical organization, professionalized through specialization and division of labour, and trained through a modern educational system that would equip monks with both secular knowledge and Buddhist learning and cultivation (Jiang 1998: 439–466; Pittman 2001: 229–236; Goodell 2012: 98–105; Lai 2013: 121–129). While most of Taixu's plans for the *sangha* could never be carried out, he did have an important impact in education. Taixu's Wuchang Buddhist Academy served as the model for modern Buddhist seminaries in republican China. These seminaries and the textual communities anchored by them further served as the breeding ground for a reconceptualization of monastic identity: the "student monk" or "new monk", educated young monastics who saw themselves as citizens of the republic and the vanguard of Buddhist progress (Lai 2013).

This-Worldly and Other-Worldly

In this final section, we take up the dyad of "this-worldly" vs. "other-worldly". A "this-worldly" soteriology is often said to be a defining feature of modern religiosity. This world is both the arena of salvific action and religious fulfilment. In contrast, the classical goal of a blissful, other-worldly afterlife is de-emphasized or demythologized (Pittman 2001: 293).[5] Yet this is not what we find in republican-era Chinese Buddhism. Pure Land thrived not only among the poor and uneducated but also among the elite. Moreover, concerns for "this world" and for "other worlds" were closely connected. Other-worldly Pure Land was more associated

Buddhist Modernity in Republican China 61

with social action in this world and this-worldly Human Life Buddhism more concerned with rebirth in other worlds than one might expect.

Long the most popular form of Chinese Buddhism, Pure Land was infused with new vitality in the republic through the efforts of Yinguang. Far from promoting a demythologized vision of the Pure Land, Yinguang vigorously defended the position that Amitabha's paradise was a real place, in contrast to the more Chan-inflected position that pure land was simply an expression of pure mind. Only in this pure land was salvation to be found. This world was a burning house to be escaped (Jiang 1998: 420–423; Jianzheng 1998: 65–71). Where the "new monks" were deeply concerned with world events, Yinguang commented on the troubles of his time only to reinforce the need to seek rebirth. Yet it would be a mistake to see this concern for other worlds as excluding concern for this one. Yinguang was well aware that in the Mahayana, benefitting oneself necessarily depended upon benefitting others. He held ethical action to be the foundation of the path and a prerequisite for advancement (Jiang 1998: 424; Wei 2007: 45–47). Hongyi, who knew and deeply admired Yinguang, added that practitioners should "exert themselves strenuously in all meritorious deeds . . . beneficial to the masses in order to provision themselves for rebirth in the West" (Chen and Deng 2003: 370). Certainly, the Pure Karma Society in Shanghai saw extensive charitable activity and service to the nation as appropriate activities for aspirants to the Pure Land (Jessup 2010).

Likewise, although Taixu is known for his focus on this world, this was not so exclusive as has sometimes been imagined. Taixu is best remembered today for Human Life Buddhism (*rensheng fojiao* 人生佛教). Just as one might expect, Human Life Buddhism entails a refocusing of religious life on the human world and ethical action in it. Improvement of the human world through ethical action, however, is only the first of four aims of Human Life Buddhism identified by Taixu. The second is advancement in the next life through favourable rebirth; the third, liberation from *samsara*; and the fourth, Buddhahood. Taixu demonstrates a bit of ambivalence about the other-worldly second and third aims. These goals, represented by Pure Land and Esoteric Buddhism on the one hand and eremitic self-cultivation on the other, had been overemphasized in the past. Human Life Buddhism, he asserts, advances directly from the first aim to the fourth. However, this does not exclude them but "incorporates them seamlessly" (Taixu 2006).[6] We can get some sense of what he might mean by this from his ideas about Maitreya and his pure land. Taixu held that through ethical action in the world paired with devotion to Maitreya, one could contribute to the gradual purification of this world, while with the selfsame action securing one's progress on the path through rebirth in Maitreya's Inner Court in Tuṣita Heaven. When in the distant future the world would be fully purified, this would stimulate Maitreya to descend to this world, inaugurating the true Pure Land on Earth and bringing all the activist-devotees down with him to receive the prediction of Buddhahood (Ritzinger 2010). This demonstrates the complex interrelation of this-worldly and other-worldly in republican-era Buddhism and complicates portrayals of Taixu as a secularizing figure.

Epilogue

Buddhists in republican China thus navigated a complex landscape marked by novel developments that both threatened the religion and offered new opportunities. It was a landscape transformed by modernity but still shaped and informed by tradition. The major figures of the era continued to draw upon established sources of power and charisma to varying degrees, even as novel institutions and practices opened up new avenues to prestige and influence. The category of religion reconfigured the Chinese religious field, establishing a new model of acceptable religiosity—organized, useful, and pure. Among China's religious traditions, Buddhism was relatively successful at remoulding itself in this image and avoiding the label of "superstition" that would have marked it unfit for a modern nation. Based on the common idea of the time that religion was an essential part of a nation's character, Buddhists argued that their religion had an essential role to play in the project of national salvation, developing an inverted Buddhist nationalism in which the project of religious reform came to be infused with the discourse of national crisis. At the same time, the new conception of Buddhism as a "world religion" brought new exchanges with foreign co-religionists, exchanges that were sometimes put in the service of the nation. The clear identification implied by "religion" helped to foster a new lay Buddhist identity that sometimes encroached on monastic prerogatives. This encroachment, along with criticism from foreigners and Chinese elites, created a sense that the monastic institution was in a crisis that could be resolved only through the restoration of the purity of the past or a comprehensive reorganization to meet the needs of the present. Finally, while this world received new attention and new valorization as an arena of religious activity, the call of other worlds remained strong. Pure Land enjoyed a new vigour, and pure lands remained important even for those deeply engaged with this world.

The communist revolution in 1949 brought the period to a close and reshuffled the deck for Buddhists again. In the People's Republic, they continued to try to show their utility in the construction of a new China until the state began to liquidate the religious sector in the mid-1950s and attempted to eradicate it entirely in the Cultural Revolution (Welch 1972; Jessup 2012). In Taiwan, refugee Buddhists from the mainland struggled amongst themselves for status and resources, while the exiled republican government continued to constrict the religion's social space through its state corporatist policies and preferential treatment of Christianity (Jones 1999: 97–177; Ritzinger 2010: 311–341; Goossaert and Palmer 2011: 213–217). Small wonder Holmes Welch, writing in *Buddhism under Mao*, gloomily offered the "pragmatic" assessment that "Buddhism as a living religion" had disappeared for good in China (Welch 1972: 380). Yet in recent years, Buddhism has flourished in Taiwan and been reborn in the People's Republic. While the ultimate shape of these developments remains to be determined, the importance of patterns established in the republic is clear (Birnbaum 2003a; Ashiwa 2009). Welch thought that modernism had put Buddhism on a path to extinction that the communist revolution only hastened (Welch 1968: 268). Today, we can see that the current revival is built upon the foundations laid in the republic.

Notes

* This chapter benefitted from the helpful suggestions of Brooks Jessup, Hwansoo Kim, and Beverley McGuire. Any remaining errors or infelicities are my own.
1. For a recent survey of the period, see Zarrow (2005).
2. For a comprehensive overview of the transformation of Chinese religion in the republic and beyond, see Goossaert and Palmer (2011).
3. This figure is based on the number of articles for which he is the author according to the digital index to the 259-volume photo-reprint collection of republican-era Buddhist periodicals and its first supplement, the *Minguo fojiao qikan wenxian qikan ji bubian ziliaoku* 民國佛教期刊文獻集成及補編資料庫.
4. Although this includes some reprints, that does not detract from the point.
5. The distinction between "this-worldly" and "other-worldly" derives from Weber, of course, but he used it instead to designate religious activity undertaken within society vs. in seclusion from it (Weber 1978: 541–544; 2001).
6. For a much more detailed, diachronic account of Taixu's Human Life Buddhism, see Goodell (2012).

References

Ashiwa, Yoshiko. 2009. "Positioning Religion in Modernity: State and Buddhism in China." In *Making Religion, Making the State: The Politics of Religion in Modern China*, edited by Yoshiko Ashiwa and David L. Wank, 43–73. Stanford, CA: Stanford University Press.

Aviv, Eyal. 2011. "Ambitions and Negotiations: The Growing Role of Laity in Twentieth-Century Chinese Buddhism." *Journal of the Oxford Centre for Buddhist Studies* 1: 39–59.

———. 2013. "The Root that Nourishes the Branches: The Role of the *Yogācārabhūmi* in 20th-Century Chinese Scholastic Buddhism." In *The Foundation for Yoga Practitioners: The Buddhist Yogācārabhūmi Treatise and Its Adaptation in India, East Asia, and Tibet*, edited by Ulrich Timme Kragh, 1078–1091. Cambridge, MA: Harvard University Press.

Birnbaum, Raoul. 2003a. "Buddhist China at the Century's Turn." *China Quarterly* 174: 451–467.

———. 2003b. "Master Hongyi Looks Back: A Modern Man Becomes a Monk in Twentieth-Century China." In *Buddhism in the Modern World: Adaptations of an Ancient Tradition*, edited by Steven Heine and Charles Prebish, 75–124. Oxford: Oxford University Press.

———. 2007. "The Deathbed Image of Master Hongyi." In *The Buddhist Dead: Practices, Discourses, Representations*, edited by Jacqueline Stone and Bryan Cuevas, 175–207. Honolulu: University of Hawai'i Press.

Chen, Bing. 2008. "The Tantric Revival and Its Reception in Modern China." Translated by Monica Esposito. In *Images of Tibet in the 19th and 20th Centuries*, edited by Monica Esposito, 387–427. Paris: École française d'Extrême-Orient.

———. 2013. "Reflections on the Revival of Yogācāra." Translated by Justin R. Ritzinger. In *The Foundation for Yoga Practitioners: The Buddhist Yogācārabhūmi Treatise and Its Adaptation in India, East Asia, and Tibet*, edited by Ulrich Timme Kragh, 1054–1076. Cambridge, MA: Harvard University Press.

Chen, Bing 陳兵, and Deng Zimei 鄧子美. 2003. *Ershi shiji zhongguo fojiao* 二十世紀中國佛教 [Chinese Buddhism in the twentieth century]. Taipei: Xiandai chan 現代禪.

Dikötter, Frank. 2008. *The Age of Openness: China before Mao*. Berkeley, CA: University of California Press.

64   *Justin R. Ritzinger*

Goodell, Eric. 2012. "Taixu's (1890–1947) Creation of Humanistic Buddhism." PhD diss., University of Virginia.

Goossaert, Vincent, and David A. Palmer. 2011. *The Religious Question in Modern China*. Chicago: University of Chicago Press.

Hammerstrom, Erik J. 2015. *The Science of Chinese Buddhism: Early Twentieth-Century Engagements*. New York: Columbia University Press.

Jessup, James Brook. 2010. "The Householder Elite: Buddhist Activism in Shanghai, 1920–1956." PhD diss., University of California, Berkeley.

———. 2012. "Beyond Ideological Conflict: Political Incorporation of Buddhist Youth in the Early PRC." *Frontiers of History in China* 7: 551–581.

Jiang, Canteng 江燦藤. 1998. *Zhongguo jindai fojiao sixiang de zhengbian yu fazhan* 中國近代佛教思想的諍辯與發展 [Controversies and developments in modern Buddhist thought]. Taipei: Nantian 南天.

Jianzheng 見正. 1998. *Yinguang fashi de shengping yu sixiang* 印光法師的生平與思想 [The life and thought of master Yinguang]. Taipei: Fagu wenhua 法鼓文化.

Jones, Charles. 1999. *Buddhism in Taiwan: Religion and the State, 1660–1990*. Honolulu: University of Hawai'i Press.

Katz, Paul R. 2014. *Religion in China & Its Modern Fate*. Waltham, MA: Brandeis University Press.

Kiely, Jan. 2010. "Spreading the Dharma with the Mechanized Press: New Buddhist Print Cultures in the Modern Chinese Print Revolution, 1866–1949." In *From Woodblocks to the Internet: Chinese Publishing and Print Culture in Transition, circa 1800 to 2008*, edited by Cynthia Brokaw and Christopher A. Reed, 185–210. Leiden: Brill.

Lai, Lei Kuan Rongdao. 2013. "Praying for the Republic: Buddhist Education, Student-Monks, and Citizenship in Modern China (1911–1949)." PhD diss., McGill University.

Minguo fojiao qikan wenxian qikan jicheng ji bubian ziliaoku 民國佛教期刊文獻集成及補編資料庫 [Catalogue database of republican-era Buddhist journals]. n.d. Accessed 18 March 2016. http://buddhistinformatics.ddbc.edu.tw/minguofojiaoqikan.

Nedostup, Rebecca. 2009. *Superstitious Regimes: Religion and the Politics of Chinese Modernity*. Cambridge, MA: Harvard University Asia Center.

Pittman, Don A. 2001. *Toward a Modern Chinese Buddhism: Taixu's Reforms*. Honolulu: University of Hawai'i Press.

Ritzinger, Justin R. 2010. "Anarchy in the Pure Land: Tradition, Modernity, and the Reinvention of the Cult of Maitreya in Republican China." PhD diss., Harvard University.

———. 2013. "Dependent Co-Evolution: Kropotkin's Theory of Mutual Aid and Its Appropriation by Chinese Buddhists." *Chung-Hwa Buddhist Journal* 26: 89–112.

———. 2014. "Original Buddhism and Its Discontents: The Chinese Buddhist Exchange Monks and the Search for Pure Dharma in Ceylon." Paper presented at Asian Buddhism: Plural Colonialisms and Plural Modernities, Kyōto, 12–14 December.

Scott, Gregory Adam. 2011. "The Buddhist Nationalism of Dai Jitao 戴季陶." *Journal of Chinese Religions* 39: 55–81.

———. 2014. "Navigating the Sea of Scriptures: The Buddhist Studies Collectanea, 1918–1923." In *Religious Publishing and Print Culture in Modern China, 1800–2012*, edited by Phillip Clart and Gregory Adam Scott, 91–138. Berlin: de Gruyter.

Sheridan, James E. 1975. *China in Disintegration: The Republican Era in Chinese History 1912–1949*. New York: Free Press.

Taixu 太虛. 2006. "Rensheng fojiao de kaiti" 人生佛教的開提 [Remarks on Human Life Buddhism]. In *Taixu dashi quanshu* 太虛大師全書 [Collected works of Master Taixu].

Vol. 3, edited by Yinshun 印順, 217–222. Included in *Yinshun fashi foxue zhuzuo ji* 印順法師佛學著作集 [Master Yinshun corpus]. CD-ROM, version 4.0. Yinshun wenjiao jijinhui 印順文教基金會, 2006.

Tarocco, Francesca. 2007. *The Cultural Practices of Modern Chinese Buddhism: Attuning the Dharma*. London: Routledge.

Tuttle, Gray. 2005. *Tibetan Buddhists in the Making of Modern China*. New York: Columbia University Press.

———. 2008. "Tibet as the Source of Messianic Teachings to Save China." In *Images of Tibet in the 19th and 20th Centuries*, edited by Monica Esposito, 303–326. Paris: École française d'Extrême-Orient.

Weber, Max. 1978. *Economy and Society*. Berkeley: University of California Press.

———. 2001. *The Protestant Ethic and the Spirit of Capitalism*. New York: Routledge Classics.

Wei, Tao. 2007. "Pure Mind, Pure Land: A Brief Study of Modern Chinese Pure Land Thought and Movements." Master's thesis, McGill University.

Welch, Holmes. 1968. *The Buddhist Revival in China*. Cambridge, MA: Harvard University Press.

———. 1972. *Buddhism under Mao*. Cambridge, MA: Harvard University Press.

Xu Yun. 1988. *Empty Cloud: The Autobiography of the Chinese Zen Master*. Translated by Charles Luk. Shaftesbury: Element Books.

Xue Yu. 2005. *Buddhism, War, and Nationalism: Chinese Monks in the Struggle against Japanese Aggressions, 1931–1945*. London: Routledge.

Zarrow, Peter. 2005. *China in War and Revolution 1895–1949*. London: Routledge.

5 Seeking the Colonizer's Favours for a Buddhist Vision

The Korean Buddhist Nationalist Paek Yongsŏng's (1864–1940) Imje Sŏn Movement

Hwansoo Kim*

The modernity of Korean Buddhism is distinct in three respects. First, it emerged under the influence of Japanese colonialism and Buddhism, whereas Buddhist modernity, in most other Asian countries, grew under the dominance of Western colonialism and evangelical Christianity. Second, as a result of centuries-old marginalization of Korean Buddhism under the Neo-Confucian government of the Chosŏn dynasty (1392–1910), the Korean clergy's social status was radically different from that of their Japanese counterparts. Japanese Buddhism rose to be a symbol of Buddhist modernity at the time. Third, the Japanese colonial government and Buddhist missionaries used this unique history of Korean Buddhism as a leitmotif in their engagement with Korean Buddhists. As a result, modern Korean Buddhism can be characterized as, in Songt'aek Cho's words, "Buddhism in dilemma" (Cho 2013: 55). Korean Buddhists not only had to recover from their past traumatic memory and experience, but also had to reconstitute the social and institutional status of their marginalized religion. They had to accomplish these goals by navigating complicated relationships with colonizers with whom they shared a similar identity in terms of ethnicity, culture, and religion. Thus, Korean Buddhists predicated their effort to modernize Korean Buddhism on two exigencies: de-traumatizing from their stigmatized position and reconfiguring Korean Buddhism in response to and in emulation of Japanese Buddhism, as well as Christianity. Yet scholarship of modern Korean Buddhism tends to deemphasize this dilemma among Korean Buddhist monks and assumes that they were fully ready to resist against Japanese colonialism and imperial Buddhism for the Korean nation.

In this chapter, I will introduce a prominent monk, Paek Yongsŏng (1864–1940), and examine his life and Buddhist practice to present an example of this contradictory feature of modern Korean Buddhism. In so doing, I will challenge and add nuance to a one-sided image of him in current scholarship of being a heroic nationalist unfettered by the historical reality that Buddhism was placed under. Paek is one of the two most revered Buddhist monks in the historiography of colonial-era Korean Buddhism. In scholarship, both Paek and Han Yong'un (1879–1944) have been described as uncompromising nationalists at a time when

Paek Yongsŏng's Imje Sŏn Movement   67

most Korean monks did not reject the thought of collaborating with the Japanese colonizer.

However, when it comes to preserving the identity and tradition of Korean Buddhism, Paek overshadows Han. In contrast with Han's support of clerical marriage and his openness to Japanese Buddhist influence, Paek vigorously safeguarded clerical celibacy and rejected the Japanese form of Buddhism (Kim Kwangsik 2008). Thus, Paek is believed to be the defender of both Korean nationalism and the true Korean Buddhist identity (Kim Kwangsik 2002; Han 2010). This ethnocentric, one-dimensional interpretation has been a dominant lens through which to examine Paek's life and activities,[1] simplifying his otherwise diverse behaviours and thoughts that would, more broadly, elicit a dynamic feature of Korean Buddhist modernity.

Thus, this chapter illuminates a distinct modern Buddhist discourse in the context of colonial Korea, a discourse that is often silenced by nation-centred Buddhist narratives. Paek's primary concern was not to fight against Japanese colonialism and Japanese Buddhism but instead to restore Buddhism from marginalization to prominence in the country's centre by disseminating his version of modern Korean Buddhism, namely Imje Sŏn (Jp. Rinzai Zen or Ch. Linji Ch'an), one of the five major Ch'an schools. If analyzed from this viewpoint, Paek's life exhibits a much richer drama centred on his Buddhist vision, which was both modern and traditional. The promotion of Imje Sŏn-centred Buddhism and Paek's tireless efforts to create a centralized Buddhist institution under the Imje lineage can be exemplified by his 1913 interactions with three actors: the visiting Sri Lankan Buddhist leader Anagarika Dharmapala (1864–1933), the influential, though non-governmental Japanese Buddhist Abe Mitsuie (1862–1936), and the colonial authorities. With Dharmapala, Paek clearly exhibited his belief that the Imje Sŏn was superior to other forms of Buddhism. Abe, also a devoted Rinzai practitioner with political influence, was considered an ally by Paek. Abe abetted Paek in keeping alive his institutional vision for Korean Buddhism and, as a result, Paek actively sought Abe's assistance. Although Paek's contact with two Asian Buddhists was short-lived, their long-term impact on Paek was significant in terms of his decision to establish a new Buddhist religion.

Paek is not unique in prioritizing his religious vision over other discourses. Other Asian Buddhist reformers include Taixu (1890–1947) in China, Tanxu (1875–1963) in Manchukuo, and Dharmapala and Hikkaduve Sumangala (1827–1911) in colonial Sri Lanka, who likewise strove to protect, unify, and advance their own versions of Buddhism in the face of colonialism, nationalism, and modernity.[2] To this end, these individuals not only appropriated modern, traditional, and transnational ideas in their works but also employed multiple social and political affiliations even with colonizers. In her examination of Sumangala, Anne Blackburn terms this aspect the "locative pluralism" (Blackburn 2010: 209–211) that colonial-period Sri Lankan Buddhist leaders, including Sumangala, employed to rejuvenate their religion. Even somebody like the nationalist Paek took a similar trajectory as Sumangala in a different colonial context.

68 Hwansoo Kim

Relying on untapped primary materials, including Abe's collections (*Abe Mitsuie kankei bunsho*, hereafter *AMKB*)[3] of the letters[4] he exchanged with Paek, other Korean monks, and journals and newspapers, I seek to prove that Paek was a much more flexible figure than previously believed. By using a wide network of relationships, even with the colonizer, he opened the door to other options in an effort to accomplish his Buddhist vision. Paek's case attests to the complex colonial realities and colonial Buddhist modernity that prompted Koreans and Japanese alike to employ multiple visions and identities, including religious affiliation, around which they could build personal and group networks, however perilous and short-lived these transnational networks might have been.

Colonial Seoul as a Contentious Site for Buddhism

Colonial Seoul in the early 1910s and 1920s was a city of opportunities and challenges for Korean monastics. The centuries-old denial of access to the capital city imposed upon them during the Chosŏn era (1392–1910) was officially lifted. Thus, Korean monastics finally flocked into the centre of the city to reaffirm the presence of their religious tradition and also to pursue personal interests and group visions. Their dreams and institutional visions, however, had to be compromised and negotiated because of a new political reality. After opening Korea through gunboat diplomacy in 1876, Japan pushed China and Russia out of Korea during two modern wars in 1894–1895 and 1904–1905, a feat that transformed Japan into the only non-Western empire in the modern era (Myers and Peattie 1984: 6). Korea became a victim of this transformation and, as a result, was made a Japanese protectorate in 1905 and a formal colony in 1910. Korean Buddhists readjusted their survival tactics to deal with Japanese colonial rule (Tikhonov 2004).

Despite the upheaval, the situation of Korean Buddhists was better than under the previous Neo-Confucian government (1392–1910), as the colonial government considered Korean Buddhism an important asset for effective rule over Korea and took a conciliatory policy towards Buddhism. In addition, Korean monastics quickly realized that Buddhism fared much better in Japan, and Japanese Buddhist priests enjoyed greater political, social, and economic prestige compared with Korean Buddhists. Quite a few Korean monastics turned to Japanese Buddhists, who had the ability to provide access to modern education and opportunities. At the same time, Korean monks used the Japanese to leverage Korean officials, who denigrated their own monks and were still reluctant to bring monastics to the centre of the capital city. In 1908, two years prior to Japan's official colonization of Korea, Korean Buddhist leaders such as Yi Hoegwang (1862–1933) and Kang Taeryŏn (1875–1942) established the first modern Korean Buddhist institution, called Wŏnjong. Together they strove to bring the physical presence of Korean Buddhism back to Seoul. Lacking political capital, they were forced to turn to the powerful Japanese Buddhist Sōtōshū sect in an effort to influence the Korean and Japanese governments to permit a modern Korean Buddhist institution to be installed in central Seoul. In mid-1910, Yi succeeded in building a temple, Kakhwangsa, in central

Seoul, which was a watershed moment in modern Korean Buddhism. However, his effort to receive state recognition for the Wŏnjong ran into major roadblocks. Later that year, Yi and other Buddhist leaders decided to form an institutional alliance with the Sōtōshū to promote their goal more aggressively. This attempted alliance prompted Korean monks in opposition to Yi to form their own sect, Imjejong (Linji Sect). The Japanese Buddhist traditions, divided into thirteen sects and fifty-six branches at the time, also reacted to this alliance negatively. More importantly, the colonial government did not welcome internal Buddhist conflicts in addition to the Koreans' brewing resistance and bitterness over Japan's annexation of Korea (Kim Hwansoo 2013). The colonial government brought Korean Buddhism under direct government control through the 1911 Temple Ordinances (Kim Sunsŏk 2003). Bypassing both the Wŏnjong and the Imjejong, the government brought the thirty head temples of Korean Buddhism under its direct control under the same institutional title that the previous Chosŏn government had used, namely Sŏn Kyo Dual Sect (Sŏn Kyo Yangjong, hereafter Dual Sect). As a result, debates over lineage and power struggles surrounding this new institution soon intensified. Paek emerged as one of the most ardent dissenters from this Dual Sect arrangement since it placed the Kyo (sutra study) on par with the Sŏn (Zen practice). Japanese Buddhists were not mere bystanders but were deeply involved in changing the course of these debates, thereby complicating the configuration of modern Korean Buddhism. Thus, a tripartite relationship between Korean monastics, colonial authorities, and Japanese Buddhists defined many Korean Buddhist reformers' behaviours and thoughts, and Paek was at the centre of this complex triangle.

Paek as a Buddhist Propagator

When Paek, at the age of forty-two, arrived in Seoul in November 1905, he had already been known among Buddhist monastics and lay believers as a Sŏn master who was also well versed in Buddhist sutras and charismatic in his teaching. Born in 1864 to a Confucian family in southern Korea, Paek grew up learning the Confucian classics. However, as he recollected later, during his childhood, he suffered from his stepmother's "excessive abuse", which forced him to leave home at age sixteen (*Samch'ŏlli* 8/12 [December 1936]: 82). He commenced his monastic training under the guidance of Master Hwawŏl at the Haein temple and, at twenty-one, received the Bhikśu ordination at the T'ongdo temple. He undertook a series of meditation retreats at Sŏn monasteries around the country, exchanged spiritual experiences with Sŏn masters, and perused major Sŏn classics. At age forty, he commenced his teaching career, and when teaching at the Mang'wol temple in northern Seoul, the court ladies, aware of his fame, would visit the temple to have an audience with him (Han 1998).

In 1907, less than three years after Korea became a protectorate of Japan, Paek seized the opportunity to visit China, the motherland of Ch'an. During this six-month trip, he met many Chinese Ch'an practitioners and Buddhist leaders and engaged in Ch'an dialogues. In early 1908, he returned to central Seoul and, staying at a lay Buddhist's house, resumed teaching (Han 1998). Less than a year

Figure 5.1 Paek Yongsŏng
Source: *Maeil sinbo*, 1 February 1914

later, however, Paek left Seoul, because of his inability to raise the funds needed to establish a temple. In 1910, he wrote a book, *The Return to the True Teachings* (Kwiwŏn chŏngjong), to counter criticism of Buddhism by other religions, especially Christianity (Han 1999: 16–17). Four months after Japan colonized Korea in August 1910, Paek returned to Seoul and resumed his Sŏn teaching at the house of a lay Buddhist, determined to disseminate his version of Buddhism to the people of the city (Kim Kwangsik 2000: 68).

At this time, Paek's activities were primarily religious and did not exhibit any overt nationalist commitment. When he returned to Seoul and observed the religious landscape there, he was deeply saddened by the popularity of other religions, namely Christianity, and the lack of presence of his own religion. As he later wrote, he faced palpable discrimination against monks and was resolved to open a preaching hall to undertake Buddhist propagation. But though he gained hundreds of members, he again failed to muster enough financial support to build a centre (Kim Kwangsik 2000: 67–68).

It was in May of 1912 when Paek entered the public scene as he joined the Imje movement to counter the aforementioned Wŏnjong-Sōtō alliance. Han Yong'un and others had established the Imje Sect and positioned the headquarters of the Imjejong, the Central Preaching Hall of the Imje Sect of Korea (Chosŏn Imjejong chungang p'ogyodang), in Seoul. Paek was nominated as its propagation director (Kim Kwangsik 2000: 68). In a sense, it was a win-win situation for both men. Han, in order to undermine the Wŏnjong Sect, needed somebody like Paek, a

Paek Yongsŏng's Imje Sŏn Movement   71

charismatic Imje Sŏn teacher and an ardent propagator, who could challenge the stature of Yi Hoegwang. Paek, for his part, finally gained an already established temple to serve as a more stable environment for propagating Buddhism. In addition, the argument made by Han and others that Korean Buddhism derived from the Imje lineage fit perfectly with Paek's own position. From this time forwards, Paek's teaching of Imje Sŏn became more direct, and he forcefully presented Imje Sŏn as the unifying tradition for Korean Buddhism and its institutions. In July of the same year, however, the colonial authorities nullified both sects and established the Dual Sect, as stated earlier. Thus, unable to claim Imjejong as a sect, Han and Paek had to rename their institution the Central Preaching Hall of Korean Sŏn (Chosŏn Sŏnjong Chungang P'ogyodang). In contrast, Yi Hoegwang and others were quick to adopt the Dual Sect and, aligning with the colonial government's policy, designated the Kakhwang temple as its centre. Debates over which one would be a legitimate inheritor of Korean Buddhism soon ensued. Paek was at the forefront of these debates, striving to disestablish the Dual Sect and replace it with an Imje Sŏn-centred institution.

Interactions with Anagarika Dharmapala

Paek's stalwart devotion to Imje Sŏn ideology can be glimpsed in his brief interactions with Dharmapala, who, on his way to China (Steven Kemper 2015: 124–125), visited colonial Seoul for three days beginning 2 August 1913. Dharmapala was the most representative Buddhist modernizer in Sri Lanka, often called the engineer of "protestant Buddhism" (Gombrich and Obeyesekere 1988: 202–240), a unique form of modern Buddhism largely emulating and responding to Protestantism and Western colonialism. In 1891, he established the Maha Bodhi (Great Enlightenment) Society in 1891 and initiated the movement to recover the Buddhist sacred temple, Bodhi Gaya, from the hands of the Hindu mahants. He had travelled around the world to galvanize the support of Buddhists to raise enough money to purchase the temple properties.[5]

When Dharmapala arrived in colonial Seoul, a special party at a Japanese restaurant, *Kagetsurō*, was arranged to welcome him. Paek, eager to meet him, did not mind joining the party, even though it was organized by the Dual Sect. Through an interpreter, Paek asked two questions of Dharmapala. Typical of the way in which Sŏn practitioners would identify their legitimacy, Paek inquired how many generations Dharmapala was removed from Śākyamuni. Dharmapala replied, "For the past several centuries, Buddhism in India has undergone both extinction and revival. Thus, I don't know." Seemingly disappointed by the fact that Dharmapala was unaware of his own lineage, Paek moved to the next question, "How many years have passed since the birth of Śākyamuni?" To this question, Dharmapala confidently answered, "It has been 2,500 years." "That is not true!" retorted Paek, explaining: "It's been 2,940 years. There are conflicting theories in sutras surrounding the birthday of the Buddha, but the historical evidence is obvious and also complies with the contents of the sutras. Even though the theory you mentioned does exist, that theory cannot be trusted" (Kim T'aehŭp

72   Hwansoo Kim

1941: 27). Apparently, the 2,939th birthday of the Buddha had been celebrated at Korean temples in the previous year (*Maeil sinbo*, 4 July 1912).

This uncomfortable exchange did not deter Paek from re-engaging with Dharmapala. The next day, Yi Hoegwang and other incumbents of the thirty head temples held a special dinner at another Japanese restaurant, *Keisenkan*. Paek again approached Dharmapala with more pointed Sŏn-style questions: "Could you tell me the most essential phrase in the eighty thousand teachings of the Buddha?" Dharmapala replied, "Be constantly diligent and mindful. If one's mind is not idle but vigilant, one can accomplish everything. All businessmen of the past and present have accomplished great works since they were mindful." Further disappointed by this lackadaisical, un-Zenlike answer by "an insignificant monk"—though Dharmapala was in fact not a monastic at the time—Paek threw a Zen koan that was entirely unfamiliar to Dharmapala, who had been trained in the Theravada tradition. Paek suddenly clenched his fist and pushed it out towards Dharmapala asking, "What is this?" Totally befuddled and struggling to respond to this unintelligible question, Dharmapala answered, "Don't you see the light [in the room]? You should know how to turn the light on and off!" To this answer, Paek laughed out loud and left the dinner (Kim T'aehŭp 1941: 28). This rather comical account of their interaction was written by a Korean monk who was present at the scene and who later compiled a collection of Paek's writings. While it is difficult to picture the detailed exchanges in their entirety, these episodes provide us with a sense of Paek's personality and his style of teaching.

A few months after Dharmapala's visit, Paek articulated his Sŏn-centred position in a letter to a Korean newspaper in early 1914. He argued that, although Buddhism had spawned hundreds and thousands of scriptures and branches, Sŏn Buddhism had existed outside of doctrinal teachings and had also been directly transmitted to Mahākāśyapa, a chief disciple of Buddha Śākyamuni. As if excoriating Dharmapala's lack of understanding of the undisrupted lineage of Buddha, Paek continued to maintain that all twenty-eight generations in India, the six generations and the subsequent five branches, along with all the following masters in China, had derived from the Sŏn lineage. In Paek's opinion, the Imje School was the only legitimate lineage for Korean Buddhism. He claimed an unbroken lineage for the Central Preaching Hall in Seoul, where he was teaching as propagation director. He criticized those monks from the Sŏn Kyo Dual Sect for obstructing his effort to bring Korean Buddhism back to its legitimate origin (*Maeil sinbo*, 1 February 1914).

Initial Meetings with Abe

Yet his effort to defeat the Sŏn Kyo Dual Sect, led by Yi Hoegwang and Kang Taeryŏn, did not fare well. First of all, the colonial authority sided with the Dual Sect. When Han, his protégé, attempted to establish two different lay associations that would operate institutionally independent of the Dual Sect, the government authorities quickly denied them permission and even arrested Han for investigation. The options possible for Paek and Han were dwindling. Emboldened, Yi and Kang intensified their attempt to absorb Paek and Han's Central Preaching Hall into the Dual Sect. Desperate, Paek turned for help to Abe Mitsuie.

Among the Japanese living in colonial Korea at the time, Abe stands out not only as one of the most influential figures in the colonial government but also as the most respected Japanese among Korean intellectuals.[6] As a close associate of the journalist and historian Tokutomi Sohō (1863–1957), Abe was invited by Governor-General Terauchi Masatake (in power 1910–1916) to become the president of the daily newspaper, *Maeil sinbo*, an organ of the colonial government, in August 1914. From that point on, Abe served as a personal advisor to Governors-General Terauchi and Saitō Makoto (in power 1919–1927) (Uchida 2011: 154) and mediated between the colonial government and Koreans. With his conciliatory approach towards many Korean intellectuals as well as entrepreneurs, Abe built a broad network of friendships. These supporters believed that Abe's intention to help Koreans was sincere, and they trusted what he said about the "harmony between Korea and Japan" (*Naisen yūwa*) (Sim 2010: 163). He was often called "the devoted supporter of Koreans" (Sim 2011b: 288) and also developed amicable relationships with Christian and Confucian scholars (Sim 2010, 2011b: 258).

Abe's popularity among Korean Buddhists was enhanced by his personal piety.[7] He was a long-time Zen Buddhist in the Rinzai tradition; his dharma name, Mubutsu (Kor. Mubul), was granted by the prominent Rinzai master Shaku Sōen (1860–1919) (Nakamura 1969: 54; Sim 2011a: 259, 264–265). Because of his personal interest in Zen Buddhism, he started, upon arriving in Korea, to engage with Korean Buddhist monks and visited temples around Seoul. Over the next few years, so many Korean monks approached or were approached by him that later a Sōtōshū priest, who was practising at Korean monasteries, said that wherever he went, Korean monks recognized Abe's name (*Chōsen Bukkyō* 119 [March 1934]: 50).

Figure 5.2 Abe   *Figure 5.3* Abe (second from left) with Terauchi (centre)
Source: *Maeil sinbo*, 4 November 1914

74 *Hwansoo Kim*

Interestingly, Paek was not an exception. Paek's first encounter with Abe was less than three months after Abe began his job as the president of the *Maeil sinbo*. The Korean baron Kim Sŏnggŭn (1835–1919), who had recently become a Buddhist (*Maeil sinbo*, 15 January 1913), invited Abe to a Buddhist ceremony, organized by Paek at the Central Preaching Hall, for the installation of an embroidered Buddha. After the opening rituals, Paek gave a sermon that was the first dharma talk in Korean that Abe heard. Abe was impressed by Paek's stature as a great speaker. After the sermon, Kim invited Abe and others to his home, adjacent to the Central Preaching Hall, and threw a party (*Maeil sinbo*, 2 November 1914). In fact, Abe's house was in the same district, within walking distance from the Hall where Paek taught (*Maeil sinbo*, 12 November 1916). Through these events, Paek and Abe established a rapport. From this time on, Abe considered Paek as a major Zen master in Korea from whom he could learn, while Paek regarded Abe as one who shared his belief in Imje Sŏn. More importantly, in Paek's eyes, Abe could be an ally for his institutional vision to unify Korean Buddhism under the Imje ideology. Apparently, Abe also gained a favourable impression of Paek. The following month, Abe invited the abbots of the thirty head temples to the headquarters of the *Maeil sinbo*. Even though Paek was not one of the incumbents, he was included among the invitees and was seated along with Yi and Kang, his key opponents, at a Japanese restaurant that the group had moved to after touring the building (Han, notably, was not invited.) (*Maeil sinbo*, 27 December 1914).

Yi and Kang's Attempt to Annex the Central Preaching Hall

In 1911, Korean Buddhism was divided into two factions, with Yi and Kang attempting to nullify Paek and Han's movement. It was obvious to Yi and Kang that the opposing movement was not viable, especially because, as previously mentioned, the colonial government sided with the Sŏn Kyo Dual Sect. In late 1914, Yi mounted pressure on the colonial government to disestablish the Central Preaching Hall.

Without political capital to counter this pressure, Paek turned to Abe and sent him a desperate letter:

> Today, the incumbents of the thirty head temples came to the Department of Local Affairs in the Internal Ministry, and we had a legal battle against Yi Hoegwang, the head of the incumbents. But [it is decided that] the authorities will implement the measure of enforcement [against the Central Preaching Hall]. This is such an urgent and pressing matter. Could you possibly help and save us by all possible means?
>
> (*AMKB* #348–4)[8]

Although the details as to how Abe could help Paek were not specified, it is quite clear that Paek was asking Abe to influence the government to block Yi's attempt. A later record indicates that Abe must have intervened in postponing the enforcement.

Paek Yongsŏng's Imje Sŏn Movement   75

In the same letter, Paek also attached the list of the thirty head temples in Korea to prove they all originated from the Imje lineage. He then accused the incumbents of twenty-nine of the temples of following the movement that Yi and others orchestrated. Paek charged them with "losing the spirit of our tradition, running after small streams, and thereby falling into the status of lineage-lessness." With mounting anger, he added that they "don't even know why Korean Buddhism was called the Sŏn Sect" or "which sutra in the eighty thousand canons is what Bodhidharma transmitted outside of sutra teachings directly pointing at the mind" (*AMKB* #348–4).

But in April 1915, Kang, the new head of the Dual Sect, intensified Yi's earlier push, garnered consensus from other incumbents of the thirty temples, and submitted a proposal to the government (*Maeil sinbo*, 3 April 1915). At this time, Paek already realized that he would not be able to accomplish his vision within the shaky existence of the Central Preaching Hall. As for Han, his activities were significantly limited because of repeated warnings by the government authorities. In early 1915, it is most likely that Abe informed Paek of the ultimate fate of the Central Preaching Hall. It is possible that Abe promised to assist Paek in promoting Imje Sŏn if Paek were to set up a new centre. In consultation with Abe, Paek relocated his residence to Changsadong and established a new centre called the Research Institute for the Imje Branch of the Sŏn Sect (Sŏnjong Imjep'a kangguso, henceforth the Research Institute). In a 1915 letter to Abe, Paek expressed his frustration and appreciation:

> The monks at the Kakhwang temple see the two words Im-je as if facing an enemy. What kind of mindset is this? The descendants of the Imje lineage are all the same. I don't know why they oppose us like this.
>
> (*AMKB* #348–3)

Then, Paek criticized the government authorities for being partial:

> What do the government's words mean that one should not breach the public order? The level of the government's dislike for the Imje Sect is as such. Relying on the government, those monks [at the Kakhwang temple] are pressuring our sect. What kinds of thousands of eons of resentment do they have with our Imje sect? I regret being born in this world!
>
> (*AMKB* #348–3)

Nevertheless, Paek did not forget to thank Abe for assisting him amidst these challenges:

> In retrospect, fortunately, the Research Institute for the Imje Branch of the Sŏn Sect will prepare to establish the Imje Sect in the future. I bow and celebrate all your utmost effort and help.
>
> (*AMKB* #348–3)

76 Hwansoo Kim

This remark indicates that Paek imparted to Han the knowledge that the Central Preaching Hall was doomed for disbandment. In a sense, Paek established the Research Institute as a third sect that, if the conditions were right, could grow into the unifying institution for Korean Buddhism.

After he took residence in Changsadong and commenced teaching Imje Sŏn at the Research Institute, Paek had one of his lay-members transcribe his talks and sent them to Abe (*AMKB* #348–1; 348–2). Abe had possibly requested that Paek provide him with the transcriptions. The collaboration of Paek and Abe deepened from this point on.

An End to Paek's Vision for the Imje Movement

Less than a year after Paek settled into the new establishment, Paek had to abandon his four-year long effort to create an Imje-centred institution of Korean Buddhism. Various obstacles hindered his goal. Most obviously, the government authorities did not heed his argument. In addition, Abe's relationship with Korean monks was not confined to Paek. Soon, Yi and Kang aggressively approached Abe and built their own friendships. Equally damaging to Paek's effort was the landscape of Buddhism in central Seoul. Paek had rivals even among those who promoted the Imje lineage. Even the Sŏn Kyo Dual Sect fully embraced the very argument that Paek had been pressing, namely that Korean Buddhism derived from the Imje Sŏn branch. Worse, there was a Japanese Rinzai (=Imje) branch temple, located close to Paek's research centre, promoting the very same form of Buddhism in its Japanese manifestation, which further rendered Paek's programme moot and superfluous. Suddenly, Paek felt wedged between many powerful players and, lacking political and economic capital to counter them, had to give up his vision and retreat from the public scene for a time.

Yi's and Kang's Approach to Abe

In fact, Yi's relationship with Abe predated Paek's. Soon after Abe was nominated as the president of the *Maeil sinbo* in 1914, Yi sent a congratulatory letter (*AMKB* #183) and visited the main office of the *Maeil sinbo* in early November, two months before Paek was invited to the same place (*Maeil sinbo*, 7 November 1914). Later, Yi closely interacted with Abe as well.

Kang's relationship with Abe had a similar trajectory. In January 1915, Abe visited the Yongju temple where Kang was the abbot. Abe's visit was timely since Kang replaced Yi as the leader of the Sŏn Kyo Dual Sect in the same month. Three months after Abe's visit to Kang's temple, Kang invited Abe to a special dinner at the Kakhwang temple, the headquarters of the Dual Sect. Abe gave a talk in the presence of the incumbents of ten head temples and other lay Buddhist leaders (*Maeil sinbo*, 3 April 1915). When Abe planned a research tour to temples on Kŭmgang Mountain and asked for institutional assistance, Kang gladly guaranteed full support and even recommended that the tour become an annual event (*Maeil sinbo*, 5 May 1915).

Interestingly, it was around this time that Kang and other incumbents were insisting on annexing the Central Preaching Hall and other Buddhist facilities that existed outside the control of the Dual Sect. Abe's rapport with Yi and Kang indicate that in spite of his regard for Paek, Abe also believed that Korean Buddhism would fare better under the sole leadership of the Sŏn Kyo Dual Sect.

In his efforts to make Paek and Han's Imje movement redundant and futile, Kang succeeded in recruiting a key teacher from Han's camp. In 1915, Kang invited the Sŏn Master Kyŏng'un (1852–1936) to the Kakhwang temple to give a series of dharma talks on Sŏn Buddhism. Kyŏng'un had been nominated by Han to be the patriarch for the Imje Sect five years earlier, in late 1910. Although Kyŏng'un declined the offer because of his old age, leaving Han to serve in that position temporarily, he was undoubtedly the symbolic head of the Imje Sect movement, which Han and Paek had initiated. Upon Kyŏng'un's arrival in Seoul, groups of monks and laypeople greeted him at the Namdaemun train station and even prepared a special carriage for him (*Maeil sinbo*, 30 March 1915). From this time on, Kyŏng'un resided in the Kakhwang temple, teaching Imje Sŏn for the Sŏn Kyo Dual Sect.

The Rise of the Rinzaishū Branch Temple

Another blow to Paek's programme was the 1915 emergence of a Japanese Rinzai branch temple as an influential player in the Seoul Buddhist world. Rinzai had been the last of the major Japanese Buddhist sects to establish a missionary post in colonial Korea (Shimazaki 2005: 89). The first missionary of the Rinzai Sect was Furukawa Taikō (1871–1968), who first came to Korea in 1908 but mostly stayed at the Pohyŏn temple in northern Korea. He later took up residence in Seoul at a small house that served as a preaching office. Gotō Zuigan (1879–1965) had replaced him by April 1915 and officially called the house a Rinzai branch temple, Myōshinji (Hagimori 1930: 34). The prominence of Abe, who was also a member of the Rinzai sect, elevated Gotō's status and influence as a Buddhist missionary in Seoul. From mid-1915, Gotō began to give regular talks at the Myōshinji to promote Rinzai Zen.

With the emergence of the Myōshinji, central Seoul became a hotbed of Imje (Rinzai) Sŏn. The Kakhwang temple of the Sŏn Dual Kyo Sect and the Central Preaching Hall of Han were in close proximity to each other. The Myōshinji and Paek's Research Institute were both in the same district and almost directly across the street, with the house numbers of 183 (Hagimori 1930: 34) and 142, respectively (see Figures 5.4 and 5.5 on the next page). In addition, these four religious establishments were located within half a mile of one another and a chorus promoting the teachings of Master Imje/Rinzai. At one point, Gotō, Kyŏng'un, and Paek lectured on Imje Sŏn on the very same day (*Maeil sinbo*, 20 July 1915). Two days later, another prominent Korean master also lectured on the teachings of Master Imje at the Central Preaching Hall (*Maeil sinbo*, 22 July 1915). Moreover, Gotō and Paek often taught Imje Sŏn at their temple and hall at the same time and on the same days. In the second half of 1915, it looked as if there was a major

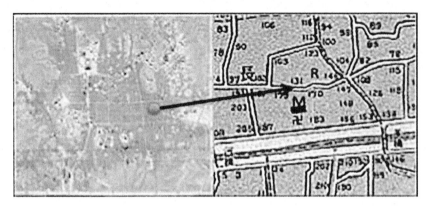

Figure 5.4 A map of Seoul in 1927

Source: *Kyŏngsŏng sigado*[9]

Figure 5.5 The location of Paek's Institute is shown with the letter "R", and the Myōshinji temple with the letter "M"

boom of Imje Sŏn in Seoul. Gradually, Han and Paek were losing ground in their efforts to use the Imje Sŏn as a major source for institutional reform.

Further troubling to Paek was the transformation of the Myōshinji temple. Not only did Gotō become a major engine for the promotion of Rinzai Zen, but he also planned a construction project to build a Japanese Zen-style temple in the same complex. Gotō officially announced the project and maintained that a new Zen training temple would "revitalize a dilapidated Chosŏn Buddhism" (*Maeil sinbo*, 11 November 1915). Abe was a key member of the Myōshinji and assisted Gotō in every possible way. He established a Zen lay group called the Gateless Association (Mumonkai), which comprised influential Japanese leaders in colonial Korea and used the Myōshinji temple as a gathering place (*Maeil sinbo*, 22 August 1916; Sim 2011a: 278–279). He also served as an executive committee member for this building project (*Maeil sinbo*, 21 March 1918). The future construction of the Myōshinji temple would certainly dwarf Paek's Institute, devastating him.

Another Desperate Plea for Help

In a deteriorating situation, Paek visited Abe, in late 1915, and made a last plea to realize his own institutional vision for Korean Buddhism. Ironically, Paek met him at the Myōshinji temple next to his own research institute. At this late evening meeting, Paek poured out his frustration and despair in the current circumstances, and even criticized Abe for not offering his cause enough support. The next day, Paek sent a letter of apology:

> I am terribly sorry and don't know what to do about my rambling last night and about disturbing your ears. I beg you a thousand times to generously

forgive me. After receiving your compassionate instruction, I feel like hundreds of thoughts were unravelled. I am going to do my duty and am not going to be attached to the idea of whether or not the Imje sect will be accomplished or whether or not it will prosper.

The prosperity or demise of our sect depends on the fortunes of time. For how could it be saved by human hands? I will just follow the cause and effect of the world and will be satisfied just with a cane, several sutras, and a table. Please forgive me for my discourtesy last night.

P.S. What I said at the Myōshinji temple last night was just to eliminate many evils. But this is also an illusion and I have decided that I will never [again] receive or ask a favour.

(*AMKB* #169)

As evidenced in the letter, the conversation with Abe was a difficult one. Abe might have persuaded Paek to accept the political reality and cooperate with the Dual Sect. Furthermore, Abe might have recommended that Paek also work with the Rinzai Sect to champion the Imje movement.

While sympathetic to Paek's reform ideas, Abe had a different concept about how to unify Korean Buddhism. Abe's fundamental position was that Korea should assimilate with Japan. No matter how conciliatory he might have been to Koreans, Korean culture, and religion, Abe, like many other Japanese, believed that Koreans should learn from the Japanese. In his first talk to Korean Buddhist leaders in April 1914, Abe emphasized that Korean monks should know the political and social situations of the entire world and exceed laypersons in knowledge and quality (*Maeil sinbo*, 3 April 1915). To Abe, Japan was where Korean monks could accomplish this goal.

Later, in a late-1920s work titled "A Personal View on Korean Buddhism" (Chōsen Būkkyō ni taisuru hiken), Abe articulated his vision for Korean Buddhism. He expressed his determination not to become involved in political matters but to dedicate his life to resolving the religious problem in Korea. Abe outlined the five major steps that needed to be taken immediately. First, Korean monks studying in Japan should be supported. Next, Korean monks in Korea should be helped to develop effective propagation methods. Third, prominent intellectuals such as Suzuki Daisetsu (1870–1966) should be invited to help improve and reform Korean monks. Fourth, monastic-training centres in Japan should be open to Korean monks, who should be encouraged to reside in these centres. Finally, young Japanese priests should be selected and sent to Korean monasteries to learn the Korean language and promote the lineage of Korean and Japanese Buddhism, and to instruct, guide, and protect Korean monks (*AMKB* #251). Although these five steps were written almost ten years after the period currently under discussion, they are indicative of Abe's underlying attitude towards Korean Buddhism. At times, Abe also acknowledged that Korean Buddhism possessed some qualities that were better than those of Japanese Buddhism, for example, the idea of keeping precepts. But he believed that Japanese Buddhism had much to offer Korean Buddhism and that instruction should come from Japan to Korea (Sim

80   Hwansoo Kim

2011a: 270). In this sense, Abe's support of Paek's ideas, along with his broad network of relationships with other Korean monks, including Yi and Kang, were all predicated on Abe's own agenda, which was to induce these leaders to embrace the influence of Japanese Buddhism.

Without doubt, Abe, like Paek, envisioned popularizing Zen-centred Buddhism in colonial Korea. An example to this end is that Abe often circulated classical Zen texts to Korean monks, who later thanked him via letters.[10] Like other monks,[11] Paek believed that Abe was committed to advancing Imje Sŏn. However, while Paek sought to establish the Korean branch of the Rinzai/Imje lineage for Korean Buddhism, Abe fundamentally regarded the Japanese branch of Rinzai/Imje as the form of Zen/Sŏn that should be popularized in colonial Korea.

Abe's talk at the Engakuji in Japan in 1917 provides a further clue about his distinct position. He declared that Korean Sŏn Buddhism derived from the Rinzai lineage. Because of the centuries-old marginalization of Korean Buddhism during the Chosŏn era, however, monks were stigmatized as one of the eight outcasts; but thanks to Governor-General Terauchi, Korean Buddhism began improving. Abe then turned to the Rinzaishū mission in Korea. He praised Gotō for bringing about a Zen boom in Korea and commended Shaku Sōen for having visited colonial Korea a number of times and disseminating Rinzai Zen. Abe concluded, "Thus, not to mention in Japan, the popularity of Rinzai Zen came to reach as far as to the lands of Korea and China, and I cannot help feeling greatly happy and pleased."[12] Here, Abe ostentatiously stressed the counterflow of Zen from Japan back to Korea and China. It is therefore no wonder why Abe assisted or instructed Paek to move to Changsadong and establish the Research Institute next to the Myōshinji temple. For Abe, Paek was a potential ally for achieving his own vision. Was it naive of Paek to let himself be drawn into this hidden agenda? While I do not have any textual evidence for such a claim, it is clear that Abe and Paek interacted with both converging and diverging interests in mind.

At any rate, from the overall tone of his letter of apology, it is clear that Paek now understood the futility of promoting his own institutional idea and also realized the incompatibility of Abe's agenda with his own. With bitterness and despair, Paek gave up his vision, resolved not to seek Abe's support[13] and decided to go his own way.

Foray into Mining and Completion of the Myōshinji Temple Building

In early 1916, a distraught Paek closed his institute in Changsadong, ending his five-year programme, and moved to Pongiktong, closer to Insadong. With Abe's political and financial clout no longer available, Paek realized that he would need to earn money to accomplish any future projects. He was determined to start a business and soon approached the former mayor of Pukch'ŏng in northern Korea, Kang Hongdo. Kang enticed Paek into assuming ownership of a gold mining business that had recently been deserted. In 1916, with no business skills or experience, Paek, out of desperation to make money, put on lay clothes, jumped into

Figure 5.6 The Myōshinji temple

Source: *Maeilsinbo*

Figure 5.7 Members in Colonial Seoul, 21 March 1918

the business and poured himself into it for three years. By 1918, he had lost everything, and it was apparent that his business had failed (Kim T'aehŭp 1941: 24). In fact, he was not alone. Many people were wrapped up in the fever of the gold rush, and their businesses failed miserably. Only rarely would some lucky person find gold. For example, Satō Sōtetsu, a Rinzaishū missionary in P'yŏngyang, found a gold mine and sold it to the Japanese Mitsui Company for an enormous amount of money (*Maeil sinbo*, 20 July 1916).

While Paek was in despair over yet another failure, Gotō at the Myōshinji temple expanded his influence and, as the leading promoter of Rinzai Buddhism in Seoul, invited the head of the Eigenji temple, Ashizu Jitsuzen (1850–1921), to visit and lecture in May 1917. Gotō even arranged a special talk for Korean monks, including Pak Hanyŏng, who used to participate in Han's movement (*Maeil sinbo*, 8 May 1917). In September 1917, another prominent Rinzai priest, Shaku Sōen (Abe's teacher), visited Seoul and gave a talk at the Myōshinji temple (*Maeil sinbo*, 12 September 1917). Later, Gotō and Abe arranged a series of talks at the *Maeil sinbo* headquarters and other places (*Maeil sinbo*, 22 September 1917).

Seizing this momentum, Gotō, abetted by Abe, was able to raise enough funds for the construction project (ten thousand yen) and started to build a 2,200-square-foot temple in March 1918. The temple was completed in August of the same year (see above). In contrast, the Central Preaching Hall, led by Han, lost its function as the centre of an Imje movement, and by 1916 it had become a mere preaching hall of the Pŏm'ŏ temple. Han went his own way by that same year (Han 2001). Now, the Sŏn Kyo Dual Sect and the Rinzaishū dominated the scene.

Starting and Ending a New Religion

Bankrupt, Paek returned to Seoul in April 1918 and resided in his old house in Pongiktong, to which he had moved in 1916 (Han 2002: 38). That same year, Abe resigned his position as the president of the *Maeil sinbo* and went back to Japan for several years. Paek restarted his teaching on a small scale. In March 1919, Han visited Paek and persuaded him to participate in the March 1st Independence

82   *Hwansoo Kim*

Movement with him. Paek was fully in agreement with Han that Korea should gain independence. As a result of his participation in the movement, Paek was sentenced to eighteen months in prison. During his prison term, he read a broad range of books, including the Christian Bible translated into Korean, and was inspired to translate Buddhist sutras from classical Chinese. At this time, he also envisioned establishing a new religion. He lamented that the centuries-old marginalization of Korean Buddhism, as he later wrote, instilled "a fixed, bad habit in the minds of people" against Buddhism and that "monks were discriminated against by people simply because they were following Buddhism" (*Pulgyo* [January 1931]: 16). He concluded that he would not be able to revitalize Buddhism with ease under its own stigmatized name.

When Paek finished his prison term in March 1921, he went back to his house in Pongiktong and launched a translation project. Because of chronic financial difficulties, though, he had to leave Seoul in 1923. He engaged in training young monks at local monasteries, although he was not satisfied with this life. A debate over clerical marriage in 1926 forced him back to Seoul.[14] The incumbents of the major head temples petitioned the colonial government to allow married monks to assume the abbotship of head temples, and Paek vehemently opposed this attempt, sending his own two petitions to both the Japanese colonial and imperial governments (*Pulgyo sibo*, 15 July 1940). In the first petition, he strongly demanded that the authorities not accept the incumbents' petition but continue to ban clerical marriage, arguing that there had been a clear distinction between monastics and laypeople throughout Buddhist history. When he received no response from either government, he softened his tone in the second petition, claiming that the government should allocate at least several head temples to celibate monks like himself so that they could continue to practise without worrying about being driven away by the married monks. The governments ignored his repeated petitions and adopted the incumbents' petition, thereby officially allowing clerical marriage. Paek lost confidence in Korean Buddhist institutions, indignantly left Buddhism, and finally opted to create a new religion, the Great Enlightenment Teaching (Taegakkyo),[15] emulating Dharmapala's Maha Bodhi Society (Masŏng [Yi Such'ang] 2010).

Paek's house in Pongiktong became the headquarters of his new religion, and he turned much of his attention to the foreign mission in northern Korea and Manchuria. This endeavour rekindled the Imje monastic spirit, which centred on the dual practice of working and meditating. Even after the establishment of the new religion, he did not entirely separate himself from Korean Buddhism but rather continued to work with like-minded monks. However, as he consolidated the institutional, ritual, and doctrinal structure of the new religion, he did not feel it necessary to continue his registration as a monk with the institution that he held responsible for the legalization of clerical marriage and for other corruptions. He officially abandoned his affiliation with institutional Buddhism in 1933 (Han 2002: 47).

Once again, after an initial success, Paek's new venture did not last long. The Great Enlightenment Teaching was categorized as a "pseudo-religion", and thus

Paek Yongsŏng's Imje Sŏn Movement   83

did not gain much legal protection. When Japan occupied Manchuria, established the Manchukuo state in 1932, and planned to go to war against China in 1937, the colonial government tightened its control over Korea for war mobilization. As part of this move, the government began cracking down on "pseudo-religions", including Paek's. He was given two options: either disestablish the temples that belonged to his religion in Korea and Manchuria, or annex them to the Korean Buddhist institution. Eventually, Paek opted for the latter, saying some time later that "the centre was handed over to Buddhism [more specifically the Pŏm'ŏ temple]" (*Samch'ŏlli* 8/12 [December 1936]: 85). Under pressure from the colonial government, Paek also had to close the temple and farm that he had founded in Manchuria. The members of this temple accused Paek of deceiving them to gain their investment in building the temple and running a large farm. They asked for compensation, and Han Iksŏn, representing forty-seven households and 326 members, went to Seoul to demonstrate in front of a police office (*Maeil sinbo*, 27 December 1939), but their protest was in vain.

After this disconcerting setback, Paek restored his affiliation with the Korean Buddhist institution that he had left. Now, he had to be content with saving the centre in Pongiktong, where he continued to teach until mid-1937 (Han 2002: 61). Interestingly, his centre donated fifty yen as a contribution to Japan's war effort, as if to avoid the wrath of the colonial government (*Maeil sinbo*, 5 August 1937). However, Paek was a tenacious monk. Although he had faced countless difficulties, this new setback did not prevent him from rekindling his lifelong vision for promoting Imje Sŏn. He replaced the Great Enlightenment Teaching and instituted another new organization called the Monastery of Korean Sŏn Buddhism (Chosŏn Pulgyo Sŏnjong Ch'ongnim) in 1938 (*Pulgyo sibo*, 15 July 1940; Han 2002: 63; Kim Kwangsik 2013). Eventually, age and illness overtook Paek's indefatigable zeal, and he passed away on 24 February 1940.

Conclusion

In a eulogy, the Korean monk Kim T'aehŭp (1899–1989) remembered Paek as somebody whose lifelong resolution was to eliminate the social stigma imposed on Buddhist monastics and thereby improve and modernize Korean Buddhism. Kim wrote that people often called Paek "a man of ambition" and that Paek suffered from rumours and the criticism of others (*Pulgyo sibo*, 15 July 1940).

It is true that Paek was a man of ambition and charisma. In 1910, he came to Seoul at the age of forty-two with the sworn goal of upholding Sŏn Buddhism and, as of 1911, Korean Imje Sŏn in particular. And the trajectories of his ideas and activities for the next thirty years until his death were unswerving: to promote his own institutional vision for Korean Buddhism. The lay members who knew him respected Paek so much that at one point the ointment that Paek made to treat his illness sold well among the members, who believed that it contained a special healing power (*Maeil sinbo*, 1 October 1925). Apparently, though, he was not that well received by his fellow monks, because of his intransigent personality. As a result, his path was rocky and filled with challenges, frustrations, and plenty of trials and

84   *Hwansoo Kim*

errors; as Paek summed it up, "everything [about my life] is nothing more than anguish and grief" (*Samch'ŏlli* 8/12 [December 1936]: 85).

However, even the uncompromising Paek sought to work with the Buddhist colonizer to quell factionalism in his tradition and accomplish his religious vision. Like other Asian Buddhist reformers, Paek tried to find a viable way to accomplish his goals through, in Blackburn's terms, "collectivities of belonging" (Blackburn: 214) with colonizers and Buddhists from other countries to maximize the odds of his religion's recovery from trauma and its future survival. Paek's plural, situational networks based on this *belonging* can be seen in his trip to China to seek a true Buddhism, his engagement with Abe, his spirited encounters with a transnational figure (Dharmapala) whose visit was partly facilitated by the colonial authorities, his petitions to both the Japanese colonial and imperial governments, and his organization's donation to Japan's war effort.

Unquestionably, Christian influence also loomed large in Paek's works. Borrowing the Christian model for his Imje-centred religious movement is another flexible dimension of his actions. He incorporated print media, capitalism, and Christian missionary worldviews and techniques into enforcing his version of Buddhism, which can be identified with "Protestant Buddhism" (Gombrich and Obeyesekere 1988: 202–240). The success of Christianity in Korea prompted him to establish a major temple in Seoul, to translate Chinese-language Buddhist scriptures to the vernacular *hangul*, to found a new religion in protest of the existing Buddhist institution, and to envision domestic and foreign missions.

As Richard Jaffe has aptly demonstrated, however, Japanese Buddhists were indebted to their fellow Buddhists in other Asian countries when reimagining their own religion (Jaffe 2004), and intra-Asian Buddhist contacts were as equally influential as East-West exchanges in the making of Asian Buddhist modernity (Blackburn: 215–217; Bocking et al. 2014). When it comes to Korean Buddhism, Korean Buddhists' interactions with other Asian Buddhists operated as a more immediate force in shaping Korean Buddhists' modern institutional and religious identity.

Do these new findings in Paek's life story undermine the recent endeavour among Korean Buddhists to canonize Paek's legacy as an unbending nationalist? There is no conclusive answer. But one can at least state the following: if anti-Japanese nationalism and anti-Japanese Buddhism continue to be the leitmotifs for evaluating Paek's thoughts and activities, our understandings of him[16] that his activities elicit will neither accurately reflect the dynamic reality in which he and other Buddhist leaders lived nor illuminate the distinct features of Korean Buddhist modernity.

Notes

* A longer version of the chapter has previously been published in 2014 in the *Sungkyun Journal of East Asian Studies* 14 (2): 171–193.
1. Two leading scholars on Paek are Han Pogwang and Kim Kwangsik.
2. For Taixu, see Pittman (2001); for Tanxu, see James Carter (2009, 2014); for Dharmapala and Hikkaduve, see Anne Blackburn (2010).

Paek Yongsŏng's Imje Sŏn Movement 85

3. The whole collection is available on microfilm at Japan's National Diet Library.
4. I would like to thank Ellie (Yunjung) Choi, an assistant professor of modern Korean literature and intellectual history at Cornell University, for kindly sharing this source with me.
5. For more details on Dharmapala's life and activities, see Blackburn (2010).
6. For Abe's life, see Kim Hwansoo (2009) and Sim (2011b).
7. For more details, see Sim (2011a).
8. I would like to thank Dr Tongch'un Pak for translating from Classical Chinese to Korean the letters exchanged between Abe and Korean monks, including those of Paek.
9. Available at http://gis.seoul.go.kr.
10. See Abe's letters to Korean monks in Abe's collections (*Abe Mitsuie kankei bunsho*).
11. See the Korean monk Kim Poryun's letter to Abe, in which Kim thanked Abe and rearticulated the prominence of Imje Sŏn in Korean Buddhism (*Maeil sinbo*, 25 March 1915).
12. *Zendō* (August 1917), quoted from Sim (2011a: 293–294).
13. Despite Paek's emotionally charged tête-à-tête with Abe at this time, their friendship was not entirely severed. Later, when Suzuki Daisetsu's visit to Korea in 1934 was imminent, Abe sent a letter notifying Paek of the visit and reported on Suzuki's subsequent trip to China (*Chōsen Bukkyō* 104 [1934]: 8.). Abe must have intended to introduce Suzuki to Paek, though extant sources do not tell us whether such a meeting took place.
14. For more details, see Kim Kwangsik (2008).
15. Paek, "My Confession" (1936: 85).
16. For a similar reevaluation of Han's life, see Lee (2012).

References

Primary Sources

Abe Mitsuie kankei bunsho [Documents Relating to Abe Mitsuie] (1991; 1993). Tokyo: Kokuritsu kokkai toshokan.
Chōsen Bukkyō [Korean Buddhism] (1924–1945). Keijō: Chōsen Bukkyō sha.
Maeil sinbo [The Korea Daily News] (1904–1910). Seoul: Maeil sinbosa.
Pulgyo [Buddhism] (1924–1933). Keijō: Pulgyosa.
Pulgyo sibo [Buddhist News] (1935–1944). Keijō: Pulgyo sibosa.
Zendō [The Way of Zen] (1910–1922). Tokyo: Zendōkai.

Secondary Sources

Blackburn, Anne. 2010. *Locations of Buddhism: Colonialism and Modernity in Sri Lanka*. Chicago: University of Chicago Press.
Bocking, Brian, Phibul Choompolpaisal, Laurence Cox, and Alicia M. Turner, eds. 2014. *A Buddhist Crossroads: Pioneer Western Buddhists and Asian Networks 1860–1960*. New York: Routledge.
Carter, James. 2009. "Buddhism, Resistance, and Collaboration in Manchuria." *Journal of Global Buddhism* 10: 193–216.
———. 2014. *Heart of Buddha, Heart of China: The Life of Tanxu, a Twentieth Century Monk*. Oxford: Oxford University Press.
Cho, Sungtaek. 2013. "Reconsidering the Historiography of Modern Korean Buddhism: Nationalism and Identity of the Chogye Order of Korean Buddhism." In *Buddhism and*

86 Hwansoo Kim

Violence: Militarism and Buddhism in Modern Asia, edited by Vladimir Tikhonov and Torkel Brekke, 54–74. New York: Routledge.

Gombrich, Richard and Gananath Obeyesekere. 1988. *Buddhism Transformed: Religious Change in Sri Lanka*. Princeton, NJ: Princeton University Press.

Hagimori, Shigeru. 1930. *Chōsen no toshi: Keijō to Jinsen*. Keijō: Tairiku jōhōsha.

Han, Pogwang. 1998. "Yongsŏng Sŭnim ŭi chŏnban'gi ŭi saengae" [The early life of Master Yongsŏng]. *Taegak sasang* 2. http://www.taegak.or.kr/re/sasang01/hbk.html.

―――. 1999. "Yongsŏng Sŭnim ŭi chungban'gi ŭi saengae" [The midlife of Master Yongsŏng]. *Taegak sasang* 3: 13–46.

―――. 2001. "Hae-Yong ŭi mannam" [The meeting between Manhae and Yongsŏng]. *Yusim* (December 10). http://yousim.buddhism.org/html/2001-win/plan-bo-kwang.htm.

―――. 2002. "Yongsŏng Sŭnim ŭi huban'gi ŭi saengae" [The later years of the life of Master Yongsŏng]. *Taegak sasang* 4: 9–74.

―――. 2010. "Paek Yongsŏng Sunim ŭi minjok undong" [Master Paek Yongsŏng's national movement]. *Taegak sasang* 14: 9–40.

Jaffe, Richard M. 2004. "Seeking Śākyamuni: Travel and the Reconstruction of Japanese Buddhism." *Journal of Japanese Studies* 30 (1): 65–95.

Kemper, Steven. 2015. *Rescued from the Nation: Anagarika Dharmapala and the Buddhist World*. Chicago: University of Chicago Press.

Kim, Hwansoo. 2009. "The Adventures of a Japanese Monk in Colonial Korea: Sōma Shōei's Zen Training with Korean Masters." *Japanese Journal of Religious Studies* 36 (1): 125–165.

―――. 2013. *Empire of the Dharma: Korean and Japanese Buddhism, 1877–1912*. Cambridge, MA: Harvard University Asia Center.

Kim, Kwangsik. 2000. "Paek Yongŏng ŭi Pulgyo kaehyŏk kwa Taegakkyo undong" [Paek Yongŏng's Buddhist reform and the Taegakkyo movement]. *Taegak sasang* 3: 65–98.

―――. 2002. "Paek Yongsŏng ŭi sasang kwa minjok undong pangnyak" [Paek Yongsŏng's thought and strategies for the national movement]. *Hanguk tongnip undongsa yŏn'gu* 19 (December): 67–95.

―――. 2008. "Yongsŏng ŭi kŏnbaeksŏwa taech'ŏyuksik ŭi chaeinsik" [Yongsŏng's petition and the reconsideration of clerical marriage and meat eating]. *Sŏn munhwa yŏn'gu* 4: 213–251.

―――. 2013. "Taegakkyo ŭi Chosŏn Pulgyo Sŏnjong ch'ongnim ŭro ŭi chŏnhwan kwajŏng" [The transition process of the Taegakkyo into the monasteries of Korean Sŏn Buddhism]. *Taegak sasang* 20: 63–98.

Kim, Sunsŏk. 2003. *Ilche sidae Chosŏn Ch'ongdokpu ui Pulgyo chŏngch'aek kwa Pulgyogye ŭi taeuŭng* [The Buddhism policies of the government-general in the Japanese colonial period and the reactions of the Buddhist community]. Seoul: Kyŏngin munhwasa.

Kim, T'aehŭp. 1941. *Yongsŏng Sŏnsa ŏrok* [The discourse record of Sŏn Master Yongsŏng]. Keijō: Samjang yŏkhae.

Lee, Jung-Shim. 2012. "A Doubtful National Hero: Han Yongun's Buddhist Nationalism Revisited." *Korean Histories* 3 (1): 35–52.

Masŏng (Yi Such'ang). 2010. "Han'guk Pulgyo wa Sangjwa Pulgyo wa ŭi mannam ŭi yŏksa wa kwaje" [The history of the encounter between Korean Buddhism and Theravāda Buddhism and its issues]. *Pulgyo p'yŏngnon* 44. http://www.budreview.com/news/articleView.html?idxno=985.

Myers, Ramon Hawley, and Mark R. Peattie, eds. 1984. *The Japanese Colonial Empire, 1895–1945*. Princeton, NJ: Princeton University Press.

Nakamura, Kentarō. 1969. *Chōsen seikatsu gojū nen* [Fifty years of my Korean life]. Kumamoto: Seichōsha.

Paek, Yongsŏng. 1936. "Na ŭi ch'amhoerok" [My confession]. *Samch'ŏlli* 8/12 (December): 82–85.

Pittman, Don Alvin. 2001. *Toward a Modern Chinese Buddhism.* Honolulu: University of Hawai'i Press.

Shimazaki, Gikō. 2005. *Inryōken Gotō Zuigan rōshi jiseki* [A memoir of Master Gotō Zuigan of the Inryō ken]. Tokyo: Fukurō shuppan.

Sim, Wŏnsŏp. 2010. "Nakamura Kentarō ŭi Abe Mubul ong ŭl ch'umoham" [Nakamura Kentarō's remembering of Mr Abe Mubul]. *Chŏngsin munhwa yŏn'gu* 33: 161–181.

———. 2011a. "Abe Mitsuie ŭi Han Il Pulgyo kwallyŏn hwaltong" [Abe Mitsuie's activities related to Korean and Japanese Buddhism]. *Hanil minjok munje yŏn'gu* 21: 257–299.

———. 2011b. "Abe Mitsuie ŭi saengae kich'o yŏn'gu" [A basic study of Abe Mitsuie's life]. *Han'gukhak yŏn'gu* 25: 287–317.

Tikhonov, Vladimir. 2004. "The Japanese Missionaries and Their Impact on Korean Buddhist Developments (1876–1910)." *International Journal of Buddhist Thought and Culture* 4 (February): 7–48.

Uchida, Jun. 2011. *Brokers of Empire: Japanese Settler Colonialism in Korea, 1876–1945.* Cambridge, MA: Harvard University Asia Center.

Part 2

Revivals and Neo-Traditionalist Inventions

6 Buddhism in Contemporary Kalmykia

"Pure" Monasticism versus Challenges of Post-Soviet Modernity

Valeriya Gazizova

Based on a combination of historical analysis and fieldwork research conducted in 2008 and 2012, this chapter explores the restoration of Buddhist institutions and the problems that accompany it in Kalmykia, one of the major Buddhist areas of Russia, along with Buryatia, Tuva, and the Altai Republic. Situated in the region of dry steppes to the northwest of the Caspian Sea and thus the only Mongol and Buddhist enclave in Europe, Kalmykia has the status of an autonomous republic within the Russian Federation. Although it is a highly multi-ethnical region, home to numerous Slavic and Asian groups, Kalmyks, an ethnic group of Mongol descent, comprise 60 per cent of the republic's total population of approximately 300,000.

Even though Kalmykia is probably one of the least-known regions of Russia, it is a unique field with regard to the questions concerning the survival and change of socio-cultural systems under the influence of persecution and repression. The history of the Kalmyks is a series of tragic events that have gradually undermined the traditional foundations of their society, leading to a substantial loss in their cultural heritage. After decades of a severe persecution of Buddhism by the Soviet government, the end of the 1980s marked the beginning of a cultural, religious, and ethnic revitalization in Kalmykia, as well as in other regions of the Russian Federation. Buddhism in all its dimensions has become the focus of ethnic identity for most Kalmyks, being perceived as an essential constituent of the ethnic cultural heritage even by those who do not consider themselves Buddhists. Historically, the Kalmyks adhere to the Gelugpa (Tib. *dGe lugs pa*) school of Tibetan Buddhism, which arose in the late fourteenth century from the teachings of the Tibetan monk Lobsang Drakpa (Tib. bLo bzang Grags pa), better known by the name of Tsongkhapa (Tib. Tsong kha pa), after Tsong kha, the region of his birth.

The primary focus of this chapter is on the policy of Telo Tulku Rinpoche, the incumbent head of the Kalmyk Buddhists, especially in regard to his support of monasticism of the Gelugpa order, as well as on the formation of the Central Kalmyk Buddhist Monastery, which to a large degree is the result of this policy. A distinctive characteristic of the Gelugpa order is its insistence on the *Vinaya* discipline,[1] which includes celibacy. Nonetheless, despite the head lama's efforts to restore celibate monasticism, most of the authorized Buddhist specialists in the republic have not been ordained according to the rules of the

92 *Valeriya Gazizova*

Vinaya, and they keep only the lay vows of *genin* (Tib. *dge bsnyen*). Building on different views expressed by informants, including monks and lay practitioners, the chapter examines why a revival of full-scale monasticism has been problematic in Kalmykia. It also discusses certain tendencies typical of emergent non-monastic communities. To understand the reconstruction of Buddhism in present-day Kalmykia, it is useful to begin with a brief look at its localization and history among the Kalmyks in order to see what place Buddhism had in traditional Kalmyk society.

The Historical Background

The direct ancestors of the Kalmyks were known as Oirats, who consisted of several ethnically and linguistically related West Mongol tribes living in southern Siberia. At the beginning of the thirteenth century, they inhabited the territory around the upper reaches of the Irtysh River and the west side of the Altai Mountains, namely the region of Jungaria. By 1218, the Oirats had been subdued by Chinggis Khan and become subjects of his empire. In the thirteenth and fourteenth centuries, they took part in the Mongol military campaigns throughout large parts of Asia and the Near East. Military success, together with family relationships to the Chinggisids,[2] helped the Oirats to gain political influence. The climax of Oirat authority in Mongolia was reached during the reign of Esen Khan (1451–1455), his military campaigns extending as far as Korea (Halkovic 1985).

At the beginning of the seventeenth century, a substantial part of the Oirats—that is, the main part of the Torgut tribe under Kho-Orluk Khan and some of the Derbet Oirats led by their ruler, Dalai-Baatyr—left their home territory in Jungaria and went northwest along the banks of the Irtysh River, thus reaching the Russian border. The primary reasons for the Oirat exodus were internal conflicts due to a shortage of pastureland, the unstable political situation among the Mongol tribes, and a constant strife with the neighbouring Kazakh khanate (Khodarkovsky 1992: 74–76). The Oirats became subjects of the Russian Empire in August 1609, when the first charter between the Russian Tsar, Vasili IV, and the Oirat Khans was signed. They were permitted to nomadize within the allotted area along the Irtysh and Tobol rivers and were guaranteed Russia's military support against the Mongols and the Kazakhs, but were obliged to protect the southern borders of Russia and to participate in Russian military campaigns. Through the charters of 1655, 1657, and 1661, the northern Caspian steppes on both sides of the Volga were allotted to the Oirats, and in 1664 this territory received the status of the Kalmyk khanate, an independent polity ruled by a khan.[3]

The Oirats who had migrated to Russia began to be called Kalmyks, this word being found in Russian historical sources and legal documents of that epoch. While scholars give different interpretations of the origin and semantics of this term, the prevailing opinion is that the name *kalmyk* is derived from the Tatar *kalmak*, which means "remaining" or "separated", and was given to the Mongols who had migrated to the Volga steppes by their Turkic-speaking neighbours (Erdniev 2007: 98–100). Although the word *kalmyk* appeared in Russian sources as

Buddhism in Contemporary Kalmykia 93

early as the beginning of the seventeenth century, it became a self-designation for the Volga Oirats almost a century later.

Until the mid-eighteenth century, the Russian government did not interfere in the khanate's internal political affairs and did not lay claim to the right to appoint the khan and his deputies. In 1771, however, approximately 70 per cent of the total population of the khanate led by Khan Ubashi left the Volga steppes to return to Jungaria. The reasons for this exodus were an exhaustion of Kalmyk pastures and severe economic crisis in the khanate, which had been caused by the governmental policy of colonizing the Volga steppes with Russian peasants from the 1730s on (Khodarkovsky 1992: 220–235). Fearing that more Kalmyks would leave for Jungaria, the Russian Tsarina Catherine the Great issued a decree abolishing the independence of the Kalmyk khanate in October 1771. According to this decree, the title of "khan" was annulled, the Kalmyk nobility became subordinate to the governor of Astrakhan, and Russian police officers were appointed to every Kalmyk settlement (*ulus*).

Buddhism began to spread among the Mongols, including the Oirats, during the rule of Chinggis Khan, who was tolerant with regard to all religions existing in the Mongol Empire. However, there is an opinion that the Oirats, in contrast to other Mongolian groups, came into contact with Buddhism as early as the ninth century through the neighbouring Turkic peoples, the Sogdians and Uighurs (Kitinov 1996: 35–36). The successors of Chinggis Khan contributed to the propagation of Buddhism in the Mongolian world, of great importance being the role of Godan Khan (reigned 1229–1241) and especially that of Khubilai Khan (reigned 1260–1294), the founder of the Mongol dynasty in China, in Chinese referred to as the Yuan dynasty (Heissig 1980; Sagaster 2007). When the Oirats became subjects of the Russian Empire, they brought Buddhism as their main religion, thus becoming the first Buddhist community in Europe. Buddhism, predominately in its Gelugpa variant, became the state religion of the Kalmyk khanate. Until the end of the eighteenth century, the Kalmyks had close ties with Buddhist centres in Tibet and Mongolia. The religious policy of the khanate was conducted under the leadership of Tibet, and the head of the Kalmyk Buddhists was appointed by the Dalai Lama. Moreover, from 1690 until the abolition of the khanate in 1771, the Kalmyk khans were also appointed by the Dalai Lama. The organization of the Kalmyk sangha, that is, the community of Buddhist monks, conformed to that of the Gelugpa order.

In contemporary Kalmykia, both a monastery and a temple are called *khurul*, which means "assembly". Before the nineteenth century, however, a monastery and a temple were referred to by different terms, with *süm* and *kiid* being the names for "a temple" or "a prayer house". This shift in terminology took place under the influence of the anti-Buddhist reforms implemented by the Russian administration after the abolition of the Kalmyk khanate. Besides prohibiting contact with Tibet, the government decided that the number of monks in one monastery should not exceed 100. In order to maintain their numbers, the Kalmyk clergy began to name each prayer house as *khurul*, "assembly of monks" or "monastery" (Bakaeva 1994: 24–25). In this way the term *khurul* acquired additional meanings.

94 *Valeriya Gazizova*

At the beginning of the twentieth century, the Russian government once more changed its policy towards the sangha. According to the regulations adopted at the summit conference of 1905, Buddhist monasteries were allowed to open printing houses and schools, and the monks were permitted to go abroad and to bring back Buddhist literature and ritual objects. As a result, contacts with Tibet and Mongolia were resumed. By 1917, the Kalmyks had ninety-two khuruls (twenty-eight big monasteries and sixty-four smaller khuruls) with 2,090 monks. At the congress of the Kalmyk clergy and laity (*S"ezd dukhovenstva i miryan*) in July 1917, it was decided to increase the number of khuruls to 119 and that of monks to 2,730 (Ochirova 2011: 48).

After the Bolshevik revolution, Kalmykia became the Kalmyk People's Autonomous Region, but in 1935 it was redefined as an autonomous republic. The period from the 1930s to the late 1980s is referred to as "non-religious" in the history of Kalmykia because during this time Buddhism was severely persecuted in the republic by the Soviet government (Bakaeva 1994: 38). The thrust of anti-religious repression in the Soviet Union took place in the late 1930s. Out of more than 100 khuruls registered in Kalmykia in the 1920s, seventy-nine had been abolished by 1937, and by the beginning of World War II all Kalmyk monasteries had ceased to exist. The majority of monks were arrested and forced to renounce their vows, and monastic property was confiscated or destroyed (Ochirova 2011: 54). Among the most tragic events in Kalmyk history was the deportation of 1943, when the entire population of Kalmykia was exiled to different regions of Siberia, having been accused of treason against the Soviet Union.[4] By a decree of the Supreme Soviet, the Kalmyk autonomous republic ceased to exist on 27 December 1943. Approximately 120,000 Kalmyks were deported, with more than 40 per cent of the exiled people losing their lives during the years of deportation.[5] Only in 1957 were the Kalmyks given the right to return to the steppes of the Volga. Although the republic was officially restored in 1958, any attempt to revive Buddhism was strictly opposed by the government until the late 1980s.

During the Soviet period, Buddhism was officially allowed to be practised only in Buryatia. Although Buddhism in Buryatia suffered severe repression in the 1930s, two Buddhist temples (*datsan*) were opened there in 1946: one was built in the settlement of Ivolga, near the republic's capital Ulan-Ude, while the other was reopened in one of the temples of the former Aginsky monastery. The change in the religious policy of the Soviet government with regard to Buryatia had ideological grounds. After World War II, the government reopened a small number of temples, churches, and monasteries of different confessions in order to show that people in the USSR were free to practise any faith. Nevertheless, the activity of the Buddhist temples in Buryatia was strictly controlled by the local KGB organs (Zhukovskaia 2010). In the same year, the Central Religious Board of Buddhists of the USSR was set up with the primary aim of controlling the two *datsan*.

Religious Revival from the Late 1980s

In October 1990, the Federal Law on "the Freedom of Consciousness and Religious Organizations" came into force, thereby opening the way to a religious revival. The first Kalmyk Buddhist community was registered even earlier, in October 1988, following an officially permitted lecture given by Alexander Berzin, an American scholar and translator of Tibetan Buddhist texts. In 1989, a small house converted into a khurul was opened in Elista and received the name of Elista Khurul. It was consecrated the same year by Kushok Bakula Rinpoche (1917–2003), a reincarnated lama originally from Ladakh and the Indian ambassador to Mongolia from 1990 until 2000. He was the first high-ranking Buddhist monk to visit Kalmykia after the collapse of the Soviet regime, and while there he initiated the first group of novices. The next step in the revival process was the foundation of a centralized religious organization, namely the Kalmyk Buddhist Union (*Ob"edinenie buddistov Kalmykii*), in 1991. The newly established union announced its autonomy from the Central Religious Board of Buddhists of the USSR.

The main problem with regard to full-scale Buddhist activity was the absence of qualified clergy. Because of the persecution of religion during the Soviet period, the lineages of Kalmyk monks had been interrupted, so from the end of the 1930s there had been no Buddhist educational establishments in Kalmykia. By the beginning of the post-communist religious revival, only three old monks with a proper Buddhist education were still alive in the republic. Hence, at the end of the 1980s mostly Buryats from Ivolginsky Datsan were invited to assist in the revival process. Tuvan Dorj, the first head lama of the Kalmyk Buddhists, acting from 1989 until 1992, was a Buryat. In contemporary Kalmykia, the title of the head of the Buddhists is the Shajin Lama, the word *shajn* meaning "religion".[6] Although Tuvan Dorj was officially elected to this post in 1991, he had actually been in charge from 1989.

Many Kalmyks were unhappy with the fact that the Buddhist revival in the republic was in the hands of Buryats and wished to revive their own Kalmyk sangha. This discontent resulted in a strike in the summer of 1992, when seven young Kalmyks in Elista Khurul who had taken the lay vows of *genin* (Tib. *dge bsnyen*) went on a hunger strike, demanding the resignation of Tuvan Dorj and a reelection of the Shajin Lama. The hunger strike continued for an entire week and attracted great attention in the media. Finally, an emergency conference of the Kalmyk Buddhist Union was held, with more than 180 people taking part in it, and it was decided to remove Tuvan Dorj from the post of the head lama and to appoint Sandji Ulanov (1903–1996), better known as Sandji Gelüng, the only Kalmyk *gelüng* (Tib. *dge slong*), that is, a fully ordained monk, still alive and residing in Elista at that time. Because of his advanced age, however, he refused to occupy such a demanding position. It was then decided to invite Telo Tulku Rinpoche to be the leader of the Kalmyk Buddhists.

A citizen of the United States, Telo Tulku (Erdni Ombadykov) was born in 1972 in a family of Kalmyk immigrants in Philadelphia. He studied at the Drepung Gomang monastery in India for twelve years, and it is owing to the fourteenth Dalai Lama's support that he was able to study there. At the end of the 1980s, he was recognized by the Dalai Lama as the current incarnation of Tilopa, an Indian yogi of the eleventh century. Telo Tulku came to Kalmykia for the first

96　*Valeriya Gazizova*

time in 1991, accompanying the Dalai Lama. A fully ordained monk from Drepung Gomang, Kalmyk by descent and a recognized reincarnation, he seemed ideal for the post of the Shajin Lama. Soon after his election in 1992, he began to implement the principles of monasticism in Elista Khurul, the only khurul in the republic at that time. The khurul's status was officially changed into that of a monastery, and a few years later it developed into the Kalmyk Central Buddhist Monastery. The revival of Buddhism has first and foremost been regarded by Telo Tulku as the revival of the community of celibate monks, the monks being one of the three major constituents, the Three Jewels, of Buddhism. Consequently, married clergy were obliged to leave the monastery, with most of them later founding their own Buddhist communities.

The election of Telo Tulku as the head of the Kalmyk Buddhists brought about a re-establishment of the institute of the *tulku* (Tib. *sprul sku*), a recognized reincarnation of an important religious personality or an emanation of a deity, or both. The tradition of *tulku* had been lost in Kalmykia already in the seventeenth century, its re-introduction being a distinctive feature of the post-Soviet Buddhist revival.[7] In 1993, Telo Tulku left for the United States, and in 1995 he renounced his monk's vows and married. However, he remained the Shajin Lama of Kalmykia and consequently the president of the Kalmyk Buddhist Union. In his absence, from 1993 to 1995, he was substituted by Jampa Tinley, a renowned teacher of Tibetan Buddhism and a representative of the fourteenth Dalai Lama in Russia. Telo Tulku returned to Kalmykia and resumed his work there in 1995, with his views and policy regarding monasticism not having changed. Even though he is no longer a celibate monk, he advocates the development of monastic Buddhism and controls the activities of the Central Monastery.

An important contribution to the Buddhist revival has been made by the Dharma Centre of Kalmykia, a centre for studying Buddhism, which was established in Elista in 1991. Its main goal was, and still is, to develop non-monastic Buddhism and to educate the laity in the basic philosophy, history, and practice of Buddhism. Courses of the Tibetan language and Buddhist logic were also organized there during the 1990s. The centre also invited Buddhist teachers of different Tibetan traditions.[8] By the end of the 1990s, a number of lay Buddhist communities had developed on the basis of the Dharma Centre.

Buddhism is not the only religious confession in Kalmykia. The second dominant religion in the republic is Russian Orthodox Christianity, which is not surprising, given that Russians constitute the second largest ethnic group. Moreover, some Kalmyks converted to Christianity in the pre-Soviet period.[9] There are over twenty Orthodox churches currently functioning in Kalmykia. In 1995, the Kalmyk Orthodox Eparchy (a diocese of the Moscow Patriarchate) was established by the decision of the Holy Synod and the Patriarch of Moscow and All Russia. There is a parish of the Roman Catholic Church in the republic's capital, with its adherents primarily being descendants of migrants from Poland, Germany, and Estonia. In 1996, a Franciscan monastery was built in Elista. Protestant congregations, such as Baptists, Adventists, and Pentecostalists, are also present, being usually supported by missionary organizations from Western Europe and the United States.

The Muslims in Kalmykia are mainly Chechens, Ingush, Adygeis, and Dargins, who have traditionally adhered to Islam. Over the last twenty years, the influx of migrants from the republics of the north Caucasus has increased, thereby leading to the growth of Muslim communities. A mosque, the first and so far the only one in Kalmykia, was opened in the village of Prikumskoe in 1995.

While the Russian federal government does not interfere in Kalmyk religious affairs, the government of Kalmykia has been taking an active part in the religious revival. Of special importance here is the role of the first head of Kalmykia, Kirsan Ilyumzhinov, who was elected to this post in 1993 and occupied it until 2010, having been reelected three times. Although the constitution of the Russian Federation separates religious institutions from the state, from 1993 to 1996 religion was declared by Ilyumzhinov to be an essential part of the state policy of Kalmykia. During these years, a special department for religious affairs functioned as the executive agency under the head of the government of Kalmykia. It was established with the aim of assisting in the religious revival in the republic. Large subsidies were collected by the department and donated for the building of khuruls and churches. By the beginning of 1994, eleven khuruls were opened with regional funds. Kirsan Ilyumzhinov also sponsored the construction of Buddhist temples and Christian churches from his private funds. In fact, sponsoring the Dalai Lama's third—and so far last—visit to Kalmykia in 2004 was part of Ilyumzhinov's election campaign.

The Central Kalmyk Buddhist Monastery

The largest Buddhist organization in Kalmykia is the Central Monastery, Geden Sheddup Choi Korling (Tib. dGa' ldan shes sgrub chos 'khor gling). It was given its name by the fourteenth Dalai Lama during his first visit to the republic in 1991. Most monks working in Elista or its suburbs reside in the monastery precincts in Arshan, a village just outside Elista. In 1996, the main temple of the monastery complex, Säküsn Süm ("The Temple of Guardians"), was built there. Its construction was financially supported by the state, along with President Ilyumzhinov's personal support. It was the biggest khurul in the republic and perhaps the largest Buddhist temple in Europe until 2005, when the Central Khurul of Kalmykia, Burkhn Bagshin Altn Süm ("The Golden Abode of Buddha Shakyamuni"), was constructed in only nine months. The initiative to build a large Buddhist temple in the centre of the republic's capital came from Kirsan Ilyumzhinov while he was still the head of state in Kalmykia, the funds for its construction having been donated by private business organizations. Its design embodies the revival of traditional Kalmyk Buddhist architecture, with stupas (Buddhist monuments containing relics) being used as decorative elements; the main temple of the khurul complex is a seven-storey building, sixty-four metres in height, the fourth storey of which is an open gallery decorated with four stupas, one in each corner.

The Golden Abode of Buddha Shakyamuni, also referred to as the Central Khurul, is the headquarters of the Kalmyk Central Monastery, and includes a residence for Telo Tulku, as well as one for the Dalai Lama. Although monks do not

98   *Valeriya Gazizova*

live there, it is the place they work for the benefit of the laity. The Central Khurul is seen by many as the icon of religious revival in Kalmykia. It has also become an important educational centre for the laity, with open lectures on Buddhist philosophy and practice, in addition to yoga and meditation classes being given there on a weekly basis. There is also a museum of the history of Buddhism in Kalmykia, a library with a substantial collection of Buddhist texts, and a centre of traditional Tibetan medicine, which is quite popular, judging by the queue to the office of the *emch* (Tib. *em chi*). Although registered as separate religious organizations, a number of smaller Gelugpa monasteries in other parts of Kalmykia are affiliated with the Central Monastery. Hence, the monastery Geden Sheddup Choi Korling is also the centre of a network of Gelugpa monastic khuruls and is therefore called "centralized". Moreover, it has close ties with the reconstructed Drepung Gomang monastery in Karnataka State in India and can be regarded as being affiliated with it. The abbot of the Central Kalmyk Monastery is Andja Gelüng (Andja Khartskhaev, born 1979). From 1997 until 2006, he studied at Drepung Gomang in India. The Shajin Lama of Kalmykia, Telo Tulku Rinpoche, also supervises the activities of the monastery, including recruiting monks and assigning duties to them.

During our conversation in the summer of 2008, Telo Tulku insistently used the adjective "pure" and its derivatives with regard to Buddhist practice. Similarly, the words "pure", "purity", or "purification" are frequently used by the Shajin Lama—as well as by journalists writing about him—when explaining his stance on the development of Buddhism and the politics of religion in Kalmykia. But what exactly does this idea of "purity" imply, and how is it being implemented in the Kalmyk monastery?

Both Telo Tulku and Andja Gelüng maintain that "pure" Buddhism is inseparable from the *Vinaya* and monasticism because only monks with full vows can be regarded as the true teachers of Buddhism. Adherence to strict monastic discipline and careful observation of the Buddhist vows, including celibacy, and many years of intensive scholastic studies are all considered to be crucial factors for becoming an authoritative source of Buddhist knowledge. This approach is in strict conformity with the Gelugpa order, where celibacy is an indispensable condition of the sangha. As Andja Gelüng explained,

> "Pure Buddhism" is the traditional approach to the sangha, without any innovations, and without adding new elements under the influence of external factors. Yes, life is changing, but the *Vinaya* remains the same. Therefore, when monks take vows, they must follow these vows no matter what is happening around them.
>
> (interview, October 2012)

The attempt to revive monasticism in the Central Kalmyk Monastery is in contrast to a relative laicization of sangha, that is, a partial deviation from the *Vinaya* and a gradual disappearance of the strict distinction between monks and laity in contemporary monasteries of Buryatia and Mongolia, where monks are allowed to marry and live with their families outside the monastery precincts.

So what is it like to be a "pure monk" nowadays, especially for someone who grew up in the Soviet Union, where religious activity was rejected as superstitious and harmful? And is it at all possible to observe the precepts of the *Vinaya* in the modern world? As mentioned earlier, the monks of Geden Sheddup Choi Korling live in the monastery precincts in Arshan, a suburb of Elista, but most of them have daily duties in the Central Khurul in the capital. The monastic community consists of roughly twenty monks, so it is possible to allot a separate room to each. A regular working day in the Central Khurul starts at 9 a.m. and finishes at 5 p.m., consisting primarily in performing ritual services. From 9 to 9:30 a.m. there is a common worship in the main altar-hall, while the period from 11 a.m. until 4 p.m. is devoted to individual appointments with the laity. In addition, some monks have various administrative tasks, which constitute an inevitable part of the monastery bureaucracy. Before and after work, monks have their individual religious practice, which usually consists of reading prayers and studying texts.

In accordance with the Labour Code of the Russian Federation, every monk gets a monthly salary. Besides monks, there are lay-people, mostly women, working in the Central Khurul who also receive their monthly salary from the monastery; they are administrative workers, accountants, librarians, cooks, caretakers, and so on. Although the lay personnel are not involved in ritual matters, they attend to the monastery needs. Religious institutions in Kalmykia, including the Central Buddhist Monastery, do not receive any subsidies from the government, neither from the federal nor from the republic's budget, with offerings and sponsorship being the only sources of income. It must be stressed, however, that neither the Central Khurul nor any other Buddhist organization in Kalmykia demands payment or expects a fixed sum of money from a devotee for performing religious services, which is a distinctive feature of Kalmykia. In contrast to other post-Soviet centres of Buddhism, for instance Mongolia (Abrahms-Kavunenko 2012), the khurul in Kalmykia has not become a sector of the republic's economy, one important reason being people's strong disapproval of religion turning into a commercial enterprise:

> Here, it is a matter of principle. Our people still remember the old *gelüng*, who during the Communist era secretly conducted religious ceremonies for lay believers, risking being arrested for it: they never charged a fee for their help. Religion has never been a money-making activity in Kalmykia as it is believed that only a pure-minded person can become a monk.
>
> (interview with Andja Khartskhaev, October 2012)

Nevertheless, it is customary among devotees to bring offerings of food—such as butter, tea, and milk products—and money when visiting any khurul. Kalmyk monasteries and lay Buddhist communities also receive donations from foreign organizations, including from Korean, Japanese, and Western Buddhists. Besides

100   *Valeriya Gazizova*

offerings and donations, another source of income for the Central Khurul, as well as for other Buddhist communities, is selling images of Buddhist deities, amulets, rosaries, incense, and similar Buddhist paraphernalia. The trade in religious material objects, which are often regarded as sacred by devotees, has become a vivid tendency in the post-Soviet context. Driven by forces of global capitalism, Buddhism in Kalmykia is also gradually becoming commercialized, in spite of the popular aspirations of the general public.

Following the rules of the *Vinaya*, the monks of the Central Kalmyk Monastery are prohibited from having private property, such as an apartment or a car, but they can use the monastery cars in connection with their duties, although they themselves do not drive. Monks are allowed to have mobile phones, but only for the business of the monastery; they cannot use them for private matters. They do not have television sets in their rooms, and in general try to avoid watching TV or listening to music for entertainment. However, they do have computers and frequently use the Internet, regarding it as a useful modern tool for spreading knowledge, for educating the public in Buddhism, and for being in contact with the rest of the world. There is also an official Internet site of the Central Khurul,[10] and young monks often have their own pages on social websites on the Internet.

Besides the monks' strict adherence to the *Vinaya*, the notion of "pure" Buddhism as endorsed by Telo Tulku and the Central Khurul includes an orientation towards the Tibetan Gelugpa institutions and the Tibetan government in exile as the highest religious authority. Since Telo Tulku was elected as the Shajin Lama of Kalmykia, he has advocated a closer connection between the Kalmyks and Tibetans, stressing that this relationship is long-standing and goes back to the epoch before the Oirat migration to Russia. He points out that, until the communist era, it was Tibetan monasteries that were the main educational establishments for Kalmyk monks. At present, the usual place for the training of Kalmyk monks is the reconstructed Drepung Gomang monastery in Karnataka State in India, whereas some students are also directed to the Tibetan School Village and to the College of Traditional Medicine and Astrology (Tib. sMan rtsis khang) in Dharamsala. Although there are qualified Buddhist teachers from India and Tibet residing in Kalmykia, Telo Tulku considers Drepung Gomang in India to be the most suitable school for monks. He believes that the novices should be trained in the authentic environment of traditional Gelugpa educational establishments, so that they can understand the atmosphere and adjust to the lifestyle of a big monastery, which is impossible to experience in contemporary Kalmykia (interview with Telo Tulku, June 2008). In 2006, owing to the efforts of Telo Tulku, a separate hall of residence for Kalmyk monk-students was opened in Drepung Gomang. At the time of my last fieldwork trip in 2012, fifteen Kalmyks were living and studying there.

Telo Tulku frequently points to an affinity between Kalmykia and Tibet with regard to the shared experience of political oppression and religious persecution, emphasizing that Tibetans are currently undergoing a cultural and religious suppression somewhat similar to the deportation of the Kalmyks and the abolition of

Kalmykia in 1943. During his presentation at the 2013 International Association of Tibetan Studies conference in Ulan Bator, he addressed the Tibetans present by saying, "Do not become a second Kalmykia! Do not let them make you forget your language, your religion, your culture!"[11]

In the same talk, he said that he viewed Russia as "the great Dharma bridge between East and West because of the geopolitical location of its traditional Buddhist republics" and stated that, in the next decade, Russia, and Kalmykia in particular, would be the main centre of Buddhism in Europe. He emphasized that since Tibet as an independent region no longer exists, and since it is no longer possible to practise Buddhism freely inside Tibet, he considered it to be the responsibility of Kalmykia—as well as that of Mongolia—to preserve and carry on the tradition of Tibetan Buddhism. On the one hand, numerous people in Kalmykia and other Buddhist republics of Russia support this approach; on the other hand, a number of Kalmyk Buddhist organizations and lay believers disagree with the policy of Telo Tulku, particularly with regard to his insistence on monasticism and his viewing Kalmykia as an "enclave" of Tibetan Gelugpa monasteries.

Disjunctive Trends: Rejection of Monastic Life and New Buddhist Categories

Despite Telo Tulku's efforts to revive and promote monasticism, the majority of the Buddhist communities in Kalmykia today are non-monastic. Out of approximately thirty khuruls built since the beginning of the 1990s, twenty-five are headed by non-celibate Buddhist specialists, referred to as "lamas". Some of these "lamas" do not have a monastic background, having only taken the lay vows of *genin* (Tib. *dge bsnyen*), while others have renounced their monk's vows after a few years of celibate monasticism. The current use of the word "lama" is an innovation for Kalmykia, brought about by the revival process. In the pre-communist period, the term "lama" was used to denote only the head of the Kalmyk sangha, whereas all the other monks were called *khuvrg*. At present, the Kalmyk word *khuvrg* is rarely used and only with reference to young lay novices or to monks of the lowest degree of ordination. One of the possible reasons for this shift in terminology is the influence of Buryat Buddhist clergy working in Kalmykia in the early 1990s, in addition to Mongolia and Buryatia being among the usual places for the training of Kalmyk non-celibate Buddhist clerics. Well-known institutions for the education of contemporary non-monastic Buddhist specialists, the so-called Kalmyk lamas, include Gandan Tegchinlen in Ulan-Bator, the Aginskiy and the Ivolginskiy monasteries in Buryatia and Datsan Gunzechoinei in St. Petersburg. However, in present-day Kalmykia, in contrast to many other Buddhist contexts, the term "monk" is restricted exclusively to the celibate members of the sangha, always being the opposite of "non-celibate".

Most temples headed by non-celibate lamas are situated in smaller settlements throughout the republic, including the suburbs of Elista. While some clergy reside permanently in the khurul, others live in separate private apartments or houses. In terms of the ritual dress of the Kalmyk lay lamas, they usually have a shaved

102 Valeriya Gazizova

head and wear traditional Kalmyk robes of a red colour, with some also wearing monk's maroon robes with a ritual mantle.

As a rule, Kalmyk lay clergy receive their ordination from Tibetan teachers of different traditions; their practice is primarily based on Tibetan texts, with Tibetan being the ritual language. But in contrast to the Central Monastery, non-monastic khurul communities try to impart a Kalmyk flavour to their Buddhist activity, which appeals to many devotees, especially from smaller settlements. For instance, there is a tendency to translate Tibetan texts into Kalmyk, using it as a second ritual language. Another prominent tendency among lay clergy is a non-sectarian approach with regard to Buddhist practice, with many khuruls being registered as not being affiliated with any particular school. Before the Soviet era, all Kalmyk monasteries were listed by the Russian administration as Gelugpa (Bakaeva 1994: 15–16). At present, however, although non-celibate clergy often receive their Buddhist education in Gelugpa institutions abroad, they tend to emphasize that their religious activity spans teachings and practices of different Tibetan Buddhist traditions. Accordingly, one and the same "Kalmyk lama" often has spiritual teachers of different lineages, and in one khurul there can be practitioners adhering to different Tibetan schools. A typical example of a non-sectarian approach to Buddhism is the khurul founded in 1993 in the village of Troitskoe, half an hour's drive from Elista. Its current abbot is Aleksey Dorzhinov (born in 1966), a lay Kalmyk lama, better known in the republic as Agvan Yeshey,[12] the spiritual name given to him by Kushok Bakula Rinpoche in 1989. Although he received his clerical training in Gelugpa establishments in Buryatia, having studied for three years in the Ivolginskiy monastery and one year in Aginskiy Datsan, he asserts that his main mentor is Namkhai Norbu Rinpoche, a renowned teacher of Dzogchen (Tib. *rDzogs chen*), a system of teachings and meditation techniques in the Nyingma tradition. Two other lay practitioners serving in the khurul position themselves as adherents of the Nyingma and the Kagyu schools. The khurul invites teachers of different Tibetan Buddhist traditions from abroad and organizes various religious activities attended by people from different parts of Russia.

This situation of inter-sectarian dialogue or Buddhist pluralism—which I understand to be a combination of teachings and practices of different schools as well as a coexistence of specialists affiliated to distinct Buddhist traditions within one community—can be explained by a number of factors. First of all, according to the rules of the Gelugpa order, monastic ordination is obligatory for the sangha, which is not the case with other Tibetan Buddhist traditions. Hence, if a non-celibate officiant insists on his commitment solely to the Gelugpa school, it creates a contradiction and, more importantly, it violates the fundamental rules of the Gelugpa order. Second, a sectarian affiliation is often associated with Tibetan political history, including numerous power struggles between different Buddhist orders, and is therefore perceived as being alien to the regional form of Buddhism. A number of researchers argue that, although monks of the Gelugpa school were the most numerous in Kalmykia, other traditions of Tibetan Buddhism were also present (Bakaeva 1994: 15–18).[13] Additionally, a common argument in favour of

Buddhism in Contemporary Kalmykia 103

a non-sectarian approach states that there are many paths to enlightenment and that different Buddhist lineages supplement one another, whereas a commitment to one order is regarded as a constriction. Consequently, a situation of what Geoffrey Samuel (2005) has called "guru-shopping" has been created in present-day Kalmykia, when both the laity and clergy can try to choose among different Buddhist teachers, often combining several.

The category of non-celibate Buddhist specialists, as well as the private ownership of Buddhist temples, is a new phenomenon in Kalmykia, because, before the Soviet period, the Kalmyk sangha was exclusively monastic and generally conformed to the Gelugpa order. At present, many Kalmyks *do* want to become practising Buddhists; they establish their own Buddhist communities, build temples and retreat centres, and some even organize Buddhist summer schools for children and courses in Buddhist philosophy for adults. Nevertheless, they prefer to do it as lay-people and not as ordained monks. In the early 1990s, after the first visits of the Dalai Lama to the republic, many young Kalmyks were enthusiastic about becoming monks; however, this enthusiasm proved to be short-lived. The first group of twenty-two novices went to India to be educated there in 1992, and, since then, more than sixty others have been sent to Buddhist educational establishments abroad, but most of them have relinquished the monk's vows. In fact, only one of the twenty-two Kalmyks ordained in 1992 is now a celibate monk. As compared with contemporary monasteries in other Buddhist contexts, the number of monks in Kalmykia is very small. In total, by 2013 there were only six Kalmyks who had taken the 253 vows of *gelüng*. The majority of monks in the Central Kalmyk Monastery are Tibetans from exile communities, and most of them do not speak Kalmyk or Russian.

Why has the revival of full-scale monasticism been problematic in Kalmykia? What are the possible reasons for the rejection of monastic life? A widespread but perhaps superficial answer is that the monastic discipline is too constricting and therefore difficult to follow in our time; people want to have spouses and children, and they want to own property and enjoy the opportunities of the post-Soviet era (Sinclair 2008). In the course of my fieldwork, however, it became obvious that the answers are more diversified and complex. Many of my informants, including the abbot of the Central Kalmyk Monastery, attribute the small number of monks among the Kalmyks to the seventy years of religious persecution in the Soviet Union, which created not just a rupture but a wide gap in the continuity of Kalmyk Buddhism, having destroyed the monastic lineages. Buddhist monasticism in pre-communist Kalmykia was the result of a sustained cultural development based on numerous social, political, and economic factors. Contemporary Kalmykia lacks the economic, political, and socio-cultural bases to support the full-scale development of traditional celibate monasticism. As Baatr Elistaev, a lay Kalmyk lama and the founder of the Dharma Centre in Elista, put it,

> Monastic Buddhism, the way it was in pre-revolutionary Kalmykia, cannot appear at once or develop over a decade just because somebody says it is the proper way to practise Buddhism. Monasticism is the end product of an

104 *Valeriya Gazizova*

epoch, of a whole culture. In Kalmykia, in contrast to Buryatia for instance, all monasteries were destroyed, all lineages of monks were exterminated, and nothing survived. We had to start from scratch. My first teacher, a now-deceased Kalmyk monk, Sandji Ulanov, said that restoring monastic Buddhism would take at least fifty years. I was too young and optimistic then, so I sincerely thought he was exaggerating. But he was right! More than twenty years have passed, and we are still at the initial stage as concerns traditional monasticism.

(interview, September 2012)

In the Kalmyk khanate, as well as after its abolition, monasteries were important centres of political and economic activity. Before the Soviet period, Buddhism in Kalmykia was inseparable from monasticism, constituting an integral part of traditional society, and there existed a number of customs and regulations regarding the relationship between monasteries and society. For instance, it was a rule to send the youngest son to be ordained as a novice at the age of five to seven, while some children were dedicated to monasteries at birth and hence raised as monks. At the age of seven to ten years, the first ten monastic vows of *manj* (Tib. *rab byung*) were taken, and at the age of fifteen or seventeen the vows of *getsul* (Tib. *dge tshul*) were received; the full monastic ordination of *gelüng* (Tib. *dge slong*) was usually received around the age of twenty-three (Bakaeva 1994: 41). According to the Kalmyk tradition, however, an only son in the family was not allowed to become a celibate monk, as he was obliged to continue his family line. Present-day families are much smaller than those of the pre-communist epoch, with many having only one son, so parents are often strongly against their son becoming a monk and being unable to give them grandchildren. The demographic situation in contemporary Kalmykia also differs from that of the pre-Soviet time. According to the 1897 census, approximately 200,000 Kalmyks resided in the Russian Empire, with 90 per cent living on the Kalmyk steppes. In the 2010 census, the Kalmyk population of the Russian Federation comprised only slightly over 180,000. The primary reason for the decline in the Kalmyk population is the anti-Kalmyk persecution during the Soviet period. Thus, by the 1959 census, that is, after the official restoration of Kalmykia, the Kalmyks in the Soviet Union numbered only 106,000. Furthermore, in contrast to what was the case before the 1920s, new requirements regarding the age and educational status for those who want to become students at monastic establishments must be followed, and, first of all, it is necessary to have completed at least nine years of compulsory education.

Consequently, the failure to restore full-scale traditional celibate monasticism can be explained by the present-day conditions and demands of Kalmyk society. Non-celibate lamas and non-monastic khuruls present a more secularized alternative to the Central Kalmyk Monastery, combining ecclesiastical and lay elements. The laicization of the sangha seems to be part of a larger pattern in post-Soviet communities, as parallel developments can be observed in Buryatia and Mongolia (Bareja-Starzynska and Havnevik 2006; Abrahms-Kavunenko 2012). The emergence of a novel—at least for the Kalmyk context—type of authorized Buddhist

Buddhism in Contemporary Kalmykia 105

specialists that does not require full monastic commitment to a more advanced Buddhist practice is an adaptation to the contemporary situation, which also reveals certain global tendencies in the development of Buddhism, often referred to as "Buddhist modernism" or "Buddhist modernity" (Sharf 1995; Baumann 2001, 2002; Lopez 2002; McMahan 2008). So what are the dominant tendencies of such a "Buddhist modernism"? And what are the discourses of post-Soviet modernity that influence the development of Buddhism in Kalmykia? The rest of the chapter will attempt to give at least some preliminary answers to these complicated questions.

"Multiple Buddhist Modernities"

The establishment of the term "Buddhist modernism" as a scholarly category is attributed to Heinz Bechert, who described it as a revival movement that reinterpreted Buddhism "as a system of philosophical thought with the sole aim of showing a way to salvation from suffering and rebirth" (Bechert 1984: 275), its key features being rationality, individualism, egalitarianism, and an emphasis on canonical texts and meditation. Its emergence was connected with socio-political changes in south Asia, particularly in Burma and Sri Lanka, in response to European colonialism. A similar form of Buddhism that was developing in Sri Lanka from the second half of the nineteenth century has been named "Protestant Buddhism" by Gombrich and Obeyesekere (1988), as it was influenced by Protestant Christianity and at the same time protested against colonization and Christian missionaries. This new variety of Buddhism supported a greater lay involvement with the sangha, the traditional distinction between monks and lay practitioners having been diluted. The movement of early Buddhist modernism was often regarded as a rediscovery of "true Buddhism", which was perceived as being embodied in canonical texts, while the ritual side and traditional cosmology were rejected as "inessential accretions or modifications of Buddhism accumulated during its long historical development" (Bechert 1984: 275–276).

A parallel and at the same time somewhat different Buddhist reform movement, known as "renovationism" (Rus. *obnovlenchestvo*), began in Buryatia and Kalmykia around the early 1920s. Its aim was also to return to "pure Buddhism", which presupposed a revival of monastic discipline, intensification of Buddhist scholastic studies, and—most importantly—purging Buddhism of "folk superstitions", such as the belief in miracles, traditional cosmological assumptions, the worship of relics, and popular rituals for everyday problems. In fact, these reforms were intended, first and foremost, to make Buddhism compatible with the communist ideology, aiming at a compromise with the Bolshevik authorities (Lindquist 2011: 74).[14] In Kalmykia, "Buddhist renovationism" was represented by the activities of Mönke Bormanzhinov (1855–1919), the leader of the Don Kalmyks from 1903, and Badma Bovaev (1880–1917), the head of one of the two *tsannid chöra* (Tib. *mtshan nyid chos rva*) monasteries, the main Kalmyk educational centres for Buddhist monks at that time. Consequently, the concepts of "purity" and "purification" with regard to Buddhism are not novel for the Kalmyk

106 *Valeriya Gazizova*

context. Nonetheless, the early modernist approach differed from the idea of "pure Buddhism" as advocated by the incumbent head of the Kalmyk sangha, even though in both cases a particular emphasis is on the canonical aspect. While the reformists of the early 1920s aimed at adapting Buddhism to the changing context, the policy of the current Shajin Lama is intended to reaffirm the Gelugpa tradition of Tibetan Buddhism, including a reconstruction of celibate monasticism, notwithstanding the changing conditions and demands of Kalmyk society.

However, Buddhist modernism cannot be restricted to one historical or cultural context. Having traced its development from the mid-nineteenth century, David McMahan (2008) maintains that Buddhist modernism is a heterogeneous phenomenon represented by different forms, both in Asia and in the West, that have evolved under the influence of the dominating "forces of modernity" (McMahan 2008: 6). "Modernity" is a multifaceted and contested concept, and scholars in different disciplines subsume various ideological and social phenomena, such as rationalism, scientific naturalism, individualism, egalitarianism, global capitalism, democracy, gender equality, and liberalism, under this category (Beck 1994; Giddens 1994; Bauman 2000; Berger 2014). Nonetheless, modernity should not be regarded as a static combination of structures, but rather as a cluster of partially interrelated processes that have become prominent during the last two centuries on the global scene. In his recent book, Peter Berger (2014) argues that the primary consequence of modernity is pluralism—that is, a coexistence of different groups having distinctive ethnic origins, cultural forms, religious beliefs, and moral systems in one society—as modernity sets in motion and intensifies the major developments that lead to pluralism, such as urbanization, literacy, higher education, mass migration and tourism, technological progress, and global TV and IT communication. The modern world is dominated by a plurality of institutions, lifestyles, worldviews, beliefs, and choices, with individual faith also becoming a matter of choice.[15] Berger admits that his initial assumption, the so-called secularization thesis—that modernity inevitably leads to a decline of religion in society, an idea that for several decades has been an influential paradigm for the study of religion—has proved to be empirically unfounded. Modernity does not necessarily exclude religious thought and practice. On the contrary, the last two decades have witnessed a great upsurge of religious activity in different parts of the world, with the former Soviet Union being an illustrative example. Attempting to explain the complicated relation between modernity and religion, Berger (2014) proposes a paradigm of "two pluralisms", which, as he argues, should replace secularization theory. While the first aspect of pluralism is a coexistence of different religious systems in one society, the second is a coexistence of secular and various religious discourses in a shared social space. Just as modernization has become a global phenomenon, religious pluralism, in both of its aspects, is also spreading globally and affecting both individual faith and the character of religious institutions. Central to this interpretation of modernity—which is helpful for understanding the development of Buddhism in post-Soviet Kalmykia—is the idea of "multiple modernities" proposed by the Israeli sociologist Shmuel Eisenstadt. Utilizing this concept, Berger argues that there is also a plurality of

Buddhism in Contemporary Kalmykia 107

various patterns of modernity in different contexts, as well as in the same context. Hence, modernity pluralizes and is pluralized at the same time. Applying this pluralistic paradigm to the study of Buddhism, we can contend that there are multiple Buddhist modernities where various elements and discourses—both secular and ecclesiastical, traditional and modern—overlap and coexist in variegated patterns. Furthermore, different Buddhist modernities often coexist in one society, with contemporary Kalmykia being a telling example.

Contemporary Buddhist institutions in Kalmykia are acquiring new forms under the influence of the major post-Soviet discourses. As Berger (2014) justly contends, the secular enters the domain of religion, becoming an inalienable constituent of contemporary religious institutions. The two examples he gives are the discourse of market economics and that of bureaucracy, both being among the determining factors in the formation of Kalmyk Buddhist institutions. The relations between the state and religion (including Buddhism) in the Russian Federation are based on the Federal Law on the Freedom of Consciousness and Religious Associations of 1997, the regional laws of the early 1990s having been abolished. The law states that a "religious association" is a voluntary union formed with the aim of professing a confession of faith, dividing all religious associations into "religious groups" and "religious organizations". While the former function without a registration, the latter are officially registered juridical entities. The concept of "religious organization" has been inherited from the communist era. If a religious community was recognized and permitted by the Soviet government, it was officially registered as a "religious organization", which was done with the aim of controlling all religious activity in the Soviet Union. At present, the status of a "religious organization" gives a number of privileges, such as tax exemption, the right to set up educational establishments, the right to build constructions for worship and pilgrimage, and the possibility of organizing public events and inviting foreign missionaries.

Religious organizations can be either "local" or "centralized", that is, consisting of at least three local religious organizations.[16] A local organization is independent if it has no fewer than ten members permanently residing in the same area; otherwise, it is to be affiliated to a centralized religious organization. Kalmykia is a rural country, consisting of small village-like settlements, and people want to have a khurul in their village. Hence, the number of Buddhist temples is constantly growing, though they are usually understaffed, with many having only one officiant. Therefore, there are no independent local Buddhist organizations in the republic, all being affiliated to some centralized organization. There are two centralized Buddhist organizations in Kalmykia, the Kalmyk Buddhist Union and the Central Monastery, both supervised by the Shajin Lama, Telo Tulku Rinpoche. Accordingly, concepts of legal discourse that were inherited from the Soviet period have shaped the organizational aspects of Kalmyk Buddhist institutions, predetermining the major tendencies in their development. It is the discourse of post-Soviet bureaucracy that creates the possibility of consolidating religious authority through the status of "centralized religious organizations". The fact that the Central Kalmyk Monastery is at the centre of a network of affiliated khuruls

108   *Valeriya Gazizova*

located in different districts of the republic indicates an obvious attempt to centralize Buddhism. However, a number of Kalmyk Buddhist leaders object to this tendency of centralization and disagree with the general policy of the incumbent head of the Kalmyk Buddhists, especially with regard to his orientation towards exiled Gelugpa monasteries, with this being another argument in favour of a non-sectarian approach. For a Kalmyk khurul to be registered as Gelug presupposes affiliation with the Centralized Kalmyk Buddhist Monastery. As Agvan Yeshey, the abbot of the khurul in the village of Troitskoe, explained,

> According to the regulations of the Kalmyk Buddhist Union, if a khurul positions itself as Gelug, it is necessary to indicate what monastery it refers to. As a rule, it has to be the Central Kalmyk Monastery and, ultimately, Drepung Gomang in Karnataka. In this way it loses its independence, becoming just another branch of the Central Khurul.
>
> (interview, October 2012)

Disagreements and internal tensions between certain members of the Kalmyk Buddhist Union led to the creation of rival centralized organizations. In 2000, the Alliance of Kalmyk Buddhists (*Soyuz buddistov Kalmykii*) was set up. A few years later, however, it had to be dissolved, having failed to renew its registration. The initiative to establish an alliance independent of the Kalmyk Buddhist Union came from Agvan Yeshey. After an unsuccessful attempt to create another centralized Buddhist organization in Kalmykia, Agvan Yeshey, together with the former Khambo Lama of Buryatia, Choi Dordji Budaev,[17] founded the Central Religious Board of Buddhists of the Russian Federation in Moscow, which was officially registered at the federal level in 2004.[18] By the end of 2012, Kalmyk members constituted the majority, with six out of approximately ten communities in the CRBB being registered in Kalmykia. Consequently, a two-way process of simultaneous centralization and decentralization characterizes the development of Kalmyk Buddhism.

Whereas the key concepts of the post-Soviet discourse of bureaucracy stem from the communist era, the discourse of market economics arrived after the collapse of the communist regime. Commercialization of religious activity is an inevitable consequence brought about by religious pluralism and religious freedom. Investigating the connection between religion and economics in contemporary Russia, Caldwell (2006) illustrates that the commercial aspect has become an important characteristic of the religious pluralism found in the former Soviet Union. Different religious traditions, as well as different schools and denominations within the same religious tradition, compete with each other, creating a specific sort of so-called religious market. With regard to Buddhism, this type of market is referred to as "the Dharmic market place" (Samuel 2005). Present-day Kalmykia is not an exception to the general rule, with different Kalmyk Buddhist communities and organizations both cooperating and competing for devotees, the primary source of financial support. Even though, as has been stated earlier, there are no price lists and fixed rates for ritual services in Kalmyk khuruls, Buddhism in Kalmykia has acquired a competitive and entrepreneurial character. As there is no possibility of discussing the issue of commercialization of Buddhism in the post-Soviet context in greater detail here, it will suffice to underline that, while in many cases a "religious organization" in Russia (including Kalmyk khuruls) can be regarded as a post-Soviet workplace with new employment opportunities, in certain cases it has become a clearly commercial private enterprise. Even the Central Khurul in Elista—although it cannot possibly be referred to as a profit-making organization—has been reconstructed as a sort of workplace with regular salary payment and fixed working hours for both monks and laity, as well as for monks from abroad, mostly from Gelugpa monasteries in India, who work in Kalmykia on a temporary contract basis and who constitute the majority of the monastery sangha.

Two opposing tendencies in the development of Buddhist communities in Kalmykia are at hand, which can be broadly referred to as *re-traditionalization* and *de-traditionalization*, both of which McMahan (2008) cites as representative aspects of Buddhist modernity. While the former is an attempt to reconstruct more orthodox forms of Buddhism, the latter is a modification of traditional aspects, leading to new types of Buddhist specialists and institutions and to novel settings for Buddhist activity, such as Dharma centres, meditation retreats for the laity, and Buddhist workshops and seminars. Representing an open perception of Buddhism with an emphasis on individual choice, it permits an introduction of unconventional elements, which creates hybridity. Kalmyk khuruls run by non-celibate practitioners with a pan-sectarian approach to Buddhism, who also incorporate new texts and folk religious elements into their ritual practice, represent a clear manifestation of detraditionalization. This process can be understood as a reinterpretation of a religious tradition as a means of its adaptation to the given context and can be compared to a translation procedure, when one cultural system is rendered into the terms of another in order to become viable in a new environment (Berger 1980: 94–124; McMahan 2008: 16–59).

Re-traditionalization or *neo-traditionalism* is the reverse process of returning to tradition, that is, a reestablishment of its more orthodox aspects notwithstanding the changing conditions and even in response to certain changes. Neo-traditionalism usually presupposes a reconstruction of conventional religious institutions and practices; it tends towards sectarianism and centralized control, and therefore often entails strong community ties and rigid hierarchical structures. McMahan defines "retraditionalized" forms of Buddhism as "postmodern", regarding them as after-effects or—in his words—"products of modernity", since although they do not repudiate modernity completely, they oppose certain innovations brought about by modernity in favour of reasserting and maintaining more conservative aspects of Buddhism (McMahan 2008: 246–250).

The attempts to restore celibate monasticism of the Gelugpa order and the traditional hierarchical organization of the sangha in the Central Kalmyk Buddhist Monastery, as well as the efforts to revive the close contacts with Tibetan monasteries that Kalmykia had before the persecution of Buddhism, are definite indicators of retraditionalization. The combination of traditional monasticism and

110   *Valeriya Gazizova*

affiliation to the major Tibetan Gelugpa institutions and the Tibetan government in exile are promoted as "purification" of Kalmyk Buddhism, which will elevate Kalmykia from the Buddhist periphery closer to the centre—that is, the Dalai Lama—and perhaps even transform it into one of the major international Buddhist centres and an important pilgrimage site. Even though Kalmykia is touted as one of the traditional Buddhist regions of Russia, it has always been—and still is—on the periphery of the traditional Buddhist world. Despite the approach of the Central Monastery, it is impossible not to comply with the laws of the Russian Federation and to disregard the secular discourses of post-Soviet modernity, as well as to ignore the demands of modern Kalmyk society. Hence, a partial transformation of tradition as a method of its adaptation to the contemporary context is unavoidable. Even though the monks of the Central Monastery keep their vows, they do not reject all aspects of modernity: they use modern technologies and global IT communication to educate the public in Buddhism, they receive secular secondary education before joining the Buddha's path and—more importantly—they perceive monasticism as a career ladder with new opportunities, including studying in prestigious institutions abroad.

Consequently, different categories of Buddhist specialists and diverse forms of Buddhist institutions and communities—whether monastic or non-celibate—that are developing in Kalmykia represent different models of so-called Buddhist modernities with distinctive, intertwining patterns that mix orthodox and heterodox aspects and secular and ecclesiastical discourses. These forms can be regarded as variegated Buddhist modernities coexisting in a shared social space and time, with this heterogeneity being the most important characteristic of the Kalmyk Buddhism scene.

Conclusion

Buddhism in contemporary Kalmykia is far from being homogeneous, consisting of different—at times even discordant and conflicting—factions and communities. The principal divide within the Kalmyk Buddhist milieu is between the Central Monastery, adhering to the Gelug order, and non-monastic khuruls run by practitioners with the lay vows of *genin*, the latter often tending towards a nonsectarian approach to Buddhism, as their rejection of celibacy means they cannot legitimately position themselves as Gelug.

The Centralized Kalmyk Monastery is largely the result of the efforts of the incumbent Shajin Lama, Telo Tulku Rinpoche, who regards the restoration of the community of celibate monks as his fundamental task. The policy of "pure" Buddhism pursued by the Central Monastery and Telo Tulku is a type of neotraditionalism directed against the laicization of the sangha and hybridization of Buddhism, including the incorporation of indigenous folk religious elements into the institutionalized form of Buddhist activity. But the revival of full-scale monasticism has proved to be problematic, the Kalmyk celibate sangha being tremendously limited in numbers. The rejection of monastic life has resulted in the emergence of a type of Buddhist specialist that is new to Kalmykia, and has

Buddhism in Contemporary Kalmykia 111

brought about new developments in Kalmyk Buddhist terminology, the word "lama" having become a general term denoting all types of Buddhist professionals. The category of non-celibate "lamas" with an open approach to the Dharma is an adjustment to the post-Soviet context, being a response to the contemporary need for more inclusive, less hierarchical, and less centralized religious institutions.

The present-day Kalmyk Buddhist scene is a clear manifestation of the controversy and interplay between tradition and modernity, being characterized by contradictory tendencies and two-way processes, such as simultaneous centralization/ decentralization and innovation/neo-traditionalism. Following the perspective developed by Berger (2014) on the issue of the relations between modernity and religion, I have argued that all forms of Buddhist communities in Kalmykia represent different variants of Buddhist modernity, with each variety being an amalgamation of the local and the transnational, and the historical and the newly introduced. Having been reintroduced in Kalmykia after a seventy-year rupture to its continuity, Buddhism had to adjust to the new circumstances and could not have possibly assumed the form it had in the pre-communist period. The post-Soviet cultural and religious revival in Kalmykia has not just entailed a revitalization and reform of Buddhism; it has become a "second conversion" of Kalmyks to Buddhism. The "Kalmyk Buddhist modernities", that is, the variegated forms of Buddhism that have developed in the republic since the early 1990s, have resulted from the interaction of a set of factors, among the most influential being: the post-Soviet secular discourses, including categories inherited from the Soviet epoch; the missionary activity of exiled Tibetan teachers of different Buddhist schools; international lay Buddhist networks; Buddhist educational centres in Buryatia and Mongolia; and an aspiration to reconstruct what is regarded as the "local Kalmyk Buddhist heritage". A creative recombination of these ingredients in different proportions has produced the types of Buddhist communities that exist in Kalmykia today.

Notes

1. The *Vinaya* consists of texts containing regulations for the Buddhist monastic community.
2. In the thirteenth century, a number of intermarriages between the lines of Oirat chieftains and the family of Chinggis Khan occurred (Baskhaev and Dyakieva 2007: 27–28).
3. The structure and political system of the Kalmyk khanate was typical of other Mongolian polities of that period (Erdniev 2007: 101–131). For an account of the Oirat entry into the Russian Empire, see Khodarkovsky (1992: 76–99) and Erdniev (2007: 43–58).
4. The Kalmyks were accused of fighting against the Soviet Army in German military detachments.
5. For the Kalmyk deportation of 1943, see Bugay (1991), Maksimov (2004) or Guchinova (2006: 23–42).
6. Before the abolition of the Kalmyk khanate, the head of the Kalmyk Buddhists had the title of Khambo (Tib. *mkhan po*) Lama, which was also abolished in 1771 by the Russian government.

112 *Valeriya Gazizova*

7. Although recognized reincarnations were referred to in pre-communist Kalmykia by the Kalmyk word *khüvlhn*, the Tibetan term *tulku* is used at present.
8. For example, Ole Nydahl, a well-known Danish lama in the Karma Kagyu tradition and the founder of a worldwide network, Diamond Way Buddhism, came to Kalmykia in 1993. In 1995, the Dharma Centre organized the visits of the Sakyapa hierarch, Sakya Trizin Ngawang, and Khenchen Palden Sherab Rinpoche and Khenpo Tsewang Dongyal Rinpoche, eminent scholars and teachers in the Nyingma tradition.
9. Christianization was imposed on the Kalmyks by the Russian government as early as in the second half of the seventeenth century. It was intended to assimilate them with the Russian Orthodox population and to weaken the Kalmyk nobility, making them less independent of Russia (Khodarkovsky 1992).
10. http://khurul.ru.
11. During the years of the Kalmyk deportation (1943–1956), the Kalmyk language was practically superseded by Russian. A substantial part of the Kalmyk population communicates exclusively in Russian.
12. He was among those who went on a hunger strike in 1992, demanding the resignation of Tuvan Dorj.
13. Iconographic material also attests to the existence of different Tibetan Buddhist traditions in pre-revolutionary Kalmykia (Batyreva 2005).
14. "Renovationism" as a tendency of adjusting to the Soviet regime was also advocated by certain Orthodox Christian leaders, which created a temporary schism in the Russian Orthodox Church in the 1920s.
15. The idea of fate becoming choice under the influence of modernity is also discussed in Berger's earlier works (Berger 1980).
16. Khuruls, Buddhist centres, and monasteries are different examples of "local religious organizations" in Kalmykia.
17. Aleksandr Budaev (Choi Dordji) was the Pandito Khambo Lama, that is, the leader of the Buryat Buddhists, from 1993 until 1995.
18. It must not be confused with the Central Religious Board of the Buddhists of the USSR, which after the fall of the Soviet Union broke into two separate communities: the Buddhist Traditional Sangha of Russia, headed by the Pandita Khambo Lama Damba Ayusheev, and the Religious Board of Buddhists of Russia, headed by Nimazhap Ilyukhinov, both consisting mainly of Buryat communities.

References

Abrahms-Kavunenko, Saskia. 2012. "Religious 'Revival' after Socialism? Eclecticism and Globalisation amongst Lay Buddhists in Ulaanbaatar." *Inner Asia* 14 (2): 279–297.

Bakaeva, Elza. 1994. *Буддизм в Калмыкии* [Buddhism in Kalmykia]. Elista: Kalmytskoe knizhnoe izdatelstvo.

Bareja-Starzynska, Agata, and Hanna Havnevik. 2006. "A Preliminary Study of Buddhism in Present-Day Mongolia." In *Mongols from Country to City: Floating Boundaries, Pastoralism and City Life in the Mongol Lands*, edited by Ole Bruun and Li Narangoa, 212–236. Copenhagen: NIAS Press.

Baskhaev, Araltan, and Raisa Dyakieva. 2007. *Ойрат-калмыки: XII-XIX вв.: история и культура калмыцкого народа с древнейших времен до начала XIX века* [The Oirat-Kalmyks: The twelfth to nineteenth centuries: The history and culture of the Kalmyk people from ancient times to the beginning of the nineteenth century]. Elista: Kalmytskoe knizhnoe izdatelstvo.

Batyreva, Svetlana. 2005. *Старокалмыцкое искусство XVII-начала XX века* [Old Kalmyk art from the seventeenth century to the beginning of the twentieth century]. Moscow: Nauka.

Bauman, Zygmunt. 2000. *Liquid Modernity*. Cambridge: Polity Press.

Baumann, Martin. 2001. "Global Buddhism: Developmental Periods, Regional Histories, and a New Analytical Perspective." *Journal of Global Buddhism* 2: 1–43.

———. 2002. "Protective Amulets and Awareness Techniques, or How to Make Sense of Buddhism in the West." In *Westward Dharma: Buddhism beyond Asia*, edited by Charles S. Prebish and Martin Baumann, 51–65. Berkeley: University of California Press.

Bechert, Heinz. 1984. "Buddhist Revival in East and West." In *The World of Buddhism: Buddhist Monks and Nuns in Society and Culture*, edited by Heinz Bechert and Richard Gombrich, 273–285. London: Thames & Hudson.

Beck, Ulrich. 1994. "The Reinvention of Politics: Towards a Theory of Reflexive Modernization." In *Reflexive Modernization: Politics, Tradition and Aesthetics in the Modern Social Order*, edited by Ulrich Beck, Anthony Giddens, and Scott Lash, 1–55. Cambridge: Polity Press.

Berger, Peter L. 1980. *The Heretical Imperative: Contemporary Possibilities of Religious Affirmation*. London: Collins.

———. 2014. *The Many Altars of Modernity: Toward a Paradigm for Religion in a Pluralist Age*. Berlin: Walter de Gruyter.

Bugay, Nikolay. 1991. *Операция "Улусы"* [Operation "Ulus"]. Elista: Jangar.

Caldwell, Melissa L. 2006. "A New Role for Religion in Russia's New Consumer Age: The Case of Moscow." *Religion, State and Society* 33 (1): 19–34.

Erdniev, Uryubdzhur. (1970) 2007. *Калмыки* [The Kalmyks]. Elista: Kalmytskoe knizhnoe izdatelstvo.

Giddens, Anthony. 1994. "Living in a Post-Traditional Society." In *Reflexive Modernization: Politics, Tradition and Aesthetics in the Modern Social Order*, edited by Ulrich Beck, Anthony Giddens, and Scott Lash, 56–109. Cambridge: Polity Press.

Gombrich, Richard, and Gananath Obeyesekere. 1988. *Buddhism Transformed: Religious Change in Sri Lanka*. Princeton, NJ: Princeton University Press.

Guchinova, Elza-Bair. 2006. *The Kalmyks*. London: Routledge.

Halkovic, Stephen. 1985. *The Mongols of the West*. Bloomington: Research Institute for Inner Asian Studies, Indiana University.

Heissig, Walther. 1980. *The Religions of Mongolia*. Los Angeles: University of California Press.

Khodarkovsky, Michael. 1992. *Where Two Worlds Met: The Russian State and the Kalmyk Nomads, 1600–1771*. Ithaca, NY: Cornell University Press.

Kitinov, Baatr. 1996. "Kalmyks in Tibetan History." *Tibet Journal* 3: 35–46.

Lindquist, Galina. 2011. "Ethnic Identity and Religious Competition: Buddhism and Shamanism in Southern Siberia." In *Religion, Politics, and Globalization: Anthropological Approaches*, edited by Galina Lindquist and Don Handelman, 69–90. New York: Berghahn Books.

Lopez, Donald S., Jr., ed. 2002. *A Modernist Buddhist Bible: Essential Readings from East and West*. Boston: Beacon Press.

Maksimov, Konstantin. 2004. *Трагедия народа: репрессии в Калмыкии 1918–1940-е годы* [The tragedy of people: The repressions in Kalmykia from 1918 to the 1940s]. Moscow: Nauka.

McMahan, David L. 2008. *The Making of Buddhist Modernism*. Oxford: Oxford University Press.

Ochirova, Nina. 2011. *История буддизма в СССР и Российской Федерации в 1985–1999 гг.* [The history of Buddhism in the USSR and the Russian Federation 1985–1999]. Elista: Fond Sovremennoi Istorii.

114   *Valeriya Gazizova*

Sagaster, Klaus. 2007. "The History of Buddhism among the Mongols." In *The Spread of Buddhism*, edited by Ann Heirman and Stephen Peter Bumbacher, 379–432. Leiden: Brill.

Samuel, Geoffrey. 2005. "The Westernisation of Tibetan Buddhism." In *Tantric Revisionings: New Understandings of Tibetan Buddhism and Indian Religion*, edited by Geoffrey Samuel, 317–344. Aldershot: Ashgate.

Sharf, Robert H. 1995. "Buddhist Modernism and the Rhetoric of Meditative Experience." *Numen* 42: 228–283.

Sinclair, Tara. 2008. "Tibetan Reform and the Kalmyk Revival of Buddhism." *Inner Asia* 10 (1): 241–259.

Zhukovskaia, Nataliia. 2010. "The Revival of Buddhism in Buryatia: Problems and Prospects." In *Religion and Politics in Russia: A Reader*, edited by Marjorie M. Balzer, 197–215. Armonk, NY: M. E. Sharpe.

7 Buddhist Modernity and New-Age Spirituality in Contemporary Mongolia

*Hanna Havnevik**

Contemporary Ulaanbaatar is a million-plus city with a centre choked by traffic and pollution. There are construction sites at every other corner, where shopping centres, offices buildings, and even skyscrapers are rising up. In between such commercial buildings and apartment houses, Buddhist temples, Christian churches, and mosques—presently there are two—are spread out in the cityscape. Two decades ago, Buddhist monks wearing Mongol robes and laypeople dressed in traditional Mongolian dress (*del*) could often be observed in the streets hurrying to and from their daily tasks. Robed *sangha* members are now more seldom seen, and apart from during seasonal festivals, only some elderly wear *del* in the city. Today, the urban young parade Peace Avenue dressed in the latest South Korean or international fashions as Ulaanbaatar is rapidly transforming into a metropolis. At the northern and western edges of the city, tent or *ger* suburbs continue to grow, housing more than half a million people. Although more well-organized and affluent than during the first decade after the collapse of communism in 1990, when urbanization started to accelerate, the city still lacks a sewage system, and the inhabitants have to drag handcarts with water containers to their households.

After the peaceful revolution in 1990 ended seventy years of communist rule, the former Mongolian People's Republic was renamed Mongolia. Parliamentary democracy replaced a one-party totalitarian political system, and the country gradually opened up for multinational capitalism. In order to meet spiritual needs suppressed for nearly three-quarters of a century, Mongol Buddhist leaders and practitioners began to found monasteries, temples, and organizations both in the countryside and in urban centres, and the large, historical monasteries such as Gandantegchenlin (abbr. Gandan), Erdene Zuu, and Amarbayasgalant started to function again as religious institutions. Religious freedom and the separation between "church" and state were granted in the new constitution of 1992. Since then, the state has contributed to the restoration of key Buddhist sites, but does not—as a rule—subsidize Buddhism.

Several scholars have studied new forms of Buddhism emerging from its interaction with modernity. Already in 1966 Heinz Bechert called this new development "Buddhist modernism"; Richard Gombrich and Gananath Obeyesekere used

116 *Hanna Havnevik*

"Protestant and Post-protestant Buddhism" for the Buddhist transformations they found in Sri Lanka in the early 1980s, while Donald Lopez employs the term "modern Buddhism" (2002). According to David McMahan (2008, 2012) Buddhist modernism is a transnational genre of Buddhism with roots in the late nineteenth and early twentieth centuries and is shaped by its interaction with dominant cultural and intellectual forces of modernity, such as the European Enlightenment, scientific rationalism, romanticism, Protestantism, psychology, and modern social and political thought (McMahan 2012: 160). According to McMahan, other central features of Buddhist modernism include de-mythologization of traditional cosmologies; a de-emphasis of ritual, image worship, "folk" belief and practices, "priesthood", and hierarchy; and an emphasis on this-worldly matters, social and political engagement, and democracy (2012: 16). Scholars agree that Buddhist modernism is a dynamic set of processes based on a plurality of local and global causes and emphasize that Buddhist revival processes in Asia are often combined with nationalist movements spurred by reactions to colonialism.

This chapter discusses how Mongol Buddhist leaders have combined traditional and new religious elements in innovative ways to create modern or post-modern religious institutions in Ulaanbaatar since the turn of the century. Three changes illustrating how Buddhist modernities localize in contemporary urban Mongolia will be analysed: innovations within the Gelugpa tradition; an increase in temples belonging to non-Gelugpa Buddhism; and the growth of Buddhist institutions founded by female religious leaders. Each in their way, these transformations illustrate a wide spectrum of Mongol Buddhist responses to modernity—from a rationalized, normative,[1] and elitist version of Buddhism, on the one hand, to a non-normative "folk" version with an emphasis on rituals, image worship, occultism, and this-worldly benefits, on the other.

Buddhism in Mongolia in a Historical Perspective

Buddhism is seen by many Mongols as their national religion. Historically, Buddhism replaced shamanism in the seventeenth century when the Mongols converted to Buddhism (Heissig 1953; Bareja-Starzyńska and Havnevik 2006: 214–215). But since its introduction, Mongolian cosmology has been shaped by normative Tibetan Buddhism, as well as by beliefs in benevolent and malevolent spirits inhabiting a sacred landscape. Mongols negotiate—often through religious specialists—with these numina in order to obtain benefits such as prosperity and good health and to avert accidents, crises, and natural disasters (see e.g. Davaa-Ochir 2008). By the nineteenth century, Buddhist temples and monasteries were scattered throughout Mongol lands, and a high percentage of the male population, some say over 100,000, were "monks".[2] Up till the revolution in 1921, a localized form of Tibetan Buddhism, also called Mongolian Buddhism, was the main religion and the dominant cultural force in the country. In 1924 the Mongolian People's Republic was established and controlled by the Soviet Union until 1990/1991, and during the communist purges, particularly during the 1920s and

1930s, Buddhism was almost eradicated.[3] In 1958, only 200 monks were officially listed in five monasteries that had survived. Soviet communism dominated social, political, and economic life, and socialist modernity—including secular education—replaced the important educational role of the *sangha*.

With democracy, formally established from 1990, Buddhists actively re-established and built new Buddhist temples (see Bareja-Starzyńska and Havnevik 2006). The new constitution of 1992 allowed any religious group to register with the Ministry of Justice and Home Affairs in order to function legally within the country, and the law opened for proselytization. Soon Mongolia was seen as a new missionary field where global religions established their satellites (Wazgird 2011). The country's rapid exposure to globalization—including new means for spreading religious messages, such as home pages and social media on the Internet, digitalization of religious texts, and the active and free use of television and radio—opened the scene not only for aggressive evangelical Christian preachers, but also to internationally experienced and high-profile Tibetan and Asian Buddhists. Mongols were soon exposed to global Buddhist modernity with its novel forms of religious organization, demands for social involvement, worldwide ecological awareness, vegetarianism, engagement in peace movements, and gender inclusiveness (McMahan 2008, 2012: 157–305).

Innovations within the Gelugpa Tradition

New Centres and Projects

The Buddhism that resurfaced in Mongolia after seventy years of communist rule was one that had been moulded by the atheist regime's attempts to eradicate it by laying almost all Buddhist monasteries and temples in ruins, burning the canonical scriptures, killing elite and learned monks, and forcing ordinary monks to marry. Slowly, Buddhism re-emerged from the ashes, but is still in a formative phase. The Dalai Lama, who has travelled to Mongolia nine times, including twice during communism,[4] is actively engaged in promoting a modernized form of Tibetan Buddhism in the country—devoid, as he says, of "mystical" elements. In a recent statement in support of the new Grand Maitreya Project, with its plan to build a fifty-four-metre-high Maitreya statue and a 108-metre-high stupa surrounded by an ecological city to the south of Ulaanbaatar, the Dalai Lama emphasizes the need to build a modern Buddhism for the twenty-first century by eliminating superstition and by founding it solidly on Buddhist philosophy and modern science.[5] He has sent a number of highly educated doctors of Buddhist philosophy (*geshes*) to Mongolia to teach and wishes to re-establish a strict enforcement of the Vinaya that was abolished by the communist regime in the 1930s. Young Mongol monks, often sponsored by exile-Tibetan institutions, are sent to Tibetan monasteries in India to be trained in Gelugpa monasteries. The Dalai Lama expresses that Mongolia is still in a state of transition, but already in 1991 made eight regulations appropriate for "modern" Mongolian monks—rules that are, according to Geshe

118   *Hanna Havnevik*

Luvsanjamts, largely disregarded by temple leaders and monastics in the city. Abbots in the city follow their own opinions, says the geshe, who explains that it is difficult today to distinguish between a monastery and something that looks like a Buddhist office or a modern enterprise.

The Jebtsundampa Khutugtu Centre

Tension exists between Gelugpa monasticism spearheaded by Gandan Monastery—seen by many as the leading monastic institution in the country—and individual Buddhist clerics eager to create a dynamic and viable form of Mongolian Buddhism relevant in contemporary society. The pioneering initiatives of Nyamsambuu Gabj are examples of modernistic reforms within the Mongolian Gelugpa tradition. The Jebtsundampa Khutugtu Centre, established in 2004 by lay students of the Tibetan Jhado Rinpoche, has since recently been directed by Nyamsambuu. In 2011 the centre relocated to a commercial building in central Ulaanbaatar and is funded by the Mongolian business community. Nyamsambuu teaches Buddhist philosophy for free to young laypeople in Club 21, while in the Vajra Youth Class he teaches university graduates and older students. After his studies at Zanabazar Buddhist University at Gandan and ten years at Drepung Monastery in South India, Nyamsambuu—who has good command of English—also joined a distant learner's programme at the University of Sunderland for two years and taught for another two years (2008–2009) at the Foundation for the Preservation of the Mahayana Tradition (FPMT), the Mongolian branch of the Tibetan-Western Dharma Centre.

Like several Buddhist modernists in Asia, Nyamsambuu names his Buddhist activities in English to attract young followers. Having taught Buddhist philosophy for three years at the FPMT in Ulaanbaatar, Nyamsambuu has adopted Western pedagogical methods in teaching a modernized form of Tibetan Buddhism. He believes in communicating philosophy in a simple language, and already as a young monk he started an evening-class programme at Gandan teaching Buddhism to the laity. Nyamsambuu uses modern media to spread Buddhism in a competitive religious market. He directs the only Buddhist radio station in Mongolia, Lavain Egshig ("the Voice of the Conch", FM 97.5), established in 2008 as a Buddhist alternative to the controversial Eagle TV, which aired Evangelical Christian programmes, news, and entertainment from 1994 until 2011. Nyamsambuu is engaged in social work and teaches Buddhism in hospitals and prisons, and he is interested in "mindfulness" and wants to study it further at the Oxford Mindfulness Centre at Oxford University's Department of Psychiatry.

There are three other Dharma centres in Ulaanbaatar, all of which are exile-Tibetan missionary enterprises introducing a modernized form of Buddhism: the aforementioned FPMT;[6] the Asral Charity, founded in 2001 as an offshoot of Jampa Ling, which started in Ireland by the Tibetan Panchen Ötrul Rinpoche;[7] and the Tarema Association, established in 2001 by Geshe Sonam Dorje (b. 1954) from Zangskar. Among the Dharma centres in Ulaanbaatar, only the Jetsundampa Khutugtu Centre has been founded by a Mongol and is supported by the Mongol business community rather than by money from Buddhist centres abroad. While all three Dharma centres emphasize the teaching of meditation, engagement in social work, and reaching out to young Mongols, only the Tibetan-founded ones emphasize Vinaya ordination for clerics, and the FPMT has hired Western Vinaya-abiding nuns ordained in the Tibetan tradition as directors since 2004.

The Kalachakra Culture Centre

Modernizers of Gelugpa Buddhism in Mongolia emphasize more than new ways to teach Buddhist philosophy and meditation to laypeople. While the Mongolian clergy has been criticized for reciting prayers in the Tibetan language that only a few elite monks understand, several Buddhist organizations translate Buddhist

Figures 7.1 Computerized transliteration of Kagnyur and Tengjur from Uighur script into Cyrillic

Photos: Havnevik 2013

120 Hanna Havnevik

prayers and scriptures into modern Mongolian in order to make them widely accessible. Instead of mechanically reciting religious texts only in Tibetan, learned Mongols today emphasize a hermeneutical understanding of their scriptures. A substantial undertaking is presently being made at the Kalachakra Culture Centre, established by the Mongolian monk Gombodorj Buyandelger in 2008, of translit-erating the entire Tibetan Buddhist canon, the Kangyur and Tengyur, from classical Mongolian (Uighur script) into the Cyrillic script used in modern Mongolia.[8] By April 2013, sixty modern bound volumes had been completed, while the full set of 400 will be published by 2016. The books are given to universities and monasteries upon their formal reuqest. Although educated segments of the population will be able to read the canon, to what extent the scriptures will be studied and understood is an open question.

Like other modern Buddhist undertakings, the Kalachakra Culture Centre is based on monastic-lay collaboration. Its monk leader has employed thirty young laymen and women—all graduates from the Zanabazar Buddhist University at Gandan Monastery and the School of Language and Culture at the National University—to do the computerized transliteration. Arjia Rinpoche (b. 1950), the former Mongolian abbot of the Tibetan Khumbum Monastery in Qinghai Prov-ince, is the advisor of the project, which is funded by donation.[9]

While elderly Mongolian monks saw it as their duty during the first phase of the revival during the 1990s to re-establish "traditional" Buddhism and protect monastic traditions and hierarchies, contemporary Buddhist reformers often go outside established monasteries to implement their programmes, and small Dharma centres can more easily spearhead reforms. Ganden remains a bureau-cratic and conservative force in religious life, although Gandan too attempts to meet modern demands and challenges posed by active Christian proselytization. Its Zanabazar Buddhist University, which includes both traditional Buddhist and secular subjects in its four-year educational programme, has opened its pro-gramme to both monastics and lay of both genders.[10]

Increase in Temples Belonging to Non-Gelugpa Buddhism

After the first chaotic phase of religious revival in Mongolia, many small, inde-pendent Buddhist temples—several of which belong to non-Gelugpa traditions and headed by "self-made" male and female religious innovators—are being consolidated in the capital. Gandan Monastery, which unofficially represents the "normative" tradition, has, according to Geshe Luvsanjamts, failed to enforce common rules for all Buddhist temples and monasteries in the country, particu-larly in the thirty-some Buddhist institutions in Ulaanbaatar, which vary in their school affiliation, size, organizational structure, and in terms of their ritual calen-dar. They are privately funded and owned and are autonomous when it comes to decision-making. As in all Buddhist temples, their clerics receive fixed salaries and carry out services for set hours per day, and the majority live outside the temple compounds with their families.

Contemporary Mongolia 121

Red Tradition Temples in Ulaanbaatar

Soon after democratization in 1990, also non-Gelugpa practitioners, adherents of what is named the Red Tradition (*ulaan shashin*, lit. "Red Religion"), started to found temples.[11] Soon *chod* (Tib. *gcod*) was revived—a religious practice brought from India to Tibet in the eleventh century and later spread among Mongols, where it survived on the margins of Gelugpa monasticism (see e.g. Havnevik 2015). *Chod*, which has many similarities with tantric practices, was maintained also during the communist era by individual male and female practitioners; they often wandered in small groups to meditate at various charnel grounds and haunted places on the steppe. In 1990, Banzar (c. 1915–2011) established the first *chod* temple, Namdoldechelin, in a poor *ger* suburb at the northern edge of the capital. Today, altogether fourteen independent satellite temples have spread in Ulaanbaatar and in the near countryside, reflecting not only the popularity of the tradition, but also the decentralized establishment of new temples.[12] The strong economic growth in Mongolia during the last two decades has secured generous funding for these institutions, while the absence of a head monastery administering strict rules and the lack of enforcement of celibacy have led to a steady recruitment of clerics.

At present there is a "tug of war" between normative Gelugpa Buddhism represented by Gandan Monastery, supported by Mongol monks trained in exile-Tibetan monasteries, and self-taught clerics who run their private temples or enterprises, many of whom adhere to the Red Tradition. The resistance to the Gelugpa hegemony of Gandan, with its close links to the Tibetan exile establishment, is partly fuelled by Mongol identity politics and nationalism. Tantric practitioners operated on the fringe of established monasticism in Tibet as well, and charismatic tantrics are known for their strong critique of scholasticism and dogmatism of the Gelugpa school. In the past, their wandering lifestyle made them hard to control, and they had wide appeal among ordinary people.

In Mongolian Red Tradition temples, *chod*, which is primarily connected with the Tibetan Nyingma and Kagyu traditions, is the main religious practice. Currently in Mongolia, some criticism is voiced that Red Tradition clerics lack proper training, implying that they do not know the philosophical background of the Kagyu and Nyingma traditions or the "correct" ways of performing their prayers and rituals. There is, therefore, some pressure to make Red Tradition temples develop in a "normative", that is, Tibetan direction. If Mongolian Red Tradition clerics were to receive extensive training in exile Tibetan monasteries, this might in the future lead to a change from a general Red Tradition identity to the development of separate Nyingmapa and Kagyupa temples in Mongolia. In order for that to happen, charismatic Tibetan reincarnations belonging to these schools would have to invest time and resources in Mongolia. Red Tradition leaders in Mongolia have so far not established wide networks in exile-Tibetan communities abroad and base their temple practices on local traditions. It was only recently (17 July 2013) that Kyabje Taklung Tsetrul Rinpoche, the head of the Tibetan Nyingmapa tradition, arrived in Ulaanbaatar as the first high Nyingmapa reincarnation to visit the country, indicating that the Red Tradition practices in Mongolia might be more closely followed by representatives of the Nyingmapa leadership in exile in the future.

The Role of the Ninth Jebtsundampa

Since 2010, a large *chod* communal prayer session has been organized within the precincts of Gandan Monastery by the Jebtsundampa's monastic household or *labrang* (Tib. *bla brang*). The late Ninth Jebtsundampa (1930–2012), the Tibetan reincarnation of the last theocratic leader of Mongolia, attempted to spread *chod* in its Gelugpa lineages in Mongolia before he passed away. Being an exiled Tibetan, he was able to play only a minor religious role in the country during the first two decades of the Buddhist revival, but returned to Mongolia in 2011 and visited a number of temples in Ulaanbaatar, including those belonging to the Red Tradition, where he encouraged the practice of Gelugpa *chod*.

The Ninth Jebtsundampa was officially recognized by the government as the spiritual head of Mongolia and enthroned ceremonially at Gandan in November 2011, three months before he passed away in March 2012. The establishment of the Jebtsundampa's *labrang* in Gandan, the scheduled display of his mummified body in the former library, and the plan to keep his body in a silver stupa in a new main assembly hall[13] show the interest of Mongolian Buddhists and the leadership of Gandan in maintaining and promoting Jebtsundamapa's legacy. Tolerating the Jebtsundampa's practice of *chod*—a tradition that has been discouraged in Gelugpa monasteries in both Tibet and Mongolia—may be an attempt by the Gandan to bring *chod* under its control and to combat Tibetan Buddhist pluralism and the influence of the Red Tradition.

Figure 7.2 The Ninth Jebtsundampa visiting the female temple Narkhajidin Sum, 12 November 2009

Photo: Courtesy of Narkhajidin Sum

Growth of Buddhist Temples Founded by Female Religious Leaders

Female Temples

Transnational Buddhist modernity is characterized by an increased involvement of women (McMahan 2012), and the establishment of Buddhist monasteries, temples, and centres by and for women after 1990 represents an innovation in Mongolian religious history. Apart from emanations of Tārā, individual female

Figures 7.3 Narkhajidin Sum and *khandamaas* dressed for Vajrayoginī Tshogchod as five *ḍākinīs*

Photos: Courtesy of Narkhajidin Sum

124   Hanna Havnevik

chod practitioners, and *chavgants* (i.e. women who take lay vows late in life), there were no professional religious roles open for women in the past, and a Mongolian *saṇgha* of nuns was never established. After democratization, however, Mongolian women have created a new, hybrid role for themselves as lay tantric practitioners or ritualists; they are called *khandamaa* (Skt. *ḍākinī*). This is the main platform from which they engage in public religious life, and during the early 1990s three female temples were established: Dara Ekh, Togsbayasgalant, and Narkhajidin Sum (see Bareja-Starzyńska and Havnevik 2006: 226–228).

In spite of incessant attempts by Tibetan masters and Western Buddhists to encourage Mongol women to choose celibacy during the twenty-five years of religious freedom, few have done so, and the number is declining. While forty to fifty novices were ordained during the first ten or fifteen years of religious freedom, there were less than twenty ordained novices in Ulaanbaatar in 2013.[14] When FPMT took over the responsibility for Dara Ekh in 2001, it was made into the only celibate nunnery in Mongolia, under the name Drolma Ling. Seven novices lived here in 2013, and the number was reduced to three in 2014.[15] In Mongolia, strong cultural norms encourage women to marry and have children, and for them the intermediate position as "semi-renouncers" or "lay-nuns" is preferred because it gives them the option to combine religious and secular life. Instead of choosing the asexual role of the celibate Buddhist nun, urban Mongolian female religious professionals, who are generally well educated, emphasize their femininity; they keep their hair long, use makeup, and wear Mongolian robes only during "work hours" in the temple.

Female Chod Temple and Its Oracle

Although shunning celibate religious careers, women continue to influence the revival of Buddhism in Mongolia. One example is Dulumjav (b. 1952), who founded her own temple, Janchuvdechinlin, in a poor northern suburb of Ulaanbaatar in 2005. She worked as a kindergarten teacher under the communist regime, but having grown up in a devout Buddhist family, she practised Buddhism in secret and joined Benzer's *chod* temple as soon as she could practise religion openly in 1990. The temple, which is well funded, was expanded in 2011, and currently some twenty male clerics are employed for ritual services. Like Japanese Buddhist temples, Janchuvdechenlin is run like a family enterprise with Dulumjav's son Shinendentsel functioning as the director and her grandsons enrolled as "monks". In addition to her activities in her temple, Dulumjav serves clients in their private houses and has travelled several times to serve diaspora Mongols in Germany, Hungary, Poland, and South Korea.

Dulumjav's temple belongs to the Red Tradition and serves the nearby community of migrants who have come from the countryside to the city in recent years. Lately, the family has made public Shinendentsel's ecstatic possessions, which had been kept secret for ten years.[16] In 2014, they rented the Buyant Ukhaa sports stadium, where the oracle went into a trance in front of 4,000 people, according to Dulumjav.[17] This is the stadium where also the Dalai Lama and evangelical preachers hold mass meetings for thousands while visiting Ulaanbaatar.

The oracular tradition is recognized in normative Tibetan and Mongolian Buddhism, and the present Nechung oracle, formerly one of the state oracles in Tibet, regularly visits Ulaanbaatar.[18] Recently, another oracle, a young man named Tseden-Ish from Zavkhan Province, is said to be an oracle of Vajrapāṇi, and his fame has rapidly spread in Buddhist circles in the capital.[19]

Oracles who perform convincingly and are recognized by tradition are likely to develop a large following of devotees—as well as considerable wealth. The highest reincarnation in Mongolia at present, Zaya Paṇḍita, says he regrets that he is unable to control the young Vajrapāṇi oracle and that the young man has developed a passion for money and fast cars provided by rich devotees. The other oracle, Shinendentsel, is possessed by the god of wealth, Namsrai (Skt. Vaiśravaṇa) and, in ecstasy, channels the communication from a deity granting material gratification to his believers. Along with the instalment of around fifteen reincarnations, the recognition of oracles is a recent addition to the growing plethora of Buddhist religious specialists in Mongolia[20] contributing to a "mystification" rather than a "rationalization" of tradition.

Figure 7.4 Dulumjav, her son Shinendentsel, and grandson
Photo: Courtesy of Dulumjav 2014

126   *Hanna Havnevik*

Female Business Temples

Gandan Darjaalin

During the last ten years, a new type of innovator has been remarkably successful in building Buddhist "business temples". Two such temples headed by women, which use modern methods of advertisement and management, have been established in suburbs at the edge of the city. These two female religious innovators, Enkhsaikhan and Sarandavaa Bat-Ochir, have each in their own way experienced great economic success performing divination, astrology, and New Age healing. Enkhasaikan is a woman in her thirties who established the Gandan Darjaalin, a building combining Mongolian temple and Christian church architecture, in the *ger* district Bayan Khoshuu in 2013. Enkhsaikhan performs divination, offers ritual protection for individuals and families, and also provides ritual insurance for private companies. For the various ritual services she charges from 5,000 to 274,000 togrog (or around 2.50 to 150 US dollars). According to the reportage of a critical journalist, Enkhsaikhan may earn as much as 5.6 million togrog (around 3,000 US dollars) per day.[21] Enkhsaikhan is a laywoman who dresses fancily— like a fashion model—and monks are employed in her service to perform dice divinations. Customers line up in front of the gate to her temple every day, but Enkhsaikhan's female manager controls admittance to only thirty to forty clients per day.

Mongol Aura and Energy Centre

The Mongol Aura and Energy Centre is located in Khailaast, another *ger* suburb north of Ulaanbaatar. The founder, Sarandavaa Bat-Ochir, entitles herself president of the Mongolian Academy of Meditation, Animism, Astrology, and Psychology. On the walls, there are diplomas of her PhD and ScD degrees, and in her thirty-some books she explains religion from the point of "science and energy". In her private sanctuary, the central image is Namsrai, the god of wealth, and from her office-temple she monitors the healing activities in her centre on closed-circuit television. In the building's numerous energy healing rooms, therapy is offered by the use of sacred water, oxygen cocktails, energy stones, sound, and so forth. Tantric and shamanistic techniques, astrology, and massage are ingredients in the healing programme.

In building her image, Sarandavaa uses elements that are Mongol shamanist and nationalist, Tibetan and Mongol Buddhist, and New Age. One of her publications provides a variety of illuminating photos: Buddhist deities important to her; her Mongol Buddhist teachers; herself and her grandchildren dressed in costumes from the time of the Mongolian empire; herself posing with Tibetan and Mongolian monks; herself abroad in India and in different places in Mongolia (Bat-Ochir 2009). At the entrance to her centre, a life-size statue of Chinggis Khan is flanked by leaders and kings of the Mongol Empire, along with Chinggis Khan's consorts. Since 1993, more than 250,000 customers have consulted Sarandavaa, and the

Figure 7.5 The Protective Deity Room, where adherents pray to obtain visas to South Korea, the United States and Canada

Photos: Havnevik 2014

tenth anniversary of her centre in 2012 was celebrated with 3,300 people attending. Sarandavaa, who is a laywoman, has some twenty employees, many of them women, but also three monks. At regular performances, Sarandavaa performs a ritual of summoning money (Mongonii Dallaga) in large halls where hundreds, many of them young people, stretch their hands above their heads with paper slips calling back money, séances reminiscent of sermons given by Evangelical revivalist preachers.

Sarandavaa has also founded a Tārā temple located next to her centre. The architecture of the tall building is postmodern, with large windows and a glass canopy. The temple contains a three-dimensional Twenty-one Tārā *maṇḍala*, a labyrinth said to remove the sins of those who pass through it and make childless women fertile; statues of the Twenty-one Tārās; and an enormous statue of Green Tārā. The ceiling is decorated with planetary constellations, giving the temple a touch of New Age spirituality.

Conclusion

From the early 1920s until 1990, Mongolia was dominated by a communist regime that enforced radical economic and political changes and thoroughly secularized society. Contrary to earlier theories postulating that religion would disappear in the face of industrialization and modernization (Berger 1967; Wilson 1976), the forced secularization in Mongolia did not eradicate religious beliefs. While global Buddhist modernity has been identified as rooted in the late nineteenth and early twentieth centuries and, in Asia, connected with opposition to colonialism (McMahan 2012), few studies have analyzed Buddhist modernity in post-communist states in depth. But like the nationalist Buddhist

128 *Hanna Havnevik*

movements in Sri Lanka at the turn of the twentieth century, the rebuilding of Buddhism in Ulaanbaatar is intimately connected with nationalism. Common to all Mongol Buddhist leaders is their emphasis on a localized form of Buddhism and opposition to foreign control. After democracy was introduced in 1990, the normative Buddhist tradition represented by the historical Gelugpa monasteries was soon re-established. The Gelugpas also dominate the religious scene in contemporary Mongolia. The revival was based on pre-communist, "orthodox" Buddhism mediated by years of socialist rule. Soon, however, modernist ideas promulgated by Asian and Western Buddhist missionaries or brought home by young Mongol monks studying abroad influenced the course of events.

A number of Mongol religious leaders try to maintain and promote features and customary practices perceived as uniquely Mongolian, including the support of Mongol reincarnations, preference for Mongolian-style robes, acceptance of married clergy, Buddhism's closeness to folk religious practices, Mongolian as a clerical language, and the cult of Chinggis Khan.[22] Some of these elements are easier to accommodate in the Red Tradition. While Mongol Buddhists have strong faith in the Dalai Lama, and the elite clerics share his vision of Buddhist modernism influenced by Western ideological developments such as individualism, scientific rationalism, psychology, human rights, and ecological awareness, they still envision an "indigenous" Buddhist religion headed by Mongol masters. While the Gelugpa school continues to be the largest in Mongolia, there is resistance to Gandan's hegemonic position, as well as a silent opposition to the influence of high Tibetan clergy (see also King 2012: 24–25).

While transnational Buddhist modernity supports gender equality, Mongolian women, who were excluded from formal positions in Mongolian Buddhism in the past, have since 1990 participated in the revival of "traditional" Buddhism. A few have built institutions modelled on male temples, while other women— seeking to construct a new spirituality based on elements from shamanism (Tengrism), Buddhism, or New Age—have established religious institutions never seen in Buddhism or Mongolia before (for New Age religion, see e.g. Hanegraaff [2001] 2009). The charismatic Sarandavaa Bat-Ochir has responded to post-socialist modernity by creating a hybrid religious institution combining elements from Buddhism and New Age. Her accomplishments, as well as those of Enkhsaikhan, are striking because of their eclectic choice of religious elements, new styles of leadership, paid employment of robed male Buddhist clerics, and unconventional methods used to respond to their clients' immediate needs. These needs include relief from poverty, success in business, good grades for their children in school, safe travelling, prosperity for relatives and their livestock on the steppe, and good health for immediate family and kin. In the name of Namsrai, the god of wealth, Sarandavaa's ritual sessions of summoning money draw devotees in the thousands. Ordinary women's religious engagement is strong in contemporary Mongolia, while those who become religious specialists and leaders also earn a living.

Contemporary Mongolia   129

Urbanization, unemployment, or arduous jobs in the mining industry and the commercial sector have left segments of the population alienated, and many face insecure and often miserable conditions in shanty towns. In recent years, after Mongolia became one of the most rapidly growing economies in the world, the income has increased also in the *ger* towns; still, many feel disappointed because of failed expectations of upward social and economic mobility and because of the loss of their traditional lifestyles on the steppe. Leaders of small Buddhists temples and Buddhist New Age "businesses", several of them established in the *ger* towns at the city's margin, are criticized by Tibetan exiles, elite Mongolian monks, and Western converts alike for their lack of Buddhist training, spreading of superstition, and commodification of religious services. Commodification is, however, a development we find in all Mongolian religious institutions; the business-like management of temples is an economic necessity for their survival in a harsh capitalist economy and an increasingly competitive religious market.

Notes

* This research is part of a project on the Buddhist revival in Mongolia after 1990 that includes two specialists on Mongolian and Tibetan Buddhism, Dr Agata Bareja-Starzyńska and Byambaa Ragchaa (University of Warsaw), and Ganzorig Davaa-Ochir (Pethub Monastery, Ulaanbaatar). I thank Agata Bareja-Starzyńska and Ganzorig Davaa-Ochir for their valuable comments on a draft of this article, and the latter also for arranging interviews in Ulaanbaatar in 2008, 2013, and 2014.

1. By "normative" and "orthodox" tradition, I mean Buddhism as it is taught and practised in leading Tibetan monasteries in exile. What "correct" Buddhism should constitute in the different Tibetan traditions is, however, contested.

2. Even (2012: 251) writes that there were 80,000 monks in 1936. The communist regime used the high percentage of monks in Mongolia as an argument to combat Buddhism, saying they were "unproductive" members of society. Many Buddhist "monks" in the Mongolian countryside were, however, only part-time clerics and took part in practical chores and lived with families (Byambaa Ragchaa, personal communication).

3. During 1937 and 1938, all monasteries but a handful were destroyed. The monk population was reduced from more than 100,000 in 1924 to 15,000 in 1939; head monks were killed or exiled to Siberia, and ordinary monks were laicized (Moses 1977). According to Abbot Choijamts of Gandan, 20,000 monks were executed, and altogether 70,000 monks were killed or disappeared during the various purges. Of 1,200 monks in Gandan, only ten remained (interview 5 June 2008). See also Atwood (2004: 47–48), Diluv Khutagt (2009: 117–165), and Even (2012).

4. The Dalai Lama's first visit was 15 June 1979 at the invitation of Khambo Lam Gombojav, the previous abbot of Gandan (1901–n.d.). Interview with Amgalan and Soninbayar, the Research and Culture Centre at Gandan, 11 April 2013.

5. See http://english.ikhmaidar.mn/content/6905.shtml (accessed 23 June 2014). Recently the Chinese government, through the Bank of China, has proposed to invest in Buddhist temples in Mongolia. More than fifty abbots from private temples, headed by Dambajav, the head of Zuun khuree, and Natsagdorj, the abbot of Manba datsan, participated recently in an investment forum. The condition for sponsoring temples is that Mongols follow the Chinese Panchen Lama. E-mail communication, Ganzorig Davaa-Ochir 4 March 2015.

130 Hanna Havnevik

6. The FPMT supports monasticism by funding Idgaachoiling Datsan at Gandan and Drolma Ling.
7. Panchen Ötrul's exposure to Irish Catholicism gives Asral an ecumenical profile.
8. See also http://www.chakra.mn. The Kangyur was translated into Mongolian before the Qing Dynasty, and the Tengyur during the Qing Dynasty.
9. In 1998, Arjia Rinpoche defected to the United States, where he became the director of the Tibetan Mongolian Cultural Center in Bloomington, Indiana (Arija Rinpoche 2010). For the Kalachakra Culture Centre, see http://chakra.mn.
10. The four-year degree is equivalent to a BA in Buddhist Studies. The Zanabazar Buddhist University was named the Buddhist University of Mongolia when it was established in 1970. Gandan also organizes the Young Buddhist Association where, since 2010, lectures on Buddhism are held every Friday evening, and through their Gurvan Erdene (Triratna) Buddhist Association, Gandan publishes a monthly Buddhist newspaper, *Bilgiin Melmii* ("Wise Eye"), featuring Buddhist events.
11. The Gelugpa tradition is named the Yellow Religion (*sharyn shashin*); see Havnevik et al. (2007: 226).
12. See Bareja-Starzyńska and Havnevik (2006). During the first phase of the Buddhist revival in Mongolia (i.e. from the 1990s to 2005) there were only a few such *chod* temples, all said to belong to the Red Tradition, but, since, then the tradition has not only flourished but also changed in several respects. What was earlier identified as the Red Tradition is now more often named Nyingmapa.
13. The building is sponsored by the Mongolian government as compensation for the destruction of monasteries during the communist purges. Information provided by Davaa-Ochir (personal communication, January 2015).
14. The number is based on interviews with nuns in Drolma Ling (Tsenla, Orgilmaa, and Kunkyen), FPMT (Thubten Gyalmo), and nuns studying at Zanabazar University.
15. For information about the institution in the late 1990s, see Bareja-Starzyńska and Havnevik (2006). Information about the current number of nuns in Drolma Ling was provided in an e-mail (29 June 2014) by Thubten Gyalmo, former director of Drolma Ling.
16. The oracular tradition was well known in Mongolia in the pre-communist era. The brother of the Bogd Khan (the Eighth Jebtsundampa, 1869–1924), Luvsankhaidav Chojin Lama, was the state oracle; one of Dulumjav's male relatives also served as an oracle for the Eighth Jebtsundampa, and Dulumjav says the ability to become possessed runs in her family.
17. Information provided by Dulumjav, June 2014.
18. Information provided by Davaa-Ochir, July 2014. In summer 2013 a young Tibetan female oracle, Tsering Chenga, was sent from Dharamsala to Ulaanbaatar by Zopa Rinpoche to lead a 100 million *mani* retreat.
19. Tseden-Ish was recognized by the Dalai Lama as the seventh reincarnation of Naro Panchen Khutugtu in October 2014. The oracle, says Zaya Paṇḍita, can move a *vajra*, bend iron swords, and control shamans with his mind. Interview with Zaya Paṇḍita, 7 June 1914. The current reincarnation of Zaya Paṇḍita (b. 1975), the second highest reincarnation in Mongolia, says he has recognized Tseden-Ish's extraordinary abilities and trained him, and his fame has rapidly spread in Buddhist circles in the capital. According to normative Tibetan Buddhism, Vajrapāṇi would not possess a human medium, because of his high spiritual level (Skt. *bhūmi*).
20. Fifteen Mongolian reincarnations had been recognized by 2014.
21. http://www.grandnews.mn/content/read/50309.htm, published 16 May 2014 (accessed 11 June 2014).
22. For a discussion of Chinggis Khan as Vajrapāni, see Sagaster (2007) and Wallace (2015: 179–202).

Contemporary Mongolia 131

References

Atwood, Christopher P. 2004. *Encyclopedia of Mongolia and the Mongol Empire*. New York: Facts On File.

Bareja-Starzyńska, Agata, and Hanna Havnevik. 2006. "A Preliminary Survey of Buddhism in Present-Day Mongolia." In *Mongols from City to Country: Floating Boundaries, Pastoralism and City Life in the Mongol Lands*, edited by Ole Bruun and Li Narangoa, 213–237. Copenhagen: NIAS Press.

Bat-Ochir, Sarandavaa. 2009. *God Helps Those Who Help Themselves*. Ulaanbaatar: Mongolian Academy of Meditation, Animism, Astrology and Psychology.

Berger, Peter L. 1967. *The Sacred Canopy: Elements of a Sociological Theory of Religion*. New York: Doubleday.

Davaa-Ochir, Ganzorig. 2008. "Oboo Worship: The Worship of Earth and Water Divinities in Mongolia." M.Phil. thesis, University of Oslo.

Diluv Khutagt. 2009. *The Diluv Khutagt of Mongolia: Political Memoirs and Autobiography of a Buddhist Reincarnation*. Translated by Owen Lattimore and Fujiko Isono. Ulaanbaatar: Polar Star Books.

Even, Marie-Dominique. 2012. "Ritual Efficacy or Spiritual Quest? Buddhism and Modernity in Post-Communist Mongolia." In *Revisiting Rituals in a Changing Tibetan World*, edited by Katia Buffetrille, 241–272. Leiden: Brill.

Hanegraaff, Wouter J. (2001) 2009. "New Age Religion." In *Religions in the Modern World: Traditions and Transformations*, edited by Linda Woodhead, Hiroko Kawanami, and Christopher Partridge, 339–357. London: Routledge.

Havnevik, Hanna. 2015. "Tibetan Chöd as Practiced by Ani Lochen Rinpoche." In *Meditation and Culture: The Interplay of Practice and Context*, edited by Halvor Eifring, 175–186. London: Bloomsbury Academic.

Havnevik, Hanna, Byambaa Ragchaa, and Agata Bareja-Starzynska. 2007. "Some Practices of the Red Tradition in Contemporary Mongolia." In *The Mongolia-Tibet Interface: Opening New Terrains in Inner Asia*, edited by Uradyn E. Bulag and Hildegard G. M. Diemberger, 223–237. Leiden: Brill.Heissig, Walter. 1980, *The Religions of Mongolia*. Translated by Geoffrey Samuel. Berkeley and Los Angeles: University of California Press.

King, Matthew. 2012. "Finding the Buddha Hidden below the Sand: Youth, Identity and Narrative in the Revival of Mongolian Buddhism." In *Change in Democratic Mongolia: Social Relations, Health, Mobile Pastoralism, and Mining*, edited by Julian Dierkes, 17–31. Leiden: Brill.

Lopez, Donald S., Jr., ed. 2002. *A Modern Buddhist Bible: Essential Readings from East and West*. Boston: Beacon Press.

McMahan, David L. 2008. *The Making of Buddhist Modernism*. Oxford: Oxford University Press.

———, ed. 2012. *Buddhism in the Modern World*. London: Routledge.

Moses, Larry W. 1977. *The Political Role of Mongol Buddhism*. Bloomington: Indiana University Press.

Rinpoche, Arjia. 2010. *Surviving the Dragon: A Tibetan Lama's Account of 40 Years under Chinese Rule*. New York: Rodale.

Sagaster, Klaus. 2007. "The History of Buddhism among the Mongols." In *The Spread of Buddhism*, edited by Ann Heirman and Stephan Peter Bumbacher, 379–431. Leiden: Brill.

132 *Hanna Havnevik*

Wallace, Vesna. 2015. "How Vajrapāṇi Became a Mongol." In *Buddhism in Mongolian History, Culture, and Society*, edited by Vesna Wallace, 179–202. Oxford: Oxford University Press.

Wazgird, Alexandra. 2011. "God on the Steppe: Christian Missionaries in Mongolia after 1990." Master's thesis, University of Oslo.

Wilson, Bryan. 1976. "Aspects of Secularization in the West." *Japanese Journal of Religious Studies* 3–4: 259–276.

8 Yumaism

A New Syncretic Religion among the Sikkimese Limbus

Linda Gustavsson

Introduction

At present, the modern syncretized religion[1] Yumaism, or Yuma Samyo, is being created by the Limbus in Sikkim, an Indian state in the eastern Himalayas.[2] Based on data collected during fieldwork in Sikkim between August and December 2012, this chapter analyzes how Yumaism is created as a response to modernity and how local conditions affect the invention of this new syncretic religion. Yumaism draws on elements from indigenous religious traditions, Tibetan Buddhism, Christianity, Hinduism, scholarly and orientalist discourses, and modernism in general.

The Buddhist kingdom of Sikkim was abolished upon its incorporation into India in 1975, leading to massive political and social transformations in Sikkimese society. Tibetan Buddhism still holds a prominent position in the state, yet the ethnic composition is extremely diverse with over twenty different groups, each of them keeping their distinct cosmological beliefs and practices. After the implementation of India's reservation policies in 1978, which includes affirmative action policies, ethnic groups are seeking to negotiate with the state for better access to its resources. In this political climate, groups are competing for recognition and to obtain preferential treatment. Consequently, the politicization and awareness of ethnic and religious identities and boundaries have increased, offering new scope for religious creations and revivals within the democratic Indian state. In Sikkim's ethnically polarized political climate, Limbu religious identity is currently undergoing a profound transformation because of rapid social changes in general and the political ambitions of the community and its middle-class leadership in particular. New religious forms are being fused together with the idea of Limbu ethnicity in order to form a unique narrative of Limbu identity. In this narrative Yumaism plays a crucial role.

Yumaism shares some similarities with so-called Protestant Buddhism in Sri Lanka in the 1960s, as described by Richard Gombrich and Gananath Obeyesekere (1988). Other researchers have suggested terms like Buddhist modernism (Bechert [1984] 1991; McMahan 2008, 2012) and modern Buddhism (Lopez 2002). Modernity is difficult to define, however—as is Buddhism, for that matter. Following McMahan (2008: 6), this chapter understands modern Buddhism, or

134 Linda Gustavsson

Buddhist modernism, as a revisionist movement, essentially a hybrid tradition, rooted in the European Enlightenment, Protestant Reformation, the scientific revolution, romanticism, and its own religious history, that through interaction with modernism has resulted in localized "forms of Buddhism that have emerged out of an engagement with the dominant cultural and intellectual forces of modernity". According to McMahan and Lopez, such modern forms of Buddhism encompass a number of characteristics, such as the rise of the middle class, detraditionalization, individualization, religious privatization, and internalization, claims that the tradition is a philosophy rather than a religion, dependence on English-language concepts, spiritual egalitarianism, and an appeal to privileged and urban segments of the population. The present chapter will argue that the development of the localized, syncretic religion of Yumaism can be closely related to such modernist trends within Tibetan Buddhism.

Within an anthropological perspective, these matters will be examined closely in relation to the local context. Moreover, grasping the modern creation of Yumaism and the complexities, hybridities, and multivocality of the religious and historical ideas, accounts, and practices shaping it requires an actor-oriented and processual approach (Comaroff and Comaroff 1992, 1993; Arce and Long 2000; Eriksen 2010). It will be investigated to what extent the creation of Yumaism can be seen as part of a broader global Buddhist modernistic trend as described by McMahan and others.

Borderland of Buddhism

> The so-called Buddhist population is practically shamanist and a large number of mediums: *Bönpos, Pawos, Bunting* and *Yabas* [Limbu shamans] of both sexes, even in the smallest hamlets, transmit the messages of gods, demons and the dead.
> (Alexandra David-Néel [1932] 2007: 7)

Sikkim is geographically and culturally a borderland, with Nepal located to the west, China (the Tibet Autonomous Region) to the north, and Bhutan to the east. As David-Néel's description of Sikkim's "Buddhist population" indicates, religious and ethnic borders and identification are complex and fluid in the Himalayas. In the localized religious modernist developments within the Limbu community, religious and ethnic identification processes play a central role. As will be shown below, religious identification among the Limbus is both emically and etically complex and has become increasingly politicized since the 1970s.

Many Limbus, as they have been throughout Sikkim's history, are enrolled in some of the Buddhist education institutes affiliated with the major Sikkimese monasteries, for example the Denjong Pema Choling Academy near Pemayangtse monastery in Pelling. Recently, however, identification with Tibetan Buddhism appears to be largely rejected in the political context.[3] The reasons for their rejection are manifold, but Limbus tend to highlight two factors. Many educated Limbus often express a complex relationship with the past. The Buddhist Namgyal dynasty's reign, from 1642 to 1975, is often described as culturally oppressive,

Yumaism 135

marking a period when the Limbu community lost many of its political and economic rights.

Despite the Limbus' historically close ties with monastic Buddhism, they are commonly categorized as Hindus in Sikkim today. Many Limbus see themselves as Hindus. They are, however, not born into Hindu castes.[4] Some Limbus, however, strongly disagree when they are grouped together with Nepalese Hindus in the present context, since they consider themselves Sikkimese with their own distinct religion.[5] Their rejection of Hinduism is a response to the negative connotations connected with being Nepalese. When Sikkim became a British protectorate in 1890, the British sought to limit Tibetan influence and encouraged Nepalese labourers to provide manpower. Immigration from Nepal, including many Limbus, contributed to great demographic changes in the area and created awareness about Nepalese and Hinduism (i.e. "foreign") presence in the state. Additionally, religious and ethnic classification as described here is, as Mélanie Vandenhelsken puts it, largely constructed on the basis of a

> combination of the Sikkimese elite's relations with others and early ethnological and colonial thought that created a representation of the population of Sikkim as being divided into a Hindu majority and an autochthonous minority. Since then, the term "Nepalese" has been used to describe anyone who is neither Bhotia nor Lepcha, regardless of his or her language, religion, social organisation, or even origin.
>
> (Vandenhelsken 2011: 98)

The significant role of the Sikkimese elite and British orientalists' classification of the population in Sikkim is reflected in the Constitution Order of 1978, which declared the Bhutia and Lepcha communities of Sikkim as Scheduled Tribes (ST). The ST status granted these two communities several quotas and benefits and has since its implementation caused debate and ethnic tension in the state. This specific representation is found in H. H. Risley's *Gazetteer of Sikhim* ([1894] 1989)[6] and has influenced how both Limbus and non-Limbus have viewed the community's history and identity construction.[7]

In other British orientalist accounts from the nineteenth century, however, we find great variations regarding the origin and religious affiliation of the Limbus.[8] Also today, religious identification within the community varies. Apart from identification with Hinduism and Buddhism, we find Limbus who consider themselves Christians and/or followers of global and local religious movements, such as Satya Sai Baba, Brahma Kumaris, and the Heavenly Path. Irrespective of religious belonging (except Christian Limbus), many Limbus also use shamans or oracles to carry out rituals in or near the household. These diverse ritual practices are strongly rooted in rural areas in particular, consisting of local variations of oral narratives (*mundhum*)[9] chanted by Limbu ritual specialists. Ritual specialists from neighbouring ethnic groups are also used to carry out rituals, including Buddhist ritual specialists. These religious elements may be linked to the vague category *bön*[10] that is commonly applied to the ritual practice of Tibeto-Burman

136 *Linda Gustavsson*

groups in Himalayan and Tibetan areas.[11] Elements from the religious belief systems, as discussed above, are being redefined, rejected, or revived in the present modern construction of Yumaism.

Rise of the Limbu Middle Class

The rise of the educated middle class is a central feature of modern Buddhism. According to Lopez, in modern Buddhism educationally advantaged individuals strive to demonstrate that their reformed or constructed religion is relevant to the modern contexts in which they live (2002: xxv) and is in line with modernization developments among the Limbus. After Sikkim was incorporated into India, a system of local government was introduced along with party politics at village level. The Limbus founded a number of ethnic associations that grew stronger and more politically assertive towards the end of the 1970s.[12]

High-status members of the Limbu associations are often urban-based, middle-aged males. By promoting the Limbu community as an indigenous tribal community with their own distinct religion, they function as cultural brokers for the promotion of their culture and language, as well as for enhancing their political and economic rights. Similarly, following his studies on Kirati groups in Nepal, Grégoire Schlemmer refers to these individuals as "indigenists", that is, intellectuals belonging to the elite who often promote their own culture in their literature, and act as spokespersons for their ethnic community (2004: 120).

Documentation of the Limbus' history and culture is seen as a crucial asset in order to create and "showcase" Yumaism as a modern religion in the current political landscape.[13] As of today, however, there are hardly any historical documents regarding the Limbus. Since only limited research has been carried out on this ethnic group in Nepal and Sikkim, it is not surprising that Limbu scholars and intellectuals strive to document their language, history, culture, and religion. The writings of I.S. Chemjong (1904–1975), a Limbu professor and activist active in Darjeeling in the 1920s, are influential in the making of Yumaism. Currently, J.R. Subba, the former president of the association Sikkim Limbu Literary Society, is engaged in elaborating many of Chemjong's articulations of Yumaism on Facebook and in numerous publications, often published in English.[14] According to Subba,

> The Limboo tribal society is an autonomous social conglomeration, followers of an ancient religion called Yumaism. It is a socially, culturally and religiously strong society reinforced by traditional wisdoms refined through consistent abidance since antiquity.
>
> (Subba 2012b: iii)

Subba's assertion is a potentially powerful political statement in Sikkim. By advocating Yumaism as a single and intelligible religious category, Subba juxtaposes it with any other respected world religion.[15] This is a strategy for obtaining the Limbus' support for the new religion in order to raise awareness of or to preserve the "unique" Limbu culture and religion. Consequently, it is also a strategy for objectifying the religion in order to communicate or "sell" their ideology on the Internet to tourists, researchers, and so on. Many association members supported my research on Yumaism, believing it would be instrumental in achieving benefits for the community, in line with what Comaroff and Comaroff (2009) refer to as commodification of ethnic identity.

Christian Influences in the Invention of Yumaism

Because of the lack of sources that can document the Limbus' history, Chemjong and Subba often rely on oral traditions (migration narratives and so forth) and use elements from different discourses in their representations of Yumaism and its glorious and ancient past. This is related to what McMahan refers to as "indigenous modernity", where elements from modern Western discourses are incorporated into local indigenous discourses to form a unique, hybrid tradition (2008: 112–113). From an etic perspective, a number of elements have been manipulated or exploited in order to create Yumaism, as discussed in the following.

According to McMahan, Protestant Christian theism in particular has influenced Buddhist modernist interpretations all over the world (2008: 10–11). Subba and Chemjong, being influenced by Christianity—mainly through their education—use this Western tradition as a model when they attempt to shape the Limbu religion as a respected and distinct religion. This is evident in the exaltation of the "supreme" deity Tagera Ningwaphuma and its worldly manifestation, Yuma.[16] The deity is described as a forceful power, an omnipresent "God Almighty", and the creator of life on Earth (Chemjong [1966] 2003: 25, 99).[17] Yuma is regarded as a principal deity by most Limbus in Sikkim today.[18] Highlighting Yuma as a monotheistic and immanent god whom Limbus should personally worship, marks, however, a departure from "traditional" rituals.

An internalized and personal belief in Yuma changes the ritual specialist's role as a mediator between physical and supernatural realms. Contrasted to the new teachings promoted by Subba and the associations, "belief" does not constitute a central dimension in the traditional ritual practices. Instead, the incarnated ritual specialists are the religious experts, and ordinary people are seldom actively involved when a ritual is performed. The new Yumaist teachings emphasizing that individuals should seek the ultimate goal without any intermediaries are similar to the "Protestant Buddhism" Gombrich and Obeyesekere found in Sri Lanka in the 1960s (1988: 215). Related to this is what McMahan refers to as "detraditionalized" religion—a development at the heart of Buddhist modernism. Detraditionalized religion involves a shift where the individual's own investigation and experience are elevated over traditional practices (McMahan 2008: 41–44). This religious redefinition, or modern revival of the Limbu ritual tradition as a religion in people's minds, stands in sharp contrast to the practical and apotropaic dimensions we find in the traditional ritual tradition. When "magic" or shamanistic elements, such as soul journeys and spirit possession performed by trained

138   *Linda Gustavsson*

and incarnated ritual specialists, are downplayed, Yumaism is "demythologized" (Lopez 2002: ix; McMahan 2008: 46).

As part of strengthening the faith in Yuma, Subba urges Limbus to worship in the new Limbu temples (*mangheem*) that the Limbu associations started to construct in the 1980s. Here Limbus can participate in community worship dedicated to Yuma. Temple worship constitutes a new, yet familiar religious element. Syncretic temple worship makes Yumaism appear more like an "authentic religion" or a modern, Western "world religion". Temple worship is also demythologized, as discussed above. Accordingly, shamanistic elements, the role of ancestors, and the social dimensions of a clan and village all seem irrelevant. Instead, according to Subba, Yumaists should relate to the deity as an omnipotent parent. In this way, it is claimed, the Limbus' awareness of their religious culture and sense of belonging to the community will be enhanced (2012b: 162–163), since ordinary people are given more responsibility to preserve their Limbu identity through their beliefs. The individualization of Yumaism is necessary, since Subba believes modern lifestyles have weakened Yumaism by causing many Limbus to cease practising the customary religious norms (2012b: iii).

Modernist Influences from Tibet

So far in this chapter, we have seen that elements from Christianity have influenced the Limbu middle class' creation of Yumaism. Another important source of inspiration is undoubtedly the changes in the practice of modern Buddhism, particularly the path pursued by the current Dalai Lama and the late sixteenth Karmapa. Both religious figures have embarked upon a reformation of Tibetan Buddhism. For the Karmapa, who had his principal monastic establishment in Sikkim, this took shape in his strict opposition to animal sacrifice in village rituals (Balikci 2008: 26). His influence, combined with his association to modern Buddhism and the perception that modern Buddhism represents "development" while local religious practice represents "backwardness", has similarly spread to Lepcha and Limbu ritual practice.

The influence of Karmapa's teachings is especially evident in Subba's notions of "purity" and "backwardness" in his classification of Limbu ritual specialists and ritual practices. Classification of Limbu ritual specialists is complex. In a Limbu temple, however, the only ones "pure" enough to carry out rituals during a temple service are *phedangma* and *samba*, who are generally associated with household and ancestor rituals. In contrast, the *yema* (female ritualist) and *yeba* (male ritualist) often deal with negative and potentially dangerous spirits whose cult often involves alcohol and ritual animal sacrifice. The "pure" ritualists are grounded in a narrative that gives this type of ritual expert a more compassionate or loving background, compared to the "primitive" and "impure" *yema* and *yeba*. Ritual actions involving animal offerings and alcohol were looked upon by urban Limbus as primitive and severely damaging for the Limbu community. To donate or consume alcohol in ritual contexts is also perceived as a financial burden and therefore a hindrance to the successful development of the Limbu community and the promotion of a "pure" Yumaism.

In recent years, the Dalai Lama's interest in meditation and compassion in education and the relationship between science and Buddhism philosophy has had a tremendous impact in Sikkim. In the last five years, two conferences, one on adapting Buddhism to educational needs and the other on science and the mind, have been convened in Sikkim. The move towards a more "scientific" rationale for Yumaism is similarly connected to these wider changes. According to Subba, meditation on or prayer to Yuma will purify the mind and lead to pure consciousness (2012b: 144, 147). In this psychotherapeutic vein, contemplative religious experiences will, according to Subba, lead to a better life and future for Limbu society as a whole (2012b: 192). This psychologization of Limbu religion, however, is mainly directed towards improving the status of the community instead of being an individual self-realization strategy, as described by McMahan (2008: 57, 250). It is clear that Yumaism is not in line with McMahan's and Lopez's descriptions of modern Buddhism as a religion that exalts the individual over the community and the universal over the local (Lopez 2002: ix). Yumaism, as it is being promoted in Sikkim today, reflects the present political context and is based on an ethnic and religious identity embedded in a distinct "Limbuness" grounded in ancient history and modern religion. However, the introduction of temple worship and an individualized and privatized religion erodes existing cultural and religious fluidity and diversity, as well as clan and economic divisions within the community, by lowering the cost of rituals and introducing a standardized ritual platform. Hence, Yumaism is an exclusive, egalitarian religion for all Limbus, irrespective of social and economic status or cultural differences along clan lines and geographical belonging.

Disinvesting Traditional Authority

Different processes of detraditionalization have been discussed so far in this chapter. The authority of Limbu ritual specialists is contested by the promotion of Yumaism as a religion in Limbus' minds. Similar to the modernist trends mapped by Gombrich and Obeyesekere (1988: 216), the Limbu "laity" is empowered in the new Yumaist teachings and practices compared to traditional village rituals. Yumaism, as it is propagated by Subba and the associations, incorporates a this-worldly orientation and is to a larger extent more centralized, standardized, and simplified. Since the teachings involve and address Yumaists directly, Yumaism becomes more accessible and comprehensible to ordinary people. But the ritual specialists' communication with the vast numbers of Limbu deities for the benefit and prosperity of the clan, household, and harvest is downplayed in the middle class' literary representation of Yumaism and can be understood as a strategy to contest their authority.

There has been a gradual change of emphasis in Subba's publications (2012a, 2012b) regarding the authority of ritual specialists, and he has recently written

140   *Linda Gustavsson*

about their position and authority in negative terms (2013). Subba criticizes their roles as mediums and healers, since science and biomedicine are, according to him, more effective and less of a financial burden for Limbus. He also regards them as obstacles to the attempts of the elite to institutionalize religious practice in accordance with the modern context of Sikkim. The reasons behind these negative narratives about ritual specialists are complex. Different agents compete for power to define religion and ethnicity in contemporary Sikkim. The modern and organized ethnic associations are clearly seeking to alter the roles of the ritual specialists. In order to revive and redefine elements of the ritual tradition, it is necessary for the ethnic associations to control the ritual specialists by institutionalizing the existing tradition. The organized elite segments therefore try to displace the ritualists as experts or the "holders of tradition and knowledge".

The Limbu middle class is attempting to alter the role of ritual specialists, and the introduction of Limbu temples and the religious changes discussed above are adaptions to modernity in urban contexts. These forms of religious practices are, first and foremost, appealing to privileged and urban segments of the population. First, livestock and crops are rare in urban settings, and performing rituals for abundant harvests therefore seems alien. Second, the practice of ritual blood sacrifice is also less acceptable in an urban context. Third, in order to carry out an elaborate ritual, for example a death ritual, both time and considerable space are needed to accommodate guests and to perform the different parts of the ritual. Fourth, neither village structures nor mutual exchange systems can easily be transposed to an urban area, where ethnic diversity is larger and housing and population density is high.[19]

In addition, the tradition of spending many years of apprenticeship, during which the neophyte learns from an older and experienced shaman, is challenged by changing social circumstances in contemporary Sikkim. Many informants were concerned about the diminishing number of ritual specialists and what they perceived as the weakening of their powers. In order to learn the vast body of oral narratives, a novice must speak Limbu and should ideally live in his or her natal village to receive extensive training by senior ritual specialists or shamans. After the merger with India in 1975, education became more widely accessible. Good schools are often located far from local villages, and young ritual specialists may not receive any Limbu language training. As the bureaucracy expanded in the 1970s, more job opportunities also opened up both within and outside the state, as well as increased interaction with urban and international lifestyles. Consequently, fewer people choose to remain in their rural villages. One may ask whether the invention of Yumaism is a strategy to resist, adapt, and preserve their religion and culture against challenges and "threats" faced in a modern context.

Political Considerations and the Role of the State

After the Limbu community was accorded Scheduled Tribe (ST) status in 2004, the associations have started distancing themselves from being characterized as "primitive animists" by promoting what they perceive as a unique, "civilized", and "modern" Limbu religion, that is, Yumaism. The definition of the much-debated ST status includes indications of primitive traits, distinctive culture, geographical isolation, shyness of contact with the community at large, and backwardness.[20] The vague definition provides the legal definition of a tribe, and these characteristics are closely associated with, among other things, a mode of exerting colonialist notions of defining "the other" as backward. In more recent times, such representations have also become closely tied to the "development discourse", where "underdevelopment" and "Third World" have emerged as working concepts (Escobar 1988: 429). As was the case with colonial representations, the thinking in terms of "development" has affinities with ideas about human evolution—a view of a progression to a "higher" form of living.

Although modern social sciences and humanities have criticized essentialist and evolutionist approaches, they are important tools for Subba and Chemjong. Subba supports his essentialized approach by drawing upon studies from well-known Western scholars, such as Edward B. Tylor, James G. Frazer, and Mircea Eliade, which enables him to argue for the truth and homogeneity of Yumaism. Subba's depiction of Yumaism rests on an assumption of religious evolution, which allows him to argue that Yumaism has developed from an animistic and primitive stage—a stage before the community was accorded the ST status—to a higher and philosophical or spiritual stage of evolution (Subba 1998). This evolution he sees as a "crowning intellectual achievement of traditional culture of Yumaism today" (2012b: 210). Social evolutionist ideas, together with the criteria specified in the definition of ST status, have played a decisive role in the endeavours of Limbu associations to be granted ST status and in the ongoing religious transitions. The vague criteria for a tribe have been acted upon and incorporated by the Limbu middle class as aspects of the Limbu community's identification process, in which the development of Yumaism plays a central role. Such agency can potentially create successful "cultural resources" (Beyer 1994: 97–98) as a political assertion that can be used strategically to, for example, mobilize groups.

Another important dimension of the ongoing religious transitions within the Limbu community has to do with the associations seeking to negotiate with the Sikkimese state for greater access to its resources. From *Sikkim: A Statistic Profile 2004–2005* (Government of Sikkim 2004–2005: 56–59), it is clear that the propagation of Yumaism centres on the endeavour to assert a religious identity as a negotiator vis-à-vis the state. Here it is stated that the state government provides ethnic and religious communities with financial funds to develop their cultural heritage. Interestingly, the specific types of cultural activities that have been revived or proposed along with the construction of Yumaism, such as the construction of Limbu temples, education institutes, and statues and the development of religious festivals, correspond directly to the sources of financial support offered by the government. The propagation of Yumaism might therefore be understood as a way of legitimizing requirements for these specific buildings and events by grounding their functions in a religious narrative and a seemingly historical continuity. The state government's list of what they support financially is indirectly a stipulation of what a religious community is, or what institutions it should consist

142   *Linda Gustavsson*

of. Paradoxically, the ethnic groups in the state claim to be distinct from each other, yet they simultaneously strive to be granted funds that enable them to construct similar religious and cultural institutions. Hence, it can be argued that a sort of religious "uniformity" is created by the state, which may be understood as an attempt to control or regulate the religious and ethnic groups in the state.

Conclusion

This chapter has discussed localized religious-modernist developments within the Limbu community in the borderlands of Buddhism in the eastern Indian Himalayas. It has been argued that individuals from the Limbu upper-middle class are constructing a religion that shares many similarities with McMahan's and Lopez's understandings of Buddhist Modernism, as well as Gombrich and Obeyesekere's concept of Protestant Buddhism. It has also been claimed that changes in Tibetan Buddhism, particularly the path towards Buddhist modernism pursued by the Dalai Lama and the sixteenth Karmapa, are being copied by members of the ethnic associations in their creation of Yumaism. Particularly, the success and perception of Tibetan Buddhism globally, and largely as a result of the international respect enjoyed by the Dalai Lama as a modern spiritual leader of our times, is represented as a compassionate, rational, modern, and individualized "way of life". The proponents of Yumaism are similarly attempting to define their religion as such a way of life (Subba 2012b), a philosophy that is both rational and modern, while at the same time being steeped in the long historical tradition of the Limbus.

Both Lopez and McMahan provide broad meta-narratives to show how modern Buddhist forms fit into dominant Western discourses. This perspective should not be neglected, but they lose sight of important nuances of the diversity and power plays involved in the making of locally grounded modern religious formations. Through an actor-oriented and processual approach, this chapter has examined the invention of Yumaism by focusing on the Limbu middle class' agency in relation to their lived contexts. The analysis chimes with Arce and Long's assertion that ideas about modernity are "reworked from within" by local actors who appropriate symbols and practices associated with it and combine "modern" with so-called traditional features into hybrid forms of "localized modernities" (2000: 2). In this case study, "modernity" has resulted in a heightened concern with "tradition" and "culture", two elements that are objectified and commoditized and have become the subject of historical consciousness and contestation (Comaroff and Comaroff 1993: xiv). By articulating a detraditionalized (McMahan 2008: 41–44) and demythologized (Lopez 2002: ix; McMahan 2008: 46) normative foundation of Yumaism, the Limbu middle class is contesting the authority of ritual specialists by limiting their relevance and significance in ritual contexts. By institutionalizing the diverse Limbu ritual practices, they displace the role of ritual specialists as "the holders of tradition and knowledge", and they can potentially receive financial funds from the government to preserve and develop their cultural heritage.

Yumaism 143

While the process of modernization involved in the creation of Yumaism and the impact of Buddhism upon this process should not be underestimated, the dynamics of the modernization of the Limbu religion are grounded in local economic changes, politics, and ethnic relations. These local contexts raise questions about the extent to which the construction of Yumaism can be seen as a part of a broader global Buddhist modernistic trend as described by McMahan and others. The construction of Yumaism is a response to the dominant political and ethnic context in the state. The modernist elements that have been discussed can be referred to as a type of "indigenous modernity", since individuals from the middle class syncretize Western scholarly, orientalist discourses and religious traditions into local "traditional" discourses to form a distinct hybrid tradition (McMahan 2008: 112–113). In the literary representation of Yumaism, elements from the "village religion" are redefined or rejected because they are perceived as "primitive" and "superstitious", showing that Yumaism is not seeking to amalgamate all religious traditions into a coherent narrative. Instead, as Lopez (2002: xxxix) notes, Yumaism uses the present, or more specifically the needs of the Limbus in the present socio-political climate, as the reference point for the creation of religious practice.

The efforts of the association members are in line with what McMahan noticed, namely that the concept of Protestant Buddhism "replicated orientalist scholars' tendency to locate "true Buddhism" in canonical texts, while often dismissing local or village iterations as degenerate and superstitious" (2008: 7). "True" Yumaism does not include animal sacrifice or the ritual offering of alcohol in order to appease the local deities, but Limbus must rather develop a personal relationship with Yuma, the great monotheistic goddess. Subba stresses that meditation or prayer to Yuma will lead to a pure mind and consciousness (2012b: 144, 147), and the "self" is therefore considered sacred (McMahan 2008: 41–44).

In conclusion, while the creation of Yumaism is clearly motivated by the political need for a distinct and separate religious tradition for the Limbus, it cannot escape being influenced by wider trends in religious modernization. This has resulted in a distinct synthesis of religious ideas, which mirrors those in the production of Buddhist modernism. Ironically, the aspirations of the Limbus to distance themselves from the dominant religious culture of Sikkim (Tibetan Buddhism) have actually led to a process whereby elements of Tibetan Buddhist modernism are integrated in the new religious tradition.

Notes

1. I follow Rosalind Shaw and Charles Stewart's understanding of 'syncretism' as a concept that can be used to analyse processes of change rather to describe static religious forms. They emphasize agency and power plays involved in processes of religious syncretism (Shaw and Stewart 1994: 7–8).
2. Associations in Nepal, in other locations in India, and in diaspora communities also promote Yumaism. This chapter, however, will analyse Sikkimese ethnic associations' propagation of Yumaism in relation to their political endeavours in the present context. To what extent the associations in Sikkim, Nepal, and the diaspora relate to one another will not be discussed here.

144   *Linda Gustavsson*

3. Sikkimese Buddhism features elements of the local pre-Buddhist belief systems. For example, features of sacred landscapes are incorporated into the Buddhist interpretation (Bentley 2007; Balikci 2008).
4. Limbus interviewed in Sikkim clearly separated themselves and so-called caste Hindus, such as Chettri and Bahun. The situation in Nepal, however, may be different.
5. Whether the Limbus are "native" to Sikkim is complex, disputed, and highly politicized. Saul Mullard notes that borders were fluid during the early Sikkim (2011: 157), and it is important to underline the complexity of state borders in a historical perspective—one must not take for granted that the political borders functioned and were perceived in the past as they are today. The Tsongs (Limbus) are generally regarded as original inhabitants of Sikkim and more closely affiliated with Buddhism, both by scholars and among non-Limbus questioned during fieldwork.
6. Other representations of the Limbus in Sikkim often describe them as Buddhists originating from either Tibet (Hooker [1854] 2011) or Mongolia (Campbell 1869: 144). Hodgson, however, associates both the Limbus and Lepchas with Sikkim and claims that they are Buddhists despite their non-Buddhist ritual specialists ([1874] 2013: 1137–1138).
7. Even though the Limbus also have been documented in Tibetan documents, few Limbus have been able to read them. Therefore, it seems like especially British accounts are regarded as authoritative and valuable and have been used in the Limbus' identity construction.
8. Geographical and clan affiliations, as well as class within the Limbu community itself, play decisive roles in religious belonging. Economic considerations also appear to be important, since many of the Limbus questioned stated that only well-off families could afford Buddhist ceremonies such as funerals—similar to Jenny Bentley's observations among the Lepchas (2007: 64).
9. *Mundhum* appears to be a complex and vague concept, but most commonly it refers to the vast body of oral narratives chanted by the Limbu shamans. Gaenszle states that the concept is found among other Kirat groups and suggests that the root of the word, *-dum*, is related to the Tibetan term *sgrung*, meaning "fable", "legend", or "tale sung by the bards", or to the Tibetan term *dpe*, meaning "pattern", "model", or "parable" (2011: 281–282). Similar concepts can be found in other Tibetan and Himalayan groups—for example, the Lepchas' *lungten sung* (Bentley 2008: 100) and the Lhopos' *khelen*. Some of the Lhopos' oral narratives have been written down and are now included in Buddhist rituals (Balikci 2008: 93–94, 380).
10. The term *bön*, according to Per Kværne, has three meanings. First, it can describe the pre-Buddhist religious practices of Tibet, where the *bönpo* ritual specialist made sacrifices and ensured the happiness of the living and dead. A second meaning refers to a religion that appeared in Tibet in the tenth and eleventh centuries, which has similarities with Buddhism but is yet a distinct religion. Third, *bön* is used to refer to the numerous popular beliefs of local deities and conceptions of the soul (Kværne 1995: 9–10).
11. Philippe Sagant ([1976] 1996) found many "ancient Tibetan" elements in the Limbus' ritual tradition during fieldwork in rural eastern Nepal in the late 1960s. There are similarities between Bhutia village religion, which is predominately Buddhist, and Limbu village religion. According to Anna Balikci, Bhutia village religion is locally perceived as being rooted in *bön* (2008: 157, 378, 380).
12. *Sikkim Express* (1977, 1978). These types of associations are not unique to the Limbu community or to Sikkim, but can also be found elsewhere in India, Nepal, and Nepali diaspora communities.
13. The association's attempts to promote Yumaism are strongly voiced in Sikkim today and serve to make Yumaism a contested issue. The main opponent of the association's definition of Yumaism is the Yuma Mang Meditation Committee Centre (YMMCC).

Since 2004, the YMMCC has promoted a different version of Yumaism, in contrast to the ethnic association's secular leadership, the YMMCC claims a woman in her twenties is the centre's spiritual leader and worldly counterpart of the Limbu deity Tagera Ningwaphuma. These two articulations of Yumaism share many similarities, but the YMMCC actively proselytizes Yumaism as a universal religion as opposed to the association's core idea of Yumaism as an exclusive "Limbu religion".

14. Although Subba is closely involved with the associations in Sikkim, readers must be aware that there are many voices within the ethnic associations, and Subba's accounts are not necessarily in accordance with the associations' ideas and guidelines.

15. While literary representations of Yumaism appear to be consistent, it is difficult to provide a clear definition of the religion on the basis of empirical data since "Yumaistic" religious elements are constantly being re-articulated in the face of social change. In fact, the discrepancies between the actual religious practice and normative Yumaism, as it appears in literary representations, are often glaring.

16. Yuma is also often called Yuma Sam or Yuma Mang. Since Limbus often refer to Yuma as the most important deity, and do not strictly separate Tagera Ningwaphuma and Yuma, "Yuma" will be used throughout the chapter.

17. While Chemjong refers to Tagera Ningwaphuma as a male deity ([1966] 2003: 20), Subba sees the deity as a supreme goddess. Yumaism is an ancient and monotheistic religion since, according to him, ancient religions were monotheistic with a female divinity at its top. For that reason, he argues that the native Himalayan religion Yumaism is preserved in its "original" form and remained unaltered between 25,000 BC and 7,000 BC despite hardships in the past (2012b: 33, 37, 39).

18. Empirical data and secondary sources reveal discrepancies in the indigenists' and association members' accounts on Yuma and Tagera Ningwaphuma. Risley explicitly states that Tagyera Ningwa Puma is the great deity of the Limbus and corresponds to the present representation. Campbell, however, claims Sham Mungh to be the highest deity ([1894] 1989: 153). But in Maunabuthuk, eastern Nepal, Fatanagan is perceived as the most respected deity (Shanti Limbu 2011: 63). Sagant interestingly suggests that the Yuma "cult" is quite recent and believes that the female deity, Nahangma, belongs to an ancient cult, which might have given precedence to the cult of Yuma (Sagant [1976] 1996: 371).

19. These challenges may also be faced by poorer segments of the Limbu community in rural areas, as these often do not reside in the upper hills but near a bazaar or in areas where there is scarce agricultural land.

20. The definition of the ST status is found in a letter dated 21 July 1976 addressed to Shri Gyaltshen, the chief secretary of the state government in Gangtok, from O.K. Moorthy, the director of Union Home Ministry (Ministry of Home Affairs), retrieved from an association member based in Gangtok.

References

Arce, Alberto, and Norman Long. 2000. "Reconfiguring Modernity and Development from an Anthropological Perspective." In *Anthropology, Development, and Modernities: Exploring Discourses, Counter-Tendencies, and Violence*, edited by Alberto Arce and Norman Long, 1–31. London: Routledge.

Balikci, Anna. 2008. *Lamas, Shamans and Ancestors: Village Religion in Sikkim*. Leiden: Brill.

Bechert, Heinz. (1984) 1991. "Buddhist Revival in East and West." In *The World of Buddhism: Buddhist Monks and Nuns in Society and Culture*, edited by Heinz Bechert and Richard Gombrich, 273–285. London: Thames and Hudson.

146 Linda Gustavsson

Bentley, Jenny. 2007. "'Vanishing Lepcha': Change and Cultural Revival in a Mountain Community of Sikkim." *Bulletin of Tibetology* 43 (1–2): 59–79.

————. 2008. "Láso múng sung: Lepcha Oral Tradition as a Reflection of Culture." *Bulletin of Tibetology* 44 (1–2): 99–137.

Beyer, Peter. 1994. *Religion and Globalization*. London: Sage Publications.

Campbell, Archibald. 1869. "On the Tribes around Darjeeling." *Transactions of the Ethnological Society of London* 7: 144–159, 333.

Chemjong, Iman Singh. (1966) 2003. *History and Culture of the Kirat People, Part I–II*. Mahalxmisthan: Kirat Yakthung Chumlung.

Comaroff, John L., and Jean Comaroff. 1992. *Ethnography and the Historical Imagination*. Boulder, CO: Westview Press.

————. 1993. "Introduction." In *Modernity and Its Malcontents Ritual and Power in Post-colonial Africa*, edited by John L. Comaroff and Jean Comaroff, xi–xxxvii. Chicago: University of Chicago Press.

————. 2009. *Ethnicity, Inc*. Chicago: University of Chicago Press.

David-Néel, Alexandra. (1932) 2007. *Magic and Mystery in Tibet*. London: Souvenir Press.

Eriksen, Thomas Hylland. 2010. *Ethnicity and Nationalism: Anthropological Perspectives*. 3rd ed. London: Pluto Press.

Escobar, Arturo. 1988. "Power and Visibility: Development and the Invention and Management of the Third World." *Cultural Anthropology* 3 (4): 428–443.

Gaenszle, Martin. 2011. "Scriptualisation of Ritual in Eastern Nepal." In *Ritual, Heritage and Identity: The Politics of Culture and Performance in a Globalised World*, edited by Christiane Brosius and Karin M. Polit, 281–297. London: Routledge.

Gombrich, Richard, and Gananath Obeyesekere. 1988. *Buddhism Transformed Religious Change in Sri Lanka*. New Delhi: Motilal Banarsidass.

Government of Sikkim. 2004–2005. *Sikkim: A Statistic Profile 2004–2005*. Gangtok: Directorate of Economics, Statistics, Monitoring & Evaluation.

Hodgson, Brian Houghton. (1874) 2013. *Essays on the Languages Literature, and Religion of Nepál and Tibet: Together with Further Papers on Geography, Ethnology, and Commerce of Those Countries* [Cambridge Library Collection]. New York: Cambridge University Press.

Hooker, Joseph Dalton. (1854) 2011. *Himalayan Journals; or Notes of a Naturalist in Bengal, the Sikkim and Nepal Himalayas, the Khasia Mountains, etc*. Vol. 1. New York: Cambridge University Press.

Kværne, Per. 1995. *The Bon Religion of Tibet: The Iconography of a Living Tradition*. Boston: Shambala Publications.

Limbu, Shanti. 2011. "Practices of Resource Management in a Limbu Village: A Study of Maunabuthuk VDC in Nepal." Master's thesis, University of Oslo.

Lopez, Donald S., Jr. 2002. "Introduction." In *A Modern Buddhist Bible: Essential Readings from East and West*, edited by Donald S. Lopez, Jr., vii–xli. Boston: Beacon Press.

McMahan, David L. 2008. *The Making of Modern Buddhism*. New York: Oxford University Press.

————, ed. 2012. *Buddhism in the Modern World*. Abingdon: Routledge.

Mullard, Saul. 2011. *Opening the Hidden Land: State Formation and the Construction of Sikkimese History*. Leiden: Brill.

Risley, H. H. (1894) 1989. *The Gazeteer of Sikhim*. Gangtok: Sikkim Nature Conservation Foundation.

Schlemmer, Grégoire. 2004. "New Past for the Sake of a Better Future: Re-Inventing the History of the Kirant in East Nepal." *European Bulletin of Himalayan Research* 25–26: 119–144. doi: ird-00557472.

Shaw, Rosalind, and Charles Stewart. 1994. "Introduction: Problematizing Syncretism." In *Syncretism/Anti- Syncretism: The Politics of Religious Synthesis*, edited by Charles Stewart and Rosalind Shaw, 1–26. London: Routledge.

Sikkim Express. 1977. "Quit Janata." 19 November.

———. 1978. "Subba Quits SPC." 15 February.

Subba, Jash Raj. 1998. *The Philosophy and Teachings of Yuma Samyo: The Religion of Limboos of the Himalayan Region*. Gangtok: Sikkim Takthing Mundhum Saplopa.

———. 2012a. *Ethno-Religious Views of the Limboo Mundhum (Myths): An Analysis of Traditional Theories*. Gangtok: Yakthung Mundhum Saplappa.

———. 2012b. *Yumaism, the Limboo Way of Life: A Philosophical Analysis*. Gangtok: Yakthung Mundhum Saplappa.

———. 2013. Post on the Facebook group "Yakthung Original Religious Forum", 1 September. Accessed 19 January 2015. https://www.facebook.com/groups/2494 40508511417/permalink/384230221699111/#_=_().

Vandenhelsken, Mélanie. 2011. "The Enactment of Tribal Unity at the Periphery of India: The Political Role of a New Form of the Panglhabsol Buddhist Ritual in Sikkim." *European Bulletin of Himalayan Research* 38: 81–118.

Part 3

Contemporary Sangha-State Relations

9 Failed Secularization, New Nationalism, and Governmentality

The Rise of Buddhism in Post-Mao China

Koen Wellens

When Deng Xiaoping started his Reform and Opening Up (*gaige kaifang*) policies in 1978, the Chinese Communist Party (CCP) also ushered in a period of tolerance for religious practice, guided by a strong modernist belief that religion would disappear by itself as a result of economic development. At the level of political ideology, the Chinese party-state continues to preach strict secularism and atheism. Nevertheless, at another level of discourse, there are indications that point in another direction, at least for Chinese Mahayana Buddhism. A speech by President Xi Jinping in March 2014 seemed to confirm the trend of the preceding decade towards an increasingly positive official appraisal of the role of Buddhism in Chinese society. The significance of this latest development is underscored by the multitude of Chinese articles appearing in Buddhist publications that optimistically herald a new era for Buddhism in China. This chapter argues—and in this way gives some credence to the optimism of Buddhist leaders and intellectuals— that the Communist Party, in line with its transition from a Marxist to a nationalist party, is now gradually relaxing its programme of secularism. In doing so, it is especially looking towards Buddhism, co-opting it in the party's gargantuan task of governing China, and at the same time allowing it to re-enter sectors of Chinese society that until very recently were strictly off limits to religion.

The Failed Secularization of Chinese Society

One of the salient attributes of modernity is the rise of the modern state. In many areas of the globe, this rise has entailed a move towards secularism, the exclusion of the prevailing religion from nascent modern institutions, and its banishment to the private sphere. The inhabitants of the state are first of all citizens, and religious organizations become reduced to but one of the state's many institutions (Ji 2008: 236). In an explicit attempt to model itself after the powerful nation-states that threatened its territorial integrity, central political reformers at the end of the Qing Dynasty (1644–1911) also had a strong focus on secularization. The Temples-Turn-to-Schools movement initiated by Kang Youwei in 1898 can be regarded as the emblematic start of the modern secularization era in China (Goossaert 2006).

152 Koen Wellens

After the fall of the Qing in 1911, Chinese religions were drawn into the maelstrom of revolutionary change that affected the whole of society. The making of modern China entailed attempts at remoulding traditional institutionalized doctrinal teachings and ethical systems into "modern" religions modelled on Christianity (see Ritzinger in this volume). This was a formidable project for many reasons, one of them being that the Western category of religion had no exact equivalent within Chinese society. A further challenge was that reformist intellectuals and politicians subscribed to the modernist conviction that it was possible to "modernize" these traditional institutions, for example by using another new category from the West: superstition (*mixin*). By removing "superstitious" elements, it would be possible to distil these institutions into modern religions. Some reformers envisaged a modern Chinese state where a rationalized and standardized form of Confucianism or even Christianity—or a hybridization of the two—could function as a state religion, fulfilling a role similar to that of Christianity in many Western countries (Goossaert and Palmer 2011: 86–87). The majority, however, subscribed to a stricter secularism where what now became identified as religion, or *zongjiao*, was forced to take a back seat.

Buddhism, which together with Taoism and Confucianism had constituted one of the so-called Three Teachings (*San Jiao*) in imperial China, would now enter into an unsteady relationship with the successor regimes of the empire. Both Nationalist and Communist regimes made at times heavy-handed attempts at curbing the role of Buddhism in Chinese society, ranging from the "anti-superstition" campaigns of the Republic to the devastations of Communist anti-religious policies that culminated in the Cultural Revolution (1966–1976). Nevertheless, this period of over a century saw also successful attempts by Buddhists to deflect and survive some of the worst attacks and negotiate with the state for a continued presence within Chinese society. According to Prasenjit Duara, the fact that organized Buddhism was historically rather susceptible to state control gave it some protection in comparison to popular or folk religion (Duara 1991: 79). After the establishment of the People's Republic of China (PRC) in 1949, Buddhism was assigned a limited and clearly fenced-in space where it could continue to operate until the chaos of the 1960s and 1970s wiped out religion from public life, and, to a large extent, from private life as well (on this Buddhist space, see Ashiwa 2009). Liberal post-Cultural Revolution policies on religion heralded a new dawn for Buddhism in China, and the beginning of the 1980s saw an ever-increasing number of temples being repaired, taken into use, and eventually also filled with monks, nuns, and lay practitioners.

The reinstatement by Deng Xiaoping of more tolerant state policies towards religion did by no means imply that practitioners of different forms of Buddhism within China proper, and within its Tibetan regions, would now enjoy comprehensive religious freedom on a par with their co-religionists in Taiwan, Japan, or South Korea. The party-state's strict control of civil society, through limiting its citizens' freedom of expression and freedom to organize, also affected religious practice. State supervision and interference with religious activities, the education of religious professionals, and the establishment of religious venues presented

Buddhism in Post-Mao China   153

substantial hindrances in the process of reclaiming and expanding the place of Buddhism in Chinese society.

However, the party-state also attempted to contain religion in a less categorical manner. While affirming explicitly, in the constitutional revision of 1982, that Chinese citizens enjoyed religious freedom, official discourse unambiguously reiterated Marx's negative view on religion. At the level of political ideology, the party-state firmly upheld secularism and promoted atheism. The past policies of suppressing religion were viewed not only as destabilizing, but first and foremost as unnecessary. Party Document 19 of 1982 (quoted in e.g. MacInnis 1989: 25–26) optimistically predicted that after socialist development people would adopt "a conscious scientific viewpoint, and no longer have any need for recourse to an illusory world of gods to seek spiritual solace".

Mayfair Mei-hui Yang (2008: 4) describes secularization as a process "whereby traditional religious orientations, rituals, and institutions lose their grip on social life, no longer seem viable in modern urban, industrial, and commercial society, and gradually decline". Surprisingly—at least to the CCP, though less so to others—this "natural" fading of religion did not take place in post-Mao China. On the contrary, not only did the secularization theory prove wrong in China, as it did in many other places in the world (Casanova 1994), but a veritable "religious fever" (*zongjiao re*) erupted throughout Chinese society in the 1980s, prompting sociologist Richard Madsen to characterize the post-Mao period as post-secular China. He points out that if the party-state continues to insist on a strict secular agenda of containing the religious field, its policies are doomed to fail (Madsen 2009).

How can we explain this demise of secularism in Chinese society? Have all the efforts by the Maoist regime to rid the Chinese people of the "false consciousness" and "alienating forces" of religion been in vain? Monika Wohlrab-Sahr and Marian Burchardt, in their analysis of secularism from a comparative perspective, suggest that when it comes to the enduring success of the secularist agenda of communist regimes, the jury is still out:

> Further research is still needed to identify to what degree the secularism in Communist societies remained only on the level of political ideology and repressive practices, and to what degree it was able to create a long-lasting culture of secularity, even if some religious rituals and practices may have been revived after the fall of Communism.
>
> (Wohlrab-Sahr and Burchardt 2012: 902)

The general picture is indeed as yet indeterminate. The strong revival of religion and its "deprivatization"—to use a term coined by Jose Casanova—is obvious in post-communist countries from Poland to Mongolia and must in one way or another be a reflection of deeply held religious beliefs that did not completely subside under policies of radical secularization and religious repression. Observers of post-communist Russia, on the other hand, are more dubious as to whether the apparent revival of Orthodox Christianity is the product of genuine belief in this country. In his analysis of media discourse on religious

154 *Koen Wellens*

revival in Russia, Alexander Agadjanian (2001: 352) suggests that Orthodox Christianity has become instrumentalized to create a new Russian nationalism, and as such has been perceived in public discourse as "a repository of cultural arguments, collective memories, and the symbolic strength needed to build new national, group, and individual identities".

Although, as I will return to below, the latest developments in China display some striking analogies with the post-communist religious revival in Russia, the "religious fever" of the early post-Mao period presented two important differences. First, the Reform and Opening-up policies at the end of the 1970s led to a liberalization of many aspects of society but not to the demise of the Communist Party and its claim to continued ideological hegemony. At the level of political dogma, the CCP stuck to some Marxist basics, and this included a secularist agenda. Second, unlike in Russia, where Orthodox Christianity has historically enjoyed a privileged position, China had a long tradition of religious plurality. The emperor was the patron and protector of the different religious schools recognized as orthodox teachings. Confucianism—which is often categorized as a non-theist religion—did enjoy a strong identification with the imperial state and its ruling and intellectual elites, but this was not to the detriment of the different Buddhist and Taoist schools, or even of several local cults. It was precisely this relation to the former elites that had turned Confucianism into a target of Maoist ire and resulted in its complete institutional eradication in the People's Republic. The liberalization policies towards religion at the end of the 1970s were not aimed at Confucianism, and, to most ordinary Chinese people, Confucianism at this moment in history had little spiritual or ritual appeal. At the same time, none of the more clearly identifiable traditional religions such as Buddhism or Taoism possessed enough shared symbolic capital to play a role in establishing a common Chinese post-Mao national identity, or nationally shared spiritual and ideological bedrock. Han Chinese Buddhism did offer a potential for locally anchored identity, and most studies of religious practitioners indicate that what turned people towards Buddhism was, above all, a genuine interest in, and adherence to, its doctrines and creeds rather than as a symbolic resource for a national or more localized communality (Ashiwa and Wank 2006; Wellens 2010a; Fisher 2014).

It seems safe then to suggest that the religious revival of the 1980s was *not* first and foremost produced by a desire for creating a national identity after the ideological trauma resulting from the period of extreme Maoism. Furthermore, the sheer magnitude[1] of the revival indicates that, unlike in the former Soviet Union, the strict secularist policies of the previous decades had not been effective in eradicating people's religiosity. There might be several reasons that have contributed to this. One is the obvious fact that the most extreme anti-religious policies did not last more than one generation, a period insufficient to entirely stamp out ritual knowledge and cosmological beliefs. During fieldwork on the revival of religious practice in villages in southwest China between 1991 and 2006, I discovered that local traditional ritual practices were now taught either by grandfathers to grandsons, jumping over the "lost" generation that grew up during the Cultural Revolution, or by the ritual specialists who had been inactive for two decades but gradually took up their trade again after Deng Xiaoping came to power (Wellens 2010b: 159–164). Indeed, the first waves of post-Mao worshippers that started filling the churches, temples, and mosques again all over China were also mostly older people.

Another reason explaining the scale and speed of the post-Mao decline of secularism in Chinese society is that, in many ways, the worshipping of Mao Zedong himself constituted a temporary substitute for more traditional forms of religious practice. Mao was keeping the seat warm until Buddha, Allah, Jesus, and countless other deities all over China could regain their place. This does not mean that a very clear-cut replacement took place everywhere, but rather that the Mao cult to a varying extent either integrated with local cosmological beliefs or weakened them. Villagers in southwest China were ambiguous in their responses when I asked them how they managed to keep evil spirits out of the house during the Cultural Revolution, when they were not allowed to conduct exorcising rituals or rituals to invoke the help of the protector deities: Mao told them there were no evil spirits, and *if* there were, they counted on him to protect them (Wellens 2010b: 161). It is, of course, not possible to know what people really thought or believed at the time. Nevertheless, new studies on popular religion show several fascinating cases of Mao being integrated within the local pantheon. In a recent field study of a rural community in Hebei Province, Mikkel Bunkenborg observes the worship of Mao along with other deities and remarks:

> Many private homes in Fanzhuang have a poster or a bust of the chairman, and elderly people tend to treat such representations in the same ways as images that are recognizably religious. One elderly woman thus enumerated the gods venerated in her home and ended the list with the Goddess of Mercy and the chairman.
>
> (Bunkenborg 2014: 578)

Defeating the evil spirits of class enemies and redistributing the land has put Mao on a par with the Goddess of Mercy, the bodhisattva Guanyin. This can be seen as rather emblematic of the failed secularization project. Not only did the party-state fail in its objective, it even looks like its founding father and unassailable hero has been shanghaied by those seeking comfort in the "illusory world of gods". Recent signals from the top leadership of the CCP might now also suggest that Marxist orthodoxy has to give way to an even more pragmatic approach by the party-state towards at least some religions.

Buddhism and New Chinese Nationalism

During a speech held at UNESCO headquarters in Paris in March 2014, Chinese president Xi Jinping touched upon Buddhism's position in China:

> Buddhism originated in ancient India. After it was introduced into China, the religion went through an extended period of integrated development

156 Koen Wellens

with the indigenous Confucianism and Taoism and finally became the Buddhism with Chinese characteristics, thus making a deep impact on the religious belief, philosophy, literature, art, etiquette and customs of the Chinese people. Xuanzang (Hiuen Tsang), the Tang monk who endured untold sufferings as he went on a pilgrimage to the west for Buddhist scriptures, gave full expression to the determination and fortitude of the Chinese people to learn from other cultures. I am sure that you have all heard about the Chinese classics Journey to the West, which was written on the basis of his stories. The Chinese people have enriched Buddhism in the light of Chinese culture and developed some special Buddhist thoughts. Moreover, they also helped Buddhism spread from China to Japan, Korea, Southeast Asia and beyond.[2]

For the casual observers of official utterances by Chinese leaders, the president's speech didn't ruffle any feathers. Nevertheless, the above-quoted passage did not go unnoticed among Buddhists in his home country. It constituted one more affirmation that Buddhism would not be left out from Xi's hallmark concept of "the China Dream" (*Zhongguo meng*). The China Dream was first mentioned in November 2012 and elaborated when he became president at the National People's Congress in March 2013, Xi stated that to "fulfil the China Dream of the great rejuvenation of the Chinese nation, we must achieve a rich and powerful country, the revitalization of the nation, and the people's happiness" (Callahan 2014). Intellectuals and policy-makers were quick to catch up, and a wide public discourse developed in the media and academic publications.[3] William A. Callahan sees the dream discourse as part of an ongoing debate produced by a post-socialist moral crisis. It is the result of widely felt concerns about a so-called value crisis in a society that is too focused on material gain. The solution proposed by the top leaders and policy-makers is to be found in combining core socialist values with traditional Chinese values such as filial piety and thrift (Callahan 2014). While taking note that advocates of political liberalization and the rule of law were unsuccessful in being included in the dream, Buddhist leaders and intellectuals were seeing an opening for Buddhism to step in—cautiously.

In his article in the Buddhist magazine *Voice of Dharma* with the telling title "The Buddhist Dream and the Chinese Dream", Li Hujiang (2014: 41, my translation), a Buddhist scholar from Sichuan University, discerns three important messages in Xi's UNESCO speech: "First, Buddhism is an important constituent part of Chinese civilization. Second, Buddhism has a wide-ranging and deep influence on the Chinese people. Third, Sinified Buddhism (*Zhongguohua de fojiao*) brings a positive influence to world civilization." While the focus of Xi's speech was to underscore the cultural cross-fertilization between China and the rest of the world, Li is mainly concerned with establishing the Chineseness of Buddhism. In an article with a similar title, "Buddhism and the China Dream", well-known Buddhist scholar and philosophy professor Fang Litian argues that Buddhist values of

Buddhism in Post-Mao China   157

attaining Buddhahood, showing compassion, and helping those under Heaven are totally in agreement with ideals of social progress:

> The values of Buddhist ideals and the China dream agree and understand each other, they make up a force uniting Buddhist circles; together they achieve the ideological foundation of the struggle and the dream of the great rejuvenation of the Chinese nation.
>
> (Fang 2013: 28, my translation)

One could easily dismiss the optimistic assessment of Xi Jinping's speech by these Buddhist scholars as a combination of unrealistic wishful thinking and a partisan attempt to promote the role of Buddhism in Chinese society. In a country where free political debate is not possible, a subtle public communication still takes place in which stakeholders cautiously probe whether they can influence the ruling party and push their agendas. In 2002, I was part of a Norwegian delegation invited by the State Agency of Religious Affairs (SARA), the government department responsible for the administration of religion in China. The visit included countless exchanges with religious leaders at all levels, and one general impression that stuck with the delegation was a marked optimism regarding new possibilities for religion in China. The main basis for this positive appraisal of the situation turned out to be a recent speech by then-president Jiang Zemin where the CCP for the first time acknowledged that religion could play a positive role in society. By referring to the speech time and again in front of the delegation and its accompanying hosts from SARA, the religious leaders were amplifying the message in an attempt to further the case for enlarging the space for religion in China (Wellens 2010a: 57–58).

As to the Xi Jinping speech, there are signs the party is listening, and one can also find articles referring to the speech that can be viewed as a more official endorsement of a changed role for Buddhism. A November 2014 issue of the Chinese journal *China Religion* contained the transcript of a talk held by Jiang Jianyong at a meeting of the China Buddhist Association. What made this noteworthy is that *China Religion* is a periodical published by SARA, and Jiang Jianyong is one of the agency's vice-directors. Jiang starts his talk by quoting Xi Jinping on the broad and deep influence that "Buddhism with Chinese characteristics" has had on the Chinese nation and China's traditional culture. He acknowledges that Buddhist circles in China have been elated about the speech, and he goes on to state that, since Chinese culture has enriched Buddhism, Buddhists have a responsibility to carry on Chinese traditional culture. They should do this by intensifying the study of Buddhism and putting more effort into publishing and disseminating Buddhist texts (Jiang 2014: 57). Again, the message that is delivered here is the importance of the link between "Chinese traditional culture" and Buddhism. Buddhism becomes a brick in the construction of Chinese nationalism.

The CCP's shift from a Marxist-Leninist-Maoist party to a nationalist party has been a gradual process. It gained momentum after the suppression of the 1989

158   Koen Wellens

protests when young people had to be coaxed in a new direction, away from Western liberal ideas. In accordance with China's growing economic clout internationally, the self-confidence and sense of entitlement of a new generation of Chinese people followed suit. The CCP actively encouraged nationalist sentiment through, for example, patriotic education, including a narrative of 150 years of humiliation by Western nations and Japan. When popular sentiment became too violent and was considered counterproductive for its agenda, the party-state would put on the brakes (see e.g. Gries 2004; Zhao 2013). Although CCP nationalism and popular nationalism are not always aligned with each other, the party does what it can to steer the content of the nationalist narrative. This is not a straightforward and consistent plan of action towards the well-defined goal of strengthening the Chinese people's national identity. Different leaders have different angles and hobbyhorses, and the party can launch new ideas and campaigns that might get picked up by enthusiastic academics and receive much support throughout society, or, as sometimes happens, remain largely inconsequential. A case in point is the attempt at reviving Confucianism sometime during the previous decade. The move was mainly initiated by intellectuals and focused on Confucian textual study (*ruxue*) and so-called national study (*guoxue*). Many of the public debates were concerned with the religious dimension of Confucianism and as a national or state religion. Some even advocated a "Confucian socialist republic" (*rujia shehuizhuyi gongheguo*, Goossaert and Palmer 2011: 344–346). In 2004, the first Confucian Institute outside China was established in Seoul, a move that clearly demonstrated that the party-state was squarely behind the inclusion of Confucianism in assembling national identity. Some researchers have shown that the embrace of Confucianism as a grassroots repository of moral and, to some extent, religious values gained some traction (Billioud and Thoraval 2008). However, the lack of well-developed institutions and its protracted and thorough eradication during a large part of the last century have, as of now, inhibited the establishment of a broad popular revival of religious Confucianism.

Buddhism and Governmentality

Coming to terms with the continued existence of religion, the CCP seems to be moving in a direction where it is finding ways to use religion to further the agenda of the party. To construct and maintain a "harmonious society" or realize "the China Dream", China's leaders need all the help they can get. While the position of Chinese Mahayana Buddhism is not on a par with that of Confucianism, as a shared icon of Chinese civilization, state power, and social morality it does have the advantage of being the most prevalent institutionalized religion in China. And, as indicated earlier, its two-thousand-year trajectory within Chinese polities and society has resulted in a high level of Sinification manifested in a Chinese-language textual canon, salient Chinese-style temple architecture, and, not the least, an extensive native development of Chinese doctrinal schools, such as Chan Buddhism. As such, Chinese Mahayana Buddhism is equipped with solid credentials as an inherent component and expression of traditional Chinese

Buddhism in Post-Mao China 159

culture. Indigenous Taoism is too marginalized and localized to be a worthwhile ally for the CCP in this regard. Chinese leaders are wary of Christianity and Islam because of their association with foreignness, although in the post-Mao period this is seldom expressed directly in official discourse. In 2006, Ye Shaowen, the then director of SARA, underscored the superiority of Buddhism in being capable of playing a positive role in Chinese society by helping believers "cope with the fast-changing society, now plagued by a huge wealth gap and increasing social unrest" (Chan 2006). Speaking at the opening of the first World Buddhist Forum, held in Zhejiang, he acknowledged that "other religions such as Christianity and Islam could also contribute to the building of a harmonious society, but Buddhism, which pursued an idea of harmony that was close to that in the Chinese outlook, could make a 'distinctive contribution'" (Chan 2006).[4]

Of course, while the Chineseness on display in Chinese Mahayana Buddhism can be co-opted into the new nationalism of post-Mao China, there were other grounds for the positive reappraisal in recent years of this religion in official discourse. Several aspects of the "religious fever" have been worrying the party-state on and off since the reintroduction of limited religious freedom in the early 1980s. The relationship between the party-state and Buddhism is to a large extent a relationship of governmentality in the Foucauldian understanding of the term (Foucault et al. 2007: 108). Buddhism becomes a technology of the modern Chinese state to influence the behaviour of its citizens. Already in the early years of CCP rule, secularization did not mean that Buddhism was forced into the private sphere or totally suppressed, but rather, that it was remoulded and utilized by the party-state (Ji 2008: 239). And a substantial segment of the Buddhist sangha has been receptive to this role and adapted its institutions to both the agenda of those governing and the perceived needs of those governed. In the fight to suppress Falungong in the late 1990s, Buddhist leaders unambiguously supported the official anti-cult campaign, partly, it has been argued, because Falungong was considered a religious competitor, but more critically because institutionalized Buddhism under the administration of the Chinese Buddhist Association is a compliant participant in the party-state's governmentality project. When the state wanted to get rid of a perceived threat by a vast uncontrollable social organization through the application of the criminalizing category of "evil cult" (*xiejiao*), it needed experts on religious orthodoxy to help legitimize its clampdown. But also historically in China there have been periods where the state and Buddhist clergy found each other in common projects. In his discussion of the role of Buddhism in the suppression of Falungong, Benjamin Penny draws parallels to Buddhists in medieval China working together with rulers in their concern to impose new orthodoxy. In attacking local deities, Buddhists strived to gain a form of symbiosis with the state (Penny 2008: 147).

In recent years, concerns about the spread of "foreign" religions have added yet new incentives for a closer partnership between the party-state and Chinese Mahayana Buddhism. According to some reports, local authorities sent in Buddhist monks to hold ceremonies in front of Christians trying to stop the destruction of their church cross in Huzhou in Zhejiang in July 2015 (Radio Free Asia

160   *Koen Wellens*

2015). Except for the very visible and tabloid removal of crosses from churches in Zhejiang that started in 2014, a more discreet campaign is taking place to counter the growing Christian influence, especially in higher educational institutions. In a survey on religious beliefs among 2,840 university students in Liaoning Province, 31 per cent of the students stated that they either believed in or were considering "taking" a religion (*guiyi zongjiao xiangfa*). Of those, about 54 per cent believed in Buddhism and 29 per cent in Christianity. The authors express their concern about these numbers and warn that "the next urgent task for colleges and universities should be resisting religious infiltration by foreign hostile forces". This can be achieved, according to them, by instilling a more scientific attitude towards life among students, and by giving them psychological support in order to better bridge the step from family life to the loneliness of student life without running to religion for support (Zhang and Rong 2012: 59). The major focus on the "foreign hostile forces" leaves no doubt that the core of the problem is the spread of Christianity and to a lesser extent Islam. In view of the fact that almost double as many religious students report being, or about to become, Buddhists, this is a noteworthy appraisal of the position of Buddhism in Chinese society.

> Foreign hostile forces, however, make religious infiltration into a means of political struggle; they utilize foreign Protestant, Catholic, and Islamic organizations. By means of modern media, they communicate reactionary information to the students in our country and infuse them with harmful ideology, making students who possess a strong thirst for knowledge but who lack judgment become interested in foreign religion. After that, they destroy the students' traditional value system and correct worldview, ultimately managing to shake the social purpose of our country.
>
> (Zhang and Rong 2012: 59, my translation)

In governing this huge and increasingly complex country, the CCP is cautiously enlarging the space for religious organizations (as well as other societal organizations) to help it with challenging tasks such as disaster relief, poverty reduction, tackling environmental threats, and taking care of the handicapped, orphans, and the elderly. Being extremely concerned with keeping its monopoly on power, the party tries to keep as much control as possible over these organizations.[5] As Susan McCarthy (2013) has shown in a seminal article, for religions this new social task also provides opportunities for discreetly filling some of the designated space with religious content. Since these organizations are not supposed to bring religion into their social work, McCarthy defines such mild insubordination as a form of resistance to the state, albeit of the loyal and evasive sort. Again, in view of the concerns held by the party relating to loss of its power monopoly and influence by foreign forces, if Buddhists manage well in filling up the space, there is less need and room for Christian organizations. It is certainly no coincidence that the first overseas NGO to receive permission from the Ministry of Civil Affairs to set up a nationwide charity foundation in August 2010 was the Taiwanese Buddhist charity Tzu Chi.[6] The meeting in 2013 between Xi Jinping and Hsing Yun from

Buddhism in Post-Mao China 161

Fo Guang Shan, the international Taiwan-based Buddhist charity, was a further official acknowledgement of the increasingly important role Buddhism is being allowed to play in today's China.

Conclusion

This chapter has explored recent developments in the relationship between two implausible partners, the Communist Party and China's largest religion, Buddhism. In spite of its history of ideological secularism—at times even of a radical variety—the party has in recent years changed considerably in its assessment of Chinese Mahayana Buddhism. The reasons for the shift are manifold, and the debate about whether the current policies of the CCP should be categorized as *post*-socialist or *neo*-socialist has not been settled (see e.g. Pieke 2009). There is, however, no discussion about the fact that the CCP is China's ruling party and has clear ambitions to remain so. Therefore, China's leaders are highly concerned with both governmentality and legitimacy: how to rule effectively while safeguarding the party's monopoly on power. The CCP's main focus is to continue providing the conditions for further economic growth, creating a strong China in the world, and bringing into being prosperous and, hopefully, happy and grateful citizens. While Chinese strength and happiness is largely predicated on achieving economic growth, the leadership also realizes that people aspire to more in their lives than material wealth, and that it therefore needs to deliver also in those areas of government. This calls for a pragmatic course, and the political leadership is looking for expedient means where it can obtain them. Marxism-Leninism is still the official party ideology, but on an implicit and operational level. Nationalism has partly replaced it as a source for emotional mobilization around a common cause. In search of a repository of common moral and philosophical values, Chinese leaders and intellectuals have looked towards Confucianism, but these endeavours have as yet not really been widely successful. Increasingly, though, Chinese Mahayana Buddhism has emerged as a thriving and viable alternative. It has proven to be a willing partner in the party-state's task of governmentality, complementing the state in providing social services, lending its religious authority in ridding the country of perceived threats by "evil cults", and, not least, providing Chinese people with moral and spiritual resources. With the secularist ideology still simmering in the background, both partners are well aware that they have to tread carefully in this collaboration.

Notes

1. Both the tendency of the Chinese government to play down the number of religious believers and the continued reluctance of believers to stand out for their beliefs, even after the liberalization policies make it hard to quantify the revival starting at the end of the 1970s. In his discussion on the "number game", Daniel Bays (2003: 491) mentions estimates for Protestants from around one million in 1949 to "maybe" fifty million by the year 2000, giving some indications of exponential growth.

162 Koen Wellens

2. The entire speech can be read at the web page of the Chinese Ministry of Foreign Affairs: http://www.fmprc.gov.cn/mfa_eng/wjdt_665385/zyjh_665391/t1142560. shtml.
3. A simple search on the China Academic Journals database with "China Dream" in the subject heading in May 2015 produced no less than 29,390 titles, all written in a period of two-and-a-half years.
4. The statement was quickly picked up by foreign media, especially Christian outlets, with headings such as "Buddhism can reduce social divisions better than Christianity and Islam" (AsiaNews.it 2006).
5. For an interesting article looking at the problems and challenges of allowing religious organizations to conduct charity in China, see e.g. Dong (2012).
6. In China, NGOs must normally register as businesses with the Ministry of Commerce. See also Lim (2010).

References

Agadjanian, Alexander. 2001. "Public Religion and the Quest for National Ideology: Russia's Media Discourse." *Journal for the Scientific Study of Religion* 40 (3): 351–365.
Ashiwa, Yoshiko. 2009. "Positioning Religion in Modernity: State and Buddhism in China." In *Making Religion, Making the State: The Politics of Religion in Modern China*, edited by Yoshiko Ashiwa and David L. Wank, 43–73. Stanford, CA: Stanford University Press.
Ashiwa, Yoshiko, and David L. Wank. 2006. "The Politics of a Reviving Buddhist Temple: State, Association, and Religion in Southeast China." *Journal of Asian Studies* 65 (2): 337–359.
AsiaNews.it. 2006. "Buddhism Can Reduce Social Divisions Better Than Christianity and Islam." 11 April. Accessed 15 June 2015. http://www.asianews.it/news-en/Buddhism-can-reduce-social-divisions-better-than-Christianity-and-Islam-5887.html.
Bays, Daniel H. 2003. "Chinese Protestant Christianity Today." *China Quarterly* 174: 488–505.
Billioud, Sébastien, and Joël Thoraval. 2008. "The Contemporary Revival of Confucianism: Anshen Liming or the Religious Dimension of Confucianism." *China Perspectives* 3: 88–106.
Bunkenborg, Mikkel. 2014. "From Metaphors of Empire to Enactments of State: Popular Religious Movements and Health in Rural North China." *Positions: East Asia Cultures Critique* 22 (3): 573–602.
Callahan, William A. 2014. "What Can the China Dream 'Do' in the PRC?" *The Asan Forum* 3 (2). Accessed 21 May 2015. http://www.theasanforum.org/what-can-the-china-dream-do-in-the-prc/.
Casanova, Jose. 1994. *Public Religions in the Modern World*. Chicago: University of Chicago Press.
Chan, Siu-sin. 2006. "Buddhism Held Up as Healer of Social Divisions." *South China Morning Post*, 11 June.
Dong, Dong. 2012. "Zongjiaojie kaizhan gongyi cishanshiye wenti yanjiu" [A study of the issue of religious circles developing welfare and charitable enterprises]. *Shijie Zongjiao Wenhua* 1: 47–51.
Duara, Prasenjit. 1991. "Knowledge and Power in the Discourse of Modernity: The Campaigns against Popular Religion in Early 20th-Century China." *Journal of Asian Studies* 50 (1): 67–83.
Fang, Litian. 2013. "Fojiao yu Zhongguo meng" [Buddhism and the China dream]. *Zhongguo Zongjiao* 12: 28–31.

Fisher, Gareth. 2014. *From Comrades to Bodhisattvas: Moral Dimensions of Lay Buddhist Practice in Contemporary China* [Topics in Contemporary Buddhism]. Honolulu: University of Hawai'i Press.

Foucault, Michel, Michel Senellart, François Ewald, and Alessandro Fontana. 2007. *Security, Territory, Population: Lectures at the Collège de France, 1977–78*. Basingstoke/New York: Palgrave Macmillan.

Goossaert, Vincent. 2006. "1898: The Beginning of the End for Chinese Religion?" *Journal of Asian Studies* 65 (2): 307–336.

Goossaert, Vincent, and David A. Palmer. 2011. *The Religious Question in Modern China*. Chicago: University of Chicago Press.

Gries, Peter Hays. 2004. *China's New Nationalism: Pride, Politics, and Diplomacy*. Berkeley, CA: University of California Press.

Ji, Zhe. 2008. "Secularization as Religious Restructuring: Statist Institutionalization of Chinese Buddhism and Its Paradoxes." In *Chinese Religiosities: Afflictions of Modernity and State Formation*, edited by Mayfair Mei-hui Yang, 233–260. Berkeley, CA: University of California Press.

Jiang, Jianyong. 2014. "Ning xin ju li: cujin fojiao jiankang fazhan" [Focus attention and unite efforts: Promote the healthy development of Buddhism]. *Zhongguo Fojiao* 11: 57–59.

Li, Hujiang. 2014. "Fojiao meng yu Zhongguo meng" [The Buddhist dream and the China dream]. *Fayin* 359 (7): 41–43.

Lim, Benjamin. 2010. "Taiwan Buddhist Charity Tzu Chi Sets Up Shop in Atheist China." *Blog Entry*, 20 August. Accessed 15 June 2015. http://blogs.reuters.com/faithworld/2010/08/20/taiwan-buddhist-charity-tzu-chi-sets-up-shop-in-atheist-china/.

MacInnis, Donald E. 1989. *Religion in China Today: Policy and Practice*. Maryknoll, NY: Orbis Books.

Madsen, Richard. 2009. "Back to the Future: Pre-Modern Religious Policy in Post-Secular China" [Templeton Lecture on Religion and World Affairs]. Accessed 15 June 2015. http://old.fpri.org/articles/2009/03/back-future-pre-modern-religious-policy-post-secular-china.

McCarthy, Susan K. 2013. "Serving Society, Repurposing the State: Religious Charity and Resistance in China." *China Journal* 70 (July): 48–72.

Penny, Benjamin. 2008. "Animal Spirits, Karmic Retribution, Falungong, and the State." In *Chinese Religiosities: Afflictions of Modernity and State Formation*, edited by Mayfair Mei-hui Yang, 135–154. Berkeley, CA: University of California Press.

Pieke, Frank N. 2009. *The Good Communist: Elite Training and State Building in Today's China*. Cambridge: Cambridge University Press.

Radio Free Asia. 2015. " 'Chanting Monks' Deployed in Standoff over Cross Demolition in China's Zhejiang." Accessed 5 September 2015. http://www.rfa.org/english/news/china/china-churches-07272015103543.html.

Wellens, Koen. 2010a. *Freedom of Religion or Belief in China: Experiences from the Sino-Norwegian Human Rights Dialogue*. Oslo: Unipub.

———. 2010b. *Religious Revival in the Tibetan Borderlands: The Premi of Southwest China* [Studies on Ethnic Groups in China]. Seattle: University of Washington Press.

Wohlrab-Sahr, Monika, and Marian Burchardt. 2012. "Multiple Secularities: Toward a Cultural Sociology of Secular Modernities." *Comparative Sociology* 11 (6): 875–909.

Yang, Mayfair Mei-hui. 2008. "Introduction." In *Chinese Religiosities: Afflictions of Modernity and State Formation*, edited by Mayfair Mei-hui Yang, 1–40. Berkeley, CA: University of California Press.

Zhang, Junsheng, and Rong Han. 2012. "Jiaqiang daxuesheng xinyang jiaoyu—diyu jing-wai zongjiao sixiang shentou—yi Liaoning wo suo gaoxiao daxuesheng zongjiao xin-yang zhuangkuang weili" [Strengthen the university students' belief education and resist foreign religious thought penetration: Taking the situation of students' religious belief at five Liaoning colleges as an example]. *Meitan Gaodeng Jiaoyu* 30 (6): 57–60.

Zhao, Suisheng. 2013. "Foreign Policy Implications of Chinese Nationalism Revisited: The Strident Turn." *Journal of Contemporary China* 22 (82): 535–553. doi: 10.1080/10670564.2013.766379.

10 Militarized Masculinity with Buddhist Characteristics

Buddhist Chaplains and Their Role in the South Korean Army

Vladimir Tikhonov*

Introduction: Chaplaincy and the State-Religion Nexus

Chaplaincies in the South Korean army constitute a critical nexus in the relations between the actors in the religious market, the state, the military (as one of the crucially important parts of state bureaucracy), and the military's ideology of statist nationalism, traditionally underpinned by strong anti-communist sentiments. Theoretically, South Korea is a religiously pluralist society. It is a market where diverse religions—primarily, various Protestant denominations, Catholics, Buddhists, and a host of smaller new religious groups—compete relatively freely for the sympathies and (financial) support of the consumer.[1] The reason "market" may constitute an appropriate metaphor for describing the religious situation in South Korea is both the absence of state religion and the remarkable degree of dynamism in the changing patterns of the religious affiliations during more than six decades of South Korea's history as a separate state founded in 1948.

The very concept of religious affiliation, of exclusively and personally belonging to a certain religious group, was brought to Korea in the nineteenth century by the spread of Christianity and, generally, modern consciousness (Baker 2006a). It was South Korean history, however, that saw an explosive growth in such a belonging. From 1964 to 1996, the number of the people who could identify their religious affiliation increased sixfold (A. Kim 2002). In a way, growth in religious belonging coincided with the development of South Korean capitalism.[2] The mutual influence of these two phenomena provides grounds for talking about a "religious market" in the South Korean case. Religions have been acquiring their followers in fierce mutual competition, in which—until the mid-1990s— Protestants were emerging as victors. From around 3 per cent in the early 1950s, they increased their following to 19.7 per cent by 1995. This was largely due to their ability to offer opportunities for social networking and drastic increase in social capital to the urban middle classes and newly urbanized workers. Furthermore, "religion" is often understood in South Korea as trading contributions to the religious bodies for this-worldly favours from the supernatural forces these bodies claim connections to. In a 1998 survey, around 40 per cent of the Protestant respondents agreed that donating money to church brings more prosperity in return, thus viewing religion as an investment of sorts (A. Kim 2002).

166   *Vladimir Tikhonov*

But even if religious market theory may be applied to the South Korean case, it does not mean that this market is, or ever was, "perfect". Indeed, that would be difficult to expect given the decisive role that the state has been playing in the development of South Korean capitalism (Woo 1991). Of course, the role of the state is not the only limitation on the supposed rationality of the market choice made by the religiously affiliated South Koreans. Just as elsewhere, some inherit their religious belonging, and the choices in many other cases are heavily conditioned by class, gender, and regional identities.[3] Still, as I will argue in the present chapter, in the particular South Korean case, the state—while officially pursuing a laissez-faire approach to the religious sphere—does exert an important influence on the configuration of the religious market. It is the military chaplaincy that functions as one of the key instruments of such influence. Whereas the contemporary Chinese (PRC) state attempts to regulate the religious market through a system of controls and prohibitions resulting in the growth of "grey" market sectors (Yang Fenggang 2006), the South Korean state, by contrast, does not attempt to control the market as a whole but provides advantages to the chosen actors via such channels as access to the military chaplaincy. Very importantly, this interplay between the state/military and religion also affects the socio-political horizons of the religions involved, institutionalizing and cementing their acceptance of the militarized patterns of modernity and citizenship that South Korea has developed (Moon 2005). On the one hand, according to a 2003 opinion survey, 72.2 per cent of the South Korean Protestants believed that war could not be justified in *any* case (Hansin Taehakkyo Haksurwŏn Sinhak Yŏn'guso 2004: 36). On the other hand, the conservative majority of South Korea's Protestants opposes the perspective of establishing alternative civil service for conscientious objectors, being afraid that it would benefit their Jehovah's Witness competitors, who are commonly regarded as non-Christians in the South Korean Protestant world, and undermine the all-important national defence (Yun 2014). Such a cognitive dissonance of sorts—war as such is opposed, but military service is accepted and obviously is *not* regarded as a part of preparation for war—demonstrates the degree to which the statist logic of "national defence first" permeated the religious consciousness in South Korea, the topic on which I will specially focus below.

Article 20 of the existing constitution of South Korea provides for religious freedom and denies any religion the status of state religion. However, institutions such as military chaplaincy emphasize the fact that certain (presumably larger and more mainstream) denominations allowed to run their chaplaincies in the military are given a state recognition of their established positions, while the rest of the religious organizations are de facto denied such a right. Given the crucially important role that religious propagation in the military plays in South Korea, a hard-core conscription society (see Moon 2005) that maintains a 639,000-strong standing army—numerically the seventh largest in the world—access to the military personnel for proselytizing purposes gives a denomination an effectively oligopolic status. It puts a denomination on a qualitatively

Chaplains in the South Korean Army 167

different level vis-à-vis its competitors. At the same time, such access implies the willingness of the religious group in question to moderate or adjust its doctrines to conform to the military's specific objectives, namely encouraging the conscripts to endure the hardships of their mandatory service terms for the presumed greater good for oneself and community. The religious groups in question also have to legitimize the skills that conscripts have to learn, namely skills in depriving state-designated enemies of their right to live. While running a chaplaincy does not necessarily imply a militaristic overemphasis in the doctrines of the denominations in question, it does necessitate giving a decidedly important place to the state in the structure of the religious doctrine. The state's willingness to provide access to the captive audience in the military for proselytizing has to be reciprocated by the denomination's willingness to provide the state with a certain place in their belief systems.

Currently, the South Korean military has chaplaincies from four denominations (Hwang 2008): Protestant (262 chaplains, 979 military churches), Buddhist (136 chaplains, 404 military temples), Catholic (86 chaplains, 282 military churches), and Won Buddhist (two chaplains, one military temple). In principle, access to the military is not denied to other denominations. However, sending chaplains requires extensive paperwork. The denomination in question must persuade the Ministry of Defence that it possesses enough followers currently enlisted in the ranks, and moreover that its doctrinal structure is fully compatible with military requirements. It has to demonstrate that it will not create unnecessary problems if allowed to operate a chaplaincy. For example, the Buddhist chaplaincy is currently monopolized by the Chogye order, which is the largest and supposedly most representative one, in that it claims to be the inheritor of the orthodox Dharma lineage of Korea's Meditation School Buddhism. The attempts by the traditionally rival T'aego order (the heirs of the colonial-era monastics who accepted the Japanese Buddhist practice of clerical marriage) or the third-largest Ch'ŏnt'ae order (claiming to inherit the Dharma lineage of Korean and generally East Asian Tiantai tradition) to send chaplains on their own were so far unsuccessful (Pŏphyŏn 2011). Seen in this light, dispatching chaplains should be regarded as a privilege of sorts granted by the state to the denominations deemed most useful for the purposes of the state in general and the military in particular.

The number of chaplains each denomination is allowed to dispatch is also subject to a political negotiation process. In 1994, for example, President Kim Youngsam (Kim Yŏngsam, in office in 1993–1998) increased the number of Buddhist chaplains by seventy-five persons, in accordance with the statistical percentage of Buddhists among the country's religious population (the Ministry of Defence orders no. 358 and no. 402, issued on 2 February 1994). According to South Korean Buddhist chaplains, this was an attempt to mollify the Buddhist electorate agitated over the perceived preference the devotedly Protestant president gave to the Christians in appointments to the top state positions, including positions in the military. Yet another factor in the decision was a number of anti-Buddhist actions taken by Christian officers in the army, for example when a Buddha statue was

168 *Vladimir Tikhonov*

destroyed and burned during a removal of a military temple in the 17th Infantry Division on 1 April 1993 (see Hwang 2008: 277–289), which could potentially have endangered the Protestant president's standing among the Buddhist electorate. In a way, the number of Buddhist chaplains allowed into the army served as a trade-off in the complicated game of give-and-take between the Protestant president and the leadership of the Buddhist community. The latter felt embattled because of the dominant positions Christians occupied in many sectors of South Korean society, and on account of the zealous support many Protestants, especially Evangelicals, rendered to "their" president during the elections (T. Lee 2006). The fact that the decision was never fully carried out—the number of Buddhist chaplains was to be 170 by the year 2000, but even now (2016) it is only 136—bespeaks also the difficulties that Buddhists, with their relatively weak political influence vis-à-vis Catholics and not least Protestants (Kim Sŏngho 2011), have in negotiating the details of the chaplaincy arrangement with the Ministry of Defence bureaucracy (Hwang 2008: 289).

Buddhist chaplains belong to a borderline zone of sorts in South Korean society: being uniformed officers—they wear their monks' robes only during the Buddhist religious ceremonies—they at the same time belong to the Special Military Religion District (Kunjong t'ŭkpyŏl kyogu) of the Chogye order, established in 2005, and, as such, they are fully ordained, regular Buddhist monks. Until 2009, however, only the military chaplains had the privilege of being allowed to marry in the otherwise strictly celibate Chogye order. The revocation of this "chaplain exception" was seen as a sign of the Chogye order gradually recovering its sovereignty over the disputed bodies of its half-monastic and half-military members (Yi 2009). At the same time, military monks are not allowed to vote at the Chogye order's internal elections. While proselytizing in the military is seen as strategically important, chaplains, because of their limited status as half-monks, are accorded somewhat less prestige than regular monks who follow the proper regimen of study and meditation (Pak Puyŏng 2008).

Why, then, do the young monks studying at Dongguk University and Central Sangha University (Chung'ang Sŭngga Taehak)—the only two educational institutions qualified to produce Buddhist chaplains—decide to take the chaplain recruitment examination and serve for at least three obligatory years at the institution the purposes of which are far removed from the world of religion? Why do some of them make chaplaincy into their lifelong careers? How do they rationalize their relations with the military in doctrinal and ideological terms? Do they see any similarity between monastic and military life? How do they proselytize, and what functions do they perform in the military beyond administrating Buddhist rituals and preaching the doctrine to soldiers and officers? What models of masculine behaviour are they supposed to suggest to the soldiers under their charge? And how do they construct their relationship with their Protestant and Catholic colleagues-cum-rivals? The present chapter builds on the interviews I conducted with South Korean Buddhist chaplains in Seoul, South Korea, in July 2013, and attempts to answer these and other questions by taking the insider's view on the functioning of the Buddhist chaplaincy system into perspective. The

Chaplains in the South Korean Army 169

in-depth interviews were taken with four active and two retired chaplains, whose names have been changed in order to ensure their confidentiality (for a summary of the interviewees, see the references section here.

Buddhist Chaplains: Motivations, Self-Legitimization, Duties

The reasons given by the Buddhist chaplains for choosing their career varied from one generation to another. The older chaplains, in their forties and fifties, often mentioned their belief in the importance of chaplaincy for the Buddhist community as a whole. By contrast, the younger chaplains in their twenties appeared more individualistic, emphasizing more personal concerns and interests. Typically, the older-generation Kang K. informed me that he ventured into chaplaincy service because it was seen as a crucial instrument in competing against the Christians, who had been expanding rapidly since the 1960s. At a time "when even Buddhist broadcasting did not exist"—it was established first in 1990, whereas the Protestant broadcasting station had existed since 1954—Buddhist chaplaincy was envisioned as marching in the forefront of Buddhist missionary work (interview with Kang). Personal career reasons did play their part, as there were few venues in the South Korea of the 1970s and 1980s to earn one's living with the degree in Indian Buddhist philosophy Kang K. possessed. But the priority motivation was the anxiety about Buddhism's perceivably weak competitive position vis-à-vis Christians. Conversely, younger Hŏ Ch. openly admitted that chaplaincy allowed him to deal away with the mandatory military service—from which even the clergy is not exempted in South Korea—in a most convenient way. After all, serving as an officer (chaplain) entails much less hardship than serving as an ordinary conscript. At the same time, as ordination is a precondition for serving as a Buddhist chaplain, Hŏ welcomed the opportunity to be ordained and thus obtain first-hand knowledge of the realities of Korean Buddhism. Lastly, he considered his religious duty to care for Buddhist soldiers throughout the trials of military life. Generally, younger-generation chaplains seemed to care less about the competition against Christians and more about their personal career choices, their life experiences, and the opportunities to help their fellow Buddhists as individuals rather than the Buddhist community as a totality.

Although the obvious contradictions between the objectives of the military and Buddhism's first precept against killing—the first and most important of the Five Basic Precepts, or *pañca-śīla*, Kor. *kŭnbon ogye*—seemed to vex the younger chaplains somewhat, they did not seem to present any particular issue to the older ones. Rather, these older chaplains argued in various ways for why Buddhism was fully compatible with the military. First, they formulated the view of the state that made it look more like an all-embracing totality rather than a contract-based association of citizens. As Kang K. phrased it, "the individual exists only if the state survives; religion can exist only if the state survives". The (South Korean) state, in his view, was the precondition for the existence of both Korean Buddhism as an institution and Korean Buddhists as individuals. Thus, defence of the state was the individual's primary and existential duty, which *no* religious

170   *Vladimir Tikhonov*

considerations could ever negate. The Social Darwinist traits visible in Kang's phrasing of his view were also present in the view stated by older retired chaplain, Chŏn Ch.: "The army teaches winning. It teaches to always take first place. If you come second, it means that you are already dead. And Buddhism in the army has to teach how to win, so that my country survives, so that we all survive."

Second, the older chaplains tended to refuse connecting military or military service with "killing" (Kor. *salsaeng*) as prohibited by Buddhist canons. Typically, Chŏn insisted that chaplains were to "pray for peace" and serve in the military with the hope it would never go to war. Yet another elder colonel at the chaplaincy service, Chi S., insisted that the purpose of the military was to "establish harmony in the world and inside society, defend the peace and spearhead the construction of the Pure Land paradise on earth, while taking the state as a bigger and more inclusive form of life than an individual or any other collective". In a word, peace was viewed by the chaplains as militarized peace, or "peace by strength". Basically, it amounted to a carefully maintained mutual balance between the well-armed states, each of which was to claim that it "defends peace" by maximizing its military advantage. While such a view of peace—reminiscent of the assumptions of the realist school in international relations (see Donnelly 2000)—may well be congruent with the intellectual culture of the South Korean army, it was somewhat surprising to hear it from the people who concomitantly are also full-time religious practitioners. However, it looks as if in the questions of war and peace, Buddhist chaplains tended to rely more on the military part, rather than the religious part, of their dual identity.

Third, and very importantly, the doctrinal appropriateness of chaplaincy was defended on the basis of Korean Buddhist tradition. While Chi also pointed out that avoiding military service was in practice impossible for Korean monks, ever since the state began to forcibly draft them during the all-out anti-communist mobilization in the time of the Korean War (1950–1953), and while serving as a chaplain hardly qualitatively differed from being forced to serve as a conscript, all the chaplains I have talked with defined the Korean Buddhist tradition as "state-protective" (Kor. *hoguk*). Interestingly, at least some of the chaplains were seemingly aware that such a tradition was not necessarily in harmony with the socio-political views and practices of earlier Indian Buddhists. An older-generation chaplain, Kim Ch., emphasized, for example, that "unlike Indian states, Korean states tended not to grant their Buddhist communities extraterritorial privileges". But the fact that this tradition was Korean (or more broadly East Asian—some of the chaplains were aware about the history of monks' militias, or *sōhei*, in Japan), rather than pan-Buddhist, did not devaluate it in the eyes of the chaplains—rather the opposite.

Silla's famed priest Wŏn'gwang (541–630) and his Five Commandments for Secular Life (Kor. *Sesok ogye*) were commonly understood by the chaplains, young and old alike, as the earliest archetypical expression of the state-protective tradition.[4] In this connection, it is no accident that the chief Buddhist military temple attached to the Ministry of Defence was named Wŏngwangsa, in honour of the priest. The fact that Wŏn'gwang's commandments—which forbade both

Chaplains in the South Korean Army 171

retreating and the random taking of life, rather than the taking of life as such—were aimed at secular warriors rather than monks (which chaplains formally are) did not seem to influence the chaplains' view of them as fully legitimizing their activities.

Yet another important precedent the Buddhist chaplains constantly invoked was the military activity of the Korean monk militias (Kor. *sŭngbyŏng*), headed by the high-ranking priests Sŏsan (Hyujŏng, 1520–1604) and Samyŏng (Yujŏng, 1544–1610), during Hideyoshi's invasion of Korea (1592–1598). In fact, the official Korean sources, *Chosŏn Wangjo Sillok* (*The Veritable Records of Chosŏn Dynasty*), make it clear that neither monk ever *volunteered* to fight against the invaders. While there were some scattered clashes between the Japanese and the monks' local self-defence militias attempting to defend their temples from looting, the pan-national monks' militia was organized only after King Sŏnjo summoned Sŏsan in the ninth lunar month of 1592 and *ordered* him to start recruiting the monks.[5] Before the royal orders to Sŏsan, the monks' militia was in fact sometimes mustered locally by the provincial administrators, and always operated as part of the governmental army. The fact that Sŏsan and Samyŏng acted on royal orders—which they could not violate without heavily endangering the very existence of Buddhism in the neo-Confucian Chosŏn Kingdom—is well-established in the South Korean historical scholarship (e.g. Yang Kŭnyŏng and Kim Tŏksu 1992: esp. 221–236). However, the Korean Buddhist chaplains tended to present both of their role models as patriotic volunteers of a sort; such a (mis)interpretation of history was most likely intentional.

In contending that their chaplaincy activities in the military did not contradict the Buddhist precepts against violence, the younger chaplains—though apparently more concerned about this possible incongruence—hardly differed from the older ones in actual practice. For them, however, the system of argumentation was noticeably different. The state as a precondition for the existence of the individual or as a peace maintainable only by force was hardly mentioned, and neither were the putative state-protecting traditions. But the younger chaplains did emphasize that, in the situation when the majority of able-bodied South Korean males *have* to undergo the mandatory military service, helping them in the capacity of chaplains could be a part of the altruistic commitment of a monk.

Typically, Hŏ Ch. mentioned that taking part in the military training helps chaplains to understand what the soldiers must go through, thus enabling them to assist these soldiers in the best possible way. And as long as supporting soldiers is an altruistic pursuit, it should not violate the Buddhist precepts in their broad and essential sense. Hŏ also specifically mentioned that he did not consider state-protecting Buddhism a suitable topic for preaching to his charges; my impression was that he viewed the mandatory military service as an inescapable trial of sorts in which monks were to help the laymen. Interestingly, anti-communism almost never figured in the answers, although Kim mentioned in passing that the South Korean army "defends our people from the forces of evil". Beyond this, however, North Korea, the South Korean army's most likely battlefield enemy, was not named at all. It looked as if the chaplains viewed the mandatory military service

172   *Vladimir Tikhonov*

and their part in strengthening the "spiritual fighting capacity" (Kor. *chŏngsin chŏllyŏk*) as just a part of the routine business of the state, as "business as usual", without any reference to South Korea's specific problem of national division and North-South confrontation (interview with Hŏ).

Some of the chaplains mentioned the specific difficulties that monks—both chaplains and the younger monks conscripted for their obligatory service periods (currently twenty-one months for the infantry)—encounter in the barracks. Faced with a social atmosphere where drinking and boasting about one's sexual exploits is seen as a crucial trait of authentic masculinity, some conscripted monks prefer to hide their status to evade teasing and possibly heavier bullying. At the same time, some of them get accustomed to drinking and brothel visits, and their newly acquired habits later put their monasteries in dishonour (interview with Chi). Chaplains, even while considering themselves primarily as monks, have to drink and eat meat together with the other officers, especially in the presence of their superiors, as their monastic status is no excuse. In practically all cases, they conform to these unwritten rules of the military life (interview with Chŏn). At the same time, the disciplined atmosphere of army life does resonate, to a degree, with the strictly regimented life of the Korean monasteries (interview with Chi). In fact, discipline is one of the things that Buddhist chaplains' instruction is supposed to strengthen. As related to me by one of the younger chaplains I interviewed, Captain Yŏm Ch., the foremost task of the Buddhist chaplain is "strengthening the spiritual force" (Kor. *chŏngsinnyŏk kanghwa*) of the soldier through developing his "religious fighting capacity" (Kor. *sin'ang chŏllyŏk*). One of the crucially important elements of such a "cultivation strategy" (Kor. *kyohwa chŏllyak*) is destroying soldiers' propensity to rebel (Kor. *panhangsim ŏbs'aegi*). It is supposed to be done by carefully working with the soldier's mind-heart (Sin.-Kor. *sim*, Kor. *maŭm*), persuading him to accept reality as it is, to conform to it and to find a secure position in it, rather than harbouring a grudge or trying to be critical.

"Stabilizing" the internal life of the soldiers should help them to end their stints without accidents or disciplinary violations, but also to submit themselves voluntarily to a plethora of rules and regulations that together constitute the totality of barrack life. An older chaplain, Chi, also informed me that the mind-heart, and the ways to cultivate and control it so that one's behaviour would answer the army's expectations, constituted the core of his preaching and consulting work with the soldiers. He even found a doctrinal source for this in the Buddhist teachings of *kṣānti* (Kor. *in'yok*), or patience, one of six and ten *pāramitās* ("perfections"). A younger chaplain, Hŏ, agreed with this view, and added that "harmonization of an individual's human relations"—centred on developing the ability to satisfy one's superiors and conform to their demands—is grounded in the core Buddhist teaching of *anātman* (Kor. *mua*), or denial of the existence of permanent and independent self. On understanding that one's instinctive urge to resist the army's regimental environment is nothing more than a fallacious attachment to an illusion of self, the soldier should be able to cultivate himself into a person ideally suited to the barrack life (interviews with Chi S. and Hŏ Ch). Following this line

Chaplains in the South Korean Army 173

of reasoning, any breach of military discipline may be seen as a religious failure. It will be a failure of self-cultivation, a failure to develop oneself spiritually to the degree that one's internal urges would fully conform to the needs of the Ministry of Defence. And following on one's unconscious urges to rebel is nothing more than clinging to the erroneous views on self, drifting further and further from the ideal of Enlightenment—as seen by the Ministry of Defence version of Buddhism.

Buddhism, Patterns of Masculine Self-Disciplining, and Religious Market Strategies

Behavioural correction of the type described above is done during the regular "character tutoring" (Kor. *inkyŏk chido*) sessions, both collectively and individually. These sessions are usually done on Wednesdays and Sundays, which are the days generally reserved in the military for religious events. Aside from the admonitions on relinquishing the attachment to one's self, these sessions may give soldiers a more practical opportunity to voice their complaints about beatings by their superiors and senior soldiers, as well as other forms of mistreatment. The ample use of corporal punishment by officers, non-commissioned officers, and senior soldiers alike is a "tradition" of the South Korean military most likely inherited from the Japanese imperial army (Moon 2005: 26–28), in which the majority of the founding members of the South Korean military forces served (Yang Pyŏnggi 1988). As all the chaplains I have talked to unanimously testify, the brutal mistreatment of soldiers remains a feature of the South Korean army, especially in the cases of its elite Marine (*haebyŏngdae*) or Special Warfare Command (*t'ŭkchŏnsa*) units (interview with Hŏ). At the same time, it was pointed out that the amount of abuse has been drastically reduced under the liberal administrations of Kim Dae Jung (Kim Taejung, 1998–2002) and Roh Moo Hyun (No Muhyŏn, 2002–2007).

Aside from the ideological commitment to eradicating the modes of discipline strongly associated with the legacies of the Japanese colonial state and South Korea's authoritarian past, the liberals in power were worried by frequent lethal "incidents" in the military. On top of suicides, the victims sometimes took justice into their own hands and massacred their victimizers. News of such "incidents" further tarnished the already rather problematic image of South Korea's armed forces, strongly associated in the minds of many South Koreans with authoritarian ruthlessness and negation of human dignity (Kim Yongsam 2007). In one particularly stunning case, on 19 June 2005, Private Kim Tongmin, serving in a unit close to the demilitarized zone between North and South Korea, killed eight soldiers and officers as revenge for the abuse he allegedly suffered. He was later sentenced to death (Kim Hyŏn'gil 2008). Preventing such emergencies was seen as one of their most important duties by all the chaplains I interviewed. Usually, chaplains are supposed to report any complaints of mistreatment to the commanding officer and then keep pressing to have the grievances properly dealt with; it is considered commonsensical that Buddhist soldiers find it psychologically easier to reveal their traumas to the Buddhist chaplains (interview with Chi).

174   *Vladimir Tikhonov*

The "character tutoring" the chaplains are involved with gives them ample grounds to defend themselves from the accusations that their contribution to the military contradicts the basic rejection of violence found in Buddhist doctrine. In fact, the chaplains I interviewed were all quick to mention that they viewed their activities as violence prevention rather than as participation in state-directed militarist violence. Spontaneous outbursts by bored, over-stressed, or rebellious soldiers directed against one another were seen as authentic violence, while neither the army nor any other state/official institution was viewed as being inherently violent. Consequently, the masculine ideal, from the viewpoint of the chaplains interviewed, was a well-disciplined man fully able to fit himself into any sort of "organizational culture" (*chojik munhwa*) he had to deal with by reining in his emotions and following the pre-existing order of things. This idea seemed also to apply to the Buddhist chaplains themselves, who usually get along with meat-eating and drinking in order not to break the "human harmony" (*inhwa*) within the military organization.

In fact, Buddhist chaplains are often used as exemplary "organizational men" inside the Buddhist community. One recent article in a Buddhist newspaper, describing the two-month-long training the future Buddhist chaplains were to receive at Kŭmnyŏnsa military temple in Pusan in spring 2013, noted, for example, that practical experience of "[right] behaviour in the world" (*ch'ŏse*) was even more important for the aspiring chaplains than the knowledge of Buddhist rituals and doctrine: "Since the military is strictly a part of organizational life, one has to know how, for example, to deal with inflexible commanding officers" (Chang Yŏngsŏp 2013). In this context, of course, dealing with the rigidities of military life means fitting in rather than raising questions or making trouble. This is the gist of the message that Lieutenant Colonel Hŏ Hyŏn'gu (2013), a Buddhist Air Force chaplain, sends to the soldiers under his charge: "Nothing changes if you simply say that you cannot adjust yourself, that you want to be transferred somewhere else, that you would prefer to have no senior servicemen (*koch'am*) above you. And in civil life you meet even harder challenges. So, what is important is the willingness and efforts towards wisely overcoming yourself." As viewed by the Buddhist chaplains, mature men are those who are skilled at adjusting themselves to the pre-existing social order rather than questioning it. It is also taken as a given that the state-sanctioned order represents the antithesis to violence rather than institutionalized violence as such.

Nothing of this, of course, is especially surprising—or specifically Korean. In the age of late capitalism, conformism is no longer as shameful as it could be, for example, for the intellectuals of the Romantic Age or the counter-cultural rebels of the 1960s. On the contrary, the self-adjustment capabilities are treated as an important instrument for middle-class "success", for men and women alike. While quasi-religious methods of self-adjustment and fitting into the existing order, such as yoga or mindfulness training, seem to sell better among women than among men,[6] males are by no means excluded from the middle-class self-improvement fashion. On the contrary, self-adjustment is increasingly treated as being most necessary for typically "male" occupations. The global managerial class, for example, is still mostly male-dominated: the proportion of women among senior managers is 18 per cent in North America and 21 per cent globally (King 2012). These predominantly male managers are bombarded now by messages on the supposed positive effects that mindfulness training has on sales and managerial decisions. One of the core postulates of mindfulness as applied to business/management is to eschew "judgmental thinking" and accept both people and things the way they are (Beard 2014). Essentially, "overcoming oneself" and other forms of "character tutoring" practised by the Buddhist chaplains in the South Korean army boil down to a similar attitude.

Mindfulness, meditation, and yoga are utilized now even by the bastion of quintessential maleness, the United States Marine Corps (Associated Press 2013). The absence of overtly religious references may distinguish it from the preaching of Korea's Buddhist chaplains, but the essential attitudes towards "character training", based on unquestioning acceptance of the existing order/ hierarchies and willingness to fit into them while suppressing one's rebellious ego, are quite similar. Inasmuch as mindfulness represents a late-capitalist commercial appropriation of Buddhist meditation techniques (*Economist* 2013) permeated with the middle-class ideology of conformity and "niceness", this similarity is not even accidental. Both Korean and Euro-American character tutors/trainers—in the military, business, and elsewhere—are essentially utilizing the traditional methods of mental self-regulation for a similar set of institutional and ideological purposes, constructing fully comparable models of docile, disciplined masculinity.

What is interesting, however, is the striking similarity between the sort of masculinity constructed and popularized by the Buddhist chaplains in the South Korean military, and the models of masculinity that are popular inside South Korea's corporate community. Typically, South Korean guidebooks on achieving success inside the corporate jungles recommend that aspiring managers and would-be CEOs should always control their emotions. They are advised to do their best to adjust themselves to the personal styles of their superiors and high-level managers in general, to change themselves instead of complaining, and to avoid at all costs being seen as someone different from the majority (see e.g. Chang Suyong 2001, 2012). It is not accidental that some corporations use Buddhist temples and other Buddhist facilities for their corporate training sessions. The Chogye order's Korean Culture Training Centre estimates, for example, that around 10 per cent of its clients are corporations which aspire to teach their employees a "traditional communal spirit" through collective meditation sessions (Sŏ 2014).

To which degree this model of masculine behaviour is traditional for Korean Buddhism is, however, open to debate. It is true that the Meditation School (Kor. Sŏn, Ch. Chan, Jap. Zen) temples in East Asia were indeed known for their highly disciplined way of life centred on a clearly defined set of regulations, the origins of which were commonly attributed to Master Baizhang Huaihai

176 *Vladimir Tikhonov*

(720–814) (Yifa 2002). At the same time, the religious personalities of meditation masters in the countries of the region were expected to defy the boundaries of formal discipline and self-restraint, demonstrating in such a way the unobstructed mind, enlightened enough to no longer need to cling to any sort of formal codes. "Enlightened" masters routinely shocked their disciples into breaking down the wall of conventional thinking by yelling at them or even beating them. They generally could allow themselves to behave in eccentric, trickster-like ways, disregarding the time-honoured customs and practices, along the pattern of unconventional behaviour associated with the legends about Taoist immortals (Faure 1991: 115–125).

The same expectations applied to the Korean masters as well as their Chinese and Japanese counterparts, indeed until the twentieth century. Kyŏnghŏ (1849–1912), known for his revival of meditational traditions, was also notorious for his eccentric patterns of behaviour (*kihaeng*), including reported illicit love affairs (Pak Chaehyŏn 2009: 15–47). A meditation monk of the next generation, Han Yong'un (1879–1944), was famed both for his physical strength and fist-fighting abilities, and, being a staunch opponent of Japan's colonization of Korea, reportedly used to beat up those of his friends and acquaintances who dared to speak Japanese in his presence or voice pro-Japanese views (An 1979: 259–299). Seen in this light, the disciplinary work in which the Buddhist chaplains are engaged appears to represent a facet of institutional Buddhism's modern self-invention, or conscious adjustment to bureaucratic and market discipline. Army chaplains, as well as the monks engaged in training corporate employees, essentially attempt to deliver what both state and capital forces expect from them, with the explicit aim of self-preservation and maximizing their share of South Korea's highly competitive religious market.

Aside from troubleshooting and disciplinary work, chaplains busy themselves with competitive proselytizing. On Wednesdays and Sundays, chaplains from all the denominations conduct their religious ceremonies—Buddhist services (Kor. *pŏphoe*) in the case of Buddhist chaplains. On these occasions, the Buddhist chaplains always have to compare their participant numbers with that of their Protestant and Catholic rivals. While the relations with Protestant and Catholic chaplains are usually described as collegial, often even warm, the sense of competition, according to the Buddhist chaplains, is always present. The success in competition vis-à-vis other chaplains is determined by the number of soldiers who undergo the Buddhist ritual of receiving five basic precepts (Kor. *sugye*) and thus count in the statistics as Buddhist believers. Once precepts are received, such soldiers are expected to appear in the military temples every Sunday until they get discharged from active duty.

One of the reasons why the sense of competition against Christians is so acute is the relative lack of Buddhist success, even despite the relative stagnation of Protestantism in South Korean society in general after the early 1990s (Baker 2006b). The number of registered Buddhist believers in the military climbed throughout the 1970s and reached over 123,000 adherents in 1984, compared

Chaplains in the South Korean Army 177

with the Protestants' estimated following of 226,000 (Kim Tŏksu 1986: 161). The Buddhist following then levelled down, however, and was estimated in 2007 at around 114,000, against the over 215,000 Protestants (Hwang 2008: 691). According to the 2005 population census, Buddhists represent around 22 per cent of the South Korean population, compared with the Protestants' 18 per cent (Ko et al. 2011: 22), but they still prove unable to win over their Protestant rivals in the military. This failure is attributed by chaplains themselves to the inferiority in the number of chaplains and military temples, as compared with the numbers of military churches. As Christians—both Protestants and to a lesser degree Catholics—are still perceived as religiously dominating the military, the Buddhist chaplains evaluate their work as nevertheless being of enormous importance for the position of Korean Buddhism in South Korea's religious market.

The religious loyalties acquired during compulsory military service tend to last long and to influence other family members when discharged soldiers establish their own families (interview with Chi). Military chaplaincy allows South Korean Buddhism to escape the trap of greying: while Buddhists outnumber Protestants among those above forty, the numbers tend to be roughly similar for younger South Koreans. This phenomenon indicates the relative successes of Protestant missionary work among the younger age cohorts. Buddhist chaplaincy is one of the few mechanisms that allow Buddhists to check somehow this success of their rivals (interview with Chŏn). Indeed, among South Koreans aged 25–29 there are only 11 per cent more Buddhists than Protestants, compared with the 75–79 age cohort, where there are 65 per cent more Buddhists than Protestants (the statistics are for 2005; see Ko et al. 2011: 21). Seen in this light, the maintenance of the military chaplaincy is undoubtedly an important element in the self-marketing strategy of South Korean Buddhists, since it allows them to cover these segments of their potential consumers which otherwise are difficult to reach out to; indeed, in South Korean society, temple visits are customarily perceived as something more fitting the aged, especially older women, rather than the young.

Conclusion

All in all, the military chaplaincy in general—and its Buddhist segment in particular—constitutes an important link between the state power apparatus and the religious market. The state bestows privileged access to the captive audience of several hundreds of thousands conscripts to the chosen mainstream religious groups and thus further boosts their market position. The religious denominations reciprocate this by sanctifying the military apparatus of the state. Of course, such legitimation is hardly of any crucial meaning to the South Korean military. Already by the early 1970s, it succeeded in making military service part of the normative lifecycle of a "normal", able-bodied South Korean male, an organic part of both gender identity ("only in the military can you become a real man") and the political identity as a South Korean citizen (Moon 2005).

178　*Vladimir Tikhonov*

Still, the Buddhist stamp of approval for the state-imposed military service obligation is not unimportant, as Buddhism, Korea's age-old popular religion, enjoys a general appeal even outside the Buddhist religious milieu. According to a 2014 survey by Christian Ethics Practice Movement (Kidokkyo Yulli Silch'ŏn Undong), a Christian NGO, 28 per cent of self-proclaimed atheists named Buddhism as their most trusted religion, while 29 per cent named Catholicism and 21 per cent named Protestantism. Buddhism is widely seen as a living embodiment of the Korean tradition, although its societal contribution—through the provision of, for example, medical and welfare services—is generally viewed as deficient (Yang Sŭngnok 2014). Thus, the Buddhist acquiescence to military service for all the able-bodied South Korean men, including both lay and monastic Buddhists, as a part of their historical state-protective function, along with its vision of the military being an instrument of peace (rather than war), does seem to contribute to turning military service into a self-evident norm.

Such a norm cannot be compromised even by the revelations about regular and systematic abuses (beatings, etc.) in the ranks. The legitimation of the military service by the institutional Buddhist presence there seems to help to motivate the young South Korean Buddhists not to even try to protest or avoid their mandatory service, despite the reputation for ruthlessness the South Korean military has earned since its establishment. Its understanding of the state as all-embracing totality preceding the individual and creating the preconditions for his or her very existence—obviously harking back to the Japanese imperial ideology of the 1930s and early 1940s—should counter the more individualistic tendencies in the thinking of the younger Koreans, who, unsurprisingly, tend to prioritize their own economic survival, rather than the defence of the state, in the current neo-liberal age.

Buddhist chaplains' insistence on the religious (Buddhist) dimension of conformity to the disciplinary rules—conformity being regarded as a sign of successful self-cultivation—works to further legitimize the disciplinary norms of the military, the harshness of which obviously contrasts the more liberal tendencies in post-authoritarian South Korea. In fact, the emphasis on self-control and self-regulation as crucial masculine virtues amounts to a modern re-invention of Buddhism. It differs significantly from the sort of spontaneity, often bordering on eccentricity, which was expected from meditation masters in traditional times. It rather resembles the patterns of behaviour control in the corporate world, both inside and outside South Korea.

In a word, institutional Buddhism and the South Korean military reached a mutually beneficial symbiosis which appears to ultimately influence both sides. The military becomes the first ever place where the majority of the younger South Korean males—overworked in their high schools because they strive so hard to enter the most prestigious universities—obtain the free time to enjoy organized religious activities, including the Buddhist ones. In a way, religion becomes an essential feature of the barrack life, with religious discipline being conflated with the military disciplinary norms. At the same time, the existence of the chaplaincy

Chaplains in the South Korean Army 179

makes the South Korean Buddhist community into an avid supporter of its military. Any negative sides of the over-militarization of South Korean society are thus conveniently overlooked by the majority of Buddhist clerics. In this way, institutional Buddhism ultimately fails to play the role of the peace religion in South Korea—ironically, given the usual (and in reality rather misleading) associations between Buddhism and pacifism in the West. The symbiosis between institutional Buddhism and the military constitutes an important part of the lived reality of many South Korean Buddhists, many of whom start going to temple while serving in the military. Thus, it definitely merits further study by the scholars of Korean religion.

Notes

* The present article is a modified version of an article previously published in 2015 as "Militarized Masculinity with Buddhist Characteristics: Buddhist Chaplains and their Role in the South Korean Army", *Review of Korean Studies* 18 (2): 7–35.
1. On religious markets and their effects on the popularity of religion, see Iannaconne (1991).
2. On the development of capitalism in South Korea, see Amsden (1992).
3. On the general limitations of religious market approaches, see van der Veer (2012).
4. For an English translation of Wŏn'gwang's original biography from *Haedong Kosŭngjŏn*, or *The Lives of Eminent Korean Monks*, see P. Lee (1993: 78–83).
5. See the *Sŏnjo Sillok* (Fascicle 26, twenty-fifth year, ninth lunar month, twelfth day *kisa*), http://sillok.history.go.kr/inspection/inspection.jsp?mState=2&mTree=0&clsName=&searchType=a&keyword=%ED%9C%B4%EC%A0%95+%EC%8A%B9%EA%B5%B0), accessed 24 September 2015.
6. In 2012, 82.2 per cent of all yoga practitioners in the United States were women (*Yoga Journal* 2012).

References

Amsden, Alice. 1992. *Asia's Next Giant: South Korea and Late Industrialization*. Oxford: Oxford University Press.
An, Pyŏngjik. 1979. *Han Yong'un*. Seoul: Han'gilsa.
Associated Press. 2013. "U.S. Marine Corps Members Learn Mindfulness Meditation and Yoga in Pilot Program to Help Reduce Stress." *Daily News*, 23 January. Accessed 10 March 2014. http://www.nydailynews.com/life-style/health/u-s-marines-learn-meditate-stress-reduction-program-article-1.1245698.
Baker, Donald. 2006a. "The Religious Revolution in Modern Korean History: From Ethics to Theology and from Ritual Hegemony to Religious Freedom." *Review of Korean Studies* 9 (3): 249–275.
———. 2006b. "Sibling Rivalry in Twentieth-Century Korea: Comparative Growth Rates of Catholic and Protestant Communities." In *Christianity in Korea*, edited by Robert Buswell and Timothy Lee, 283–309. Honolulu: University of Hawai'i Press.
Beard, Alison. 2014. "Mindfulness in the Age of Complexity: An Interview with Ellen Langer by Alison Beard." *Harvard Business Review*, March. Accessed 10 March 2014. http://hbr.org/2014/03/mindfulness-in-the-age-of-complexity/ar/1.

180 Vladimir Tikhonov

Chang Suyong. 2001. *Chikchang'in ŭl wihan Sŏnggong ch'ŏseron* [The theory of successful behavior for salaried employees]. Seoul: Chŏllyak Kiŏp Consulting.

———. 2012. *Sŏnggonghanŭn saram ŭi in'gan kwan'gye* [Interpersonal relationships of successful people]. Seoul: Hyŏndae Midio.

Chang Yŏngsŏp. 2013. "Kunpŏpsa silmu ik'igo: Kyŏnghŏm paeugo" [Accustoming oneself to the practical aspects of military chaplaincy: Learning from experience]. *Pulgyo Sinmun*, 14 January. Accessed 10 March 2014. http://www.ibulgyo.com/news/article View.html?idxno=123541.

Donnelly, Jack. 2000. *Realism and International Relations*. Cambridge: Cambridge University Press.

Economist. 2013. "The Mindfulness Business: Western Capitalism Is Looking for Inspiration in Eastern Mysticism." 16 November. Accessed 10 March 2014. http://www.economist.com/news/business/21589841-western-capitalism-looking-inspiration-eastern-mysticism-mindfulness-business/.

Faure, Bernard. 1991. *The Rhetoric of Immediacy*. Princeton, NJ: Princeton University Press.

Hansin Taehakkyo Haksurwŏn Sinhak Yŏn'guso. 2004. *Han'guk Kidokkyoin ŭi Chŏngch'i, Sahow Ŭisik Chosa* [Research on the socio-political consciousness of the South Korean Protestant Christians]. Seoul: Hanul.

Hŏ Hyŏn'gu. 2013. "Hamkke iyagihamyŏn ihaehaji mothal kŏs i ŏpta" [Nothing is beyond understanding if we talk together]. *Magazin Konggam*, 11 April. Accessed 10 March 2014. http://afzine.kr/90170993858.

Hwang, Ilmyŏn. 2008. *Pulgyo Kunjongsa* [The history of Buddhist military chaplaincy]. Seoul: Kunjong t'ŭkpyŏl kyogu.

Iannaconne, Laurence. 1991. "The Consequences of Religious Market Structure: Adam Smith and the Economics of Religion." *Rationality and Society* 3 (2): 155–177.

Kim, Andrew Eungi. 2002. "Characteristics of Religious Life in South Korea: A Sociological Survey." *Review of Religious Research* 43 (4): 291–310.

Kim, Hyŏn'gil. 2008. "GP ch'onggi nansa Kim Ilbyŏng p'agi hangsosim esŏdo sahyŏng" [Private first class Kim, who randomly shot (colleagues) at the guard post, has his death sentenced confirmed by the appeals' court]. *Kuki News*, 7 May. Accessed 21 November 2013. http://news.naver.com/main/read.nhn?mode=LSD&mid=sec&sid1=100&oid=14 3&aid=0001948072.

Kim, Sŏngho. 2011. "Sahoejŏk yŏnghyangnyŏk k'ŭn chonggyo kaesin'gyo, chonggyogye todŏk, ch'ŏngnyŏmsŏng hwangnip sigŭp" [The religion with strong social influence is Protestantism; religions need to urgently establish their ethics and integrity standards]. *Sŏul Sinmun*, 21 November.

Kim, Tŏksu, ed. 1986. *Pulgyo Kunjong sa* [The history of Buddhist chaplaincy]. Seoul: Kunpŏpsadan.

Kim, Yongsam. 2007. "Chŏngbo munmyŏnggi Han'ggukkun ŭi pyŏngyŏng munhwa kaesŏn panghyang" [The ways of improving South Korean military's barrack culture in the age of the informational civilization]. *Chŏngsin Chŏllyŏk Yŏn'gu* 38: 225–251.

King, Dominic. 2012. "Women in Senior Management: Still Not Enough." *Grant Thornton International Business Report 2012*. Accessed 10 March 2014. http://www.international businessreport.com/files/ibr2012%20-%20women%20in%20senior%20man agement%20master.pdf.

Ko, Pyŏngch'ŏl, Kang Ton'gu, and Pak Chongsu, eds. 2011. *Han'guk ŭi chonggyo hyŏnhwang* [Current status of religions in South Korea]. Seoul: Munhwa Kwan'gwangbu.

Lee, Peter, ed. 1993. *The Sourcebook of Korean Civilization*. Vol. 1. New York: Columbia University Press.

Chaplains in the South Korean Army 181

Lee, Timothy S. 2006. "Beleaguered Success: Korean Evangelicalism in the Last Decade of the Twentieth Century." In *Christianity in Korea*, edited by Robert Buswell and Timothy Lee, 330–350. Honolulu: University of Hawai'i Press.

Moon, Seungsook. 2005. *Militarized Modernity and Gendered Citizenship in South Korea*. Durham, NC: Duke University Press.

Pak, Chaehyŏn. 2009. *Han'guk Kŭndae Pulgyo ŭi T'aja tŭl* [The others of modern Korean Buddhism]. Seoul: P'urŭn Yŏksa.

Pak, Puyŏng. 2008. "Sinbun ŭn chongdan sŭnim kwŏlli nŭn chehan" [Status as order monks, but rights are limited]. *Pulgyo Sinmun*, 5 July.

Pŏphyŏn. 2011. "Kun p'ogyo wa Pulgyo taehak, Pulgyo Ŏllon" [Military chaplaincy and Buddhist universities, Buddhist media]. *Pulgyo Focus*, 30 November. Accessed 14 November 2013. http://www.bulgyofocus.net/news/articleView.html?idxno=64429.

Sŏ, Hyŏnmuk. 2014. "Pulgyo chŏnt'ong yunghap: Yŏnsu taejunghwa ikkŭlgetta" [The synthesis of Buddhism and tradition: Will lead the popularization of training]. *Pulgyo Dotcom*, 4 March. Accessed 11 March 2014. http://www.bulkyo21.com/news/articleView. html?idxno=24246.

Van der Veer, Peter. 2012. "Market and Money: A Critique of Rational Choice Theory." *Social Compass* 59 (2): 183–192.

Woo, Jung-eun. 1991. *Race to the Swift: State and Finance in Korean Industrialization*. New York: Columbia University Press.

Yang, Fenggang. 2006. "The Red, Gray and Black Markets of Religion in China." *Sociological Quarterly* 47 (1): 93–122.

Yang, Kŭnyŏng, and Kim Tŏksu, ed. 1992. *Imjin Waeran kwa Pulgyo Ŭisŭnggun* [Imjin Japanese invasion and the Buddhist Militias]. Seoul: Kyŏngsŏwŏn.

Yang, Pyŏnggi. 1988. "Ch'ogi Han'guk Kunbu ŭi hyŏngsŏng kwa chŏngch'ihwa yangsang" [Formation of the early South Korean military establishment and its politicization]. *Kukche Munhwa Yŏn'gu* 5: 203–226.

Yang, Sŭngnok. 2014. "Sahoe Pongsa nŭn Kidokkyo ga, Silloedo ga Kat'ollik i 1 wi" [The first place in social service is taken by Protestant Christians, and the highest trust is enjoyed by Catholics]. *Tŭlsori Sinmun*, 14 February. Accessed 25 August 2014. http://www.deulsoritimes.co.kr/news/articleView.html?idxno=28034.

Yi, Kangsik. 2009. "Kun pŏpsa kyŏrhon si sŭngjŏk pakt'al" [Military chaplains are to be disrobed if they marry]. *Kŭmgang Sinmun*, 20 March.

Yifa. 2002. *The Origins of Buddhist Monastic Codes in China: An Annotated Translation and Study of the Chanyuan Qinggui*. Honolulu: University of Hawai'i Press.

Yoga Journal. 2012. "Yoga Journal Releases 2012 Yoga in America Market Study." 6 December. Accessed 10 March 2014. http://www.yogajournal.com/article/press-releases/yoga-journal-releases-2012-yoga-in-america-market-study/.

Yun, Yongbok. 2014. "Hyŏndae Han'guk Sahoe esŏ Yŏhowa Chŭng'in ŭi Wich'I" [The position of Jehovah's Witnesses in contemporary South Korean Society]. *Sinchonggyo Yŏn'gu* 30: 29–56.

Personal Interviews

Chi S.: A chaplain in his 50s, currently on active service.

Chŏn Ch.: A retired chaplain, colonel of the reserve, in his sixties; served in chaplaincy in 1982–2002.

Hŏ Ch.: 29, retired chaplain who served in 2010–2013, currently a PhD student at Dongguk University.

182 *Vladimir Tikhonov*

Kang K.: Infantry colonel in his fifties, ordained as a Chogye order monk in 1978.
Kim Ch.: A chaplain in his fifties, currently on active service.
Yŏm Ch.: An active-service chaplain in his twenties, a recent graduate of Dongguk University.

The interviews were carried out 17–19 July 2013 at the Buddhist Wŏn'gwangsa temple attached to the Ministry of Defence, and also Dongguk University (Hŏ Ch.) and the Buddhist P-sa temple in northern Seoul (Chŏn Ch.).

11 Re-Enchantment Restricted

Popular Buddhism and Politics in Vietnam Today

Aike P. Rots

Vietnam is a country of paradoxes, not least when it comes to religion.* According to some statistics, Vietnam is one of the least religious countries in the world, as more than 80 per cent of the population is not officially affiliated with any religious institution.[1] Other statistics, however, suggest that a similar percentage have "religious beliefs" (Nguyễn 2012: vii). Apparently, then, a large proportion of the population has some sort of "religious belief" without being listed as "religious". Likewise, it is difficult to establish how many adherents Buddhism has: according to official statistics, there are between ten and fifteen million Buddhists in Vietnam,[2] but the number of people who take part in Buddhist ritual practices and regularly worship Buddhas and/or bodhisattvas is probably much higher.[3] Although not backed by official statistics, recent academic literature suggests that Vietnamese society is highly religious indeed, more so today than in the recent past: religion in Vietnam is said to have been "thriving in recent years", and places of worship are "offering signs of fervent faith and unmistakable religious vitality" (Taylor 2007a: 2). Thus, Vietnamese society has been described as characterized by widespread "re-enchantment" (Taylor 2007b).

In fact, it may be argued that Vietnamese society has never been truly "disenchanted", and that, therefore, the term "*re*-enchantment" is not entirely apt. Rather than re-enchantment, then, perhaps we are witnessing the de-privatization and reinvention of practices previously conducted more privately or even secretly, and the public popularization of beliefs that were not shared widely before. But whatever the terminology, there is no denying the fact that Vietnamese society is characterized by a remarkable religious vitality and diversity, more visible today than, say, twenty or thirty years ago. This applies to officially recognized religious institutions as much as to unofficial and popular worship practices. It most certainly also applies to Buddhism, which remains one of the most visible and prominent religious traditions in the country, socially and economically as well as politically.

Despite optimistic reports of religious vitality and diversity, however, there is no complete freedom of religion in Vietnam. Individuals and institutions are free to engage in worship practices only within certain parameters; activities that are considered subversive (for whatever reason) by police or Party officials are not tolerated. Accordingly, international NGOs such as Human Rights Watch

184   *Aike P. Rots*

regularly report on the persecution and harassment of members of certain religious organizations in Vietnam, including, but not limited to, Buddhists. Indeed,
Human Rights Watch (2014) has suggested that the situation has deteriorated
significantly since 2013. Thus, the image of a "re-enchanted" society characterized by a "flourishing" religious diversity is one-sided at best: paradoxically, the
revitalization of religion in Vietnam has gone hand in hand with an increasing
repression of religion—some types of religion, at least.

In this chapter, I will discuss the recent popularization of Buddhism in Vietnam in the light of this paradox. Vietnamese Buddhism, I hold, is not simply a
"religious tradition" going back to ancient times, which has lingered until today;
rather, it is a set of practices, institutions, and ideological resources that have been
subject to continuous reinvention and adaptation, and which constitute an integral
part of Vietnamese modernity. Indeed, it may be argued that Buddhism played a
central part in Vietnam's modernization and the construction of the Vietnamese
nation-state. Of course, the terms "modernity" and "modernization" are somewhat diffuse and carry different meanings in different contexts. That said, in the
case of Vietnam, it is possible to distinguish two periods of widespread societal,
technological, economic, and cultural change, influenced by transnational flows
of knowledge and capital, which we may refer to as "modernization". The first
period lasted roughly from the 1920s until World War II. This period saw the
emergence of a range of new ideas and criticisms of existing practices and power
structures; an emerging nationalist intellectual elite (French- and/or Japanese-
educated); the growth of new social movements and ideologies, most notably
reform Buddhism and Marxism; the abandoning of Chinese characters as a strategy for the democratization of knowledge, and so on. Significantly, as different
scholars have pointed out, Buddhist actors were among the most influential social
activists and reformers in this period, actively rallying for social justice and education and against anything they considered a hindrance to "modernization" and
emancipation, including so-called superstitious practices within Buddhism itself
(McHale 2004; DeVido 2007).

Arguably, Vietnam's second period of modernization started with the *đổi
mới* reforms in 1986[4] and continues until today. This period is characterized
by economic liberalization, diversification, and increasing consumption; rapid
urbanization and corresponding social changes; and new types of transnational
connections, made possible by new mass media (the Internet, in particular), the
availability of global brands and popular culture, and easy contact with Vietnamese overseas. It is this second type of modernity that is discussed by Philip Taylor in relation to "re-enchantment" (2007a, 2007b), and it is this modernity with
which I engage in the present chapter. The chapter consists of two parts. I will
start by drawing a picture of a contemporary Vietnamese urban centre that has
undergone significant transformations in recent years, suggesting that religious
revitalization can go hand in hand with economic development and may even
be enforced by it. Buddhism, I show, constitutes an important part of contemporary Vietnamese cityscapes, and devotional practices are closely intertwined with
local politics. Following this example, I proceed to discuss the topic of the state

Buddhism and Politics in Vietnam Today 185

patronage of Buddhism more in general. Drawing on the arguments of Taylor and Soucy, I will show that (diaspora) Buddhist authors as well as state actors have framed "Zen" as an authentically Vietnamese tradition, thus trying to appropriate the symbolic capital of this globally successful concept.

In the second part of this chapter, I will focus on the most famous of these diaspora Vietnamese Buddhists: Thích Nhất Hạnh (born 1926). I will first provide some historical context, briefly discussing the ambiguous position of Buddhism in post-1954 Vietnam. As this overview makes clear, Thích Nhất Hạnh may well have reinvented certain ideas and practices in order to make them more appealing to Western audiences, but there is nonetheless clear evidence of continuity with earlier Vietnamese modern Buddhist ideology. I will then move on to examine the tumultuous series of events following Thích Nhất Hạnh's 2005 visit to Vietnam, in relation to the twin topics of religious revival and repression. As this case shows, political patronage can easily give way to polarization and persecution. In theory, Vietnam has a legally guaranteed freedom of religion and a strict separation of religion and state. In reality, however, state attitudes towards religion are ambiguous, and religion and politics are closely intertwined.

A Modern City

With a population of approximately one million, Da Nang (Đà Nẵng) is the largest city of central Vietnam and its main economic centre. In recent years, the cityscape has changed almost beyond recognition: local authorities have invested heavily in ambitious construction projects, and impressive skyscrapers, suspension bridges, and other modern architectural achievements now line the boulevards of this formerly provincial port city. Although the construction boom appears to have come to a temporary halt—in 2013, real estate prices dropped significantly, leaving many building projects unfinished (*Thanh Niên News* 2013)—foreign investors and tourists alike are gradually finding their way to the city. For the time being, Da Nang remains less congested and polluted than Hanoi and Ho Chi Minh City, Vietnam's two main urban centres, located in the country's far north and south, respectively. Its geographical location, moreover, is enviable: located on the Hàn River and flanked by high mountains in the west and the South China Sea in the east, it not only has good transport connections but also houses an increasing number of high-end beach resorts.

According to classical theories of modernization and corresponding secularization narratives, urbanization and economic diversification generally lead to widespread disenchantment and, consequently, the gradual disappearance of religion from the public sphere.[5] In Da Nang, however, the opposite is the case. This emerging modern metropolis is home to various religious communities and places of worship, many of which are thriving. As in other parts of Vietnam, *lên đồng* (spirit medium rituals) and similar practices are conducted increasingly frequently and publicly, reflecting their recent reclassification in Vietnamese academic and public discourse from the negative "superstition" (*mê tín*)[6] to the positive "tradition" (*truyền thống*), and their corresponding popularization nationwide.[7]

186   *Aike P. Rots*

Likewise, various local and translocal festivals, such as those associated with the worship of the whale deity Cá Ông,[8] are now conducted out in the open, attracting followers from coastal towns in neighbouring provinces as well as overseas Vietnamese. In addition, Da Nang continues to be home to sizeable Catholic and Cao Đài communities. Not surprisingly, then, places of worship constitute an integral part of the changing cityscape, as temples (*đền* or *miếu*), pagodas (*chùa*),[9] community worship halls (*đình*), family shrines (*nhà thờ tộc*), whale god shrines (*lăng Cá Ông*), and Christian churches are renovated and, in several cases, built anew throughout the city and surrounding suburban areas.[10] Thus, the religious landscape of Da Nang is dynamic and diverse; although not all worship practices are classified as "religion" (*tôn giáo*) by the actors involved, ritual life throughout the city confirms the impression of a society characterized by widespread re-enchantment and religious revival.

Buddhism is no exception to this rule. Indeed, Buddhist pagodas constitute a highly visible part of today's cityscape. Arguably the most impressive of Da Nang's various Buddhist pagodas is the newly built Chùa Linh Ứng, located on the rugged Sơn Trà Peninsula, several kilometres north of the city's main beach. Construction of this pagoda commenced in 2004. It was inaugurated on 30 July 2010: a festive event attracting large numbers of people (monks, nuns, and lay Buddhist practitioners as well as local government officials and crowds of interested Danangians, many of whom would probably not define themselves as "Buddhists"), where so-called religious elements such as sutra recitations and ritual offerings mingled with apparently "secular" elements such as dance performances. The inaugural festival thus confirmed the impression that in Vietnam the boundaries between "the sacred" and "the secular" are often blurred, if existent at all—even though Vietnam is a "communist" state with a strictly secular state apparatus, at least in theory. In Vietnam, as elsewhere in the world, performing arts, tourism, and consumerism are as much part of "religion" as ritual practices, devotion, and beliefs in transcendental beings. So, for that matter, is politics. "Secular" though they may officially be—and, in any case, not religiously affiliated—politicians and other state actors in Vietnam often associate themselves with pagodas, temples, and popular rituals, thus taking part in and sanctioning contemporary sacralization processes (as pointed out by Salemink 2009). The prominent presence of local Party officials at the inauguration ceremony of Chùa Linh Ứng is illustrative of the close intertwinement of religious institutions and state actors in post-*đổi mới* Vietnam, where patronage of popular religious institutions by local politicians serves to provide legitimacy to both.[11]

The most striking feature of Chùa Linh Ứng—indeed, one of the most striking features of Da Nang's contemporary cityscape—is its gigantic white statue of the bodhisattva Quan Âm (or Quán Thế Âm; C. Guanyin). With a height of sixty-seven metres, the statue is visible from many kilometres away. The pagoda itself is impressive, too, including a large worship hall, a lecture hall, offices, a Buddhist library, a garden, and a series of large marble statues of the eighteen arhats. It is said that a Buddhist pagoda was first built at this location during the reign of Emperor Minh Mạng (1791–1841; reign 1820–1841), when local fishermen

Buddhism and Politics in Vietnam Today 187

found a Buddha statue at the nearby beach—hence its name, Bãi Bụt ("Buddha Beach")—but it was later destroyed. Recent though the current pagoda is, it is widely regarded as a sacred place, from where Quan Âm oversees and guards the city; despite its young age, it is already surrounded by various myths and legends. For instance, according to local mythology, halos of light and double rainbows have appeared several times in the sky around the statue. Quan Âm is said to have contributed to the city's recent prosperity and to the construction of the brand-new Da Nang Cancer Hospital, and believed to have protected the people from devastating typhoons and floods (Thạch 2014). Not surprisingly, then, the pagoda today attracts a steady flow of visitors, worshippers from Da Nang, as well as tourists from elsewhere. It gets particularly crowded on Buddhist holidays and during the first days of the Vietnamese New Year. In sum, modernization does not necessarily imply secularization: in Vietnam, it has gone hand in hand with religious revival, sacralization, and an increasing intertwinement of politics and religion.

Re-Enchantment, Buddhism, and "Zen"

The success of Chùa Linh Ứng is illustrative of the so-called re-enchantment of Vietnamese society, as described by Philip Taylor and others (Taylor 2007b). Although religion never completely disappeared from Vietnamese public life, in the past two decades or so, religious institutions have seen a remarkable survival, as have popular devotional practices not directly associated with institutionalized religion (e.g. *lên đồng*-type practices). This is partly due to changing attitudes towards religious practices on the part of the authorities. The active participation of leading local politicians in the inauguration ceremony of Chùa Linh Ứng is by no means unique: in recent years, state actors have promoted and appropriated religion in various ways. As Alexander Soucy has pointed out, "the state has adopted a new stance towards religion. While it is still careful not to let religious groups engage in activities that could be potentially threatening, the state has largely allowed people to resume their traditional religious practices. It even makes use of some aspects of religion for fostering nationalism and building a national narrative that provides legitimacy" (Soucy 2012: 8; cf. Salemink 2008). Hence, Philip Taylor (2007a: 2) argues that "the endorsement of religious activities by Vietnam's religious leaders contravenes the notion that communist states are opposed to religion on ideological or institutional grounds". Interestingly, the apparent resurgence of religion in Vietnam since the 1990s corresponds to similar developments in China, Russia, and European post-communist states such as Poland, which are often mentioned by critics of the classical secularization thesis as examples of countries where economic progress goes hand in hand with an increase in religious activity.[12]

Not surprisingly, these changing attitudes towards religion have had significant impact on Vietnamese Buddhism. As indicated above, they have facilitated the increasing prominence of Buddhist organizations, symbols, and practices in public space, as exemplified by the construction of the colossal statue of Quan Âm in one of the country's largest cities. Significantly, it has also made possible

188   Aike P. Rots

increasing contacts between Vietnam-based Buddhist organizations and individuals, overseas Vietnamese, and non-Vietnamese Buddhists. This has led not only to the resurgence of Buddhist practices, but also to their transformation. As Philip Taylor points out,

> The flow of Buddhist practitioners, texts and ideas throughout Vietnam and across national boundaries sets the context for another recent development in Buddhism in Vietnam, the increasing prominence given in northern Vietnam to Zen (*Thiền*) as the quintessential Vietnamese Buddhist tradition. . . . Southern Vietnam's intense transnational connections have enabled the repatriation and the circulation to elsewhere in Vietnam of the markedly meditative form of Buddhism developed by Vietnamese émigré monks based in the United States and France. . . . Ironically, this recently imported purified form of Buddhism has come to be taken as a national tradition, a view which receives endorsement from the state, motivated, as are many lay Buddhists, to attach itself to an authentic national tradition that is not sullied by the taint of superstition. . . . Today, the Communist Party seeks to boost its legitimacy by endorsing Zen a version of Buddhism promoted by a transnational movement, as an authentic national tradition.
>
> (Taylor 2007a: 27–28; cf. Soucy 2007)

Introductory texts on Vietnamese Buddhism often claim that Zen (or Chan) is historically the most important Buddhist school in the country. As Soucy summarizes, "since at least the early twentieth century, Zen has been taken by academics and practitioners as the core of Vietnamese Buddhism. . . . This primacy placed on Zen has been assumed by Buddhists and academics alike in colonial and communist Vietnam because it fits the rhetorical requirements of the nationalist elite who continue to disparage 'folk' beliefs and practices" (2007: 343–344). By extension, some diaspora Vietnamese Buddhist leaders have even asserted that Zen represents the Vietnamese "national character" (Thich Thien-An 1975: 27, quoted in Soucy 2007: 345). It is somewhat ironic that they use the Japanese instead of the Vietnamese term (i.e. "Zen" instead of *Thiền*) when asserting that Zen is typically Vietnamese, but it is not entirely surprising, for their arguments mirror the rhetoric used by modern Japanese "Zen" ideologists such as D.T. Suzuki, who promoted an idealized version of Zen for nationalist purposes (e.g. Suzuki 1959; cf. Sharf 1993). However, it is questionable whether Zen Buddhist institutions and ideologies have had such a significant impact on Vietnamese history as commonly assumed: the number of Zen lineages and monastic institutions present in Vietnam may have been much smaller than commonly believed, and Vietnam's main "Transmission of the Lamp" text—which is supposed to prove the unbroken lineage of Zen masters in Vietnam, going back to the introduction of Mahāyāna Buddhism in the sixth century—is probably a fourteenth-century "invented history", rather than an accurate description of Zen's continuous historical presence in the country (Nguyen 1997).

Buddhism and Politics in Vietnam Today   189

In any case, there has long been a discrepancy between official, elite views of Buddhism in Vietnam—which typically identify Vietnamese Buddhism with Zen/*Thiền*, dismissing the historical importance of the Pure Land tradition and the association of pagodas with spirit worship and mediumship—and devotional Buddhism, as it was (and is) practised by the majority of the people (Soucy 2007: 356–362, 2012: 31–35). This discrepancy between elite views of Buddhism and devotional practices "on the ground" is not particularly recent: it has been present throughout modern history and has periodically caused tension. In particular, members of the nationalist revival movement that tried to reform and "modernize" Vietnamese Buddhism between the 1920s and 1950s—inspired by similar developments elsewhere in Asia, in particular China[13]—actively rallied against popular devotion, arguing that Buddhism should be "purified from superstition" in order for it to serve its role in modernizing and liberating the nation, for example by means of education (McHale 2004: 162–163; DeVido 2007: 271). In recent years, however, it has taken on a new global dimension, as Vietnamese Buddhist practices and self-understandings—especially in urban centres—are increasingly influenced by the teachings of overseas Buddhist leaders, who have reinvented their tradition in accordance with the needs and expectations of European and North American lay practitioners, for example by focusing on personal spiritual development and meditation techniques rather than, say, ritual offerings and communal prayers. As a result of this hybridization, Vietnamese monks and lay Buddhists have recently started to engage in meditation activities and to practise "mindfulness", thus transforming domestic Buddhist traditions (cf. Soucy 2007: 353–356).

Thích Nhất Hạnh: Historical Background

Undoubtedly the best known of these overseas Vietnamese Buddhist leaders is Thích Nhất Hạnh. Like others before him, he explicitly places himself in the Zen tradition; in his English- and French-language writings, he uses the Japanese instead of the Vietnamese term, presumably because of its international appeal (e.g. Thích Nhất Hạnh 1974). He received his education and was ordained as a Buddhist monk in the central city of Hue (Huế), a few hours north of Da Nang, the former imperial capital and one of the main centres of Buddhism in the country. In the 1950s, he became involved with the General Association of Vietnamese Buddhists (Tổng hội Phật giáo Việt Nam), the predecessor of the Unified Buddhist Church of Vietnam (Giáo hội Phật giáo Việt Nam Thống nhất, usually abbreviated as UBCV, also referred to as Unified Buddhist Sangha of Vietnam), which was established in Saigon in 1964. Influenced by the Buddhist modernist revival movement that had started in the 1920s (DeVido 2007), as a young monk Hạnh already subscribed to the modernist notion that Buddhism should be active "in this world", and strive for social, political, and educational reform. In 1957, he founded a new monastic "community of resistance" in the Central Highlands and taught at pagodas in Saigon (Chapman 2007: 300). His political activism,

190   *Aike P. Rots*

however, brought him into conflict with the authorities. In 1961, he went to the United States, where he studied comparative religion at Princeton University.

It was a period of high tension. Under the regime of Ngô Đình Diệm (1901–1963), who was president of South Vietnam from 1955 until the coup of 1963, several anti-Buddhist policies were implemented. In 1963, Buddhists were prohibited from displaying the Buddhist flag on Vesak, the birthday of the Buddha, one of the main Buddhist holidays. During a protest against this ban in the city of Hue in May 1963, nine people were killed by Diệm's security forces. One month later, Buddhist protesters were attacked with chemicals, and dozens were injured. These events led to further protests against the regime, including the self-immolation of the monk Thích Quảng Đức (1897–1963) in Saigon, pictures of which were published in newspapers worldwide. This contributed significantly to the US-backed coup and subsequent assassination of Diệm in November 1963.

Following the turmoil, Hạnh returned to Vietnam, where he participated in the establishment of the Unified Buddhist Church of Vietnam (UBCV).[14] As the war between North and South Vietnam escalated and American military involvement increased, he actively urged political leaders to take part in peace negotiations, thus giving shape to his ideal of "engaged Buddhism". In 1966, he founded a new monastic order, the Order of Interbeing, which "would seek to end war and work for social justice without taking sides" (Chapman 2007: 302). He subsequently embarked on a journey to Europe and the United States, where he presented a peace proposal. His suggestions were condemned by the South Vietnamese government, which accused him of being a communist, as well as the North Vietnamese government, which claimed that he was pro-American. As a result, it was no longer safe for him to return to Vietnam, and he was de facto exiled (Chapman 2007: 304).

After the annexation of the south and the national reunification in 1975, groups of monks continued to be politically active in Vietnam. The communist authorities soon restricted these activities, however, and most leaders of the UBCV were arrested. In 1981, the Vietnam Buddhist Sangha (Giáo hội Phật giáo Việt Nam, abbreviated as VBS) was established, which has since functioned as the sole government-recognized Buddhist umbrella organization. The UBCV, meanwhile, has remained active as the main diaspora Vietnamese Buddhist organization, and is known for its anti-communist orientation. Its current patriarch, Thích Quảng Độ (born 1928), who has long been one of the most vocal pro-democracy activists in Vietnam, has spent several periods in prison and under house arrest (Chapman 2007: 310–312; Nguyễn 2013). Other monks and laypeople associated with the UBCV continue to be subject to government persecution as well, as reported by human rights NGOs and by the organization's overseas branches in the United States and France, which seek to achieve international recognition for their plight.[15] The regular reports of arrests and imprisonment of monks, and of the harassment and intimidation of laypeople by police officers, do appear to be at odds with the image of a society in which Buddhist pagodas are flourishing. It most certainly raises questions regarding Vietnam's supposed "freedom of religion", on which the government prides itself.

Buddhism and Politics in Vietnam Today 191

It should be pointed out, however, that the UBCV is by no means united: there are significant differences in opinion when it comes to questions of a political nature, such as the choice between reconciliation or confrontation with the current government, and power struggles are not uncommon (Nguyễn 2013). Significantly, although he was initially involved with the organization, Thích Nhất Hạnh left the UBCV long ago; relations between the two are complicated (see King 1996). Soon after his exile, in 1969, Hạnh established his own organization, confusingly called the Unified Buddhist Church (Église Bouddhique Unifiée). The headquarters of this organization are at Plum Village monastery, the centre of the international Order of Interbeing, located in the Dordogne region in France. Like the UBCV, Thích Nhất Hạnh's Unified Buddhist Church is not recognized by the Vietnamese government. Unlike the former, however, it has a strongly international orientation, catering primarily to the needs of European and North American Buddhists, as well as non-Buddhists interested in meditation practices, spirituality, and so on. In order to do so, it has adopted a rather innovative approach to Buddhist ritual and belief. Thus, Thích Nhất Hạnh's movement arguably constitutes a more profound discontinuity with traditional Vietnamese Buddhist practices and institutional structures than the UBCV, which, despite being critical of the communist regime, remains highly Vietnamese—ethnically, culturally, and linguistically.[16] As Nguyen and Barber state bluntly,

> Thích Nhất Hạnh, though he was never known as a Ch'an master in Vietnam, has become a famous master in the West. He oversees several retreat centers in America and Europe where his disciples engage in the practice of a "New Age"-style Zen and rituals created by him that do not have any affinity with or any foundation in traditional Vietnamese Buddhist practices.
>
> (Nguyen and Barber 1998: 131)

Nguyen and Barber certainly have a point. Thích Nhất Hạnh is an influential religious innovator, who has actively adapted and transformed Buddhist ideas and practices in order to make them more suitable for Western religious markets. He has succeeded admirably: he is undoubtedly one of the best-known and most popular Buddhist leaders in the world today, and his notion of "mindfulness" has spread far beyond the limits of religion proper, to the point that it has become a buzzword used regularly in lifestyle magazines and management courses. However, one may question the extent to which such notions and practices correspond to the historical reality of Buddhism as a lived religion in Vietnam, which was (and is) characterized primarily by devotional practices (ritual offerings, sutra recitals, etc.) rather than, say, meditation practices and the pursuit of individual "mindfulness".

Nevertheless, the statement that Thích Nhất Hạnh's ideas "do not have any affinity with or any foundation in traditional Vietnamese Buddhist practices" is arguably too simplistic. In particular, his notion of "engaged Buddhism"—which is said to have been coined by himself (Queen 1996: 2)—reflects a longer tradition of Buddhist social and political activism, in Vietnam and elsewhere in

192   *Aike P. Rots*

Asia. As DeVido (2007, 2009) points out, there is a continuity between, first, the various Asian Buddhist modernist reform movements that emerged in the late nineteenth and early twentieth centuries; second, the Buddhist-nationalist revival movement that was active in Vietnam during the late colonial period; third, the political activism of Buddhist monks during the 1960s and 1970s; and, fourth, Thích Nhất Hạnh's teachings on "engaged Buddhism", which have exercised considerable influence on contemporary understandings of Buddhism in the West. In particular, she argues, his notion of "engaged Buddhism" draws on the reformist ideology of the Chinese Buddhist monk Taixu (1890–1947) and its subsequent Vietnamese adaptations, even though the terminology was probably derived from the work of the French philosopher Jean-Paul Sartre (1905–1980) (DeVido 2009: 436–437). Innovative though this transnational Buddhist reform movement was, it did represent a genuine attempt to reconcile modernity with Asian tradition and emerging notions of nationhood, and therefore cannot be referred to as simply an attempt to "Westernize" Buddhism. Thus, it may be argued that Thích Nhất Hạnh's teachings on "engaged Buddhism" are firmly grounded in East Asian traditions of Buddhist socio-political involvement, even though they are phrased and presented in such a way that they appeal to contemporary non-Asian audiences.[17]

Furthermore, the fact that Thích Nhất Hạnh's "Mindfulness Buddhism" has taken shape mainly in France and the United States, where his main monastic centres are located, does not necessarily mean it is incompatible with religious practices in Asia. In fact, in recent years Hạnh and his followers have been actively trying to spread his teaching in Asia: they have established a branch of Plum Village in Thailand, and he has embarked on teaching tours to various Asian countries, including Japan (1995), China (1999 and 2001) and Malaysia (2010).[18] Most importantly, his works have also gained significant popularity in his country of origin, in particular in the urban centres. As Philip Taylor writes, "for many years, these texts have filtered back informally to Vietnam, proving immensely popular there. Significantly, this has been at a time when Vietnam has been entering into the kinds of economic and cultural relations that have proved fertile ground in places beyond his homeland for Thích Nhất Hạnh's teachings" (2007a: 26). These teachings appeal not only to Buddhist laypeople, but also to young, well-educated members of the emerging urban middle classes, many of whom are not religiously affiliated. In other words, the social transformations which Vietnam has undergone in recent years—rapid urbanization, economic diversification, an increasing openness to foreign cultural products, the impact of consumer capitalism, and so on—may well have contributed to the great success of his teachings there, several decades after his departure. This, in turn, has contributed to the transformation of Vietnamese Buddhist self-definitions and practices, constituting an interesting example of what anthropologists and scholars of religion have called "the pizza effect": the adaptation and reinterpretation of a particular cultural practice in a different context, which in turn leads to a transformation of that practice in its place of origin (see, for instance,

Buddhism and Politics in Vietnam Today 193

Borup 2004). Thus, when Thích Nhất Hạnh finally returned to his native country in 2005, he was greeted by thousands of enthusiastic followers, who perceived him as one of Vietnam's greatest living Buddhist masters—notwithstanding the discontinuities between his ideas and more traditional Buddhist practices, or the critique that his version of Buddhism is merely a "Western" innovation (Nguyen and Barber 1998).

The Return of Thích Nhất Hạnh: Re-Enchantment Restricted

Nearly forty years since the beginning of his exile, in 2005, Thích Nhất Hạnh went back to Vietnam for a three-month tour of the country. During this period, he was accompanied by one hundred ordained monks and nuns, as well as several hundred lay followers of various nationalities. The visit was preceded by lengthy negotiations, significant diplomatic challenges, and much red tape for the monks, nuns, and laypeople accompanying him (Chapman 2007: 312–315). Eventually, however, the visit was approved, and on 12 January Hạnh landed in Hanoi. Reportedly, a "large crowd had gathered to greet his arrival. The swell of people that rushed forward to him on his exit from customs was described as more befitting a rock star than a monk" (Chapman 2007: 315). He subsequently visited several well-known pagodas in the capital city, where he gave *dharma* talks. According to John Chapman, these "were extremely well attended and at each of them the audience was engrossed in the message and manner of its presentation" (Chapman 2007: 315). Although these descriptions appear overtly hagiographic, it is probably true that Thích Nhất Hạnh's lectures were well attended and made an impression, if only among Buddhist clergy and laypeople in the cities he visited. In addition to Hanoi, he went to Hue and Ho Chi Minh City, where he gave talks in pagodas and at Buddhist institutes.

Significantly, however, he addressed not only Buddhists but also government members. During a talk at the Hồ Chí Minh National Political Institute, he reportedly stated that Buddhism and Marxism are compatible, and that "they can grow together and help one another" (Chapman 2007: 319). He even met the then-prime minister, Phan Văn Khải. Thus, his visit to Vietnam was not merely an apolitical "religious" event: it was highly politicized, providing legitimacy to the Vietnamese authorities, who used it to substantiate their claim that Vietnam has freedom of religion. As Chapman summarizes:

> The Vietnamese Government's main reason for inviting Thích Nhất Hạnh was probably to display to the international community the existence of freedom of religious belief in Vietnam, hoping thereby to facilitate its integration into the world economic system, and thus increase economic growth and strengthen its legitimacy. Another of its basic aims is to create a Vietnamese culture "imbued with national identity" which has increasingly involved official endorsement of once-criticized religious identifications. . . . There have, however, been conflicting interpretations of the reasons for this

194   *Aike P. Rots*

development: some commentators regarded it cynically as being only a short-term political manipulation; others saw it as being a positive indication that the Vietnamese government now accepts that allowing more freedom for religion could be helpful in encouraging economic development, inculcating more ethical behaviour and achieving political stability.

(Chapman 2007: 298)

Whatever the motivations, soon after Thích Nhất Hạnh's visit to Vietnam, its prime minister paid an official visit to the United States, where he met President George W. Bush—the first such visit since the end of the war between the two countries. The United States subsequently removed Vietnam from a list of countries characterized by severe violations of religious freedom. Partly as a result of this decision, in 2007, Vietnam was finally allowed to join the World Trade Organization, which its government had aspired to for many years (Chapman 2007: 331–332).[19]

It would be wrong to conclude, however, that the Vietnamese authorities were the only actors benefitting from Thích Nhất Hạnh's visit. It also provided legitimacy to his own movement, as well as positive publicity both in Vietnam and abroad. For one, his followers could now refute the arguments made by critics that his "mindfulness Buddhism" is merely an innovation well suited to the Western spiritual market, said to be "not authentically Vietnamese". The popularity of his teachings in his homeland at least suggested otherwise. Significantly, one of the most noteworthy results of Hạnh's visit was the establishment of a Buddhist monastery modelled after Plum Village, Bát Nhã (Prajna) monastery in Lâm Đồng province (Central Highlands), where several hundred Vietnamese monks and nuns settled. In addition, several of his books were translated into Vietnamese, while CDs with *dharma* talks were made "widely available" (Chapman 2007: 330).

Likewise, the visit could be seen as a powerful example of the possibility of reconciliation and forgiveness, which are central to Thích Nhất Hạnh's ethics. Thus, it provided him with significant symbolic capital. It came at a price, however. Although one of Hạnh's stated objectives was to contribute to establishing a relationship between Vietnam's two rival Buddhist associations, the UBCV and the VBS, his visit had the opposite effect. He was condemned by senior UBCV members, one of whom was quoted as saying, "He gives a precious propaganda bonus to the Vietnamese regime. But he does nothing for the cause of religious freedom and human rights in Vietnam" (quoted in Chapman 2007: 326). Although Thích Nhất Hạnh did try to arrange a meeting with UBCV leaders (including Thích Quảng Độ), who were under house arrest at the time, they refused to meet him (Johnson 2007). As a result, relations between Hạnh and the UBCV deteriorated significantly.

Nevertheless, in 2007 Thích Nhất Hạnh paid a second ten-week visit to Vietnam, which again met with strong disapproval by senior UBCV members (Johnson 2007). One reason for this visit was the performance of several three-day long commemoration ceremonies for Vietnam's war dead. In addition, Hạnh visited

Buddhism and Politics in Vietnam Today 195

and gave lectures at Bát Nhã monastery, which, according to accounts of Plum Village members, had been growing "rapidly, with retreats and monthly mindfulness days attracting thousands of people, especially the young" (Plum Village 2014). In contrast to the previous visit, however, this time Hạnh was more outspoken in his criticism of the present-day government. This may have been triggered by government interference with the commemoration ceremonies: although the initial plan had been to commemorate all those who died during the Vietnamese-American war, senior state officials objected. As one of them argued, "the spirit of the Vietnamese people doesn't agree with the idea of praying for foreign imperialists coming to kill millions of Vietnamese" (Johnson 2007). As a result, the name of the ceremony was changed, and South Vietnamese or American soldiers were no longer included—not officially, at least. Possibly in response to this interference, Thích Nhất Hạnh wrote a ten-point proposal in which he criticized government involvement with religious affairs. This proposal was presented to the president during Hạnh's official visit. It stated: "Please separate religion from politics and politics from religious affairs. Please stop all surveillance by the government on religious activities, disband the Government Department for Religious Affairs but most of all disband the Religious Police. All religious associations should be able to operate freely in accordance with laws and regulations" (quoted in Thayer 2014: 144). Importantly, the proposal was not kept internal: in January 2008, Hạnh made its contents public (Plum Village 2014). In addition, in sharp contrast to earlier statements concerning the compatibility of Buddhism and Communism, "the annual journal of Plum Village proposed that the government abandon Communism, take the word Communist out of the name of the ruling political party and remove 'Socialist' from the country's official name, Socialist Republic of Vietnam" (Ruwitch 2009). Perhaps not surprisingly, these statements contributed to the deterioration of relations between the Vietnamese government and the Plum Village movement.

In his proposal, Hạnh was calling for a more secular state apparatus, and for freedom of religion not only in theory but also in practice. These demands may sound reasonable to people living in more-or-less-secular democracies, but they are quite radical indeed in a country such as Vietnam, where religious organizations can prosper as long as they maintain good relations with local authorities, and where political patronage of certain religious actors and places of worship goes hand in hand with the oppression of others. Not surprisingly, then, Hạnh's proposal caused irritation among government officials, who may have felt that he had crossed a line—after all, by making such explicitly political demands, Hạnh violated the unwritten agreement that he steer clear of politics. The irony is, of course, that calling for the separation of religion and politics is a political act in itself. Hạnh's choice to make such demands meant that he no longer stuck to his assigned role as a "religious" leader, who was expected to cooperate with the state and legitimize its policies, not criticize them.

Nevertheless, in May 2008, Thích Nhất Hạnh visited Vietnam one more time, as he had been invited to give a keynote lecture at the United Nations Day of Vesak Celebrations in Hanoi, a large international and transdenominational Buddhist

196 *Aike P. Rots*

event co-organized by the Vietnam Buddhist Sangha. The fact that such a large-scale Buddhist event can take place in Vietnam today confirms the impression of a country with a flourishing Buddhist community, active not only in private religious institutions but also, increasingly, in the public realm.[20] Sadly, however, Thích Nhất Hạnh's 2008 visit to Vietnam may well have been his last. According to Plum Village accounts, around this time

> Government policy turned against Bat Nha monastery and, over a period of 16 months, they used police harassment, slandering, propaganda and diktats to undermine the monastery's activities. They made it impossible for monks, nuns and retreatants to come and go freely, or for the monastery to host days of mindfulness and retreats. . . . In June 2009, the government cut off water, electricity and phone lines. Finally, the government sent in a series of paid mobs to attack the monks and nuns, arrest a number and forcibly evict the rest. The monks and nuns took temporary refuge in a nearby temple, but government repression continued. Within days, hundreds of leading intellectuals, jurists, policy makers and senior Communist Party members signed a national petition begging the government not to repress but to support the young generation and their interest in mindfulness. The US Ambassador to Vietnam made a strong public statement against the government's actions, the European Parliament passed a Resolution upholding the Bat Nha monks' and nuns' right to religious freedom, and the United Nations Special Rapporteur for Religious Freedom made an official complaint. Despite all this, government repression continued until finally, in December 2009, all the Bat Nha monks and nuns were forcibly dispersed.
>
> (Plum Village 2014)

The Vietnamese government denied any involvement in these events, stating that the violence was brought about by sectarian rivalry (McCurry 2009). Indeed, it is quite possible that local rivalries played a part in the conflict, and that "the Bat Nha Monastery narrative is much more complex than simply an 'authoritarian government cracks down on the faithful' story" (Ruwitch 2009); there may have been multiple actors involved, local as well as national. There are other examples of Buddhist organizations in different parts of the country, which have met with violence because they failed to understand local sensibilities and establish connections with the surrounding community (Soucy, personal communication). Nevertheless, considering the length and scale of the intimidation, some sort of government involvement is highly likely. Even if they did not instigate the violence, the authorities did nothing to prevent it, allowing mobs to attack Buddhist practitioners who were not given any police protection. Practically overnight, Thích Nhất Hạnh had become persona non grata once again, monks and nuns associated with his movement suffered from oppression, and his publications and talks could no longer be distributed freely. Illustratively, in 2009 and 2010, none of his recently translated books were available at the state-owned Fahasa bookstores; they were still sold semi-illegally by street vendors, though, which indicates that there was still a market for them.

Soon after the events, international Plum Village members made attempts to draw attention to the plight of the monks and nuns at Bát Nhã monastery. Likewise, several human rights organizations criticized the Vietnamese government and called for international action, but to little avail. In recent years, the United States Commission on International Religious Freedom (USCIRF) has repeatedly stated that Vietnam is one of the world's violators of religious freedom and has argued that it should be categorized as a "country of particular concern" by the United States government once again. Thus far, it has not succeeded—after all, Vietnam and the United States currently have strong economic and military ties, and the United States appears to consider it a strategic partner in a region dominated by China. Nevertheless, the USCIRF regularly reports on human rights violations in Vietnam, suggesting that freedom of religion has in fact deteriorated markedly in recent years.[21] Meanwhile, Bát Nhã monastery continues to be empty, and many of its monks and nuns now live as refugees at the Plum Village centre in Thailand (Plum Village 2013).

Conclusion

Religion plays an important role in contemporary Vietnamese society and politics. Temple festivals, family rituals, spirit communication practices, and other devotional practices are omnipresent. Previously designated as "superstition" and conducted mostly underground, many of these practices now take place in public; reclassified as "cultural tradition", several of them have come to be sanctioned and appropriated by (local) political actors. Likewise, institutionalized religions appear to be growing, in terms of unofficial attendance if not in official membership rates. Buddhism, in particular, has been reinstated as a religious tradition intimately connected with the nation-state, and politicians have been quick to patronize pagodas, despite the fact that they are Communist Party members and therefore not registered as "Buddhist" (in general, Party members cannot have a religion, at least not officially). As suggested by the example of Chùa Linh Ứng, however, the patronage of a popular pagoda can be an effective tool to strengthen one's political capital. It is no coincidence that the local Party leader who played a prominent role in the pagoda's inauguration ceremony was Nguyễn Bá Thanh (1953–2015), a controversial yet highly popular Danangian politician partly responsible for the city's rapid growth and modernization, whose recent death was mourned by many in central Vietnam. Thus, although the Party and state apparatus are secular in theory, in reality Buddhism is closely intertwined with the state.

However, as Soucy has pointed out, the state has endorsed one particular expression of Buddhism, at the expense of others. According to him, the Buddhist Revival of the 1920s and 1930s led to the formation of "two Buddhisms": an elite Buddhism, which conceives of Buddhism as a "rational" tradition in line with modernity and which condemns so-called superstitious elements, and a popular, devotional Buddhism associated with Pure Land beliefs and the worship of local deities (Soucy 2012: 31–35, 38–41). State actors have tended to patronize and

198   *Aike P. Rots*

emphasize the former. It is this kind of sanitized, "modern" Buddhism that is represented by the official Buddhist umbrella organization, the Buddhist Sangha of Vietnam, and by Hanoi's most powerful Buddhist institution, Chùa Quán Sứ (Soucy 2012: 42–51). According to the official interpretation, "Zen" constitutes the authentic Vietnamese Buddhist tradition, whereas "Pure Land" devotional practices are seen as distorted and filled with "superstitious" elements. Considering the discursive association between "Zen" and the Vietnamese nation in modern times (Soucy 2007: 342–345), and the international proliferation of "Zen master" Thích Nhất Hạnh's ideas in recent years, in particular his increasingly popular notion of "mindfulness", it should come as no great surprise that the government decided to allow him to return to Vietnam in 2005 and 2007, give lectures and conduct ceremonies at prominent pagodas, and meet with high-profile politicians. After all, he had become one of modern Vietnam's most successful export products, so the association with him could provide the government with significant legitimacy, domestically as well as internationally. A product of globalization, as well as a representative of "traditional" Vietnamese values, Thích Nhất Hạnh was fast becoming a core symbol of Vietnam's newly devised modernity, along with free-market capitalism, open borders, and mass tourism.

Indeed, this is what happened during the 2005 visit, which was arguably beneficial to both parties, even though it led to the deterioration of relations between the Plum Village movement and the UBCV. However, in 2007 Hạnh made a strategic mistake: by publicly arguing for the separation of religion and politics in Vietnam (a secularist demand, in fact), he implied that currently there is no such separation, thus exposing the myth that Vietnam is a secular state. Furthermore, he suggested that the country has no real freedom of religion—a highly problematic statement, considering the fact that one of the main reasons the government had allowed him to return to Vietnam and establish his own monastic communities there was to show and convince the world (or, more precisely, the United States) that Vietnam *did* have religious freedom. By making these subversive statements—and, more importantly, by making them public—Hạnh entered the realm of politics, if only discursively. Thus, he violated his own principle that religion and politics should be strictly separated;[22] moreover, he probably alienated powerful members of Vietnam's ruling oligarchy, who may have considered him a potential ally previously but who could no longer support him now. In the meantime, however, Hạnh had gained considerable popularity among urban Vietnamese. The combination of these things must have led to the government perceiving him as a potential threat and therefore changing their policy towards him, which culminated in the oppression and forced exile of the Bát Nhã monks and nuns.[23]

In sum, as any visitor to the country can confirm, Vietnam's economic and social modernization has gone hand in hand with, to use Taylor's terminology, a process of "re-enchantment"—or, at least, a revitalization and deprivatization of ritual and devotional practices. Although the state is officially communist and secular, ritual practices are increasingly prominent in public life, and religious institutions and festivals are closely intertwined with (local) politics. This applies

Buddhism and Politics in Vietnam Today 199

to Buddhist institutions as much as to non-Buddhist temples, perhaps even more so. Pagodas constitute highly visible elements of modern cityscapes, not only in the capital city but also in relatively young urban centres such as Da Nang. However, Vietnam's re-enchantment is restricted. Freedom of religion exists only within certain parameters, which are subject to continuous negotiation and which differ from place to place. Any type of social activism that transgresses these parameters and ends up challenging existing power structures—whether by "religious" actors or by others—is repressed. Thus, when discussing the position of Buddhism in contemporary Vietnam, the conclusion can only be ambivalent. On the one hand, Buddhism thrives, and the tradition is increasingly seen as an integral part of the modern nation-state. On the other, several Buddhist organizations are actively oppressed and their leaders persecuted, not because of their beliefs or ritual practices per se but because they have challenged the ideological state apparatus, for instance by calling for multi-party democracy or criticizing official state policies. Such repression has by no means diminished in recent years; quite the contrary. Apparently, repression of religion and religious revival can coexist.

Notes

* I wish to thank Ute Hüsken, Alexander Soucy and Mark Teeuwen for their useful comments on earlier versions of this paper.
1. *The World Factbook: Vietnam*, accessed 3 April 2015, https://www.cia.gov/library/publications/the-world-factbook/geos/vm.html.
2. See, for instance, *The World Factbook*; Nguyễn (2012: vii) and Pew Research Center (2015).
3. As Soucy (2012: 2–3) writes: "In Vietnamese Buddhism, there is no systematized, formally imposed, orthodox practice that is required of all devotees. . . . The different ways that people engage with Buddhism presents a challenge to determining who we can call a Buddhist. Many practice without taking part in any formal initiation which categorically distinguishes them as Buddhist."
4. The term *đổi mới* literally means "to renovate". In this context, it refers to the economic and political reforms that were implemented in 1986. With the *đổi mới* reforms, Vietnam's socialist planned economy gave way to state-controlled capitalism and a semi-free market.
5. On the secularization paradigm, see, for instance, Bruce (2002: 1–44). For a concise overview of the academic debate on secularization, see Demerath (2007).
6. For clarity's sake: the fact that some practices are no longer classified as "superstitious" does not mean the term has disappeared from public discourse altogether. On the contrary, "superstition" remains highly important as an ideological category used to discredit certain practices and beliefs. Its category boundaries are by no means fixed, however: what does and does not count as "superstition" is subject to ongoing negotiation, and is contingent upon changing power relations. Cf. Endres (2011: 159–168).
7. As Kirsten Endres (2011: 11–12) writes, "the recent resurgence of religious activity after years of state-imposed restrictions has proved that the 'inextricable forest of Vietnamese religion' has ultimately withstood the communist party-state's zealous attempts to trim its treetops and clear the mossy undergrowth of so-called depraved customs (*hủ tục*) and harmful superstitions. The current cultural-nationalist discourse on Vietnam's cultural roots (*nguồn gốc văn hóa*) and national identity (*bản sắc dân*

200   *Aike P. Rots*

tộc) even capitalizes on the persistence of the spirit religion (*đạo thánh*) in order to claim an indigenous Vietnamese heritage that predates 'imported' religious and ethical codes such as Confucianism, Buddhism, or Christianity." Thus, various forms of spirit worship and mediumship are now no longer seen as dangerous superstition but, on the contrary, as "indigenous traditions" worthy of public support. On this topic, see also Fjelstad and Nguyen (2006) and Salemink (2008).

8. For a description of Cá Ông worship in central Vietnam, see Lantz (2009).

9. Somewhat confusingly, Buddhist places of worship in Vietnam are usually referred to as "pagodas", whereas the term "temple" is used for non-Buddhist places. This categorization goes back to the French colonial period and is different from other parts of East Asia. In Japan, for instance, the term "temple" is used for Buddhist institutions in general, whereas "pagoda" refers to the tiered towers sometimes found on temple grounds. In this essay, I will follow the convention and use the term "pagoda" to refer to Buddhist places of worship in Vietnam (i.e. as a translation of *chùa*).

10. There is a bewildering variety of terms denoting different places of worship in Vietnam. To the outsider, the difference between, say, a *đền* or a *miếu* is not immediately clear. For the purpose of this essay, it is important to point out the difference between Buddhist institutions, called *chùa* ("pagodas"; see previous footnote), and other places of worship, which are primarily concerned with non-Buddhist deities and (ancestral) spirits. The difference is not always clear-cut, however, as most pagodas have altars and shrines for non-Buddhist deities (e.g. mother goddesses) in addition to the central altar, which usually contains statues of Buddhas and bodhisattvas. Cf. Soucy (2012: 23–25, 56–57).

11. Significantly, the popular local party secretary and president of the Da Nang city council, Nguyễn Bá Thanh (1953–2015), was one of the prominent politicians involved with the inaugural ceremony, as were vice-president Nông Thị Ngọc Minh and various other local officials (Đỗ 2010).

12. See, for instance, Berger (1999) and Taylor (2007a: 2–4). It should be noted, however, that the "desecularization" narrative does not apply to all post-communist states: countries such as Estonia and the Czech Republic are generally considered to be among the least religious in Europe.

13. As Elise DeVido (2009) has demonstrated, the ideas of the Chinese Buddhist reformer Taixu (1890–1947) have strongly influenced the development of twentieth-century Vietnamese Buddhism.

14. For a discussion of Thích Nhất Hạnh's activities during this period, and his relationship with the UBCV, see King (1996).

15. See, for instance, the blog "Save the Unified Buddhist Church of Vietnam," accessed 8 February 2015, https://saveubcv.wordpress.com/.

16. Revealingly, although a significant proportion of UBCV activists and supporters now live overseas, its official website is available only in Vietnamese. The English version of the site is still "under construction"—and presumably has been so for quite some time. *Giáo hội Phật giáo Việt Nam Thống nhất*, accessed 10 February 2015, http://www.ghpgvntn.net/.

17. In his recent writings, Thích Nhất Hạnh (e.g. 2008) has addressed topics such as global inequality and climate change.

18. See *Plum Village Asia*, accessed 11 February 2015, http://www.plumvillageasia.org/. Thích Nhất Hạnh and a group of his followers were supposed to visit Japan again in 2011, but their trip was cancelled because of the tsunami and subsequent nuclear crisis that took place in March. A new trip was planned for April-May 2015. However, in November 2014, Thích Nhất Hạnh suffered a brain haemorrhage. As a result, he could not join his followers on this trip, and the lectures were given by others.

19. For a critical discussion of Vietnam's current communist-capitalist system, see Hayton (2010).

Buddhism and Politics in Vietnam Today 201

20. In 2014, this event, which usually takes place in Thailand, was organized in Vietnam again. This time it took place in Bái Đính pagoda, a popular Buddhist pilgrimage destination in Ninh Bình province. Among the speakers were members of state-sanctioned Buddhist institutions in Vietnam, Buddhist leaders from other Asian countries, and academics representing prominent Anglo-Saxon universities. See *The 11th United Nations Day of Vesak in Vietnam*, accessed on 17 February 2015, http://www.undv2014 vietnam.com/en/.
21. *United States Commission on International Religious Freedom: Vietnam*, accessed on 17 February 2015, http://www.uscirf.gov/countries/vietnam.
22. Interestingly, Thích Nhất Hạnh often stresses the importance of the separation of religion and politics; for instance, he has stipulated that monks and nuns should not become involved with party politics, and that the *sangha* must be politically independent (see the chapter by Jens Borgland in this volume). Meanwhile, however, his notion of "engaged Buddhism" implies that Buddhists should be socially active and concerned with suffering and exploitation in this world. Yet social activism very often is politically embedded, as illustrated by the Buddhist protests and self-immolations in South Vietnam in the 1960s. Thus, there is undeniably a tension between these two principles.
23. It has been suggested that this policy change was the result of Hạnh speaking out in support of the Dalai Lama during an interview in Italy. This apparently annoyed the Chinese government, which is said to have put pressure on the Vietnamese government not to invite him anymore (Plum Village 2014; Thayer 2014). Such a thing may have happened, but I doubt whether that was the main reason for the changes. Relations between China and Vietnam are ambivalent, to say the least; while the Vietnamese government often looks at China for examples on how to combine absolute one-party rule with free-market capitalism, the two countries have divergent interests, and Vietnam is wary of China's territorial claims. Therefore, the impact of Hạnh's statement about the Dalai Lama may have been overestimated. Instead, I think the policy change was primarily the result of domestic political concerns.

References

Berger, Peter L., ed. 1999. *The Desecularization of the World: Resurgent Religion and World Politics*. Grand Rapids, MI: Eerdmans.

Borup, Jørn. 2004. "Zen and the Art of Inverting Orientalism: Buddhism, Religious Studies and Interrelated Networks." In *New Approaches to the Study of Religion, vol. 1: Regional, Critical and Historical Approaches*, edited by Peter Antes, Armin W. Geertz, and Randi R. Warne, 451–488. Berlin: De Gruyter.

Bruce, Steve. 2002. *God Is Dead: Secularization in the West*. Malden, MA: Blackwell.

Chapman, John. 2007. "The 2005 Pilgrimage and Return to Vietnam of Exiled Zen Master Thích Nhất Hạnh." In *Modernity and Re-Enchantment: Religion in Post-Revolutionary Vietnam*, edited by Philip Taylor, 297–341. Singapore: Institute of Southeast Asian Studies.

Demerath, N. J., III. 2007. "Secularization and Sacralization Deconstructed and Reconstructed." In *The Sage Handbook of the Sociology of Religion*, edited by James A. Beckford and N. J. Demerath, III, 57–80. London: Sage.

DeVido, Elise A. 2007. "'Buddhism for This World': The Buddhist Revival in Vietnam, 1920 to 1951, and Its Legacy." In *Modernity and Re-Enchantment: Religion in Post-Revolutionary Vietnam*, edited by Philip Taylor, 250–296. Singapore: Institute of Southeast Asian Studies.

202   *Aike P. Rots*

———. 2009. "The Influence of Chinese Master Taixu on Buddhism in Vietnam." *Journal of Global Buddhism* 10: 413–458.

Đỗ Thế Hiền. 2010. "Chùa Linh Ứng—Bãi Bụt, Sơn Trà." *Webdanang.com*, 4 August. Accessed 13 January 2015. http://www.webdanang.com/da-nang/du-lich/tham-quan/Van-hoa-nghe-thuat/co-so-ton-giao/phat-giao-chua/chualinhung%E2%80%93bai butsontra.

Endres, Kirsten W. 2011. *Performing the Divine: Mediums, Markets and Modernity in Urban Vietnam.* Copenhagen: NIAS Press.

Fjelstad, Karen, and Nguyen Thi Hien, eds. 2006. *Possessed by the Spirits: Mediumship in Contemporary Vietnamese Communities.* Ithaca, NY: Cornell Southeast Asia Program.

Hayton, Bill. 2010. *Vietnam: Rising Dragon.* New Haven, CT: Yale University Press.

Human Rights Watch. 2014. *World Report 2014: Vietnam.* Accessed 3 April 2015. http://www.hrw.org/world-report/2014/country-chapters/vietnam?page=2.

Johnson, Kay. 2007. "The Fighting Monks of Vietnam." *Time*, 2 March. Accessed 17 February 2015. http://content.time.com/time/world/article/0,8599,1595721,00.html.

King, Sallie B. 1996. "Thich Nhat Hanh and the Unified Buddhist Church: Nondualism in Action." In *Engaged Buddhism: Buddhist Liberation Movements in Asia*, edited by Christopher S. Queen and Sallie B. King, 321–364. Albany, NY: State University of New York Press.

Lantz, Sandra. 2009. *Whale Worship in Vietnam.* Uppsala: Swedish Science Press.

McCurry, Justin. 2009. "Vietnamese Riot Police Target Buddhist Monk's Followers." *Guardian*, 2 October. Accessed 17 February 2015. http://www.theguardian.com/world/2009/oct/02/vietnam-police-buddhist-monks-nuns.

McHale, Shawn F. 2004. *Print and Power: Confucianism, Communism and Buddhism in the Making of Modern Vietnam.* Honolulu: University of Hawai'i Press.

Nguyen, Cuong Tu. 1997. *Zen in Medieval Vietnam: A Study and Translation of the Thiền Uyển Tập Anh.* Honolulu: University of Hawai'i Press.

Nguyen, Cuong Tu, and A. W. Barber. 1998. "Vietnamese Buddhism in North America: Tradition and Acculturation." In *The Faces of Buddhism in America*, edited by Charles S. Prebish and Kenneth K. Tanaka, 129–146. Berkeley, CA: University of California Press.

Nguyễn, Thanh Xuân. 2012. *Religions in Việt Nam.* Hanoi: Thế Giới.

Nguyễn, Văn Huy. 2013. "Về Phật giáo Việt Nam và hai giáo hội." *BBC*, 9 September. Accessed 7 February 2015. http://www.bbc.co.uk/vietnamese/vietnam/2013/09/130909_vn_phatgiao_hai_giaohoi.

Pew Research Center. 2015. *Religious Composition by Country: 2010–2050.* 2 April. Accessed 3 April 2015. http://www.pewforum.org/2015/04/02/religious-projection-table/2010/number/all/.

Plum Village. 2013. "Bat Nha Continues." 22 April. Accessed 17 February 2015. http://plumvillage.org/news/bat-nha-continues/.

———. 2014. "Plum Village Practice in Vietnam: Some Background." 3 January. Accessed 17 February 2015. http://plumvillage.org/blog/monastic/plum-village-vietnam-background/.

Queen, Christopher S. 1996. "Introduction: The Shapes and Sources of Engaged Buddhism." In *Engaged Buddhism: Buddhist Liberation Movements in Asia*, edited by Christopher S. Queen and Sallie B. King, 1–44. Albany, NY: State University of New York Press.

Ruwitch, John. 2009. "Vietnam's not-so-simple eviction of Buddhist monks and nuns." *Reuters*, 5 October. Accessed 11 May 2016. http://blogs.reuters.com/faithworld/2009/10/05/vietnams-not-so-simple-eviction-of-buddhist-monks-and-nuns/.

Salemink, Oscar. 2008. "Embodying the Nation: Mediumship, Ritual, and the National Imagination." *Journal of Vietnamese Studies* 3 (3): 261–290.

———. 2009. "Secularization, Sacralization and Bricolage: Syncretizing Categories of 'Religion' and 'Superstition' in Post-Secular Vietnam." Paper presented at the Consortium of African and Asian Studies Inaugural International Conference "Religion, Identity and Conflict", Leiden University, 26–28 August.

Sharf, Robert H. 1993. "The Zen of Japanese Nationalism." *History of Religions* 33 (1): 1–43.

Soucy, Alexander. 2007. "Nationalism, Globalism and the Re-Establishment of the Trúc Lâm Thiền Buddhist Sect in Northern Vietnam." In *Modernity and Re-Enchantment: Religion in Post-Revolutionary Vietnam*, edited by Philip Taylor, 342–370. Singapore: Institute of Southeast Asian Studies.

———. 2012. *The Buddha Side: Gender, Power, and Buddhist Practice in Vietnam*. Honolulu: University of Hawai'i Press.

Suzuki, Daisetz T. 1959. *Zen and Japanese Culture*. Rutland, VT: Tuttle.

Taylor, Philip. 2007a. "Modernity and Re-Enchantment in Post-Revolutionary Vietnam." In *Modernity and Re-Enchantment: Religion in Post-Revolutionary Vietnam*, edited by Philip Taylor, 1–56. Singapore: Institute of Southeast Asian Studies.

———, ed. 2007b. *Modernity and Re-Enchantment: Religion in Post-Revolutionary Vietnam*. Singapore: Institute of Southeast Asian Studies.

Thạch, Thị Sang. 2014. "Những câu chuyện linh thiêng, sự trùng hợp bí ẩn tại ngôi chùa Linh Ứng." *An ninh Thủ đô*, 16 February. Accessed 13 January 2015. http://www.anninhthudo.vn/phong-su/nhung-cau-chuyen-linh-thieng-su-trung-hop-bi-an-tai-ngoi-chua-linh-ung/536693.antd.

Thanh Niên News. 2013. "Vietnam Central City's Economic Bubble Bursts." 13 August. Accessed 30 December 2014. http://www.thanhniennews.com/society/vietnam-central-citys-economic-bubble-bursts-1365.html.

Thayer, Carlyle A. 2014. "The Apparatus of Authoritarian Rule in Vietnam." In *Politics in Contemporary Vietnam: Party, State, and Authority Relations*, edited by Jonathan D. London, 135–161. Basingstoke: Palgrave Macmillan.

Thích Nhất Hạnh. 1974. *Zen Keys: A Guide to Zen Practice*. Garden City: Anchor Press.

———. 2008. *The World We Have: A Buddhist Approach to Peace and Ecology*. Berkeley: Parallax Press.

Thich Thien-An. 1975. *Buddhism and Zen in Vietnam in Relation to the Development of Buddhism in Asia*. Rutland, VT: Tuttle.

12 "Buddhism Has Made Asia Mild"

The Modernist Construction of Buddhism as Pacifism

Iselin Frydenlund

In a discussion of Buddhism and violence in Sri Lanka, Richard Gombrich once said that a key question concerns the extent to which their religious tradition predisposes Buddhists to being less violent in public affairs than other people. He then added, "When one looks at the historical record one begins to wonder how anyone ever came by the idea that it might" (Gombrich 2006: 31). The basic question addressed in this chapter is why popular as well as academic discussions of Buddhism and violence are largely shaped by the notion that Buddhism as a whole is *essentially* based on nonviolence, and, moreover, why we are presented with the idea that Buddhism is *pacifist*. The last decade has witnessed a growing academic literature on the intersections of Buddhism and violence, both in terms of text as well as historical practice, but as will be discussed in detail later, we are still presented with the picture that "true" or "original" Buddhism is pacifist, that is, that the canonical sources express the view that war is always wrong. Surprisingly little academic attention, however, has been paid to notions of war and peace in classical sources, let alone a close scrutiny of what actually "pacifism" might mean in a Buddhist context.[1]

My aim is not to question the importance of no-harm (*ahiṃsā*) in Buddhism or the importance of this concept in defining Buddhism in relation to other religious traditions. Rather, this chapter seeks to explore why—and in what ways—Buddhist ethics and notions of nonviolence were privileged over other aspects of Buddhist teaching and practice during the nineteenth and twentieth centuries. My argument is threefold: First, by tracing European notions of religion that shaped the way Buddhism was defined and conceptualized in the nineteenth century, I suggest that the notion of Buddhism-cum-pacifism is largely the result of European "positive orientalism" towards Buddhism. Second, I suggest that the notion of Buddhism-cum-pacifism is largely a modern reshaping of ideals of nonviolence, in a modernist attempt at reformulating a new Buddhism suitable for the modern world. Third and finally, using Sri Lanka as a case, it is argued that the principle of nonviolence was strategically used by anti-colonial forces and consequently that Buddhist pacifism is largely a modern, anti-colonial, and Gandhian-inspired enterprise, with little historical precedence in Buddhist history.

Representations of Buddhism as Pacifist

Let me first illustrate the idea of Buddhism-cum-pacifism with three examples: two academic and one from a leading Buddhist monk in contemporary Sri Lanka. The view that Buddhism is pacifist is presented in many general scholarly introductions to Buddhism. Take, for example, the entry on "War and Peace" in the *Encyclopaedia of Buddhism*, where Damian Keown writes that

> Buddhist teachings strongly oppose the use of violence, analyzing it in psychological terms as the product of greed (*rāga*), hatred (*dveśa*) and delusion (*moha*). . . . The pacifist ideal of the classical sources has not prevented Buddhists from fighting battles and conducting military campaigns from a mixture of political and religious motives.
>
> (Keown 2010: 812)

According to Keown, Buddhist violence is the result of a tension between precept and practice, but he offers no explanation as to how Buddhists have rationalized—and still rationalize—the use of armed force. Along similar lines, the scholar-monk Mahinda Deegalle argues that

> Buddhism is rather well known for its explicit and uncompromising pacifist foundations with regard to warfare. . . . When Buddhist communities have been drawn or forced into warfare, their engagement in the battlefield has drawn the attention of scholars concerned with the pacifist foundations of Buddhist doctrines and its celebration of the ideals of nonviolence.
>
> (Deegalle 2014: 544)

Similarly to Keown, Deegalle asserts the "uncompromising pacifist foundations" of Buddhism, but without any further explanations of what pacifism should mean in this context. Moreover, it is argued that, historically, Buddhists have only been "drawn" or "forced" into war, and consequently that Buddhists have not engaged in aggressive warfare. Also, in Sri Lanka today, the normative discourse on issues relating to violence and Buddhism is that of pacifism. With a few exceptions, the majority of Buddhist monks in Sri Lanka would hesitate to argue that violence has a place in Buddhism. However, this normative discourse, which is justified by reference to canonical texts,[2] stands in contrast to the hegemonic militaristic position found within the Buddhist monastic order, the Sangha. The ambiguity that such a position entails is clearly illustrated in the works and engagement of the late Madihe Pannasiha (1913–2003). Being one of the most prominent monks in post-independence Sri Lanka and a leading voice of Buddhist modernism, looking at Pannasiha's view on violence is particularly interesting:

> Buddhism, more than any other religion, has indeed contributed most towards promoting world peace. It is the teaching of tolerance and love. It is also

206   Iselin Frydenlund

the doctrine of cause and effect. It places causality in a position of supreme importance within its Teaching. Without prior elimination of the cause, the effect or result cannot be nullified. If it is possible to get rid of the underlying cause, or causes that lead to war, peace becomes spontaneous. This is due to the fact that peace is diametrically opposed to war. Greed, envy and anger are the prime motives for armed hostility.

(Pannasiha 1985: 6)[3]

Pannasiha clearly engages Buddhist concepts to explain conflict: the three "unwholesome actions" (*akusaladhamma*) of "greed, envy and anger" constitute the explicatory model for conflict.[4] Such actions comprise the prime cause of conflict that have to be eliminated. In Sri Lanka, minority communities tend to explain the conflict in terms of state failure and Sinhala majoritarianism. By contrast, the dominant Sinhala discourse, including the discourse of Buddhist monks, regarded Tamil militancy in terms of "terrorism" and thus as a legitimate military target. While outright demands for military action were considered problematic by traditional Buddhist elites, monks like Pannasiha asked for *protection* of Buddhism and in manifold ways supported a military solution to the "national problem" (Frydenlund 2005, 2013).

Theravāda Buddhism and the Puzzle of Pacifism

Scholars have in recent years paid attention to the various ways in which Buddhism is associated with violence, particularly its association with state-sanctioned violence. Cross-cultural ethics has contributed to contextualize Buddhist justifications for violence within the framework of just-war ideology, pointing to the fact that in war-torn countries like Sri Lanka, most Buddhist monks and scholars defend state violence to some degree Bartholomeusz 2002). Much of this literature, including my own, seems to be driven—at least initially—by some sort of surprise of justifications of the use of military means made by Buddhist actors. Surprisingly, however, few attempts have been made to locate pacifism within ethical or political thinking in Buddhist traditions. Before I go on to explore the reasons for why I believe this is the case, and the reasons for why I suggest that pacifism assumed a new and distinct role as an identity-marker for Buddhist modernism, it might be useful to briefly review previous debates on Buddhism and war.

Pacifism (derived from Latin *pax* and *facere*, "to make peace") is a complex concept, but a common usage of the term refers to the commitment to making peace that rejects violent means to obtaining this end. Thus, war is always considered to be wrong. The concept includes a variety of positions, however, ranging from general and total nonviolence in all societal spheres to more specific anti-warism. In Western philosophy, pacifism can be distinguished between minimal and maximal pacifisms, between absolute and contingent pacifisms, as well as between deontological and consequentialist pacifisms (Fiala 2014). How wrong war and violence are deemed to be, and at what times, depends upon the position

Buddhism as Pacifism 207

one takes. In Theravāda Buddhist teachings we find maximalist and absolute pacifist notions, most importantly, the notion that the ultimate goal of religious striving is contrary to any use of violence.[5] However, this is restricted to the (intra-) personal level. In fact, with a few notable exceptions,[6] "anti-warism" or what we may call "political pacifism" is largely absent in Pāli canonical sources Schmithausen (1999: 45). Seen from a cross-cultural ethical perspective on religion and war, two things are striking in the case of Buddhism: one is the importance of *ahiṃsā* (no-harm), the other is the lack of any systematized thinking about the justified use of force, what in Western philosophy is usually referred to as just-war tradition.[7]

"Degeneration Theory": From "Ethical" to "Political" Buddhism

If we were to accept the "pacifist position" held by Damian Keown and Mahinda Degalle in that the classical sources express absolute pacifism, an interesting question arises on how to explain Buddhist justifications of violence. Should Buddhist militarism be explained as norm deviation? On the basis of contemporary debates in Sri Lanka, I will, in the following, argue that the uncritical acceptance of "canonical pacifism" expresses a view in which Buddhism degenerates from "ethical" to "political", ignoring a critical discussion of politics, kingship, and social order as expressed in canonical sources.

In Sri Lanka, although the institution of warfare is generally widely accepted by Buddhists, violence is generally regarded as "un-Buddhist" (Frydenlund 2013). According to the distinguished Sri Lankan Pāli scholar P. D. Premasiri, nonviolence is one of the core virtues of Buddhism, and the ultimate goal of Buddhism is to overcome conflict in the consciousness of the individual. Moreover, in line with the psychologizing tendency within Buddhist philosophy and ethics, conflicts at both the mental and the social level are regarded as the result of an unenlightened response to one's sensory environment. Thus, Premasiri (2006: 81) holds that "there could not be a righteous war from the Buddhist point of view". He also points out, however, that there are different degrees of moral development within any Buddhist community, and that ordinary lay Buddhists are involved in the pursuit of pleasures of the senses (*kāma*). This pursuit of *kāma* is seen as the immediate psychological cause of conflict. As most people are attached to their possessions, Buddhism considers conflict as an unavoidable evil in society. Nonetheless, Premasiri concludes, the ultimate religious goal of *nibbāna* is antithetical to acts of violence.

Again, within the growing comparative academic corpus on "religion and violence", Deegalle (2001) not only reaffirms Buddhist pacifism—as one particular position within various Buddhist traditions—but also reiterates the notion of Buddhism-cum-pacifism, arguing that "Buddhist teachings maintain that under any circumstance, whether it is political, religious, cultural or ethnic, violence cannot be accepted or advocated in solving disputes among nations". Referring to narratives that emphasize loving-kindness and compassion in a violent world, Deegalle rejects the suggestion that Buddhism can be a source for just-war ideology. In this view, the

208 Iselin Frydenlund

true pacifism of Buddhism is unquestionable, and violence committed in Buddhist societies is due to violations of the norm of nonviolence. Thus, he holds that "whatever violence found in the so-called Buddhist societies is merely a deviation from the doctrine of the Buddha and a misinterpretation of Buddha's valuable message" (Deegalle 2001: 2). The Sri Lankan anthropologist Gananath Obeyesekere (1992: 158) also questions the Buddhist identity of those who advocate violence. He argues that such arguments represent a "perversion of Buddhism" and that those who make them are rejecting their "Buddhist heritage". A distinction is also sometimes made between "the Buddhist doctrinal tradition" and Buddhist history, where violence committed in Buddhist Sri Lanka is explained as a result of the growth of ethnonationalism. For example, in *Buddhism Betrayed?*, Stanley J. Tambiah (1992: 58) writes that "as the energies of Sinhala Buddhist nationalism were translated into concrete policies . . . the substantially soteriological, ethical, and normative components of doctrinal Buddhism qua religion were weakened, displaced, even distorted". In this separation between "ethical" and "political" Buddhism, doctrinal Buddhism remains a religion of absolute nonviolence. These strong condemnations of militant Buddhism during the civil war can be understood as a particular *normative* positioning during the conflict, whereby Sri Lankan intellectuals like Tambiah and Obeyesekere sought to challenge militant Sinhala nationalism. Obeyesekere (1995: 254) even called for a "fundamentalist turn"—that is, a return to the original scriptures, to find the perceived original truth of nonviolence.

The question, then, is to what extent the precept of non-killing is explicitly discussed in relation to war in the canon, or whether non-killing is considered to be self-evident. At first sight, this would seem to be a simple issue, as the first precept to be observed—by lay Buddhists and monastics alike—is to abstain from killing. Participation in warfare, therefore, seems incompatible with this precept. As discussed above, in three (almost) identical sermons, the Buddha tells military leaders that they will go to hell, and not heaven. This position of absolute pacifism is also found in a later systematic treatise, in which it is stated that "killing is bad karma even in case of *self-defence* or when done for the sake of *defending friends*" (the *Abhidharmakośabhāṣya*, quoted in Schmithausen 1999: 48–49). Similar positions of absolute pacifism are also found in the *Jātakas*, where stories are told about rulers who, horrified with the violence connected with kingship, choose the path of asceticism or refrain from military self-defence. From this perspective, a strict application of the Buddhist ethical principal of no-harm cannot but lead to the rejection of all kinds of war, including defensive war.

But while absolute and universalist pacifism evidently is found in the canon, so is the assumption that violence belongs to a separate sphere of activity, that of the warrior caste (to which kings belong). In fact, political paradigms in the Pāli canon all accept the institution of war, in that they regard it as being within the jurisdiction of the state, and, more often than not, Buddhist injunctions against violence are related to the level of individual and inter-group relations (Gokhale 1969: 734). Furthermore, the Buddha appears to be reserved in advocating absolute pacifism with regard to kings. We can only speculate about the reason, but the Buddha may have considered political interference as detrimental to the future

Buddhism as Pacifism 209

of the monastic order (Bareau 1993: 38). Finally, although the discussion of the nature of Buddhist ethics is far from exhausted, it is difficult to argue that Buddhist ethics has a single underlying moral theory and that Buddhists at all times have made use of several moral theories.[8] For example, medieval Sri Lankan texts indicate that certain Buddhist narratives worked as "discursive sites" where contradicting moral principles concerning violence and its consequences were discussed (Hallisey 1996).[9] The ongoing debate about the nature of this diversity—whether it represents ethical particularism,[10] or ethical pluralism[11]—is beyond the scope here. Suffice it to say that, from an empirical point of view, the narratives concerning kingship, military institutions, and warfare in the Pāli canon are too complex and multivocal to render early Buddhism as pacifist in any universalist and absolutist meaning of the term. What we do find are, rather, certain "discursive sites" that can justify Buddhist pacifism—as one stream of thought among others—to be found within Theravāda Buddhist political thinking.

Nonetheless, as previously discussed, the assumption that the "true" Buddhism of the canon is unquestionably pacifist continues to be reproduced in contemporary scholarly (and popular) writings. The question, then, is where this notion stems from and why it is so persistent. In the following, I will trace some of the sources that have contributed to this development.

The Search for Origins and European Constructions of "Buddhism"

Discussions about Buddhism, violence, and nonviolence are shaped by the various ways in which the term "Buddhism" is defined. Turning to the early days of Buddhist studies in Europe, we see that there was a tendency to emphasize Buddhist philosophy as found in Pāli canonical texts at the expense of other aspects of the Buddhist traditions, such as cosmology or rituals. In a critical inquiry of "roads taken and not taken" in the study of Theravāda Buddhism, Charles Hallisey discusses how ritual was excluded in the early Western constructions of Buddhism:

> By emphasizing those aspects of Buddhist ideology, especially those which were polemically directed against Hindus, it was possible for Orientalists like Rhys Davids to make it appear that this rationalism was uncovered in Buddhism, rather than projected onto it. The appearances of uncovering the rationalist core of Buddhism were strategically supported by comparisons to Protestant and Catholic Christianity, always of course from the perspective of a Protestant representation of Catholicism as a degenerate form of Christianity.
>
> (Hallisey 1995: 46)

In Rhys Davids's view, Theravāda Buddhism paralleled Protestantism, while "Lāmaism" represented "superstitious dogma, gorgeous ritual and priestly power", not unlike Roman Catholicism (quoted in Gombrich and Obeyesekere 1988: 220). Absence of ritual and rationalism, then, were made into two of the

210 *Iselin Frydenlund*

most important markers of Theravāda Buddhism that distinguished it from Hinduism. Moreover, according to the essentialist assumptions of the day, Rhys Davids sought to uncover "the true message" of the Buddha. The "true message" of the Buddha, as it was constructed and presented in the West, was that of a rational, ethical, and ritual-free philosophy. The reduction of Buddhism into a rational philosophy was closely linked to a strong "textual attitude", to borrow Edward Said's term (Said 1978) found in Buddhist studies.[12] This textual attitude, rooted in the Lutheran credo of *sola fide, sola scriptura*, influenced early Western constructions of Buddhism by giving preference to the "pure" Buddhism of the Pāli canon, also considered to be the "earliest" form of Buddhism. Moreover, the consequences of this trend was that what was perceived as "authentic Buddhism" became located, in the words of Richard King (1999: 150) "not in the experiences, lives or actions of living Buddhists in Asia but rather in the university libraries and archives of Europe—specifically in the edited manuscripts and translations carried out under the aegis of Western Orientalists".

European Puzzlements about Nonviolence

How, then, did the early Western scholars relate to the specific issue of nonviolence? In the early nineteenth century, Buddhism was yet to be defined by European scholars as a distinct religious tradition and was located under the "Hindu umbrella". The issue of nonviolence in "Hinduism" puzzled early Western scholars. In *The History of British India* (1817), for example, James Mill (1773–1836) wrote that he found the idea of nonviolence ridiculous.[13] According to Mill ([1817] 1840: 31), "a Hindu lives in perpetual terror of killing even an insect", which he interpreted as the result of individual fear and cowardice and henceforth to India's alleged political incapability. This view, of course, served British colonial interests, and at this point nonviolence was not considered a virtue by the British colonial power.

By the mid-nineteenth century, however, Buddhism had been defined by Indologists as an independent tradition, and the very term "Buddhism" seems to have been first used in 1827.[14] The general Victorian emphasis on morality made Buddhist morality and ethics a favourite subject within nineteenth-century discussions on Buddhism (Almond 1988). Buddhist ethics were seen as inferior only to those of Christianity. In particular, virtues like patience, unselfishness, sympathy, temperance, and chastity were values that appealed to the Victorians. In Sri Lanka, civil servants such as Jonathan Forbes and William Knighton wrote texts favouring the rational and positive core of Buddhism to counterbalance the negative constructions of Buddhism promulgated by Christian missionaries. For alongside positive evaluations of Buddhist ethics went negative views of Buddhist ethical codes, the connection of Buddhist ethics to other Buddhist doctrines (e.g. rebirth, karma, and lack of a saviour god),[15] as well as the apparent failure of Buddhist societies to put these codes into practice. In one respect, however, Buddhism was seen as superior to Christianity, namely in its (alleged) tolerance of other religions and its nonviolent forms of missionary activity. Buddhism's

Buddhism as Pacifism 211

nonviolence and tolerance were contrasted with the religious wars of Islam and Christianity. For example, in 1873 the *Dublin University Review* maintained that

> its doctrines have never been enforced by persecution; its records have no Torquemada; it has never lighted Smithfield fires for heretics, nor filled dungeons with its opponents. Its disciples . . . have never condemned to everlasting torment those who refused to receive it.
>
> (*Dublin University Review*, quoted in Almond 1988: 129)

Buddhism, then, was seen as a civilizational force in the areas of Asia to which it had spread. What is striking is how the nonviolence of Buddhism is contrasted to Christian persecutions and the Inquisition. Buddhism is what Christianity is not. Tolerance was not, however, necessarily regarded as positive by European writers: some Christian thinkers condemned Buddhism's tolerance as indifference, others saw the roots of the virtues of forgiveness and meekness in "womanly, instead of manly and heroic qualities" (quoted in Almond 1988: 130).

Regardless of evaluations: by the latter half of the nineteenth century, Buddhism was established in the European mind as mild, tolerant, and nonviolent. Therefore, as Ronald Inden (1986) reminds us, not all constructions of Indian religions were negative. This "Positive Orientalism" (with strong romantic undertones) came to dominate Western perceptions of Indian religions, including Buddhism, up to the present. In the enthusiasm for this "ethical Buddhism", Buddhist justifications of violence were regarded as being wrong interpretations of "true Buddhism". For example, in his famous *Journey to Mustang 1952*, the great Italian oriental scholar Giuseppe Tucci regretted that

> like all religions, when it was a matter of defending its own interests Buddhism could find justification for war with that subtle casuistry which theologians the world over have at their shrewd disposal. The captious doctors showed how passages from the scriptures could legitimize the harsh and unavoidable necessity and even killing. . . . They were undisturbed by the fact that these were late writings, and that the Buddha had taught total pacifism.
>
> (Tucci [1953] 1993: 55–56)[16]

Several interesting views on Buddhism and violence can be identified in this text. First, Buddhist justifications for war (which admittedly do exist) are not conceptualized as an object for further analysis: they are simply explained away as the result of the use of clever arguments to trick people. Second, Buddhists themselves (unlike Tucci) are "undisturbed", something they should be in the opinion of Tucci. Third, Tucci bears with him the orientalist insistence upon the existence of a "true" and "original" Buddhism to be found in the texts, and he denounces later positions that justify violence on the grounds that these were "late writings". Moreover, he unambiguously declares that the "authentic" Buddha of the "true" sources had advocated total pacifism. This view of Buddhism stems from Tucci's own disillusion with modern Europe and what he considered to be the alienation

212   Iselin Frydenlund

of human beings in industrialized societies (Benavides 1995: 178–179). The remedy was to be found in Asian spirituality.

Finally, I would like to draw attention to the work of the sociologist Max Weber, who ended up exerting considerable influence on Western perceptions of Indian religions. He based his understanding of Buddhism on the writings of Rhys Davids and Oldenberg, and came to reproduce the accepted view of Buddhism as non-political, ethical, and philosophical. Weber's focus on Buddhism as an individualistic "salvation doctrine" also made him argue that it did not encompass a social ethic, and moreover that it was a "technology of a contemplative monkhood", in which the laity were ascribed only an inferior status (Weber [1958] 1992: 213). Moreover, according to Weber ([1958] 1992: 84) Indian urban development facilitated the emergence of the principle of *ahiṃsā* that was observed by the "pacifist salvation religions" (e.g. Buddhism and Jainism). Indologists have criticized Weber's many empirical mistakes and his heavy reliance on a particular reading of the Pāli canon. He has been criticized for not paying attention to the importance of the monastic order for individual monks, and for ignoring the importance of the laity in Pāli canonical texts. In a discussion of the standing among Western sociologists of the position set out in Weber's *The Religion of India*, David Gellner (2001: 20) suspects that it is "probably the only book on South Asia they ever read". Consequently, notions of Buddhism's social aloofness and pacifist orientation were widely spread among Western scholars.

Buddhist Modernism and the Question of Violence

European interpretations of Buddhism certainly influenced the ways in which Buddhism was modernized in Asia. It should be noted, however, that the textualization and rationalization of Buddhism discussed above was not entirely a Western, orientalist enterprise, but also among the main features of the new Buddhism that emerged out of the encounter with modernity. Thus, Buddhist modernism should be understood as a two-way process, and as pointed out by David McMahan (2008: 6), as various forms of Buddhism "that have emerged out of an engagement with the dominant cultural and intellectual forces of modernity". This cultural encounter resulted in new directions in Buddhist thought and practice that emphasized rationalism, meditation, and the recovery of canonical text, as well as de-emphasis of ritual and image worship. Important to my argument here is the Buddhist modernist insistence on Buddhism as a "rational religion" completely compatible with modern science, devoid of dogmas and ritualism.

The rationalization of Buddhism and its transformation into a philosophy—and not a religion—had a strategic advantage for reformers such as Anagarika Dharmapala (1864–1933), who not only sought the revival but also the modernization of Buddhism in British Ceylon. Why was this of importance to Buddhist modernists? Gombrich and Obeyesekere (1988: 222) point out that "if Buddhism is not a religion like Christianity, Hinduism, or Islam, that leaves open the possibility that it moves on a higher level of generality. . . . It can overcode mere 'religions', include them under its mantle." In this regard, the Buddhist modernist response in Sri Lanka shared many features with the Hindu revivalism in India in the same period. According to modernist Hindu views, Hinduism is the *sanātanadharma*, or the "eternal religion", a kind of meta-religion, "potentially ready to comprise and reconcile within itself all the religions of the world" (Halfbass 1992: 51). Moreover, tolerance and nonviolence as significant identifiers of Indian civilization became prominent in Indian nationalist writings from the latter half of the nineteenth century. For example, Hindu reformers like Vivekananda emphasized the inclusivity and tolerance of the Hindu tradition, in contrast to Christianity. Also, in spite of the militancy often associated with contemporary Hindu nationalism, Hindu nationalist writers, such as, for example, Sita Ram Goel and Harsh Narain, often stress the tolerance and nonviolence of the "Hindu civilization", which are contrasted to the alleged violent nature of Islam. In a similar vein, within the various Buddhist modernist movements in Asia we find seeds to contradictory ideas about violence: on the one hand, we find ideas and practices that emphasize Buddhist ideas of justice, equality, and world peace, but, on the other hand, we also find a certain militancy—at least at the ideological and rhetorical levels—often categorized as "Buddhist fundamentalism". Therefore, it is my contention here that Buddhist modernism contains an unresolved tension with regard to violence and, even more so, that the Buddhist modernist militants themselves represented this tension because they promoted certain Buddhist qualities—such as nonviolence—in their militant struggle to protect and accommodate Buddhism to modernity.

Nonviolence as a Strategic Tool against British Colonialism

Buddhist modernism in Asia was closely linked to national and social reform movements, and certain interpretations of Buddhism were adopted by Buddhist modernists as a tool in the struggle against the colonial power. For example, the alleged ethical superiority of Buddhism became a strategic tool used by Buddhists in Sri Lanka when confronting Christian missionaries. In the Sri Lankan city of Panadura, several important debates between Buddhist monks and Christian missionaries took place. Here, in 1873, the Buddhist monk Mohottivatte Gunananda pointed to passages in the Bible that involved violence. He claimed, for example, that Moses was a murderer and accused Christians of worshipping a violent, demon-like god. Moreover, in the writings of Anagarika Dharmapala (Dharmapala 1965) the great champion of Buddhist modernism, we see a clear polarization between "barbaric Christianity" and the "Human Religion" (i.e. Buddhism). In his characteristic polemical style, Dharmapala proclaimed that "the sweet, tender, gentle, Aryan children of an ancient, historic race are sacrificed at the altar of the whiskey-drinking, beef-eating belly-god of heathenism" (Dharmapala 1965: 484).

Dharmapala illustrates Buddhist modernism's foregrounding of the principle of nonviolence. At the Parliament of Religions in Chicago in 1893, Dharmapala made his famous speech "The World's Debt to the Buddha", in which the peacefulness of Buddhism is of utmost concern. The world parliament presented the participants,

214   Iselin Frydenlund

particularly those coming from the lesser-known Eastern traditions, with a unique opportunity to present their traditions to the increasing global religious market of the late nineteenth century. Throughout his speech, Dharmapala emphasizes Buddhism's peaceful qualities, not only at the normative level but also as a historical reality. In the opening of his speech, for example, he puts forward the idea that Buddhism "has made Asia mild", thereby assuming a causal relationship between the normative level and actual history. Moreover, he holds that

> the student of Buddha's religion abstains from destroying life, he lays aside the club and the weapon, he is modest and full of pity, he is compassionate and kind to all creatures that have life. He abstains from theft, and he passes his life in honesty and purity of heart. He lives a life of chastity and purity. He abstains from falsehood and injures not his fellow-man by deceit. Putting away slander he abstains from calumny. He is a peace-maker, a speaker of words that make for peace.
>
> (Dharmapala 1893: 862–880)

Thus, Dharmapala creates a link between the ideal of not taking life (as prescribed in the first precept) with individual conduct of how Buddhists actually behave. While the word "pacifism" is not used, it is clear that a "student of Buddha's religion" lays aside the weapon, which is tantamount even to minimalist definitions of pacifism. Then, he moves from the individual Buddhist to Buddhism as a system of thought:

> Buddhism advocates universal peace amongst nations, and deplores war and bloodshed. The rights of smaller tribes and nations for a separate existence should be protected from aggressive warfare. In the Anguttara Nikaya, Tika Nipata, Brahmanavagga, Buddha advocates arbitration, instead of war. Buddhism strongly condemns war on the ground of the great losses it brings on humanity. It says that devastation, famine and other such evils have been brought on by war.
>
> (Dharmapala 1893: 862–880)

The whole paragraph seems to imply a strong view of Buddhism-cum-pacifism, an argument that is supported by direct reference to the Pāli canon. The argument brought forward is not deontological (that war is wrong in itself), but consequentialist: war is condemned in Buddhism because it brings about other evils. The notion of "peace"—although not clearly defined in his speech—was of utmost importance to Dharmapala when communicating to a world audience, and his speech communicates a strong discourse on Buddhist pacifism as one of the prime Buddhist qualities in contrast to other world religions. The World Parliament of Religions came to widely influence popular perceptions of the world's religious traditions, so we can think of the parliament and Dharmapala's speech as the earliest and most important "sites" for the global transmittance of the notion of Buddhism-cum-pacifism.

Even more interesting, however, are the often contradictory messages of Dharmapala, in that his speeches communicate both Buddhism-cum-pacifism *and* a certain militancy.[17] This can, for example, be seen in the following exhortation to the "young men of Ceylon":

> Enter into the realms of our king Dutugamunu in spirit and try to identify yourself with the thoughts of that great king who rescued Buddhism and our nationalism from oblivion. Think that you are now surrounded by a host of enemies who encompasesth [sic] your destruction, who is trying to make you a slave in your own land by giving you to drink the poison of alcohol.
>
> (Dharmapala 1965: 510)[18]

The reference to King Duṭṭhagāmaṇi is noteworthy. One of the most famous examples of Theravāda Buddhist justifications for war is found in the Sri Lankan text *Mahāvaṁsa*, from the fifth century CE. This text tells of the Buddhist king Duṭṭhagāmaṇi (161–137 BCE), who, in order "to bring glory to the doctrine",[19] killed the (Tamil) king Eḷāra, although this king in fact is portrayed as just. As Duṭṭhagāmaṇi was feeling remorse for the slaughter, eight *arahants* come to comfort him by saying that "from this deed arises no hindrance in thy way to heaven" and that "thou wilt bring glory to the doctrine of the Buddha in manifold ways".[20] The king is not said to have committed compassionate murder, but through a strategy of dehumanizing the opponent, killing for the sake of the *Dhamma* is justified.

Thus, when Dharmapala asks the "young men of Ceylon" to be like King Duṭṭhagāmaṇi, he refers explicitly to a well-known justification for violence in Theravāda Buddhism, presumably well known to Dharmapala's audience. While Dharmapala generally regarded Buddhism and war as antithetical, his references to the island's military history and allusions to military metaphors remind us of the fine line between military symbolism and justifications of actual practices of warfare. Thus, in Dharmapala we can discern a particular ambiguity concerning violence: on the one hand, nonviolence and absolute pacifism become strategic tools vis-à-vis other religions (both Christianity and Islam), indicating Buddhism's superiority; on the other hand, Dharmapala and the Buddhist modernism associated with him built on militant symbolism and references to the island's military history, preparing the ground for Buddhist just-war ideology in post-independent Sri Lanka.

Gandhian Influence, Postwar Pacifism, and Peace and Conflict Studies

As a result of Gandhi's nonviolent strategy for political action, ideals of nonviolence in Indian religions, including Buddhism, garnered major attention across the world.[21] In Buddhist Sri Lanka, the Gandhian ideals of nonviolence inspired Buddhist social movements such as the Sarvodaya Shramadana Movement. *Sarvōdaya*, "awakening of all", was a term coined by Gandhi. The Sarvōdaya

216   Iselin Frydenlund

movement in Sri Lanka was founded in 1958 and is a Buddhist lay movement. Interestingly, the strongest Buddhist pacifist voice during the Sri Lankan civil war was lay Buddhist and not monastic. Through a blending of Gandhian ideals of nonviolence and *svarāj* (self-governance and community-building) with texts in the Pāli canon that call for nonviolence, the Sarvōdaya movement focused on peace-building through the restoration of the human spirit. According to the movement itself, "Non-violence could be utilized as a very effective weapon more than violence to bring about lasting structural changes without demeaning the dignity and worth of the human being."[22] This is often referred to as *transformational pacifism*, which aims at transforming psychological, cultural, social, and moral sensibility away from acceptance of violence and war. It includes a broad framework of cultural criticism and is often connected to a progressive interpretation of history that points towards a pacifist goal (Fiala 2014). According to Sarvodaya and its leader A. T. Ariyaratne, the conditions that permit violence arose during the colonial period. These conditions, which are still present, run counter to a Buddhist spirituality that was thought to have guaranteed peace in pre-colonial times. In fact, in Ariyaratne's view, pre-colonial Sri Lanka was Buddhist in both precept and practice (Bond 2004: 27–30). This idealized vision of the past is used as a critique against the government, and the movement seeks the restoration of Buddhist values as a way of building a peaceful society. Sarvodaya, then, represents a particular version of transformational pacifism, which is simultaneously regressive and progressive.

This romantic vision of Buddhism as peaceful became important not only in Sri Lanka but also in peace movements throughout postwar Europe, as well as in Japan. In Japan, the idea of "Buddhism as peaceful" is a postwar phenomenon, as exemplified by Soka Gakkai's peace activism. Until then, Zen Buddhism had been closely associated with military power, something that, in fact, was admired by Tucci early in his writings, but absent in his post-war writings on Tibet, as previously discussed. In addition to post-World War II sentiments, the strategy of nonviolence against Chinese occupation opted by the Dalai Lama has promoted the concept of nonviolence as the assumed primary Buddhist quality.

Finally, I would like to discuss an academic tradition that I believe has contributed in significant ways to the prevalent perception of Buddhism as nonviolent— namely peace and conflict studies. One of the leading figures within peace research, and the co-founder of the International Peace Research Institute, Oslo (PRIO), was Johan Galtung (b. 1930). I would venture that Galtung has contributed significantly to the notion of Buddhism as pacifist, even though a bibliographical search through Galtung's writings from the early 1950s indicates that it was Gandhi, not Buddhism, that provided the inspiration for Galtung's advocacy of nonviolence as a political strategy. In fact, in the first published bibliography of Galtung's writings,[23] "Buddhism" does not appear as an entry word. An explicit interest in Buddhism clearly emerges in the 1980s, however, and "Buddhism" appears in the entry list in the second edition of the bibliography of his writings, published in 1990. In the 1980s, titles such as "Peace and Buddhism", "The Role of Buddhism in the Creation of Peace", and "Buddhism: A Quest for

Unity and Peace" begin to appear. In these works, Galtung clearly regards Buddhism as the most valuable source for world peace. Moreover, in his introductory work to peace and conflict studies, *Peace by Peaceful Means: Peace and Conflict, Development and Civilization*, Galtung applies the Buddhist concepts of the Four Noble Truths and the Eightfold Path. Moreover, Galtung is linked to Buddhist lay organizations such as Soka Gakkai and the Sarvodaya Shramadana Movement, and he has published books together with their leaders, or through their publishing houses. As far as I can see, Galtung does not critically engage in discussions about the place of violence and militarism within Buddhism, but has introduced Buddhist concepts to peace and conflict studies, and to peace activism in general, as tools for world peace. This seems to represent a clear example of how the concept of nonviolence has been used in a specific political environment in postwar Europe, and subsequently how it has contributed to the perception of Buddhism as a *pacifist* religion.

Conclusion

The idea of Buddhist pacifism—the notion that war is always wrong—has yet to be the object of critical academic scrutiny, and in many ways, a notion of Buddhism-cum-pacifism has been taken for granted for far too long. In my analysis here, I have suggested that such notions are the result of a specific European understanding of Buddhism as rational and ethical, as well as a particular reorientation brought about by Buddhist actors during the colonial encounter in nineteenth-century Ceylon. Finally, several post-World War II peace movements, as well as peace and conflict studies, have uncritically promoted Buddhism as pacifist and as a source of world peace. A critical study of how Buddhism came to be defined in "positive orientalist" terms as rationalist and ethical not only adds to our understanding of how Buddhism has been conceptualized as an object of study in Western academic institutions. It has also shed new light on the ways in which Buddhism transformed itself into a modern religion fit to resist Western colonialism and how it positioned itself as superior to other religions in the global religious market in terms of its assumed rationalist, scientific, and pacifist qualities.

Notes

1. A rare critical discussion on pacifism and Buddhism from a practitioner's point of view is Fleischman (2002).
2. If not otherwise stated, "canonical texts" or "canon" refers to the Pāli canon as preserved in Sri Lanka.
3. Pannasiha belonged to one of the subgroups of the Amarapura Nikāya and resided in Vajirarama, an important centre for Buddhist modernism.
4. The text reads "greed, envy and anger", although the usual list of the three most basic afflictions (*kilesa*) includes greed, hatred and delusion.
5. This position in Theravāda Buddhism is most clearly expressed in the Abhidhamma, or "higher doctrine", which denotes scholastic analysis of religious teachings. A common interpretation of the Theravādin Abhidhamma position holds that killing can

218   *Iselin Frydenlund*

never be based on auspicious or neutral states of mind and consequently not be conducive for the ultimate soteriological goal (Gethin 2004: 11). This is in contrast to various Mahāyāna Buddhist positions, found, for example, in the *Upāyakauśalya Sūtra*, in which compassionate acts of killing can be justified (Jenkins 2010: 299–331).

6. In three (almost) identical sermons, the Buddha tells military leaders that they will go to hell, and not heaven, as the Vedic tradition held. See, for example, the *Yodhajiva Sutta*, or "The Kindered saying about headmen" (ch. 42, p. 216–217) or the *Sagāthā-Vagga*, or "Two sayings about war" (in the Sangama Sutta, p. 109–110) of the *Saṃyuttanikāya*. Also, upon hearing the story of the fighting between King Pasenadi and King Ajātasattu, the Buddha seems to argue against military action from a consequentialist position by saying that violence fosters violence in a never-ending circle of action and retribution, as told in the *Saṃyuttanikāya* 3.15 (*Sagāthā-Vagga*), "Two sayings about war" (Sangama Sutta), p. 109–110.

7. It is beyond the scope here to give a detailed analysis of the origins of Christian just-war theory or its historical developments, but it should be noted that already in the work of Augustine (354–430) and later in the writings of Thomas Aquinas (1224–1274) we find systematic theological thinking concerning the extent to which it is justifiable for Christians to participate in war. The answers to this basic question can be placed along a continuum ranging from total pacifism through just war to concepts of holy war.

8. Meta theorists like Keown (2013) hold the opposite view, arguing that ethical diversity in Buddhism does not go against a single moral theory, like for example that of pacifism.

9. See also Bartholomeusz (2002) for similar arguments on the importance of context to Buddhist ethics.

10. Particularism rejects the use of principles, rules, and norms in making moral decisions, reducing moral judgement to particular situations and contexts.

11. Ethical pluralism refers to the idea that there are several values which may be equally correct and fundamental, and yet in conflict with each other.

12. For a detailed study of British writers on Buddhism in Sri Lanka in the nineteenth century, see Harris (2006).

13. On the importance of this work as a "hegemonic account" of Indian cultural history, and its role in the education of civil servants of the East India Company, see Inden (1986: 401–446).

14. Needless to say, Theravāda Buddhists themselves distinguished their tradition from other Indian traditions in terms of *Buddha-dhamma* or *Buddha-sāsana*.

15. Moreover, Buddhist monasticism was regarded as morally bankrupt, selfish, and antisocial. The Victorian antipathy for Buddhist monasticism was informed both by the work ethic of the Victorian period and by its anti-Catholicism.

16. Exemplifying this, Tucci refers to the position in Mahayāna Buddhism that one can kill in order to save one's victim for negative karmic consequences ("compassionate violence").

17. Also, in a quote from 1892 Dharmapala writes that "the Sinhalese people have submitted with silence for the simple reason that they have not had the weapons to fight against the intrusion of the scheming missionary" (Bartholomeusz 2002: 71).

18. "A Message to the Young Men of Ceylon", a pamphlet published in Calcutta in 1922.

19. *Mahāvaṃsa* 35.3.

20. *Mahāvaṃsa* 35.109–111.

21. Gandhi himself was in fact as much inspired by European pacifist traditions, expressed for example by Ruskin and Tolstoy, as he was by Indian religious notions of nonviolence. Such Indian ideals and practices of nonviolence, however, were rarely put into political action. Rather, Gandhi's aim of transforming violence can be understood as grown out of the experiences of war and violence in North India (Devji 2012).

Buddhism as Pacifism 219

22. From the article "Sarvodaya in a Buddhist Society," available at http://www.sarvo
   daya.org/about/philosophy/collected-works-vol-1/in-a-buddhist-society (accessed
   14 January 2015).
23. Galtung has had a remarkably voluminous production of both academic and political
   writings, which has resulted in the publication of two editions of a bibliography of his
   work (Gleditsch 1980, 1990).

References

Almond, Philip C. 1988. *The British Discovery of Buddhism*. Cambridge: Cambridge University Press.

Bareau, André. 1993. "Le Bouddha et les rois." *Bulletin de l'Ecole fransaise d'Extrême-Orient* 80 (1): 15–39.

Bartholomeusz, Tessa J. 2002. *In Defense of Dharma: Just-War Ideology in Buddhist Sri Lanka*. London: Routledge.

Benavides, Gustavo. 1995. "Giuseppe Tucci and Fascism." In *Curators of the Buddha: The Study of Buddhism under Colonialism*, edited by Donald S. Lopez, Jr., 161–196. Chicago: University of Chicago Press.

Bond, George D. 2004. *Buddhism at Work: Community Development, Social Empowerment and the Sarvodaya Movement*. Bloomfield, IN: Kumarian Press.

Deegalle, Mahinda. 2001. "Is Violence Justified in Theravāda Buddhism?" *Current Dialogue* 39: 8–17.

———. 2014. "The Buddhist Traditions of South and Southeast Asia." In *Religion, War, and Ethics: A Sourcebook of Textual Traditions*, edited by Greg Reichberg and Henrik Syse, 544–596. Cambridge: Cambridge University Press.

Devji, Faisal. 2012. *The Impossible Indian: Gandhi and the Temptation of Violence*. Cambridge, MA: Harvard University Press.

Dharmapala, Anagarika. 1893. "The World's Debt to Buddha." In *The World's Parliament of Religions: An Illustrated and Popular Story of the World's First Parliament of Religions, Held in Chicago in Connection with the Columbian Exposition of 1893*. 2 vols, edited by John Henry Barrows, 862–880. Chicago: The World's Parliament of Religions Chicago: Parliament Publishing Company.

———. 1965. *Return to Righteousness: A Collection of Speeches, Essays and Letters of the Anagarika Dharmapala*. Edited by Ananda Guruge. Colombo: Anagarika Dharmapala Birth Centunary Committee, Ministry of Education and Cultural Affairs.

Fiala, Andrew. 2014. "Pacifism." In *The Stanford Encyclopedia of Philosophy*. Fall 2014 ed., edited by Edward N. Zalta. Accessed 15 August 2016. http://plato.stanford.edu/archives/fall2014/entries/pacifism/.

Fleischman, Paul R. 2002. *The Buddha Taught Nonviolence, Not Pacifism*. Chicago: Pariyatti Publishing.

Frydenlund, Iselin. 2005. *The Sangha and Its Relation to the Peace Process in Sri Lanka*. Oslo: International Peace Research Institute Oslo.

———. 2013. "The Protection of Dharma and Dharma as Protection: Buddhism and Security across Asia." In *The Routledge Handbook of Religion and Security*, edited by Chris Seiple, Dennis R. Hoover, and Pauletta Otis, 102–112. London: Routledge.

Gellner, David. 2001. *The Anthropology of Buddhism and Hinduism: Weberian Themes*. New Delhi: Oxford University Press.

Gethin, Rupert. 2004. "Can Killing a Living Being Ever Be an Act of Compassion? The Analysis of the Act of Killing in the Abhidhamma and Pali Commentaries." *Journal of Buddhist Ethics* 11: 167–202.

220   Iselin Frydenlund

Gleditsch, Nils Petter. 1980. *Johan Galtung: A Bibliography of His Scholarly and Popular Writings 1951–80*. Oslo: International Peace Research Institute.

———. 1990. *Johan Galtung: A Bibliography of His Scholarly and Popular Writings 1951–80*. 2nd ed. [Peace Research Monograph 22]. Oslo: International Peace Research Institute, Oslo.

Gokhale, Balkrishna G. 1969. "The Early Buddhist View of the State." *Journal of the American Oriental Society* 89 (4): 731–738.

Gombrich, Richard. 2006. "Is the Sri Lankan War a Buddhist Fundamentalism?" In *Buddhism, Conflict and Violence in Modern Sri Lanka*, edited by Mahinda Deegalle, 22–37. New York: Routledge.

Gombrich, Richard and Gananath Obeyesekere. 1988. *Buddhism Transformed: Religious Change in Sri Lanka*. Princeton, N.J.: Princeton University Press.

Halfbass, Wilhelm. 1992. *Tradition and Reflection: Explorations in Indian Thought*. New Delhi: Sri Satguru Publications.

Hallisey, Charles. 1995. "Roads Taken and Not Taken in the Study of Theravāda Buddhism." In *Curators of the Buddha: The Study of Buddhism under Colonialism*, edited by David S. Lopez, Jr., 31–62. Chicago: University of Chicago Press.

———. 1996. "Ethical Particularism in Theravāda Buddhism." *Journal of Buddhist Ethics* 3: 32–43.

Harris, Elizabeth J. 2006. *Theravāda Buddhism and the British Encounter: Religious, Missionary and Colonial Experience in Nineteenth Century Sri Lanka*. London: Routledge.

Inden, Ronald. 1986. "Orientalist Constructions of India." *Modern Asian Studies* 20 (3): 401–446.

Jenkins, Stephen. 2010. "On the Auspiciousness of Compassionate Violence." *Journal of the International Association of Buddhist Studies* 33 (1–2): 299–331.

Keown, Damien. 2010. "War and Peace." In *Encyclopedia of Buddhism*, edited by D. Keown and C. S. Prebish, 812–814. London: Routledge.

———. 2013. "Some Problems with Particularism." *Journal of Buddhist Ethics* 20: 443–460.

King, Richard. 1999. *Orientalism and Religion: Post-Colonial Theory, India and "the Mystic East"*. London: Routledge.

Mahānāma. *Mahāvaṃsa*. Translated by W. Geiger. 1912. London: Pali Text Society.

McMahan, David. 2008. *The Making of Buddhist Modernism*. Oxford: Oxford University Press.

Obeyesekere, Gananath. 1992. "Dutthagamani and the Buddhist Conscience." In *Religion and Political Conflict in South Asia: India, Pakistan, and Sri Lanka*, edited by D. Allen, 135–160. Westport, CT: Greenwood Press.

———. 1995. "Buddhism, Nationhood, and Cultural Identity: A Questions of Fundamentals." In *Fundamentalisms Comprehended*, edited by M. E. Marty and S. R. Appleby, 232–244. Chicago: University of Chicago Press.

Pannasiha, Madihe. 1985. *Peace Through Tolerance and Co-Existence*. Edited by S. V. Dharmayatana. Maharagama: Sasana Sevaka Society.

Premasiri, P. D. 2006. "A 'Righteous War' in Buddhism?" In *Buddhism, Conflict and Violence in Modern Sri Lanka*, edited by M. Degalle, 78–85. New York: Routledge.

Said, Edward W. 1978. *Orientalism*. London: Routledge and Kegan Paul.

Schmithausen, Lambert. 1999. "Aspects of the Buddhist Attitude towards War." In *Violence Denied: Violence, Non-Violence and the Rationalization of Violence in South Asian Cultural History*, edited by J. E. M. Houben and K. R. V. Kooij, 45–68. Leiden: Brill.

Buddhism as Pacifism 221

Tambiah, Stanley Jeyaraja. 1992. *Buddhism Betrayed? Religion, Politics, and Violence in Sri Lanka*. Chicago: University of Chicago Press.

Tucci, Giuseppe. (1953) 1993. *Journey to Mustang, 1952* [Bibliotheca Himalayica 1.23]. Edited by H. K. Kuløy. Translated by Diana Fussell. Kathmandu: Ratna Pustak Bhandar.

Weber, Max. (1958) 1992. *The Religion of India: The Sociology of Hinduism and Buddhism*. Translated by H. H. Gerth and D. Martindale. New Delhi: Munshiram Manoharlal.

Part 4
Institutional Modernity

13 Family, Gender, and Modernity in Japanese Shin Buddhism

Jessica Starling

Many recent studies have highlighted the dramatic changes undertaken by Buddhist institutions in Japan's modern period, usually thought of as encompassing the Meiji, Taisho, and early Showa eras, roughly 1868–1945. The vast majority of this scholarship focuses on the strategies of Buddhist intellectuals and institutional leaders as they responded to the imperatives of modern global discourse.[1] Lamentably few, however, have sought to document the concrete effects these changes had on local realities; even fewer have turned their attention towards the issue of gender. The question of to what extent the "Buddhist modernism" envisioned by Buddhist pundits managed to filter its way into the popular consciousness of lay practitioners remains largely unexamined. Most studies have also stopped short of tracing the effects these changes have had on Buddhism since the end of World War II, and yet Buddhists' negotiations of religious meaning, identity, and practice alongside modern social and material realities continue today in Japan as in other Buddhist countries.

Although the various sects of Japanese Buddhism have, in their own ways, struggled to adapt to a changing ideological, legal, and economic landscape after World War II, the two major sects of the Jōdo Shinshū (True Pure Land Buddhism, also called Shin Buddhism) have achieved unparalleled institutionalization of the progressive, modernizing impulses of the second half of the twentieth century.[2] In the case of the Ōtani branch of the Jōdo Shinshū (hereafter referred to as the Ōtani-ha), the ideological and institutional manifestations of modernity can be seen in two somewhat distinct currents of reform. First, there was the doctrinal emphasis on private religious experience and the democratization of the religious institution brought about by the Dōbōkai (Companions in Faith) Movement. Second, there was an outward orientation towards social justice propelled by the Marxist and human rights-based critiques of the Ōtani-ha by the Buraku Liberation League (Buraku Kaihō Dōmei).[3] Although the majority of *burakumin* are followers of the Jōdo Shinshū, the Buraku Liberation League has had a contentious relationship with the Ōtani-ha institution throughout the twentieth century, and the Dōbōkai movement and the Buraku Liberation League have often been at odds for reasons I discuss below.

The point at which these two modern currents converged, and the subject of this chapter, is the women's movement of the 1980s and 1990s and the ensuing two

226 *Jessica Starling*

decades of debate concerning the status and definition of temple wives, in the Jōdo Shinshū known as *bōmori* or temple guardians. At stake in the definition of temple wives was more than just the bureaucratic regulations describing the role of 9,000 wives of parish temple priests (*jūshoku*) across Japan. The "temple wife problem" (*bōmori mondai*) actually represented a confluence of issues—one might say existential issues—precipitated by the aforementioned modernizing discourses. Specifically, institutional leaders struggled with how to justify the continuation of the Jōdo Shinshū's centuries-old temple inheritance system in the face of modern imperatives such as gender equality, individual religious subjectivity, and the freedom of religion of temple residents, now guaranteed by Japan's constitution. It also proved difficult to reconcile the Dōbōkai movement's professed ideal of a democratic religious organization comprising a community of equally ranked practitioners (*dōbō* literally means "companions") with the birthright inheritance of temple abbacies.

While I lack the space to explore all of these issues adequately here, by tracking the temple wife problem in three different spheres of the modern Ōtani-ha—national networks of practitioners, the public discourse and regulations of the sectarian institution, and the local family temple—I hope to highlight the complex matrix of conditions in and through which modern discourses are negotiated. The first section focuses on regional and national networks of temple wives, which date back to the Meiji period (1868–1912), as they collectively exerted pressure on the male-dominated religious institution to recognize women's contributions. The activities of these networks, along with several independent women's groups formed during the 1980s, represent a robust feminist movement within the Ōtani-ha, which lasted more than a decade. The second section traces the contours of the arguments made for women's rights within the Ōtani-ha. Next, I show how the question of how to revise the official definition of *bōmori* amounted to an existential self-examination of the modern Jōdo Shinshū religious organization. In the final section, I juxtapose the efforts by institutional elites to inscribe gender equality and individual freedom of religion into the institution's bylaws with one temple daughter's attempt to put these ideals into practice in her own life. My findings support the thesis that regardless of the zeal with which institutional elites may attempt to "modernize" the Buddhist faith, for the majority of followers (both lay and clerical), local understandings of religious faith and identity remain strongly contingent on family relationships and obligations.

Modern Networks and the Ōtani-ha Feminist Movement

To understand the position of women in the modern Jōdo Shinshū, some historical background is necessary. Temple wives have existed in the Jōdo Shinshū since the movement was founded by Shinran (1173–1263), who declared himself "neither monk nor layman". Congregations and later formal temples were usually run by a priest (*bōzu*) and his wife (*bōmori*). As the national organization of Higashi Honganji, now known as the Shinshū Ōtani-ha, took shape under the Tokugawa government (1603–1867), the only clerical position created in the sectarian bureaucracy was for male priests. Women continued to live and serve

Family, Gender, and Modernity 227

in temples as family members of priests, whether mothers, wives, daughters, or daughters-in-law, but no official provision for a female clerical role was provided until early in the twentieth century. In 1925, the Ōtani-ha first added regulations concerning the *bōmori* to their bylaws, describing the position of temple wife as providing the domestic help to her husband's religious activities; her first priority was to take care of the temple's children, and make the temple an inviting place for lay followers (*Shinshū* 1925). Finally, during the Pacific War, with its temples drained of male clerical labour, the sect revised its constitution to allow women to ordain and become "proxy resident priests" (*daimu jūshoku*; Yamauchi 2006). This meant that they could become stopgap replacements for their husbands by holding the temple for a generation, but their sons were expected to take over as soon as they came of age. Even with the institution of a new sectarian constitution after World War II, the restriction that women could become only "proxy" rather than full *jūshoku*, and the assumption that the *bōmori* was a temple housewife who required no formal recognition or training, remained in place.

These temple housewives, however, had since the beginning of the twentieth century begun to organize into regional and national networks. What began as a few local temple wife study groups (*kōwakai* or *hōwakai*), which had formed as part of the push for women's education in the Meiji and Taisho periods, by 1958 became a national Federation of Bōmori Associations (Bōmorikai Renmei; see Shinshū Ōtani-ha Bōmorikai Renmei 2008: 28). These modern networks allowed for the assertion of a collective agency in lobbying the male-dominated institution for the enfranchisement of women within the sect. In the early 1980s, local associations of temple wives began to submit petitions to the central Ōtani-ha governing body, known as the Shūgikai, raising the issue of what they saw as institutionalized sexism.[4] In 1982, representatives of the Central Bōmori Conference (Chūō Bōmori Kenshūkai) presented a petition to the chief administrator of the Ōtani-ha. *Bōmori* representatives met in person with the Ōtani-ha cabinet (the chief administrator and five section chiefs, collectively known as the *naikyoku*) and raised their concerns again. Among the requests made were for female representation in the sects' governing bodies, a recognition of the status and importance of temple wives, and the removal of the special restrictions attached to the women's ordination (Heidegger 2006: 307–311).

In addition to the activities of local *bōmori* associations, which were under the administrative auspices of the sect's regional offices, 1987 saw the formation of an independent all-women's group called the Women's Group to Consider Sexual Discrimination in the Ōtani-ha (Ōtani-ha ni Okeru Seisabetsu o Kangaeru Onnatachi no Kai, hereafter Onnatachi no Kai). Its members were primarily the wives of temple priests, but most were also ordained priests (*sōryo*) themselves. Many had served as local or national *bōmori* association leaders, but felt that an independent group was necessary to confront the issue of institutionalized sexual discrimination (*seisabetsu*). They were educated in the language and literature of feminism, and most were self-described feminists.[5] Many of them, such as Obata Junko and Ukō Kikuko, went on to join the trans-sectarian Women and Buddhism Network of the Tokai and Kanto Region (Josei to Bukkyō Tōkai Kantō Nettowāku), started in 1996

228   *Jessica Starling*

by Noriko Kawahashi, a scholar, feminist, and wife of a Sōtō Zen priest. The network's two branches continue to meet regularly in both Tokyo and Nagoya, and its members have published several books (Josei to Bukkyō Tōkai Kantō Nettowāku 1999, 2004, 2011).

Like the *bōmori* associations, the Onnatachi no Kai repeatedly submitted petitions to the Ōtani-ha administration, but they also strove to raise the visibility of Jōdo Shinshū women's issues in media outside of the sect. Several members authored features or letters to the editor that were published in the *Asahi Journal, Fujin kōron, Kita Nihon shinbun*, and a publication with general readership in the Buddhist world, the *Bukkyō Times*.[6] *Bōmori* networks and independent Buddhist women's groups also teamed up with *buraku* advocacy groups, especially the Buraku Liberation League, to confront the Ōtani-ha about discriminatory policies and statements.[7] Temple wife activists found common cause with *buraku* advocacy groups in their goal of bringing about recognition of discrimination (*sabetsu*) by the Ōtani-ha. In 1987, the Ōtani-ha's chief administrator, Kurube Shinyū (on whose role as the founder of his own institutional reform movement we will hear more in the next section), was publically questioned by a temple wife from Takayama about the rules that prevented women from becoming full-fledged *jūshoku*. He responded with a slew of ill-considered, conservative remarks about the proper role of women as being to stay at home to support their husbands. These remarks, in addition to discriminatory comments about *burakumin*, prompted an extended denunciation campaign by the Buraku Liberation League, lasting from 1987 until 1989. At a 1988 meeting, the league declared that not recognizing female *jūshoku* was an act of discrimination by the Ōtani-ha. In response, the administration promised that the reality of female *jūshoku* would be implemented within five years (Ukō 1999: 133; Heidegger 2010: 186).

The temple wife leaders of the 1980s and 1990s, such as Obata Junko, Fujiba Yoshiko, Mochizuki Keiko, Miyoshi Etsuko, and Ukō Kikuko, might be called the leaders of the feminist generation of Ōtani-ha women. In the following section, I turn to the nature of the arguments made by feminists during the period in which the status of women in the Ōtani-ha was hotly contested. To understand these arguments and their relation to the two streams of modernity within the Ōtani-ha world, we must start with an introduction to the primary concerns of the Dōbōkai movement.

Framing the Debate: The Language of Ōtani-ha Feminism

Kurube Shinyū (1906–1998) helped to found the Dōbōkai [Companions in Faith] movement in 1962 and described its genesis as follows:

> During the 700 years of Jōdo Shinshū, the life, the vigour that was present in the beginning gradually hardened, fossilized. What was once alive and functioning became just a custom or convention. In short, Jōdo Shinshū became a religion of family heritage. No longer did the individual understand and therefore believe; rather the family, generation after generation, belonged to

Family, Gender, and Modernity 229

Jōdo Shinshū. This is irrelevant to one's own salvation, it's just a custom of the family. At this point you have to regain your faith based on individual self-realization. When things arrive at this stage there always arises a movement which attempts to revitalize or go back to the beginning, go back to the original vitality. Now is that very time, and this is what the Dōbōkai movement is all about—revival. That is what I initiated.

(Kurube, quoted in Hubbard 1988: 37)

Kurube's depiction represents the basic narrative of the defining Ōtani-ha reform movement of the twentieth century. Inspired by Kiyozawa Manshi's (1863–1903) theology of Spiritualism (Seishinshugi), Kurube and other reformers sought to revive the spirit of the founder Shinran by placing—or rather, re-placing— theological and practical emphasis on the interior experience of faith in Amida by the individual believer.[8] The movement's slogan was "From a family religion to a religion of individual awareness" (*ie no shūkyō kara ko no jikaku no shūkyō e*). "Feudal" models of religious identity and affiliation based on family were depicted as a degenerate and lifeless form of religion that needed to be left behind.[9]

The Dōbōkai movement was quintessentially modern in many ways: reformers sought to democratize the religious organization and increase lay participation in sectarian government by establishing a branch of the sect's congress comprised solely of laypeople, called the Sangikai, and by promoting local temples as being "a place for listening to the dharma that is open to the laity". As seen in Kurube's rhetoric above, the movement redefined religiosity as an individual, private experience rather than family affiliation. And yet, in terms of ethical activism— one of the broad patterns of Buddhist modernism identified by Gombrich and Obeyesekere (1988), McMahan (2012), and others—the Dōbōkai movement was surprisingly passive. On this front, the movement drew frequent criticism from the Buraku Liberation League. Given the *buraku* advocates' focus on reforming social structures to improve material conditions for marginalized populations, they found fault with the Dōbōkai leaders for being overly concerned with interiority of faith and therefore apathetic to social injustices.[10]

Temple wife activists in the 1980s and 1990s drew from the ideologies of both of these movements to make their case for the equal rights of women within Jōdo Shinshū institutions. From the Dōbōkai movement, they seized on the concept of *shutaisei*, which is variously translated as "autonomy", "subjectivity" or "selfhood" (I shall use the translation "autonomy" hereafter).[11] The Dōbōkai movement emphasized the primacy of individual self-reflection and awareness as the underlying principle of Shin religiosity. In the voices of the women's movement, we find an insistence on the recognition of women's "independent participation in the sect" (*shutaiteki sankaku*) and a promotion of their "autonomous religious activities" (*shutaiteki katsudō*).[12] The feminists' cooperation with the Buraku Liberation League, however, gave them an additional ideological resource, that of human rights (*jinken*). The temple wife activists thus went on to assert that this autonomy required that they be liberated from institutional and social barriers to their self-realization.

230 *Jessica Starling*

At times, temple wife activists strategically wove together liberal feminist and Shin Buddhist justifications. For instance, in 1987 the Onnatachi no Kai cited the 1981 Ōtani-ha constitution, which espoused "equal religious liberation for all human beings" (*jinrui byōdō no sukui*) through Amida's vow (Heidegger 2010: 191). Here, *byōdō* ("equality") refers to the religious equality of human beings (male or female, lay or cleric) and draws from Shinran's *Kyōgyōshinshō* and other writings. But the Onnatachi no Kai and other voices from the movement for gender equality pushed the sense of *byōdō* to apply to equal rights and status for women within the religion's social institutions.[13] In subsequent discussions, the sense of this term is solidified as referring to social status and freedom from social or institutional barriers that constrain one's self-realization. However, more frequently than *byōdō*, feminists used the expression *danjo kyōdō sankaku* (literally, "equal participation by men and women") when referring to the social equality of men and women. This term also carried the authoritative impact of Japan's gender equality legislation.[14]

The leaders of the Ōtani-ha feminist movement were by some measures very successful in making their voices heard. With the help of the Buraku Liberation League's denunciation campaign, the administration promised to allow women to become *jūshoku* going forwards. In 1991, the Ōtani-ha constitution was amended to allow for the registering of women as full, rather than just proxy, *jūshoku* in the event that there was no male successor. Further, the restriction that women must be twenty years old before receiving basic ordination was removed so that girls as well as boys could become ordained at nine years old. In addition, an Office for Women's Affairs (Josei Shitsu) was added to the Ōtani-ha's administrative offices at Higashi Honganji in 1996 to continue to address issues of sexism and other forms of discrimination. It was staffed with three men and five women, and it continues to hold yearly women's conferences (*josei kaigi*) in Kyoto where gender and discrimination issues are discussed.[15]

Nonetheless, as the feminist movement found a home in the sectarian institution, it also lost steam. The feminist generation of *bōmori* association leaders who were active in the 1980s are now in their sixties and seventies, and they have handed over the leadership of the *bōmori* associations to the next generation of mid-career temple wives. The current *bōmori* association officers, the feminists note, are much more passive. In one conversation, Obata Junko commented to me that "the *bōmori* association leaders now are so concerned with being good wives and staying in the background, that they are unlikely to make a fuss. They always choose male teachers to speak at their workshops. In my day we made sure to have female teachers, because we thought that was important." In the course of my twenty-seven months of fieldwork, I interviewed sixty temple wives, some of whom were leaders in local or national temple wife networks, and others of whom were more isolated in their home temples. The vast majority of these women were unlikely to attend events such as the annual women's conference hosted by the Office of Women's Affairs, if they were even aware of them. One *bōmori*, who is currently an officer in the national Federation of Bōmori Associations, even confided that she found the women who run the conference "scary" (*kowai*).

Family, Gender, and Modernity 231

Although the pendulum of mainstream *bōmori* attitudes may have swung back towards the more apolitical, many national leaders of the 1980s movement that first raised the temple wife problem (*bōmori mondai*) were appointed to official deliberative committees of the Ōtani-ha in 1994, 1999, and 2008, to advise the chief administrator about how to bring the bylaws that govern family temples into line with the ideals of its own democratizing reform movement, the imperative of human rights, the Japanese constitution, and anti-discrimination legislation.

Individual Choice in a Family Religion: The Temple Wife Problem

Although many complaints of the feminists were addressed in the 1991 reforms, they nevertheless sparked nearly two decades of active reconsideration of the status of *bōmori*. The term conventionally refers to a temple wife, but literally means "temple guardian"—in other words, it has historically been used to refer to the partner of the *bōzu* or "temple master". If it were now possible for women to become resident priests (*jūshoku*), would their husbands then be called *bōmori*? This seemed counter-intuitive, and the Ōtani-ha administration was confronted with a number of problems in redefining *bōmori* in a manner that both recognized the contributions of temple wives at temples, but did not restrict the freedom of individual women to choose to become religious professionals of their own accord. The sect convened deliberative committees in 1994, 1999, and 2008 to advise the administration on what definition and status the role of *bōmori* should be given in the Ōtani-ha's bylaws for individual temples (*jiin kyōkai jōrei*). The committees also solicited the feedback of active temple wives by distributing surveys to local temple wife associations (*bōmori kai*). The public debate that began in the 1980s continued on the pages of the Ōtani-ha's major journals, the *Shinshū* and the research journal *Kyōka kenkyū*, with several issues of each being devoted to the topic of women in the Jōdo Shinshū.

Many leading voices from the temple wife networks drew from tradition to make their case for the recognition of women's roles at local temples. Recall that in the Jōdo Shinshū, clerical marriage dates back to the founder Shinran's time. This means that for seven centuries the majority of Jōdo Shinshū temples and congregations have been run jointly by a male priest (*bōzu*) and a female *bōmori*. The *bōmori* leader Keiko Mochizuki, a member of the Ōtani-ha's 1994 Committee to Consider the Activities of Women in the Sect and one of the first two females elected to the Shūgikai, was one of those who wanted to model the relationship of modern-day temple wives and temple priests on that of Shinran and his wife, Eshinni (1182–1268?). Mochizuki's idea was to preserve the long-standing married clerical partnership of the Jōdo Shinshū, and in the meantime to work on concrete ways to make that partnership more equal. In a 2006 interview, she proposed heightening the status of *bōmori* by requiring temple wives to be certified religious specialists, thus encouraging equality in the division of labour at the temple:

> My understanding is that the *dōjō bōzu* [congregational priest] is the male religious specialist, and the *dōjō bōmori* is the female religious specialist.

232   Jessica Starling

So, I have said at the *bōmori* association meetings that *bōmori* should study more and take the *kyōshi* [religious instructor] certification. That's because I want the *bōmori*, as a religious specialist, and as someone who runs the Shinshū temple together with the *jūshoku*, to take that responsibility. Upon doing that, then yes, please recognize our existence, please give us status as *bōmori*—but that means us taking on the responsibility ourselves.

(Mochizuki 2006: 131)

Mochizuki's idea that the position of *bōmori* should be confined to temple wives was not ultimately adopted by the sect. In the spirit of equal opportunity of the sexes, the 2008 deliberative committee decided to leave the position of both *jushoku* and *bōmori* open to either men or women (*Shinshū* 2008). Nonetheless, Mochizuki's espousal of the *bōmori* as a specifically female religious specialist is reflective of the reality at most temples. As she notes in the same interview, in the earliest case of a female *jūshoku*'s husband having taken on the title of *bōmori*, temple parishioners told him that it seemed "unmanly", and he ultimately surrendered the title. Mochizuki herself has had trouble putting her ideal of a gender-equal clerical partnership into practice at her home temple. After describing herself and her husband as "equal partners" in running the temple with both of them holding the same ordination credentials, she noted a problem she continues to have with the temple's gardener:

Our gardener will only come by to tend to the garden if I am there. If the *jūshoku* [her husband] is there by himself, I have him take care of the three o'clock snack [and afternoon tea]. But this old man says that he could not bear to be served tea by the *jūshoku*.

(Mochizuki 2006: 131)

Women like Mochizuki remain undiscouraged by such encounters, insisting that through their example they will be able to change the culture, one parishioner at a time. My informant Sachiko, whose story I give in the final section, is less confident that this is the case.

Both individual *bōmori* and institutional leaders have struggled with whether to embrace or leave behind the *bōmori* of history. Defining the *bōmori* as a wife and mother, while reflective of the lived reality at temples across Japan, also threatens to normalize their identity as the *jūshoku*'s "domestic help" and make their status contingent on that of their husbands.[16] In addition to the problem of gender equality, codifying the *bōmori* as "wife" and *jūshoku* as "husband" is also in direct conflict with the principles of the Dōbōkai movement. Some critics claimed that this would restrict access to the clerical profession to those who had either been born or married into a temple family. According to the Dōbōkai movement and modern understandings of religious faith, shouldn't the desire to undertake a religious vocation be freely undertaken by the individual? How could it be assigned to someone on the basis of his or her birth?

Family, Gender, and Modernity 233

The question of how to define *bōmori* in the sect's bylaws was, like many debates concerning women, about more than just women.[17] It touched on the dissonance of the household inheritance system (*ie seido*) with individualized religiosity and the equality of practitioners emphasized by the Dōbōkai movement. The minority opinion of a 1996 Ōtani-ha committee report (of which Obata Junko, quoted above, was a co-author) suggested that defining the *bōmori* by virtue of her marriage relationship to the *jūshoku* would give the impression that the running of the temple is closed off to laity, dominated by the *jūshoku*'s own family line:

> Limiting *bōmori* to the spouse of the *jūshoku* presents a problem with the existence [of a temple] as "a place for hearing the dharma, which is open to the laity". . . . There is a problem with constructing the *bōmori* on the basis of her married relationship to the *jūshoku*, as well as with conducting Shinshū temples on the basis of a household system (*ie seido*), namely the transmission of temples through the line of descendants of the *jūshoku*.
>
> (*Shinshū* 2008: 31)

It was suggested that, instead, the position of *bōmori*, as the assistant to the *jūshoku*, should be open to anyone—even a layperson unrelated to the temple family—who had a sincere desire to undertake a religious vocation. However, the committee ultimately decided to keep the "spouse of the *jūshoku*" or "other designated family member" wording in their bylaws, rather than opening up this position to parishioners. Their reasoning was cited as follows:

> Under the current rules, the *bōmori* is defined as the title for the *jūshoku*'s spouse. Concerning this, when we reflect on the history and tradition of Shinshū temples, the fact that the *jūshoku* and his spouse the *bōmori* have all this time cooperatively run the temple is not necessarily related to the temples' being closed-off. On the contrary, we should value and respect the duty actively performed by the *bōmori* as the *jūshoku*'s spouse all of these years.
>
> (*Shinshū* 2008: 31)

The committee members cited the long history of husband-and-wife-led congregations in the Shinshū to support their decision to keep only members of the temple family in charge of the temples.

The next problem that had to be confronted was temple family members' rights to freedom of religion (*shinkyō no jiyū*), as inscribed in Japan's postwar constitution. Feminists within the Ōtani-ha have vociferously noted problems with the assumption that the *bōmori* must necessarily be the wife of the priest (or even another temple family member), because of conflicts with the constitutionally protected human right of individual freedom of religion (see Thomas 2014). As one woman from a Buddhist feminist group explained to me, "Religion and marriage are different. It's feudalistic to assume that a wife will just automatically

234　*Jessica Starling*

adopt the faith of her husband, that she won't want to keep her own faith." This faction maintained that a woman's choice to marry her husband should not be tied to her choice to adopt his faith, and beyond that, to devote herself to the service of his temple.

Beyond just freedom of religion, of course, the very integrity of the autonomous female subject is at stake in this definition of the *bōmori*. As noted above, a major concern of feminists in both the Ōtani-ha and the Honganji-ha was to recognize the autonomy (*shutaisei*) of women as individual religious practitioners (see Heidegger 2010: 189). Thus, in the minority opinion of a 2008 committee report, we find the concern voiced that, in defining the *bōmori* in principle as the wife of the *jūshoku*, "the *bōmori* herself has no autonomous choice in the matter" ("'Bōmori no ichizuke ni kan suru iinkai' tōshin" 2008: 32). After much debate, however, the committee concluded that women are in fact choosing a religious career when they knowingly marry a priest, as "the woman's autonomous choice (*shutaiteki erabi*) was exercised at the time of her decision to marry the *jūshoku* or *jūshoku* candidate" ("'Bōmori no ichizuke ni kan suru iinkai' tōshin" 2008: 31). Thus, the sect officially holds that a young woman is voluntarily entering into this religious position by virtue of her decision to marry a priest.

At the same time, the sect worked to locate some more visible moment of autonomous choice in the *bōmori*'s transition from a mere spouse of a priest to an important religious professional at the temple. To this end, they revived a previously dormant ceremony called a "*bōmori* installation ceremony" (*bōmori shūnin shiki*).[18] The committee stated that the purpose of the *bōmori* installation ceremony would be to "deepen the awareness of *bōmori* as *bōmori*". Although the first administration of the ceremony in 2009 was momentous, with 140 inductees (including the president of the Federation of Bōmori Associations, Fukushima Eiko, and her son-in-law, who was the first male *bōmori*), subsequent ceremonies have been much smaller in scale, and the sect has recently had difficulty gathering enough people to receive the initiation (Soshikibu 2009: 14–15). At the administration that I attended on 7 December 2010, a mere twenty-four women were present, although the Organizations Department had attempted to recruit up to 150 by promoting the event through their local and regional offices. The scene in the Founders Hall (Goeidō 御影堂) of Higashi Honganji as the women were initiated on the morning after a one-day training retreat (*kenshū*) reflected the problem with a ceremony that has very little performative power to effect an objective change in status. Of the twenty-four women being initiated, nineteen wore their priestly robes and clerical collars, which they had received from prior ordinations as priests; the remaining women wore plain clothes with their *bōmori* collars around their necks.[19] The vows they read in front of the image of Shinran were homemade, having been composed hours before in their small group meetings. This was in line with the subjective purpose of the ceremony, but it also detracted from the gravity of the ritual, and the sense that any official endorsement of their change in status had occurred.

The ceremony has, by most measures, failed to resonate on a national scale. The *bōmori* is primarily a local figure who, as housewife, mother, and daughter-in-law,

Family, Gender, and Modernity 235

as well as a hostess and event coordinator for her temple's parishioners, is in nearly constant demand at the temple. Why would a small temple in the countryside, already strapped for resources, fly their *bōmori* all the way to Kyoto to deepen her self-awareness? Who would receive guests, prepare meals, clean the temple, and care for elderly in-laws while she is gone? The need for such a ceremony is not recognized by the vast majority of temple families, which accounts for the low participation rate.

Tracking the Local Resonance of Modernizing Reform Movements

Here my investigation crosses over from the pages of public journals and minutes of the meetings of the governing bodies of the Jōdo Shinshū Ōtani-ha, and into the world of Shin Buddhism as lived at local family temples. While I cannot paint a comprehensive portrait of life on the ground at Ōtani-ha temples, I will include just one story from my fieldwork from 2009 to 2011, in order to track the local resonance[20] of modernizing reform movements of the Ōtani-ha, whether the Dōbōkai movement, the Buraku Liberation League's denunciation campaigns, or the feminist movement's agitation for a recognition of the status of temple wives.

Sachiko is a temple wife in her sixties with whom I spent many hours during my fieldwork. I include her story here because she is a bridge between the efforts of feminists and temple wife network leaders—many of whom are her friends or role models—and the more messy realities of temple family life on the ground, where familial obligations and moral relationships to parishioners, who are often very much like family, mean a great deal. Over coffee and lunch, and while we worked together at manual tasks at her temple, Sachiko narrated for me her own encounter with the Dōbōkai movement and the feminist movement that had been especially prominent in her own district's temple wife association activities.

Sachiko was the only child of the *jūshoku* of a small, urban temple in Osaka. Her responsibility for maintaining the continuity of temple succession loomed large over her youth. For as long as she can remember, her parishioners referred to her only as "the temple daughter" and teasingly reminded her of her obligation to find a good successor to the temple by marrying a nice priest. Her father, fearful that his daughter would want to leave the temple and marry a layman, forbid her to take phone calls from boys at home and restricted her extra-curricular activities at university. Sachiko, recounting her difficult teenage years to me over coffee, explained it thus: "Even as my father was participating in the sect's Dōbōkai movement and working on the problem of discrimination against the *burakumin*, he was violating the human rights of his own daughter."

When she entered college, she began plotting her escape by saving up money and making plans to elope with her boyfriend, who was not a temple son. Suddenly, however—and in Sachiko's account quite intentionally—her father "fell ill" and claimed to be unable to continue to run the temple. Her obligation to the temple had come due prematurely, and she abandoned her plans, breaking up with her boyfriend. After a few arranged dates, she picked an agreeable-seeming young

236   *Jessica Starling*

priest from Kobe to marry, and succumbed to her destiny as a temple wife. For the next two decades, she stewed in resentment while carrying out the obligations of a temple wife in form only.

When she was nearly forty, her turn finally came due to serve as an officer in her local *bōmori* association, a position she undertook with great reluctance. But it was at a workshop of the association that she heard a lecture that changed her perspective and provoked an awakening in her about the meaning of living in a temple. The lecturer gave a talk entreating temple wives to realize both the responsibilities and the opportunities they enjoyed in their position as temple resident. Sachiko was stirred by his message, which prompted her to revisit her position at the temple with a new perspective. Because she had felt constrained by her situation, she explained to me, she had become fixated on the glue that was binding her; she resented the restraint to her freedom so much that she had not bothered to notice what she was glued *to*. Surveying that which was in her own proximity, she realized that many teachers had been placed there. In Buddhist terms, Sachiko began to recognize her *en*, or the connections or opportunities that her position at the temple provided.

Fortunately for Sachiko, the teachers she encountered through her local temple wife association had a different "flavour" (*aji*) altogether than men like her father, whom she associated with the prison-like temple and its disregard for her own desires. They were women, they were minorities, they were "liberal", and their gospel was distinct from the "teachings of gratitude" that had characterized all the dharma talks she had heard growing up in the temple.[21] Sachiko chose liberal human rights causes as her mode of becoming active in the world, but she also emphasized that being a temple person was her position, or *tachiba*, for working at these causes. The Shin temple world provided her with a network, teachers, and institutions for continuing her education that she would not otherwise have had. Now in her sixties, she is currently serving a second term as president of her temple wife group, and often comments with a smile that the events she organizes "do not smell like the temple". Such a smell, for Sachiko, is redolent of the self-suppression and obligation that nearly drove her to run away when she was young, and continued to keep her at arm's length from the temple's operations and religious message as an adult. "It's important to remember that Shinran's spirit also lives outside the temple," she explained to me.

Sachiko has had very limited success, however, in instantiating the feminist ideals that she had so admired when she first found her community of liberal Jōdo Shinshū activists. Inspired by one friend who claimed to have achieved perfect equality with her husband in sharing the labour at the temple, Sachiko sought her own priestly credentials and now has ordination equal to that of her husband. After a brief stint of attempting to share the temple's ritual labour with her husband, however, Sachiko found it too uncomfortable, and too much work, to change the prejudicial views of her parishioners about women as priests. The first few times she tried to perform a monthly service at a parishioner's house, the parishioners told her she needn't have come all that way, and might as well stay home next time. She was humiliated, and now leaves the ritual work to her

Family, Gender, and Modernity 237

husband—"Anyway, what is his job, if not that?" she jokes—in order to concentrate on her own volunteer activities. These, she explains, have become her true "life's work".

In the narratives of Sachiko and my other informants, nearly all agree that authentic faith cannot be inherited, but must come from individual realization (*ko no jikaku*). This speaks to the effectiveness of the Dōbōkai reformers in making Kiyozawa Manshi's modern, spiritualist doctrine universally accepted in the Ōtani-ha. But where does individual realization come from? From what causes and conditions does it arise? In the Buddhist worldview, it is actions and conditions from one's past that come to fruition in the form of one's inclinations and opportunities in the present. At Shin Buddhist workshops and lectures for temple personnel, the message is clear that the Pure Land teachings are not transmitted in a vacuum. Human relationships are frequently emphasized as the primary occasion (*ki*) for hearing the teachings, which then gives rise to faith in Amida Buddha. For contemporary followers of the Jōdo Shinshū, the primary relationships through which their connection to Amida Buddha come to fruition are family ones.

Conclusion

How do we track the effects of modernity in the experiences of individuals or families, communities of Buddhists practising in places more or less far-flung from central Buddhist institutions? One way is to study the writings of the educated elite and organizational leaders, which was my methodology in the first three sections of this chapter. This approach needs to be complemented, however, by the person-centred ethnographic approach I employed in the final section.

The question of whether modern reforms in the Ōtani-ha "resonate" at the ground level of small family temples is brought home by Sachiko's story. Because of her birth into a temple family, Sachiko was subject to forces that obstructed her freedom to determine her own life course. She was ultimately unable to liberate herself from this predetermined life path, whether for lack of courage or because she prioritized her filial obligations over her personal desires, even as a rebellious and love-stricken twenty-year-old. Similarly, the leaders of the Shin Buddhist institution were unwilling to relinquish the principle of family as being essential to the Shin temple system, despite the logical implications of individual human rights and personal religiosity, which they themselves embraced in other instances.

As a Shin Buddhist practitioner, Sachiko eventually developed the understanding that her life had followed a mysteriously yet meaningfully predestined course, and that her position at the temple was a gift from Amida Buddha. Through this consciousness, she was able to seize upon networks, education, and opportunities to become active in engaging both her religious and political values with the world. Thus, her individual awareness (*ko no jikaku*) and her autonomous choice (*shutaiteki sentaku*)—we might say her agency—rest, for Sachiko, in an easy tension with her understanding that the opportunities and

238 Jessica Starling

connections through which her life course is played out are already inscribed in her karmic conditions and the all-encompassing compassion of Amida.

Sachiko's experience mirrors that of many of my informants, in particular her struggle to reconcile the Shin Buddhist teachings of gratitude—and their tendency to promote quietism and even resignation with regard to material or social problems—with her desire to engage the Shin teachings by improving *this* world. This struggle echoes the tension between Shin Buddhism's "two modernities"— that of the Dōbōkai members who emphasize quiet introspection and a privatized faith, and that of the *buraku* advocates and other social activists who have directed their faith outwards towards the transformation of society. Sachiko's inability to overcome entrenched expectations about gender roles at the temple also points to the continuing challenge confronting Shin modernizers to adapt the traditional Buddhist place of practice to the modern ideals of gender equality and human rights.

Despite liberal concerns about the rights of temple family members, and the modern preference for a clerical vocation to arise from individual awareness rather than inherited obligation, the social reality of family-run temples has proven to be a non-negotiable element of the Shin clerical tradition. This has resulted in a very limited local resonance of well-intentioned attempts by institutional leaders and temple wife network leaders to bring their Buddhist tradition into line with the predominant ethical discourse of modernity.

Notes

1. To cite but a very few examples, see Ketelaar (1990), Sharf (1995), Jaffe (2001), and Josephson (2012); in Japanese, see Kashiwahara (1990), Yoshida (1998), and Sueki (2004, 2012), and the journal *Kindai Bukkyō*, published by the Nihon Kindai Bukkyōshi Kenkyūkai.
2. The 1960s also saw reform movements in the Sōtō Zen, Nichiren, Jōdo, Tendai, and Shingon schools, but they arguably have been less transformative than their Jōdo Shinshū equivalents (Chilson 2012: 61). On the efforts of Tendai, Sōtō Zen, and individual priests across Japan to adjust to changing models of religious affiliation and economic conditions, see Covell (2005), Rowe (2011), and Nelson (2013).
3. *Burakumin* or *hisabetsu buraku* are a discriminated-against social group in Japan. See Amos (2011) for a complex history of the *burakumin* and Amstutz (2010) for a history of Shin Buddhism's relationship with the *burakumin* in the early modern period. The critiques of the Ōtani-ha by the Buraku Liberation League and how they intersect with the anti-discrimination efforts of the feminists are discussed below; for a more detailed treatment, see Main (2012).
4. Issues cited in the petitions included the restriction of women's ordination to adults of at least twenty years of age (whereas boys could receive ordination from the age of nine), and the inability of women to legally become the resident priest (*jūshoku*) of their own temple regardless of their ordination credentials. Further, because only registered *jūshoku* were eligible to be elected to the sect's clerical governing body (*shūgikai*), no women were eligible to participate in sectarian governance. While there was also a lay house of representatives (*sangikai*, established in the 1981 constitution), there had never been a woman elected to it.
5. On the state of Japanese feminism during these years, see Buckley (1997) and Mackie (2003).

Family, Gender, and Modernity 239

6. In addition, in 1984, a number of Shinshū women (temple wives, daughters, and *jūshoku* successors) formed a group called the Women's-only Dharma-listening Society (*Onna bakari no monbō kai*). Women who had young children brought them along to the meetings once a month, during which Shinshū scriptures were read and personal responses were exchanged in a women's-only environment (Fujisawa 2004: 193–195).

7. Shinshū Ōtani-ha (2005). Takeuchi Ryō'on (1891–1968) was a pivotal figure who engaged the *buraku* liberationists (if not always successfully) from his position within the Ōtani-ha organization. Takeuchi eventually succeeded in establishing a "Society Department" at Higashi Honganji, which by 1977 had evolved into Kaihō Undō Suishin Honbu (Office for the Promotion of Liberation Movements; Main 2010).

8. There is a growing body of literature in English regarding Kiyozawa Manshi and his philosophical movement. In Japanese, see Yasutomi (1999) and Yamamoto (2014). In English, an entire issue of the *Eastern Buddhist* (35/1–2: 2003) is devoted to studies of Kiyozawa, and Rhodes and Blum (2011) is a collection of English translations of modern Ōtani-ha thinkers in Kiyozawa's lineage.

9. The "feudal" form of religious affiliation refers to the compulsory parishioner (*danka*) registration system enforced by the Tokugawa government (see Tamamuro 2001). Kurube's account of Jōdo Shinshū history conforms to the narrative of Japanese Buddhism characterized by "degeneration and renaissance", frequently given by Meiji intellectuals and modern sectarian scholars. This narrative has been discussed and critiqued by Stephen Covell (2005: 11–12) and others.

10. Jessica Main (2010: 158–159) has pointed out that the subjectivities espoused by these two parties are somewhat contradictory, making smooth reconciliation especially difficult. Jōdo Shinshū theology sees the self as ultimately wicked (*akunin*) and in need of the salvation of Amida's compassion, while the Marxist-inspired worldview of the Buraku Liberation League saw the individual self as autonomous and worthy of respect.

11. This term has a complicated history in the context of Japanese political discourse, variously accruing connotations from Marxism, Freudian psychology, humanism, and modernism (Koschmann 1981).

12. *Shinshū* (1996: 39–40) and Heidegger (2010: 190).

13. For instance, Simone Heidegger (2010: 192) cites the Onnatachi no Kai petitions of 1991 and 1994.

14. The *Danjo kyōdō sankaku shakai kihon hō*, or Basic Law for a Gender Equal Society, went into effect in 1999 (http://www.gender.go.jp/danjyo_kihon/situmu3.html, accessed 10 January 2012). For much of the information in the two paragraphs above, I also referred to Simone Heidegger's (2010) summary of the debate in her examination of gender discrimination in the Jōdo Shinshū. For more detail on this issue historically and in modern times, see her book-length monograph in German (Heidegger 2006).

15. Other activities include curating an exhibit at Higashi Honganji, coinciding with Shinran's 750th memorial celebration, regarding gender discrimination in the history of the Ōtani-ha. Now housed in the Office for the Promotion of Liberation Movements, the Women's Affairs staff also contribute to the publication of booklets and magazines on gender issues, for example, "Between Man and Woman" (*Hito to hito no aida de* 男と女のあいだで, 1998) and a periodical called *Aiau*, which now has a men's edition (http://www.higashihonganji.or.jp/release_move/female_room/).

16. Obata (2004) and Kawahashi (2012: 120–121). Fujiba Yoshiko even ventured to suggest abandoning the name *bōmori* altogether, in favour of adopting the name "nun" as used in other Buddhist schools, so that the temple wife could be taken more seriously as a religious professional (Fujiba et al. 1995: 51).

17. Mrozik (2009: 368–369) made a similar observation about the debate over reviving *bhikkhuni* ordination in Sri Lanka and other Buddhist countries.

240 Jessica Starling

18. The committee cited that women who had undergone a similar bōmori installation commemorative ceremony (*bōmori shūnin kinen shiki*) during its administration from 1993–1998 had reported that it was "very meaningful" to them. The first ceremony of this kind had accompanied the introduction of *bōmori* regulations and a central registration system in 1925: the sect provided a special lay ordination ceremony that temple wives could take in order to receive a special *bōmori* clerical collar (*Shinshū* 87 [1925]: 1). However, the ceremony was underutilized and eventually fell out of use.

19. *Hōe* are the Buddhist priestly robes, which in the Shinshū are frequently worn over lay clothes. Although the most common image of a *kesa* (Skt. kasāya) is that of a colourful ceremonial vestment draped over a priest's left shoulder, there are in fact many varieties according to one's priestly rank and the occasion. The type worn most commonly in the Shinshū (aside from major rituals or priests who belong to the abbot's family) is the informal *tatami gesa*, which is folded up to resemble a simple collar or stole that can easily be taken on or off over one's robes. The term for a temple wife clerical collar in the Ōtani-ha is *bōmori shō*. Although these *bōmori* collars signify a different clerical identity than the priestly stole (*kesa*) and are somewhat lighter in physical weight as well, they are visually very similar.

20. In his examination of Buddhist Modernism, David McMahan (2008) combines the various concepts of "being-in-the-world (Heidegger), forms of life (Wittgenstein), *Lebenswelt* (phenomenology), habitus and *doxa* (Bourdieu)" into the rather more accessible (and deliberately vague) term of "resonance". In using this everyday term to describe the "inarticulate *feeling* of whether [something] can make intuitive sense in terms of a culture's pretheoretical understandings and social practices", McMahan highlights the way new cultural forms (in this case, Buddhist modernity as envisioned by the activist educated class and the institutional elite) either succeed in taking root, or do not (2008: 15).

21. Gratitude is a key element of Shin religiosity, but many women complain that brandishing the concept too easily or glibly, as they believe Shin preachers often do, can cover up actual social injustice and discourage people from questioning their current condition.

References

Amos, Timothy D. 2011. *Embodying Difference: The Making of Burakumin in Modern Japan*. Honolulu: University of Hawai'i Press.

Amstutz, Galen. 2010. "Shin Buddhism and Burakumin in the Edo Period." In *The Social Dimension of Shin Buddhism*, edited by Ugo Dessì, 59–110. Leiden: Brill.

Blum, Mark Laurence, and Robert Franklin Rhodes. 2013. *Cultivating Spirituality: A Modern Shin Buddhist Anthology*. Albany, NY: SUNY Press.

Buckley, Sandra. 1997. *Broken Silence: Voices of Japanese Feminism*. Berkeley, CA: University of California Press.

Chilson, Clark. 2012. "Searching for a Place to Sit: Buddhists in Modern Japan." In *The Making of Buddhist Modernism*, edited by David L. McMahan, 49–68. New York: Routledge.

Covell, Stephen G. 2005. *Japanese Temple Buddhism: Worldliness in a Religion of Renunciation*. Honolulu: University of Hawai'i Press.

Dessì, Ugo, ed. 2010. *The Social Dimension of Shin Buddhism*. Leiden: Brill.

Fujiba, Yoshiko, Watanabe Kōjun, Yamauchi Sayoko, Sakato Masako, Kondō Hiroko, and Fujiba Yoshiko. 1995. "Zadankai: Kyōdan, jiin no genjō to tenbō: mizuko kuyō o megutte, tera ni kurasu josei no shiten kara." *Kyōka kenkyū* 113: 48–71.

Fujisawa, Shōko. 2004. "Onna bakari no monbōkai kara." In *Jendā ikōru na Bukkyō o mezashite*, edited by Josei to Bukkyō Tōkai Kantō Nettowāku, 193–195. Osaka: Toki Shobō.

Family, Gender, and Modernity 241

Gombrich, Richard, and Gananath Obesekyere. 1998. *Buddhism Transformed: Religious Change in Sri Lanka*. Princeton, NJ: Princeton University Press.

Heidegger, Simone. 2006. *Buddhismus, Geschlechterverhältnis und Diskriminierung: die gegenwärtige Diskussion im Shin-Buddhismus Japans*. Berlin: LIT.

———. 2010. "Shin Buddhism and Gender: The Discourse on Gender Discrimination and Related Reforms." In *The Social Dimension of Shin Buddhism*, edited by Ugo Dessì, 165–208. Leiden: Brill.

Hubbard, Jamie. 1988. *Yielding to the New: Buddhism and the Family in Contemporary Japan* [Study Guide for "The Yamaguchi Story"]. Washington, DC: J&H Information Systems.

Jaffe, Richard M. 2001. *Neither Monk Nor Layman: Clerical Marriage in Modern Japanese Buddhism*. Princeton, NJ: Princeton University Press.

Josei to Bukkyō Tōkai Kantō Nettowāku. 1999. *Bukkyō to jendā: onnatachi no nyoze gamon*. Osaka: Toki Shobō.

———. 2004. *Jiendā ikōruna bukkyō o mezashite: Zoku onnatachi no nyoze gamon*. Osaka: Toki Shobō.

———. 2011. *Shin Bukkyō to jendā: joseitachi no chōsen*. Tokyo: Nashi no Kisha.

Josephson, Jason ānanda. 2012. *The Invention of Religion in Japan*. Chicago: University of Chicago Press.

Kashiwahara, Yūsen. 1990. *Nihon Bukkyō shi*. Tokyo: Yoshikawa Kōbunkan.

Kawahashi, Noriko. 2012. *Saitai Bukkyō no minzokushi: jendā shūkyōgaku kara no apurōchi*. Kyoto: Jinbun Shoin.

Ketelaar, James Edward. 1990. *Of Heretics and Martyrs in Meiji Japan: Buddhism and Its Persecution*. Princeton, NJ: Princeton University Press.

Koschmann, J. Victor. 1981. "The Debate on Subjectivity in Postwar Japan: Foundations of Modernism as Political Critique." *Pacific Affairs* 54 (4): 609–631.

Mackie, Vera. 2003. *Feminism in Modern Japan: Citizenship, Embodiment, and Sexuality*. Cambridge: Cambridge University Press.

Main, Jessica. 2012. "To Lament the Self: The Ethical Ideology of Takeuchi Ryō'on (1891–1968) and the ōtani-ha Movement against Buraku Discrimination." In *The Social Dimension of Shin Buddhism*, edited by Ugo Dessì, 137–164. Leiden: Brill.

McMahan, David L. 2008. *The Making of Buddhist Modernism*. Oxford: Oxford University Press.

———, ed. 2012. *Buddhism in the Modern World*. New York: Routledge.

Mochizuki, Keiko. 2006. "Intabyū: hontō no dōbōkyōdan o negatte." *Kyōka kenkyū* 135: 127–138.

Mrozik, Susanne. 2009. "A Robed Revolution: The Contemporary Buddhist Nun's (*Bhikṣuṇī*) Movement." *Religion Compass* 3 (3): 360–378.

Nelson, John K. 2013. *Experimental Buddhism: Innovation and Activism in Contemporary Japan*. Honolulu: University of Hawai'i Press.

Obata, Junko. 2004. "Shinshū Ōtaniha ni okeru 'bōmori mondai' ni tsuite: katte ni sōshūhen." In *Jendā ikōruna Bukkyō o mezashite*, edited by Josei to Bukkyō Tōkai Kantō Nettowāku, 38–54. Osaka: Toki Shobō.

Rowe, Mark. 2011. *Bonds of the Dead: Temples, Burial, and the Transformation of Contemporary Japanese Buddhism*. Chicago: University of Chicago Press.

Sharf, Robert. 1995. "The Zen of Japanese Nationalism." In *Curators of the Buddha: The Study of Buddhism under Colonialism*, edited by Donald S. Lopez, Jr., 107–160. Chicago: University of Chicago Press.

Shinshū. 1925. "Bōmori mo hōmu ga tsutomareru." *Shinshū* 88 (October 1925): 19–20.

242 *Jessica Starling*

———. 1996. "'Josei no shūmon katsudō ni kan suru iinkai' tōshin." *Shinshū* (May 1996): 28–41.

———. 2000. "'Bōmori no kitei ni kan suru iinkai' tōshin." *Shinshū* (July 2000): 84–91.

———. 2008. "'Bōmori no ichizuke ni kan suru iinkai' tōshin." *Shinshū* (May 2008): 27–33.

Shinshū Ōtani-ha, ed. 2005. *Buraku Mondai Gakushū Shiryōshū*. Kyoto: Shinshū Ōtani-ha Shūmusho.

Shinshū Ōtani-ha Bōmorikai Renmei, ed. 2008. *Shinshū Ōtani-ha bōmorikai renmei kessei gojū shūnen kinen jigyō*. Kyoto: Shinshū Ōtani-ha Bōmori Renmei.

Soshikibu. 2009. "Bōmori shūnin kenshūkai/bōmori shūnin shiki kaisai." *Shinshū* (July): 14–15.

Sueki, Fumihiko. 2004. *Kindai Nihon no shisō saikō*. Tokyo: Toransubyū.

———, ed. 2012. *Kindai to Bukkyō*. Kyoto: Kokusai Nihon Bunka Kenkyū Sentā.

Tamamuro, Fumio. 2001. "Local Society and the Temple-Parishioner Relationship within the Bakufu's Governance Structure." *Japanese Journal of Religious Studies* 28 (3–4): 261–292.

Thomas, Jolyon. 2014. "Religions Policies during the Allied Occupation of Japan, 1945–1952." *Religion Compass* 8 (9): 275–286.

Ukō, Kikuko. 1999. "Otera ni ikiru onna no ibasho to seido: Shinran no tsuma to musume wa nani to miru." In *Bukkyō to jendā*, edited by Josei to Bukkyō Tōkai Kantō Nettowāku, 127–135. Osaka: Toki Shobō.

Yamamoto, Nobuhiro. 2014. *Kiyozawa manshi to nihon kingendai shisō: Jiriki no jubaku kara tariki shisō e*. Tokyo: Akashi Shoten.

Yamauchi, Sayoko. 2006. "Kindai ni okeru Shinshū Ōtani-ha no josei kyōka soshiki." *Kyōka kenkyū* 135: 60–85.

Yasutomi, Shin'ya. 1999. *Kiyozawa Manshi to ko no shisō*. Kyoto: Hōzōkan.

Yoshida, Kyūichi. 1998. *Kin-gendai Bukkyō No Rekishi*. Tōkyō: Chikuma Shobō.

14 Theravāda Nuns in the United States

Modernization and Traditionalization[1]

Ute Hüsken

This essay deals with the process of the revival of the Bhikkhunīsaṅgha, the Buddhist nuns' monastic order, in the Theravāda tradition.[2] Since 2009, after more than thirty years of struggle, the communities of Theravāda nuns are ordaining their second generation of women. The Bhikkhunīsaṅgha thus seems to be out of troubled water. At the time of writing, we find groups of Theravāda nuns in Sri Lanka, Thailand, India, Indonesia, Germany, the United States, and Australia—in addition to individual nuns in these and other countries. The revival of the Bhikkhunīsaṅgha is thus an ongoing process, taking place in the late twentieth and early twenty-first centuries.[3]

While this can arguably be interpreted as a form of Buddhist modernity, I deal with this as a multifaceted *process of modernization*, since the situation is still continuously changing.[4] Yet with Milton Singer (1971) I do not understand "modernization" as a contrast to "tradition".[5] As this case study shows, modernization is not the change of something old and archaic into something new. Rather, it designates the integration of innovations in an existing system. This process is complete only when the innovation is successfully integrated into a perceived essential core of the tradition, "which has itself changed in order to integrate the new items". Singer (1971) describes this process as "traditionalizing". Modernization and traditionalization are thus closely interlinked. Yet the mechanisms of these processes unfold differently in the diverse Theravāda communities and regions. In this essay, I shall look specifically into this process regarding Western Theravāda nuns in the US state of California.[6]

A Short History of the Process

At the time of writing (2014), the revival of the Theravāda nuns' Saṅgha is still in the making. The process so far has been marked by crucial events. I will here first summarize some of these events.

The history of the Bhikkhunīsaṅgha goes back to the historical Buddha.[7] Yet until recently a nuns' Saṅgha continued to exist in only one surviving Buddhist monastic tradition, namely the one transmitted in Chinese. In the two further surviving traditions with their own version of monastic law (Vinaya), Theravāda and

244   *Ute Hüsken*

Mūlasarvāstivāda, full ordination for nuns ceased to be practised centuries ago,[8] thus preventing women from joining the Buddhist community as fully ordained monastics.[9] Since the late 1980s, however, more and more women have publicly asked for or acted towards the formal revival of the Buddhist nuns' order, and in spite of strong opposition, we are currently witnessing the emergence of Theravāda nuns' communities in Asian and Western countries.[10]

In order to revive the Bhikkhunīsaṅgha, the first Theravāda nuns had to be ordained by Saṅghas of Mahāyāna traditions (following the Dharmaguptaka Vinaya).[11] Other early nuns were ordained by Theravāda monks alone.[12] Especially the ordination of Theravāda nuns by a "mixed" Saṅgha (consisting of nuns of Mahāyāna traditions and Theravāda monks) initially met with strong resistance among Theravāda monastics and laypeople. The resistance is connected to the fact that the diverse Buddhist traditions developed very different practices over time. For example, Chinese Buddhists are vegetarian, while Southeast Asian Buddhists are generally not. Theravāda Buddhists also seem to suspect that (Chinese) Mahāyāna nuns are "corrupt" (see Collins and McDaniel 2010: 1392–1393). While this attitude is mainly based on differences in day-to-day practices that do not stem from differences in Vinaya regulations, it fosters resistance against "mixed" ordinations, which is then underpinned by arguments based on Buddhist monastic law (*vinaya*).[13]

Yet the later "mixed" ordinations in India and Sri Lanka in 1996 and 1998 had lasting effects, and a number of the women ordained during these occasions continue to live as Theravāda nuns until today. Since the late 1990s, nuns have been ordained every year with the support of Theravāda monks.[14] Yet the situation in the Theravāda countries is far from being uniform: while in Sri Lanka the nuns' order is now starting to take root, the official Saṅgha representatives in Myanmar and Thailand do not accept the new nuns' ordination.[15] However, as we will see, many Thai women live in fact as ordained Theravāda nuns in Thailand.[16]

In 2009–2010 another transition was successfully mastered. Since 1998, in fact, "pure" Theravāda ordinations have taken place,[17] since the nuns from the early ordinations received very soon after their own ordinations permission to ordain other nuns. However, only since 2009–2010 have the first nuns of these early ordinations attained the seniority required by the Vinaya[18] and are now on all accounts authorized to confer ordinations on other women and act as their preceptors. This is a crucial step in the revival of the Bhikkhunīsaṅgha and is therefore consciously and conspicuously staged in contemporary Theravāda ordinations.

While the revival of the Theravāda Bhikkhunīsaṅgha is on its way, I shall show here that what might seem to be *one movement* is in fact very diverse in terms of actors, motivations, processes involved, and their articulations in practice. In what follows, I will pay special attention to the perceived authority of the normative texts and contrast this with actual practices on the ground.

The Revival of the Bhikkhunīsaṅgha as a "Foreign" Cultural Product

I shall now examine whether it is helpful to distinguish between the integration of elements perceived as foreign, on the one hand, and innovations from within the Buddhist tradition, on the other, when analyzing the process of the Bhikkhunīsaṅgha revival. For the demand for a revival of a Bhikkhunīsaṅgha is often depicted as inherently Western and thus foreign to Buddhist traditions. Nirmala Salgado (2013: 4–5), for example, describes the discourse on this issue as entirely framed by the agenda of scholars and English-speaking nuns, dominated by liberal and feminist theories, suggesting that the demand for ordination is a fundamentally Western project and even a modern form of colonialism.[19] She argues that the feminist discourse is in deep complicity with a certain trend in Third World discourse, which implies that how people treat their women is indicative of how developed they are. From this perspective, Buddhist women, for example, in Sri Lanka, are "deprived subjects worthy of aid, and ultimately, of upasampadā [i.e. full ordination]" (Salgado 2013: 13).[20] This foreign intervention, Salgado argues, is thus imposed on female celibate Buddhists in Asian countries, who are not necessarily interested in joining the Saṅgha as Bhikkhunīs and even oppose the idea of the revival of a women's ordination. And in fact, the opposing voices of these Buddhist women have for a long time not been given any weight, as has been shown by Collins and McDaniel (2010) for Thailand and by Salgado (2013) for Sri Lanka. The dismissal of these voices as the opinion of uneducated women lay followers who simply repeat the opinion of the monks they serve does not correspond to reality either, since opposition is, for example, also eloquently expressed by the large group of very well-educated Mae Chis ("lay nuns")[21] in Thailand. Many of these scholarly Mae Chis perceive their own position as preferable to being Bhikkhunīs. Some among them explicitly reject full ordination because this would make them dependent and subordinated to the Buddhist monks and deprive them of the relative independence and esteem they enjoy through their status as Mae Chi scholars. As ordained nuns they would have to follow Buddhist monastic law, and many of the Vinaya rules clearly state that in the internal hierarchy even experienced nuns are always below the youngest and most inexperienced monk. These issues make full ordination seem little attractive to the scholarly Mae Chis, who have practised the celibate religious life on their own for many years and who enjoy respect and esteem by the lay communities.[22] Also in Sri Lanka many of the lay nuns do not embrace the idea of full ordination for women, as Salgado (2013) reports.[23]

The Bhikkhunīsaṅghas in Thailand and Sri Lanka

At the same time, however, it is equally incorrect to assume that Asian Theravāda women are generally *against* the introduction of female ordination. The reality on the ground is complex. There are in fact many women and men in Asian

246   *Ute Hüsken*

countries who are positive towards a revival of the Bhikkhunīsaṅgha, and despite the official claims that the ordination of women is impossible in Thailand, many Bhikkhunīs' monasteries with fully ordained Thai women as Bhikkhunīs exist in Thailand. Moreover, as with the Mae Chis, even within the different Bhikkhunīsaṅghas in Thailand we find diverse motivations, opinions, and practices. On one end of the scale, we see the Thai Bhikkhunī Dhammananda, the former Chatsumarn Kabilsingh, professor at Culalongkorn University. Bhikkhunī Dhammananda received her novice ordination in 2001 and her full ordination in 2003 in Sri Lanka, and publicly promotes the revival of the Bhikkhunīsaṅgha; she is a global player for the cause, an active member of the Shakyadhita organization and actively introduces full ordination for women in Thailand. On the other end of the spectrum, there is, for example, the Nirotharam Bhikkhuni Arama's community in Northern Thailand. This is one of the largest groups of ordained Buddhist women in Thailand today, enjoying the support of local monks and the laity (see Itoh 2013). The head nun Bhikkhunī Nanthayani also received her full ordination in Sri Lanka and encourages ordination for her fellow nuns. Yet she acts locally in the first place, without attracting media attention. She is motivated not by an ideal of gender equality, but by the understanding that *nibbāna* can be attained in this lifetime. She therefore wants to provide a monastic environment in order to make *nibbāna* accessible to as many women as possible. Thus, instead of tracing their efforts to the international movement promoting Bhikkhunī ordination, Bhikkhunī Nanthayani's monastery is a local development, mainly driven by the charisma and sincerity of the head nun, which inspires the support of the local laypeople and monks. Acknowledging Dhammananda and Nanthayani as two among many voices in Thai Buddhism, in spite of the state-promoted uniformity, is crucial to understanding female Buddhist renunciation in Thailand. It is also crucial to realize that there are always also monks who support women renunciants.

The Bhikkhunīsaṅgha as Co-Production of Asian and Western Buddhists

Ordinations performed, for example, in Thailand or the United States cannot take place without the active participation of Theravāda monks. Moreover, even while there are also Western Theravāda monks among the supporters,[24] the majority of ordinations are performed in Asia by Theravāda monks of Asian origin.[25] This points to the important aspect that this modern form of Buddhism is *not* just a phenomenon of foreign (Western) origin. Even if we should maintain that the nuns' ordinations are inspired by Western ideas,[26] Buddhists of Asian origin are as involved as Westerners in the production and practice of these new forms of Buddhism. The ordination of women in Theravāda Buddhism is thus a "co-production" of Asian and Western cultures, individuals, and institutions, in which Asian Buddhists are "co-creators of modernist versions of their traditions" (McMahan 2008: 21).

From this perspective, the generalization that the struggle for Buddhist women's ordination is at the same time a conflict of cultures, or worse, a contemporary avatāra of colonization, needs to be seriously scrutinized, looking at the details of each individual situation.[27] To me it seems rather that these movements, whether in Thailand or in California, have developed their own dynamics, internal contradictions, and global and local entanglements. It is therefore imperative that we look closely at what is actually going on.

Bhikkhunīs in Thailand and in California

One reason for the relative invisibility of the Bhikkhunīsaṅghas in Thailand is certainly the specific historical-political context.[28] Since the monks' Saṅghas do not allow the ordination of Bhikkhunīs, the logical consequence seems to be that Bhikkhunīs do not exist in Thailand, even though this impression does not correlate with the actual existence of a number of Bhikkhunīsaṅghas.

Another reason for this relative invisibility might, however, be that this change is perceived as an innovation "from within", rather than a "foreign cultural product". In this sense, the perception that the revival of the Bhikkhunīsaṅgha is a foreign innovation is nevertheless important, since it points to a major difference between the Asian and the Western nuns' ordinations and nunneries. In her work on Bhikkhunī Nanthayani's monastery, Ayako Itoh (2013) explicitly stresses the embeddedness of female renunciants in Thai history and culture—which is in stark contrast to the popular depiction that movements of female Buddhist renunciants are of foreign origin, and therefore imposed on Thai culture from the outside. Rather, Itoh argues that this movement can be understood only *within* its local history, both individual and social. This local character of the process is denied by Salgado and others who present it as an interpretation and practice of Buddhism that is imposed from the outside (Western intellectuals) on the original Asian owners of the tradition. Importantly, however, Westernization has to be distinguished from modernization. While modernization *can* encompass the assimilation of originally foreign (for example, Western) elements, modernization happens also from within a tradition. The mechanisms and the speed with which perceived foreign and "indigenous" new elements are integrated (or rejected) differ, but, in the end, the integration of new elements in both cases amounts to modernization, which is fully accomplished only if these new elements are accepted as part and parcel of the tradition (Singer 1971: 165).[29] For the California nuns, these "pure" Theravāda ordinations thus mark an important step in the process of the incorporation of the contemporary California Bhikkhunīsaṅgha, since one "foreign" element (the participation of Chinese nuns) is now removed—even though the Western nuns are still perceived as relatively foreign by the Asian monks living in monasteries in the West, if only because of their skin colour and mother tongues.[30] According to Singer (1971: 176), "for a foreign import or group to enter the hallowed realm of the 'traditional' it must become old,

248   *Ute Hüsken*

it must conform to customary or scriptural norms, and it must have an origin myth in which it is linked to a great traditional set of ancestors or precedents". In contrast, Bhikkhunī Nanthayani and her monastic community seem not to pose a threat to the tradition. She does not question the system and can thus be accepted at the margins of the system. Her modernization of the Theravāda tradition takes place within the system and is possibly seen just as a minor change within a long-established structure of accepted cultural tradition (see Singer 1971: 172).

While I agree with Singer that a change "from within" Theravāda Buddhism, such as the nunnery set up by Bhikkhunī Nanthayani in Northern Thailand, might be easier to incorporate than innovations perceived to be "foreign", I will argue here that the situation of the California nuns cannot be fully captured by the dichotomy of "foreign" and "indigenous". When analyzing this variety of modernization of the Theravāda tradition, we clearly have to look closely at the mechanisms of this process. Crucially, the Theravāda nuns' ordinations in California have to bridge many gaps—temporal (from the first ordinations during the time of the Buddha to the present), spatial (from Asian countries with a living Theravāda tradition), and cultural (Asian forms of asceticism and monasticism practised in the United States)—and they must relate to a variety of agents involved, both monastic and lay. Importantly, these new agents are female Buddhist practitioners who practise a form of asceticism that was until recently reserved for male monastics alone.

The California Nuns' Practices as Modernization *and* Traditionalization

The efforts of the Theravāda nuns in California are a modernization of a very specific kind, which is perceived and presented in many ways as the "return to an original tradition". The Western nuns are traditionalizing and modernizing at the same time—and the navigation and the balancing of these two positions poses major challenges to these women's practice and self-representation. The relationship between innovation and conservation is crucial for understanding the Bhikkhunīsaṅgha's taking root in the West. Its "newness" is played down and instead its "pastness" is emphasized (Bell 2000: 20). However, since the revival of the nuns' ordination in fact marks significant changes in Theravāda Buddhist practices, these changes need to be understood and represented as a return to an original and authentic tradition. In this process, the strong focus on the canonical text (as *buddhavacana*, the word of the Buddha) is crucial here. Reference to and reliance on the canonical Theravāda texts in many ways legitimizes the innovation as "traditional", as the return to pure, albeit imagined[31] origins. In what follows, I concentrate on the strong focus on canonical texts and especially on the reference to the text of the Buddhist monastic law (*vinaya*) as the locus of "true" and "original" Buddhism.

The Shifting Roles of the Canonical Texts:
Buddhist Monastic Law

It has often been stated that an important feature of Buddhist modernity as it emerged at the end of the nineteenth century in Southeast Asian countries is the increasing importance of Buddhist canonical texts understood to be the highest religious authority.[32] Texts were made widely available, for example by the Pali Text Society, through critical editions and prints, available for perusal not only by lay and monastic Buddhists but also by philologists and scholars of Buddhism, whose work then fed back into the perception of the Buddhist traditions from within.[33] This factor is especially important for the revival of the Theravāda nuns' order. The young tradition of Western Theravāda nuns strongly depends on the free availability of Buddhist texts. Not only are arguments *for* the revival of the nuns' ordination derived from the Vinaya texts, but the actual performance of the ordination procedures has also mainly been extracted from texts, since this ritual had not been performed in the Theravāda monastic communities for many centuries. The same holds true for the interpretation and practice of the monastic rules for nuns. According to monastic law, the rules for Buddhist monastics are "in house" documents, not to be taught to laypeople. Familiarity with the rules and their application is therefore gradually achieved in daily practice and interaction, after ordination, and before ordination through watching other monastics. This points to a basic difference between male and female Theravāda monastics: while monks have the opportunity to undergo rigorous training in monasteries in Asia and thus to develop a routine and understanding of monastic life similar to that of Asian Buddhist monks, the nuns had to reinvent their own monastic communities and monastic cultures. Not all Western nuns who went to Asia and practised Buddhism had the chance to train over longer periods of time with an established community. They are therefore exposed to many different influences and create their own style of monastic living—among them the practice of local monks' communities—often looking for guidance in the texts, and especially in the Vinaya. This text presents itself as guiding the daily life and the communal procedures of Buddhist monastics. It contains a set of rules for the individual monastics[34] and the formal acts (*kamma*) to be performed by the monastic communities (*saṅgha*), such as the ordination of new monks and nuns; significantly, it is accepted by Buddhists to be the "word of the Buddha".

The actual references to the Vinaya in the context of the revival of the Bhikkhunīsaṅgha are diverse. The text of the Vinaya is used as an argument both for and against the legitimacy of a revival of the Bhikkhunīsaṅgha.[35] In this context, the Vinaya narrative of how the order of nuns was established by the Buddha is frequently discussed, as we find therein a number of contradictory statements about the impact of Buddhist nuns on the Buddhist monastic community as a whole.[36] However, not only is the content of the Vinaya text of great importance, but the contemporary California nuns see the Vinaya rules also as the framework

250 *Ute Hüsken*

that connects female Theravāda Buddhist monastics worldwide. As one California nun said to me,

> All the different countries have one Vinaya tradition, even if it is embodied in different ways—there is a certain way that I can relate to *bhikkhunīs* all over the world, and this is a really useful universality. But the *bhikkhunīs* split up in these different forms, in Sīladharā and Mae Chi and Tila shin and so on, makes us not compatible. Then people can say "Yes, the *bhikkhunīs* cannot get on!" But the reason why we cannot get on is because we don't have the framework!

In fact, the common Vinaya rules are a vital factor in building and maintaining the local and global communities, defining the identity of monastics as distinct from laypeople, and tying the present Saṅgha to the past Saṅgha. In what follows, I discuss the role of the Vinaya text and practice for the recognition of the status and the economic survival of contemporary Bhikkhunīs in California.

Actual Practice and Vinaya Norms

Interestingly, the need for economic support of the Western Bhikkhunīs is a further key factor that ties them closely to the Vinaya regulations. In general, Western lay Buddhists do not provide a constant flow of donations and services for Buddhist monastic communities. Therefore, Theravāda monks and nuns often depend on the generosity of the Asian Buddhists living in the United States, and also on donations coming from Asia.[37] Donations to the monastic community are regular expenses and part of many Asian lay Buddhists' monthly household calculations. This generosity is based on the concept that donations (*dāna*) to the Saṅgha create religious merit (*puñña*) for the giver. Religious merit secures success and good luck in the present life and a good rebirth, and it can also be transferred, for example, to one's deceased parents, so that they have a good rebirth. However, these donations create religious merit, but are also hierarchically ordered: the most effective donation is to the Buddhist Saṅgha or to individual members of the Saṅgha.[38] In this context, it is essential that the nuns are considered to be regular members of the Saṅgha. Their status as "legally ordained" is therefore highly important for the California nuns. Yet this acknowledgment strongly depends on the Theravāda monks of Asian origin living in the West.[39] Their local support network also carries the nuns along and hinges on these monks' conviction that the nuns maintain a faultless style of living, and that their ordinations are performed according to the Vinaya regulations.

This is one of the reasons why the nuns in the San Francisco Bay Area are extremely careful to scrupulously follow the Vinaya rules when ordaining new nuns. Should the participating monks suspect that Vinaya rules are skipped or not adhered to, they might refuse to participate in these ordinations and withdraw their support for the emerging Bhikkhunīsaṅgha. The ordinations

Theravāda Nuns in the United States 251

organized by the California nuns must therefore be "strictly by the book", although the details of these rules are hardly known and difficult to understand and often do not represent a coherent legal system. Thus, on 1 November 2014 I had the chance to witness a nun's ordination in California. It was the nuns' explicit desire to "do things flawlessly", and they spent hours on the day before the ordination rehearsing the proceedings. The choreography was intensely discussed during the rehearsal, and the potential of "legal failure" was seen mainly in issues related to the boundary of the performing community (sīmā).[40] For this, however, the nuns had had to resort to Vinaya scholarship beyond their own Saṅgha. The head nun consulted extensively with the German scholar Petra Kieffer-Pülz, who was recommended to them as an expert in matters of monastic boundaries.

Interestingly, detailed knowledge of the monastic regulations is not even expected from the monastics by the Vinaya texts themselves. There are many passages in which it is assumed that the monastics know very little about the rules and regulations. Schopen has shown that the Mūlasarvāstivāda Vinaya depicts monks with a bare minimum of knowledge of the monastic rules as "Vinaya experts".[41] The contemporary reference and use of the Vinaya by the California nuns therefore differs substantially from the use and application of the Vinaya as described in the canonical texts. Yet strict adherence to all rules is understood today as the text's original intent, and the contemporary Vinaya practice of the nuns is therefore perceived as the return to the original tradition.

It should be noted that in actual practice we observe quite some flexibility among the Californian nuns, in spite of their devotion to the letter. While their monastic practices impress the onlooker as being very orthodox and traditional, and while the Vinaya is a constant matter of concern and reference, we often also see an existing flexibility in the performance and interpretation of the legal acts of the Saṅgha. During my conversations with Western Theravāda nuns during the 2013 meeting of Western Buddhist monastics, it became clear that the reality and on-the-ground experience of women who want to become Bhikkhunīs differs substantially from how it is described in public discussions about ordination. In practice, there are many ways to become a nun, and importantly the general acceptance of a nun among laypeople and among monastics does not simply depend on the details of her ordination. Thus, one senior nun, who herself acts as preceptor in many ordinations, an expert in Vinaya questions, talked as follows about her own way into nunhood:

> My ordination was unique because there was not a Bhikkhunī quorum, I was ordained by a Sri Lankan Bhikkhusaṅgha—ordained at one side. . . . Only five Bhikkhunīs were invited, and one got the flu and could not come. So I was ordained by the Bhikkhu procedure, but [*jokingly*] I converted to becoming a Bhikkhunī immediately.

While in some East Asian lineages the ordination of women "by one side", that is, by monks alone, is a standard procedure, in the Theravāda tradition such an

252   *Ute Hüsken*

ordination could be highly disputed, at least on the normative level. On the level of lived reality, however, this nun is highly respected. She is consulted not only by female monastics, but held in high regard by male monastics, too.[42]

Bell's (2000: 21) observation regarding the early British monks' Saṅgha also applies here: adherence to the Vinaya and charisma is closely interconnected and enables the actors to "maintain a creative balance between new developments and the maintenance of orthopraxy". Here, as with the Thai nun Nanthayani, reputation, charisma, and local presence are as important as Vinaya regulations and normative discourse.[43]

Thus, in spite of the Vinaya-centred rhetoric, the strict adherence to Vinaya rules is not the only indicator, nor even the most important one, as to whether a ritual performed by the Saṅgha is successful or whether it fails. Yet the globally dominant discourse is entrenched in a language of law, rights, and egalitarianism, and the ideal picture of a nun is mainly guided by textual descriptions found in the Vinaya, not by lived realities. And if someone wants to *challenge* the validity of a formal act by the Saṅgha, Vinaya arguments are the most powerful means to do so.[44]

A Return to Which Tradition?

Martin Baumann discusses the labels that are given to Buddhists who live and practise in Western countries and suggests "traditionalist" and "modernist" Buddhists (2002: 54), but cautions himself that "both forms have many internal variations" (2002: 56). However, when talking about Western women who adopt a monastic life style as Theravāda nuns in the United States, "modernist" does not capture their practices. Too much emphasis is placed on "following the tradition". Yet the nuns necessarily follow an *imagined* tradition, since the contemporary Theravāda nuns have to re-invent their own monastic culture. They necessarily do so assuming that their innovations constitute tradition. Shils makes the case that those who introduce (inevitable) modification often see these changes as being "in the spirit" of the tradition (1971: 151). Modification is presented and understood as the return to an original, pure tradition. This pattern is, as Shils argues, usually part of an "active and insistent search or demand for a tradition which is not immediately received and consensually recommended" (1971: 133). This description captures the situation of the California Bhikkhunīs well.

As McMahan (2008: 20) concedes, there are many forms of modernities. The form of modernizing Theravāda Buddhism we have been looking at here perceives innovation not as a new feature, but as a return to the authentic, original tradition. Here, modernization *is* traditionalization, and a separation of "modern" and "traditional" does not make sense. The California nuns' modernization of Theravāda Buddhism is thus a cultural process that turns the new into something old, not a cultural process that makes something new out of that which is old.[45]

Notes

1. I wish to thank Ayya Tathaloka, Petra Kieffer-Pülz, Ayya Sudhamma, Hanna Havnevik, Vladimir Tikhonov, the South Asian Studies group at the University of Texas at Austin, the members of the Asia Studies Brown Bag Seminar at Duke University, and the attendants of the conference "Buddhist Modernities" at Oslo University for their valuable input to earlier versions of this paper.
2. I use the term "Theravāda" here to refer to those traditions that accept the Mahāvihāra recension of the canon as authoritative (cf. Skilling 1993). This essay does not deal with the attempts to install a Tibetan nuns' ordination lineage, which is a related yet different process. "Nun" throughout this essay renders the Pāli term *bhikkhunī* or its Sanskrit equivalent, designating a woman who has undergone the monastic ceremony of "full ordination" (*upasampadā*). In my use of "nun", I depart from the terminology used by the vast majority of Theravāda Buddhists, who use the word "nun" rather as translation for female Buddhist practitioners *without* full ordination (Mae Chi or Tila Shin). The Bhikkhunīs in California generally render *bhikkhunī* as "female monk", "female monastic" or "monastic woman."
3. McMahan (2008: 243) mentions the efforts to revive the Bhikkhunīsaṅgha and the global organization Sakyadhita International, and also emphasizes the potentially profound effect this will have on Buddhism, but does not explore this topic further in his book.
4. McMahan describes "modernity" as a "stream" and "growing and shifting patterns" (2008: 4), rather than a specific form of Buddhism.
5. Following Milton Singer (1971), modernization is here understood as the gradual incorporation of new elements into a tradition. While Milton Singer's article is based on his analysis of these processes in urban India (Madras) in the mid-twentieth century, many of the mechanisms he describes capture the process of modernization in a variety of (religious) traditions and prove to be useful tools for the analysis of forms of contemporary Theravāda Buddhism. The ability to adapt and incorporate changes is fundamental to the survival of a tradition. For example, through its exceptional capacity to integrate local cults and gods who are subdued and then installed as "protectors of the *dhamma*", Buddhism was always undergoing modernization throughout its long history. Different forms of Buddhism have thus always "modernized" in the sense that they embraced numerous cultural adaptations (cf. McMahan 2008: 254).
6. In this article, for the sake of brevity, I speak of "Western" and "Asian" Buddhists (lay and monastic). I use the term "Western" here as shorthand for (mostly) Caucasian women and men who were not socialized in a cultural setting shaped mainly by Theravāda Buddhism. I use the term "Asian" here as shorthand for women and men of Asian descent, who were socialized in a cultural setting strongly influenced by Theravāda Buddhism, either in Asia or in the USA. This distinction emerges from the situation in the sites of my fieldwork and points to the importance of (sometimes imagined) racial distinctions in the process of the re-establishment of the Theravāda Buddhist nuns' Saṅgha in the USA and in Asia. This is, however, an issue that is not at the center of my attention for this article.
7. The historical Buddha is said to have founded first an order of monks (*bhikkhusaṅgha*), and not much later also an order of nuns (*bhikkhunīsaṅgha*). A Bhikkhunīsaṅgha might thus have existed since the fifth or fourth century BCE. The first inscriptional evidence for the existence of Bhikkhunīs is the Aśoka inscriptions. However, von Hinüber (2008) suggests that the establishment of the nuns' order took place *after* the Buddha's demise. See, however, Analayo (2013) on the issue.
8. While the reasons for the disappearance of the nuns' Saṅgha in India remain insufficiently explored, it is likely that the Bhikkhunīsaṅgha disappeared from Sri Lanka along with the Bhikkhusaṅgha in a period of political instability. While the

254 *Ute Hüsken*

Bhikkhusaṅgha was later reintroduced to Sri Lanka from Burma, the same did not or could not happen for the Bhikkhunīsaṅgha. On the disappearance of the Theravāda Bhikkhunīsaṅgha in different regions, see Skilling (1993) and Kieffer-Pülz (2000). The latest research (Kieffer-Pülz 2013) shows that, for example, in South India a sizeable Bhikkhunīsaṅgha still existed in the eleventh century. While among academics there is no agreement whether a nuns' Saṅgha ever existed in Tibet, individual fully ordained nuns did in fact live in Tibet (see, for example, Diemberger 2014); I thank Hanna Havnevik for providing me with this reference.

9. This does not, however, mean that there existed no Buddhist "professional celibate women" who might or might not have had the wish to become Bhikkhunīs. Collins and McDaniel (2010) show that scholarship on Buddhist women in fact urgently needs to take into account the many different statuses that Asian Buddhist women chose to occupy rather than being a Bhikkhunī.

10. On the international level, the revival of a full ordination for nuns has been promoted since the late 1980s, most prominently by members of the International Association of Buddhist Women, Sakyadhita. This organization continues to play an important role in spreading the idea of the revival of a nuns' lineage in the Theravāda and the Tibetan tradition.

11. As Ayya Sudhamma and Ayya Tathaloka informed me, such ordinations were performed in 1996, 1997, and 1998, and also in 2005.

12. This procedure is said to resemble the situation when Mahāpajāpatī Gotamī's female companions were ordained: there were no nuns yet, so they were ordained by monks alone. This seems also to have been the method when a Buddhist nuns' ordination was introduced in China in the fifth century CE (see Heirman 2001: 290, 297).

13. On the details of the "mix of traditions" as a Vinaya issue, see Hüsken and Kieffer-Pülz (2011). The power of this initial resistance against the first "mixed ordinations" in Los Angeles in 1988 forced some of the Singhalese women among the first batch of Theravāda nuns to defrock on their return to Sri Lanka, when they were neither supported nor acknowledged by the monks and laypeople. The same happened to the first American Bhikkhunī, Ayya Dhammapali. Yet also some of the key figures in the process of the re-establishment of the Bhikkhunīsaṅgha were ordained at that time (e.g. Ayya Khema and Dhammawati Guruma).

14. On some political aspects of the monks' involvement in Sri Lanka, see Abeyesekara (1999). Ayya Tathaloka informs me that there were also a few ordinations that took place even earlier (e.g. the 1988 ordination at His Lai in Southern California) with the support of senior Theravāda Bhikkhus.

15. A Thai law from the late 1920s forbids Thai monks to ordain women. This law remains in force (see Seeger [2006] 2008). It also needs to be mentioned that in Sri Lanka neither the official Saṅgha authorities nor the government do formally acknowledge Bhikkhunī ordinations. Consequently, the nuns do not receive monastic ID cards or government support similar to the support Bhikkhus are entitled to.

16. In early December 2014, Bhikkhunī Dhammananda planned to ordain more than 110 women temporarily as Sāmaṇerīs (female novices) in her Songdhammakalyani Monastery (see http://www.thaibhikkhunis.org/eng2014/index.html, accessed 10 September 2014; the content of the website—originally announcing the ordination in early December in Thailand—was changed). This took place in the context of a Bhikkhunī ordination that was held in Southern Thailand, Songkhla province, Koh Yoh Island, at Thippayasathandhamma Bhikkhuni Arama, on November 29th 2014. However, the National Office of Buddhism formally objected to leading Bhikkhus from abroad (in this case from Sri Lanka) entering Thailand undiplomatically and without going through proper channels, for the sake of ordaining Thai women as Bhikkhunīs. They were asked to apply for permission to enter the country for this purpose, with the understanding that permit would not be granted, as there is no process in place to grant such permission. Bhikkhunī Dhammananda now performs ordinations in Sri Lanka

Theravāda Nuns in the United States 255

(see http://www.thaibhikkhunis.org/eng2014/OrdinationSriLanka.html, accessed 12 February 2016). I thank Ayya Tathaloka for providing me with the details of these events.

17. These ordinations are not performed by a "mixed" tradition (with Chinese nuns and Theravāda monks), but here both the ordaining nuns and monks belong to the Theravāda tradition.

18. According to the Theravāda Vinaya, a nun has to be ordained for at least twelve years to be allowed to act as preceptor (*upajjhā*) in another nuns' ordination (see Hüsken 1997: 268). Importantly, again according to the Theravāda Vinaya, the fact that the female preceptors in these ordinations did not fulfil this requirement did not invalidate the ordinations.

19. This is also explicitly expressed by the Western monk Jayasaro in the documentary film *The Buddha's Forgotten Nuns* (Sati 2013). His ground to oppose a Bhikkhunī ordination is his perception that Thai women do not demand ordination.

20. Even though I argue here that this stance does not capture the whole picture, it needs to be mentioned that this stance is in fact taken by some women who are very active in the "international Buddhist nuns' movement", as a heated discussion between Tibetan nuns living in Asia and Western nuns during the 2007 conference in Hamburg made clear (Hüsken and Kieffer-Pülz 2011).

21. Collins and McDaniel (2010) see these Mae Chis as belonging to a third category, beyond the standard claimed dichotomy of house and houselessness. They also lay out powerful evidence of the high level of education that many of these Mae Chis possess, which is in stark contrast to the generally denigratory perception of the Mae Chis, perpetuated also through academic writing about the Bhikkhunī movement (Collins and McDaniel 2010: 1384 and n. 31).

22. However, even among Mae Chis internal hierarchies exist: those Mae Chis who concentrate on study and meditation often look down upon the "kitchen Mae Chi" (*mae chi krua*), who spend all their time cooking and serving the monks (see Collins and McDaniel 2010: 1396).

23. Her 2013 book is based on more than twenty-five years of conversations with female Buddhist renunciants in Sri Lanka.

24. Prominent Western monks who support the revival of the Bhikkhunīsaṅgha are for example Bhikkhu Bodhi (the United States), Ajahn Sujato and Ajahn Brahm (both Australia), and Bhikkhu Analayo (Germany).

25. Again, the situation is by no means uniform: also some of the Theravāda monks living in the United States refuse to participate in these ordinations, while others are openly positive and supportive. Yet the role of transnational Asian Bhikkhus living in the West, especially Bhante Ratanasara and Bhante Gunaratana, was extremely important in this process. These monks were exceptional in encouraging and supporting women's ordination in the West, both for women of Asian and of European or American ancestry.

26. I do not subscribe to this view, which deprives people such as nun Nanthayani of their agency.

27. While it needs to be acknowledged that, in many cases, feminist ways of thinking and feminist arguments are present in the debates, reducing (and thus dismissing) efforts to establish a Bhikkhunīsaṅgha to "feminism" and a "struggle for gender equality" is much too reductionist. The realities are far more complex.

28. For a study of the political and historical contexts of female Buddhist renunciants, especially in the Northern Thai tradition, see Itoh (2013).

29. "Modernity . . . is a permanent layer or dimension of indigenous culture and not simply a collection of recent foreign imports or the fashionable life-style of a privileged class" (Singer 1971: 175).

30. As Ayya Tathaloka informs me, even the Theravāda Bhikkhunīs in California who are of Asian ancestry are perceived as foreign by Asian Bhikkhus in the USA due to their

256 *Ute Hüsken*

being Bhikkhunīs. For the Western California nuns, there exists therefore a "double foreignness" due to being Westerners *and* being Bhikkhunīs.

31. It is important to note here that this does holds true not only for the Bhikkhunīs who are the main subject of this essay, but also for the Theravāda tradition in its entirety: "The source or model of the recreated tradition need never have existed in the form in which the seeker alleges; what is significant is that he believes that it did so exist" (Shils 1971: 133).

32. For a detailed list of characteristic features of Buddhist modernism, see Baumann (2002).

33. The Singhalese elite Buddhists, for example, obtained access to their own textual heritage through publications in English and the Pāli texts printed in Roman letters. One recent example of this kind of collaboration of Buddhists and academics is the 2007 conference in Hamburg with invited scholars and Buddhists as contributors (for details, see Hüsken and Kieffer-Pülz 2011).

34. The Theravāda tradition gives 227 rules for monks and 311 rules for nuns (see Hüsken 1997).

35. The main argument of the opponents of the ordination of women is that without pre-existing Bhikkhunīs who participate in the formal procedures, the ordination of women is impossible. Once the lineage is interrupted, it is gone until the next Buddha establishes the nuns' order again. In the Vinaya, we find the regulation that nuns have to be ordained by Buddhist monks *and* Buddhist nuns—yet we also find instances of the ordination of women by monks alone. For details on these discussions, see Hüsken and Kieffer-Pülz (2011).

36. See, for example, Hüsken (2000). While it seems to be acknowledged among many Buddhists that even a single Vinaya contains contradictory statements, the focus is now rather on the questions of which statement should be given more weight, and why.

37. As Vladimir Tikhonov suggests (personal email communication), this relationship can be characterized as quintessentially modern, as it implies the inclusion of Asia into the globalized market economy, as well as the dependence of the religious body on its success in "marketing" itself to overseas customers. This specific case also signifies some degree of (economic) power being wielded by the Asian Buddhists vis-à-vis their "Western" co-religionists, subverting the conventional centre-periphery hierarchy.

38. This difference between unordained Buddhist ascetics and ordained monks and nuns is even more pronounced in those countries in which the Buddhist Saṅgha receives state support, such as Sri Lanka, Myanmar, and Thailand. This is one major reason for the lay nuns' poverty in such places. Moreover, according to the canonical texts, the efficacy of a donation is also dependent on the donors' and the recipients' intentions and mental state.

39. This situation is very similar to what Bell (2000: 2, 10–11) describes for the early phases of Theravāda Buddhism in Great Britain.

40. On "legal" grounds for the failure of a formal act of the Saṅgha, see Bodhi (2007: 9).

41. See Schopen (2014): a monk well versed in the discipline is one who knows the four Pārājika rules—these are only the four most basic rules. Similar (though less drastic) passages are found in the Pāli Vinaya.

42. Salgado reports a similar trend when it comes to the *garudhamma* rules in Sri Lanka (Salgado 2013: 11). The authority of these rules in practice is challenged, despite a stated acceptance of them (Salgado 2008: 203).

43. See also Bell (2000: 21).

44. Salgado (2013) mentions a nun from Nepal who felt the need to undergo ordination when she was visiting the United States, since full ordination (*upasampadā*) there had become such an important marker of status within the Buddhist community.

45. "The cultural ideology of 'traditionalism' [is] one of the major instruments of modernization" (Singer 1971: 161).

Theravāda Nuns in the United States 257

References

Abeyesekara, Ananda. 1999. "Politics of Higher Ordination, Buddhist Monastic Identity, and Leadership at the Dambulla Temple in Sri Lanka." *Journal of the International Association of Buddhist Studies* 22 (2): 255–280.

Analayo, Bhikkhu. 2013. "The Revival of the Bhikkhuni Order and the Decline of the Sasana." *Journal of Buddhist Ethics* 20: 147–193.

Baumann, Martin. 2002. "Protective Amulets and Awareness Techniques, or How to Make Sense of Buddhism in the West." In *Westward Dharma: Buddhism beyond Asia*, edited by Charles S. Prebish and Martin Baumann, 51–65. Berkeley, CA: University of California Press.

Bell, Sandra. 2000. "Being Creative with Tradition: Rooting Theravāda Buddhism in Britain." *Journal of Global Buddhism* 1: 1–23.

Bodhi, Bhikkhu. 2007. *The Revival of Bhikkhunī Ordination in the Theravāda Tradition.* Penang: Inward Path.

Collins, Steven, and Justin McDaniel. 2010. "Buddhist 'Nuns' (mae chi) and the Teaching of Pali in Contemporary Thailand." *Modern Asian Studies* 44 (6): 1373–1408.

Diemberger, Hildegard. 2014. *When a Woman Becomes a Religious Dynasty: The Samding Dorje Phagmo of Tibet.* New York: Columbia University Press.

Heirman, Ann. 2001. "Chinese Nuns and Their Ordination in Fifth Century China." *Journal of the International Association of Buddhist Studies* 24 (2): 275–304.

Hinüber, Oskar von. 2008. "The Foundation of the Bhikkhunīsaṃgha: A Contribution to the Earliest History of Buddhism." *Annual Report of the International Research Institute for Advanced Buddhology at Soka University* 11 (*for the Academic Year 2007*), Tokyo: 3–29.

Hüsken, Ute. 1997. *Die Vorschriften für die buddhistische Nonnengemeinde im Vinaya-Pitaka der Theravadin* [Monographien zur indischen Archäologie, Kunst und Philologie 11]. Berlin: D. Reimer.

———. 2000. "The Legend of the Establishment of the Buddhist Order of Nuns in the Theravāda Vinaya-Piṭaka." *Journal of the Pali Text Society* 26: 43–69.

Hüsken, Ute, and Petra Kieffer-Pülz. 2011. "Buddhist Ordination as Initiation Ritual and Legal Procedure." In *Negotiating Rites*, edited by Ute Hüsken and Frank Neubert, 255–276. New York: Oxford University Press.

Itoh, Ayako. 2013. "The Emergence of the bhikkhunī saṅgha in Thailand." PhD diss., École Pratique des Hautes Etudes.

Kieffer-Pülz, Petra. 2000. "Die buddhistische Gemeinde." In *Der Buddhismus I: Der indische Buddhismus und seine Verzweigungen*, edited by Heinz Bechert, 278–399. Stuttgart: Kohlhammer Verlag.

———. 2013. "Buddhist Nuns in South India as Reflected in the Andhakaṭṭhakathā and in Vajrabuddhi's Anugaṇṭhipada." *Annual Report of the International Research Institute for Advanced Buddhology* 16: 29–46.

McMahan, David L. 2008. *The Making of Buddhist Modernism.* Oxford: Oxford University Press.

Salgado, Nirmala S. 2008. "Eight Revered Conditions: Ideological Complicity, Contemporary Reflections and Practical Realities." *Journal of Buddhist Ethics* 15: 176–213.

———. 2013. *Buddhist Nuns and Gendered Practice: In Search of the Female Renunciant.* New York: Oxford University Press.

Sati, Wiriya. 2013. *The Buddha's Forgotten Nuns.* Culture Unplugged video, 33:54. Produced by Katrina Lucas. http://www.cultureunplugged.com/documentary/watch-online/play/50345/The-Buddha-s-Forgotten-Nuns.

258 *Ute Hüsken*

Schopen, Gregory. 2014. "On Incompetent Monks and Able Urban Nuns in a Buddhist Monastic Code." In *Buddhist Nuns, Monks, and Other Worldly Matters: Recent Papers on Monastic Buddhism in India*, edited by Gregory Schopen, 47–72. Honolulu: University of Hawai'i Press.

Seeger, Martin. (2006) 2008. "The Bhikkhuni-Ordination Controversy in Thailand." *Journal of the International Association of Buddhist Studies* 29: 155–183.

Shils, Edward. 1971. "Tradition." In "Tradition and Modernity", special issue, *Comparative Studies in Society and History* 13 (2): 122–159.

Singer, Milton. 1971. "Beyond Tradition and Modernity in Madras." In "Tradition and Modernity", special issue, *Comparative Studies in Society and History* 13 (2): 160–195.

Skilling, Peter. 1993. "A Note on the History of the Bhikkhunī-saṅgha (II): The Order of Nuns after the Parinirvāṇa." *World Fellowship of Buddhists Review* 30 (4)/31 (1): 29–49.

15 Some Reflections on Thích Nhất Hạnh's Monastic Code for the Twenty-First Century

Jens W. Borgland

Introduction

Regulating the conduct of individual monks and nuns, as well as the monastic order as a whole, the Buddhist monastic law codes (*vinaya*) represent an almost 2,500-year-old legal tradition of considerable sophistication. Buddhist monastic law is the foundation of the Buddhist monastic order (*saṃgha*), which has in turn played an essential part in the spread of Buddhism both within and beyond India. Where the monastic community (*saṃgha*) has spread, so have the monastic law codes.[1] One of the core texts of these Buddhist monastic law codes is the *Prātimokṣa*,[2] containing the list of rules all individual monastics are to live by, although the degree to which its precepts have been observed has varied greatly in different places at different times.

Law, whether monastic or civil, religious or secular, is a cultural product. As such, it not only is deeply influenced by the wider culture within which it was produced, but is in many ways an expression of this culture, here understood in the widest possible sense, including material culture, technology, economic culture, and so forth, at the time of its formulation. Being composed in India close to 2,500 years ago, the *Prātimokṣa* and its rules are in large part an expression of a time and culture that is far removed from the manifold contexts in which Buddhism is today lived and practised. With the spread of the Buddhist *saṃgha* to the West, many characterize the challenges to the *Prātimokṣa* as being greater than ever, leading to gloomy predictions concerning the future of Buddhist monasticism.[3]

The spread of Buddhism to the West is here understood as one important aspect of modernity. Yet of course "modernity" encompasses many more interconnected processes and developments. Structural differentiation and secularization, industrialization, technological progress, and the rise of the hard sciences are among the central processes making up this phenomenon. So too are individualization, the weakening of gender hierarchies, and the privatization of religion. Technological progress has had an enormous impact on communications and infrastructure, changing the way in which (and the extent to which) people, including Buddhist monastics, communicate and travel, and binding the whole world together. It is especially important for this chapter that globalization, at least in some respects an extension of modernization, has brought both Buddhists (lay and monastic) and

260 *Jens W. Borgland*

"Buddhism" to the world, and that it has brought the world to traditionally Buddhist countries. All of these processes have naturally had significant impact on Buddhist monasticism, and hence on Buddhist monastic law, since the latter aims to regulate the behaviour of Buddhist monastics in relation to the larger sociocultural setting in which they exist.

One of the most interesting recent responses to the perceived challenge posed by modernity to the relevance of the *Prātimokṣa*, so far almost unnoticed or perhaps simply ignored in scholarly literature,[4] is a revised *Prātimokṣa*, published in 2004 by the well-known Vietnamese Buddhist monk, activist, and author Thích Nhất Hạnh as "A Buddhist Monastic Code for the Twenty-first Century". This revised code has, in Hạnh's own words, "substituted trainings that are no longer appropriate to our time with new trainings that are essential to protect the practice and integrity of monastic members" (Hạnh 2004: ix), with the expressed purpose of "protect[ing] the freedom and integrity of monastic practice, so that the *authentic* path of liberation can continue" (2004: x, emphasis added).

As has recently been pointed out by Tzu-Lung Chiu, studies of Buddhist monastic law have so far mostly been concerned with the past (2014: 11). This includes also my own research. As a small contribution towards remedying this state of affairs, I will in this chapter look at Hạnh's revised *Prātimokṣa* in relation to the broader history of *vinaya* adaptation, both in India and beyond. Examining his arguments for why the *vinaya*, regarded as the words of the Buddha himself, both can and should be revised, I will then take a closer look at some matters of monastic legislation that have been highlighted as particularly troubling for modern monks, and compare Hạnh's solutions to these problems with how other monastic communities have dealt with these challenges. The adaptation of Buddhist monastic law to changing circumstances and demands is an ongoing process as old as the *vinaya*s themselves, and Hạnh's code is but one of the latest, albeit untraditional, examples of this. That it is used and studied in a globalized monastic community of approximately 200 monastics makes the revised *Prātimokṣa* a significant new development in modern Buddhist monasticism, a development that warrants a closer look.

This chapter has no ambition to be exhaustive, even with regard to the goals outlined above. It is, moreover, not possible here to thoroughly and systematically compare Hạnh's rules with the canonical texts. Even though Hạnh never explains which version of the *Prātimokṣa* the term "Classical Pratimoksha" refers to, that is, which version of the *Prātimokṣa* is the basis of the revised *Prātimokṣa*, there are good reasons to conclude that it is the *Prātimokṣa* of the Dharmaguptaka school.[5] But many of Hạnh's changes can be fully understood only in light of rules found in the vast canonical commentary on the *Prātimokṣa* (the *Vibhaṅga*), as well as the sections devoted primarily to monastic procedures (the "Chapters").[6] Since no *vinaya* holds any explanatory relevance for traditions other than itself (as pointed out by Heirman 2008: 175, n. 6), a systematic investigation into Hạnh's changes, while undoubtedly interesting, would require comprehensive treatement of Dharmaguptaka materials.[7] Lastly, it is purely for reasons of brevity and

Thich Nhất Hạnh's Monastic Code 261

simplicity that I shall here contain myself to the *Prātimokṣa* for monks and not discuss Hạnh's adaptation of the *Prātimokṣa* for nuns.[8]

Hạnh, His Monastic Code, and Plum Village

Thich Nhất Hạnh, a Zen master in the Vietnamese tradition, is a world-famous Buddhist monk, author, and peace activist. Since Aike Rots's contribution to the present volume deals in depth with some of his activities, here we need only to say that, after founding the Order of Interbeing in the 1960s, a movement that has spread to many countries around the globe, Hạnh later settled in Bordeaux, France (Kay 2004: 32). There he founded Plum Village, "a Buddhist monastery for monks and nuns and a mindfulness practice center for lay people" (Plum Village 2014c). In addition to its main monastery in France, Plum Village also has practice centres in the United States, Germany, Thailand, and Australia (Plum Village 2014a, 2014c). According to the Plum Village website, approximately 200 monastics are presently spread among three such centres: Plum Village in France, Deer Park Monastery in California, and Blue Cliff Monastery in New York (Plum Village 2014a), making it a prime example of a modern, globalized Buddhist monastic community.

Although published by Hạnh, the revised *Prātimokṣa* appears to have been made by the Dharma Teacher Council of Plum Village, and so should be viewed as the result of a collective effort spanning five years (Hạnh 2004: ix).[9] According to Hạnh's preface, the revised *Prātimokṣa* is studied by ordained monks and nuns at Plum Village (2004: vii), but Hạnh explains that the revised *Prātimokṣa* also "aims to offer guidance and support to contemporary Buddhist monastics living both in Asia and in the West" (2004: ix).

Hạnh further states that the monks and nuns in the Plum Village Sangha must spend at least five years studying the *vinaya* (i.e. the Buddhist monastic legal code), and that this study includes both "the Revised and the Classical Pratimoksha" (2004: vii).[10] The revised *Prātimokṣa* contains not only rules, but also formulas for the fortnightly *poṣadha* ceremony during which the *Prātimokṣa* is recited.[11] This indicates that it is meant to be recited, and so can completely replace the "Classical Pratimoksha".

Buddhist Monastic Law, the *Prātimokṣa*, and Adaptation

The Buddhist monastic legal codes, or *vinaya*s, six of which are today extant in their entirety,[12] are canonical scriptures. These six legal codes all contain somewhat different versions of the *Prātimokṣa*,[13] and so the *Prātimokṣa* too is a canonical text,[14] containing rules regarded to have been declared by the Buddha himself. This ascription to the Buddha is ultimately the source of these rules' authority, for the Buddha is considered the only legitimate lawgiver (von Hinüber 1995: 7).

In addition to the *Prātimokṣa*, which contains the core set of rules, the *vinaya*s contain a canonical commentary on the *Prātimokṣa*, the *Vibhaṅga*,[15] as well as

262   *Jens W. Borgland*

sections known as "Chapters" (Skt. *vastu*; Pāli *khandhaka*).[16] The latter contain chapters with rules pertaining to monastic procedures and communal life. However, the "Chapters" sections also contain many rules pertaining to individual monastics. For example, the rule against monks riding in a vehicle, a rule many deem particularly problematic in modern times, is contained not in the *Prātimokṣa* but in the "Chapters".[17]

Although several different versions of the *Prātimokṣa* exist, they are all remarkably similar. Part of the reason for this is that the rules were regarded as the words of the Buddha (*buddhavacana*). But this is not in itself enough, and more importantly the *Prātimokṣa* also, in addition to its legal function, has served an important ceremonial function through its fortnightly recitation (see n. 11). It is probably the combination of these two factors that has led to the stability of the *Prātimokṣa*, and so in turn to its importance for the Buddhist monastic identity.

It is clear that the *Prātimokṣa* at a relatively early date was considered impossible to change.[18] The Buddhist tradition views this attitude as going back to the first council, held after the Buddha's death, at which it was decided that none of the rules laid down by the Buddha could be removed, despite the Buddha's reported deathbed instruction to Ānanda saying that some of the minor rules could be ignored, and that no new rules would be added. The problem was the same as it is today, namely which rules, exactly, are "minor".

That this decision was not really upheld for the *vinaya* as a whole, at least not before considerable time had passed, is clear once the *Prātimokṣa*s are compared to their later canonical commentaries, the *Vibhaṅga*s, as well as the "Chapters" sections of the *vinaya*s. One example must suffice here. Throughout the *Vibhaṅga*, "Chapters" (*Vinayavastu*), and other sections of the *Mūlasarvāstivāda vinaya* (MSV), there are many examples of monks being allowed, and even encouraged, to accept gold, money, and so forth from laypeople, despite this not being allowed in the *Prātimokṣa* (Schopen 2000: 99–103). The MSV *Prātimokṣa* forbids monks to accept[19] *jātarūparajata* ("gold and silver").[20] But, as Schopen (2000: 102) points out, "the rule does not refer to *suvarṇa*, or *hiraṇya* or *kārṣāpaṇa*s ('gold', 'silver', 'money')".[21] And it is precisely these things, and not *jātarūparajata*, that monks "own, accept, handle and inherit" in the other sections of this *vinaya* (Schopen 2000: 102). The most likely explanation for this difference is that the authors and redactors of the MSV purposefully employed different terms than those used in the *Prātimokṣa*, thus bypassing the original prohibition.[22]

This example illustrates two interesting points. First, the perceived need to adapt and change the rules governing Buddhist monastics is far from new and was prevalent even in India before the canonical *vinaya*s were closed to further redaction. But, second, and equally interesting for our purposes, is that these changes and adaptations were made without altering the *Prātimokṣa*, which was closed to redaction at a considerably earlier date than the other parts of the canonical *vinaya* and so could no longer be touched. Adaptation of Buddhist monastic law could thus for some time be achieved through redacting or adding to other sections of the

Thích Nhất Hạnh's Monastic Code 263

vinaya. But at some point—the exact time of which is unknown and depends on the *vinaya* in question—the other parts of the canonical *vinaya* were also closed to redaction and could no longer be changed. Similar adaptation then continued in the commentarial literature (Gombrich 1988: 164; Kieffer-Pülz 2007). But there were also always other ways to adapt, or get around, monastic law.

In addition to the rules of the canonical *vinaya* and the commentaries, individual monastic communities (*saṃgha*) were governed by local ordinances (*kriyākāra*).[23] Through such ordinances the *vinaya* could be augmented or adapted according to local conditions without changing the *vinaya*. Such ordinances are attested in the canonical *vinaya*s,[24] and later in epigraphic evidence from Turkestan, south India, and Sri Lanka (Kieffer-Pülz 2014: 60). In Sri Lanka, local ordinances were composed throughout the nineteenth and twentieth centuries (Ratnapala 1971: 12),[25] and similar kinds of local ordinances also developed elsewhere. In Tibetan Buddhist monasticism, the so-called monastic guidelines (*bca' yig*)[26] still play a more important role than the canonical *vinaya* (Dreyfus 2003: 40). The Chinese Buddhist tradition developed the "rules of purity" (清規 *qinggui*).[27] A prime example, which we will occasionally return to below, is the twelfth-century *Chanyuan qinggui*. This code served as the prototype for later, similar texts composed both in China and Japan (Yifa [2003] 2009: 38–45). Both in Sri Lanka and in China such local ordinances led also to the development of national ordinances (Ratnapala 1971; Yifa [2002] 2009: 48–49; Kieffer-Pülz 2014: 60; Walters 2014: 137). Buddhism has thus developed distinctly regional flavours also when it comes to discipline and monastic regulations.

Strategies for getting around certain rules were also developed through the use of "legalizers" (*kalpikāra*).[28] A legalizer, in essence, is a monastery attendant (*ārāmika*) or lay follower (*upāsaka*) who "launders" donations that monks are not allowed to receive, such as money, by using them on the monks' behalf, thus exchanging them for something else (Gombrich 1988: 92, 102–103; Kieffer-Pülz 2007: 20). In this way the legalizers may also function as a legal loophole for getting around the rule against monks "buying and selling" (Schopen 2001: 122). This practice, which is well attested in the canonical *vinaya*s and even has precedents in the *Prātimokṣa*,[29] is found also in the Chinese "rules of purity" (Yifa [2002] 2009: 62–64) and is still employed today in Sri Lanka (Gombrich 1988: 103) and Taiwan (Chiu 2014: 18–20).

Considering this, one may, as some have, describe the *Prātimokṣa* as a kind of "charter" or "constitution" providing the basis of Buddhist monastic life (Kondinya 1986: 113). As is noted by Berthe Jansen, "[t]he word 'constitution' communicates a sense of permanence, indicating that the rules are somehow fundamental" (2013: 112). This seems to be an appropriate description of how the *Prātimokṣa* has been viewed within the Buddhist tradition.[30] While there is much to indicate that it was not always, if ever, followed in all details, and that new circumstances necessitated that the rules be bent, stretched, or augmented, the importance of the *Prātimokṣa* has been just as much, if not more, its symbolic value and its role as the basis for both monastic discipline and identity. It is for these reasons that the *Prātimokṣa* has remained essentially unchanged as it was

264   *Jens W. Borgland*

transported through time, space, and cultural barriers. And it is for this reason that Hạnh's decision to revise the *Prātimokṣa* seems so radical.

Monastic Law Meets the Modern World

Adapting monastic law to the local setting, or finding ways to circumvent the rules, is thus not at all a modern phenomenon. Still, modern conditions, and especially in the West, are generally considered particularly challenging for this old monastic legal tradition. And although it seems to be widely agreed that some adaptation of the rules must be allowed, again particularly in the West, the idea of actually changing the rules of the *vinaya* has largely been dismissed (cf. Numrich 1996: 52). Numrich reports one monk comparing changing the *vinaya* to dismembering the Buddha, since the Buddha said that after his death the *vinaya* was to be the teacher (Numrich 1996: 52). Adaptation has therefore been achieved through the implementation of local ordinances and the use of legalizers. Now, as before, the problem lies in what kinds of adaptations are acceptable (see Numrich 1994: 25).

One of the early champions for adapting Buddhist monastic law in order to accommodate the different cultural and economic conditions faced in the West was the well-known Sri Lankan monk and scholar Walpola Rahula (cf. Rahula 1978).[31] Like Rahula and others, Hạnh argues for the necessity of adapting monastic law to modern conditions, although he makes no mention of the possibilities of doing this through the use of local ordinances. Characterizing the *vinaya* as "the foundation for the survival of the Sangha" (2004: vii–viii) and the *Prātimokṣa* as the "heart of the Vinaya" (2004: viii), Hạnh states that "[t]echnological developments, mass media and the spread of modern life" have influenced monastic communities. This has led to "degradation of the monastic lifestyle . . . all over the world". A revised *Prātimokṣa* is therefore urgently needed as a response to this situation (2004: ix).

Revising the precepts necessarily challenges the traditional authority ascribed to the Buddha as being the only lawgiver. Hạnh recognizes this objection, and counters that as the "children of the Buddha . . . his continuation", they are practising to carry out his wishes (2004: x). In order for the path of liberation to continue, the precepts must be revised. According to Hạnh, the essence of the precepts is "mindfulness" (2004: 3–5), and clinging to their "outer form" corresponds to the fifth wrong view described by the Buddha, and cannot lead to liberation (2004: 5–8). The precepts "guarantee our freedom and our happiness" (2004: 12), and so "[i]f a precept does not have this function, there is no need for it" (2004: 26). In essence, Hạnh's argument is that the *Prātimokṣa* was composed not only at a certain time and place, but *for* that time and place. What is most important is the essence of the precepts ("mindfulness") and their ultimate function as an aid on the spiritual path. So long as that is not altered, and the reputation and integrity of the monastic community is not jeopardized,[32] they can, and should, therefore be revised.

Thích Nhất Hạnh's Monastic Code   265

Hạnh argues that the precepts have always been dynamic (2004: 13), and that they must respond to real situations. They are not absolute truths, and so with changing circumstances new precepts must be added,[33] while precepts that are no longer applicable should be removed (2004: 17–18). To justify this, Hạnh quotes the Buddha:

> The Buddha said, "Although I have given you precepts *for this particular time and place*, if you should come to a certain place and the laws of that land are different, *you should not use the precepts that have been given to you here*. You should not practice in a way that goes against the laws of the land where you are living." The Buddha also said, "There may be precepts I have not yet devised, but *if you come to a part of the world where they are needed then you have to devise these precepts.*"
>
> (Hạnh 2004: 17, emphasis added)

Hạnh does not give any references for these quotes, which appear to be an essentially accurate paraphrase of a statement found in the *Mahīśāsaka vinaya*:

> Again [the Buddha] told the monks: although it has been stipulated by me, but elsewhere is not regarded as pure, [then] none of it should be applied. [And] even if it has not been stipulated by me, but elsewhere should be done, [then] it all must be done.[34]

The *Mahīśāsaka vinaya*, in which this passage is found, is not the basis of any ordination tradition in use today. Still, the passage is remarkable in that the Buddha here in fact appears to explicitly sanction large-scale adaptation of the discipline in accordance with what the circumstances require.[35] This is at least how Hạnh reads it, although note that Hạnh's rendering of the final statement as "devising precepts" is rather free, since this suits his argument.

Considering the role and status of the *Prātimokṣa* discussed above, and the traditional view of the Buddha as the only lawgiver, Hạnh's decision to adapt monastic discipline by revising the *Prātimokṣa* is remarkable. Nevertheless, his assertion that certain adaptations are needed seems to be widely accepted, although both the degree and mode of change that is acceptable is debated, as we shall see below. Moreover, many of the changes implemented by Hạnh concern the same issues as those highlighted in secondary literature on present-day monasticism. Although differences between traditions make direct comparison problematic, we will here take a closer look at three such issues:

* rules concerning monastic dress
* rules concerning transportation
* the use of money[36]

The degree of adaptation that is considered acceptable, even with regard to these issues, varies not only from individual to individual, but also between Buddhist

266   *Jens W. Borgland*

traditions and even distinct monasteries. Still, Paul Numrich discerns three hermeneutical principles of *vinaya* adaptation in the American Theravāda temples he has studied (Numrich 1994: 27). Not only can these three principles be extended beyond the American context, they have probably been valid throughout much of the history of Buddhist monasticism:

1. Only modification of so-called minor rules is accepted.
2. Within such minor adaptations, *practicality* is a central concern.
3. All such modification relies on *consensus* between monks and laity.

Monastic discipline has always had economic implications. One of the important functions of Buddhist monastics has been to serve as a "field of merit" (*puṇyakṣetra*) for the laity. Since they depend on lay donations (*dāna*), monastics must be sure not to act in a way that the laity finds impious or impure. This restricts what kind of adaptation is possible, although it has also prompted changes in monastic rules (see Schopen 1992, 2007).

Regarding the three issues highlighted above, we see a variety of stances and solutions in different monastic communities. All of these matters are complex. On the one hand, the rules concerning monastic dress,[37] including the rules prohibiting the use of shoes, can be viewed as culture-specific.[38] On the other hand, monastic robes, together with shaven heads, have always been important identity markers for Buddhist monks (cf. Schopen 2007: esp. 68–70). A third factor that also comes into play is climate. The rules were made in India, and did not account for icy winters. These problems are far from new. The Buddha himself is stated to have allowed some adaptations to the climate of faraway regions.[39] Once Buddhism spread to China in the beginning of the Common Era, monastic dress was adapted to Chinese culture and climate (Kieschnick 1999: 17; Hume 2013: 110), although monastics continued to shave their heads, contrary to Chinese cultural norms (Kieschnick 1999: 9).

The present-day stance on monastic dress seems to most widely be solved by keeping the traditional dress, but adding whatever extra clothing is deemed necessary due to the local climate (see Numrich 1994: 26). The rules concerning clothing in Hạnh's revised code are in this respect in themselves not at all radical, although they do incorporate Vietnamese elements.[40] Monks are explicitly allowed to use extra clothing to protect against the cold,[41] but must shave their hair[42] and are forbidden to wear lay clothes or a wig[43] or to design their monastic clothes in modern or fashionable ways.[44]

A second issue that is often highlighted as particularly problematic in modern times is the question of transportation. Not being allowed to ride vehicles unless they are ill[45] severely limits the movements of monastics in modern, urban environments where little, if anything, lies within walking distance. Walking may, moreover, be very dangerous (Numrich 1996: 48).[46] Among Theravādin monks in the United States, this has been solved in two ways. Interpreting the rule as prohibiting monks only from driving themselves, laypeople are used as chauffeurs (Numrich 1996: 48–49), thus acting as "legalizers" (*kalpikāra*). That neither the

Thích Nhất Hạnh's Monastic Code   267

problem, nor this solution, is uniquely modern is indicated by the aforementioned twelfth-century Chinese "rules of purity" text *Chanyuan qinggui*, which mentions "vehicle servers" among the kinds of servers acting as legalizers (Yifa [2002] 2009: 62). Alternatively, monks must use public transport.

Other monasteries, however, allow monks to drive (Numrich 1996: 49) through what amounts to a kind of local ordinance. Hạnh's revised code, too, allows monks to drive a car. However, monks are not allowed to own their own car, nor are they to use expensive, flashy, or brightly coloured vehicles.[47] Moreover, the revised code contains several rules detailing how monks should behave while driving. They are not to drive carelessly, swerve between cars, recklessly pass other cars, drive too fast, or race with another car.[48] While driving, they should also not joke, indulge in small talk, talk on the phone, and so forth, nor should they honk in irritation at other drivers.[49] A monk must also make sure to have all his documents (driver's licence, etc.), wear a seat belt, and make sure that the robe does not get caught in the door so it hangs outside the car.[50] Lastly, if a monk is undertaking a long drive and feels sleepy, he must have someone else drive, or stop and rest.[51]

The issue of Buddhist monastics and money[52] is a tricky one. As already noted above, ways to get around the prohibition against accepting gold, silver, and money, as well as the rule against engaging in various kinds of "buying and selling", have been devised from the very early period of Buddhist monasticism. Still, the use of money is often presented as especially pressing for modern-day monastics. According to Cheng, it is for instance common also for monks in present-day Sri Lanka to handle money, since it is viewed as inevitable "under contemporary social circumstances" (2007: 126), although it is not specified why that is.[53] In the Chinese context, Chiu explains that "[t]he majority of Chinese Buddhist monastic members in Mainland China and Taiwan report difficulties in observing the precept of not touching money, difficulties that are partly due to the social and cultural conditions they live in" (2014: 29–30).[54] Monastics need to pay bus fare and go shopping for necessities, and they also feel pressured to accept cash offerings from lay supporters (Birnbaum 2003: 443; Chiu 2014: 22–27, 36–37, 40–41).

According to Chiu, the problem of money is solved in one or two ways among nuns in China and Taiwan. Strict monasteries, such as Nanlin nunnery, use "legalizers" to handle things that are proscribed for monastics, including money (Chiu 2014: 18–20)—as is also prescribed in the *Chanyuan qinggui* (Yifa [2002] 2009: 63)—although even here exceptions are made (Chiu 2014: 38). A similar approach is reported to be used by the British Theravādin forest monasteries (Bell 2000: 18–19), but here through the innovation of the *anagārika*, a kind of cross between a layperson and a monastic that has taken the place of the novice and acts in the role of an *ārāmika* (monastery attendant) and a legalizer.[55]

Other monasteries in China and Taiwan instead show flexibility regarding the rules. For instance, the Luminary Nunnery has developed a sophisticated system for dealing with money, involving compromises on several levels, but minimizing the average nun's handling of money by certain nuns acting as "bookkeeper nuns" (Chiu 2014: 23–24), although the nuns are still left to do quite a bit of shopping. Foguangshan monastery is stated to have a similar "banking system". Both monks

268   *Jens W. Borgland*

and nuns receive a monthly wage, but are not allowed to save money privately, invest in a secular business, and so forth (2014: 24–25). In practice, if not in name, these solutions amount to solving the problem through the use of local ordinances.

Similarly, in Hạnh's code, the rules prohibiting handling money and "buying and selling", including what Borchert calls "commercial labor" (2011: 180), have either been removed or substantially altered. For instead of prohibiting the handling of money, Hạnh's code rather sets limits to how money may be obtained, held, and spent. A monk may not receive payment from the government or a political organization;[56] turn *sūtra* chanting or fortune telling into ways of earning a living;[57] raise animals or fowl in order to sell them;[58] seek to accumulate money and possessions in a way that becomes an obstacle to one's path of practice;[59] only be interested in growing or manufacturing things to sell, even if it is for the monastic community;[60] accept hired work to earn money;[61] or open a private bank account.[62] Once acquired, monks may seemingly use money to buy what they need, but are prohibited from buying and having expensive antiques,[63] buying luxurious personal items,[64] buying expensive and luxurious food items (tea, sweets, etc.) except in special cases,[65] and should not tease and joke with a vendor while shopping.[66] In addition, the many rules regulating what monks may own will set limits to what they can buy, and so monks will not be allowed to buy electronic game machines,[67] drugs,[68] and so forth.

These three examples—monastic robes, transportation, and money and trade—grant us some insight into the nature and scope of Hạnh's adaptation of monastic law vis-à-vis other such adaptation, both past and present. Disregarding for the moment the way in which these adaptations are presented, and keeping in mind the three hermeneutical principles of *vinaya* adaptation identified by Numrich, we find that Hạnh's adaptations on these three issues are not essentially different from adaptation taking place in many other monastic communities. These are by necessity driven by a pragmatic attitude and are closely related to the role of the laity. In some of the communities studied by Numrich, the laity's expectations of strict discipline set limits to the changes that may be implemented, sometimes at the expense of what is practical (1996: 49). Elsewhere, it is the laity's unfamiliarity with *vinaya* rules that creates problems, as is the case in China and Taiwan (Chiu 2014: 34–37), as well as Britain (Bell 2000: 10–12, 15–16). In order for monks to be able to survive without themselves using money, storing or cooking food, and so forth, they must receive all they need from the laity. This in turn requires a significant lay community that is ready and willing to act in its traditional role. Where such a lay community is not found, certain adaptations must be made, even among the monks of the strict Theravādin forest dwelling tradition. Hạnh's adaptations of the rules with regard to the three issues discussed above come across primarily as pragmatic, with little or no expectation of being sustained or assisted by laypeople.

What really sets Hạnh's approach apart is thus not so much *what* has been changed, or even the extent of the change, but mostly the fact that these adaptations take the form of revising the *Prātimokṣa* instead of more traditional means, namely local ordinances, while at the same time seemingly giving up the

Thích Nhất Hạnh's Monastic Code 269

traditional use of "legalizers" to get around certain rules. While the symbolic difference between these two approaches is significant, it is debatable how great the practical difference is. As noted above, local ordinances are far more important in Tibetan monasticism than the *vinaya*s, and have played an important role also in China. Since monks in Plum Village are required to study both the revised and the "Classical" *Prātimokṣa*, Hạnh's revised code could be argued to in essence be an elaborate local ordinance that imitates the structure and form of the *Prātimokṣa*.

However, unlike local ordinances, Hạnh's revised code is clearly composed to completely take the place of the *Prātimokṣa*, even in the *poṣadha* ceremony. Hahn thus rejects the authority and status attached to the original *Prātimokṣa*. But at the same time, the fact that Hạnh's revision takes the form of an updated *Prātimokṣa* can be seen as an attempt to reaffirm its status and authority. Hạnh clearly wants the *Prātimokṣa* to be relevant, and to once again correspond to the real-life conditions met by Buddhist monastics. On the one hand, this seems to have the advantage of presenting monastics with clear rules, thus avoiding constantly having to negotiate, compromise, and stretch the rules. On the other hand, by removing, for example, the rule against handling money, Hạnh's code can be seen as giving up on an ideal that, although considered by many to be impossible to live up to, has always been present as a fundament and guide. This is perhaps the very reason why the monks in Plum Village must study also the "Classical" *Prātimokṣa*, even though it does not regulate their behaviour.

Still, Hạnh's code clearly aims to safeguard the monastic vocation. It is in this regard instructive to note that while Hạnh's decision to revise the *Prātimokṣa* seems radical, and his revised code does allow monks to handle money, it also prohibits monks from accepting hired work in order to make money, or to spend too much time on money-making activities. Conversely, one of the Vietnamese abbots with whom Nguyen and Barber have worked closely during their work on Vietnamese Buddhism in America has a part-time job in order to get health benefits, while another abbot they discuss works full-time as a television repairman (1998: 140).

However, not all of Hạnh's changes can be sufficiently explained as adaptations to modern conditions or pragmatic necessities. We cannot here consider all of these. One example is the move of the rule against masturbation ("intentional emission of semen", in the "Classical" *Prātimokṣa*s) from the *saṃghāvaśeṣa* category to the *pāyattika* rules.[69] Thus, rather than involving probation, this offence needs only be confessed, which involves a considerable relaxation of the penalty. Another striking example is the rule that "[a] bhikshu who eats a non-vegetarian meal, even though he excuses himself by saying that he lacks nutrition, commits an Expression of Regret Offence" (Expression of Regret Offence [*pāyattika*] 71). No general rule against eating meat is found in any of the "Classical" *Prātimokṣa*s,[70] although the *vinaya*s do contain certain restrictions on meat-eating, most notably that a monk may not eat meat if he sees, hears, or suspects that the animal has been killed especially for him.[71]

Viewed in light of the canonical *vinaya*s, including a rule that prohibits eating non-vegetarian food in the *Prātimokṣa* is particularly striking. The reason for this

270   Jens W. Borgland

is not primarily that the *vinaya*s contain no rules prohibiting general meat con-sumption, although this is of course noteworthy, but that the *vinaya*s in fact record an episode in which a monk is said to have suggested that eating meat should be prohibited for monks. This monk was none other than Devadatta, the Buddha's cousin and arch-villain of monastic Buddhist legend, who attempted to take over the leadership of the *saṃgha* and assassinate the Buddha. Abstention from eating meat was just one among several stricter practices that Devadatta is said to have suggested become compulsory for all monks. The Buddha famously rejected this, and Devadatta then carried out his famous division of the order (*saṃghabheda*).

Hạnh is clearly aware of this episode. For in discussing the importance of the middle path between precepts being too austere and too relaxed, expressing his commitment to the "dynamic Balance we can call the Middle Way" (2004: 15), Hạnh mentions Devadatta and his attempt at making the Buddha adopt a stricter practice. But while listing some of Devadatta's points, Hạnh conveniently omits mentioning that one of the five points Devadatta advocated was that monks abstain from eating fish and meat (2004: 14–15),[72] and that the Buddha, who according to Buddhist tradition himself ate meat, explicitly denied making vegetarianism compulsory for Buddhist monks.

However, seen in light of earlier East Asian *vinaya* adaptation and practice, a pro-hibition against eating meat is not surprising. For example, the above-mentioned *Chanyuan qinggui* forbade monks from eating meat (Yifa [2002] 2009: 56). Hạnh's rule against eating meat must therefore be understood not in light of "modern con-ditions", but in light of long-standing East Asian practice based on Mahāyāna ideas.[73] As such, it could be grouped among some of the other rules that show the influence of Hạnh's Vietnamese background. Hạnh himself mentions one instance where his Vietnamese background clearly plays a role (2004: 17–18), namely, the rule that forbids monks to receive payment from the government, a political party, or a political organization (Sangha Restoration Offence [*saṃghāvaśeṣa*] 11). This is tied to Hạnh's experiences in Vietnam, some of which are discussed by Aike Rots in his contribution to the present volume. Another example, mentioned in passing above, concerns the rules about monastic dress.

Hạnh's revised code thus to some extent reflects not only the modern and global culture of which he and the Plum Village community are part, but also their Viet-namese roots, including Mahāyāna ideals, as well as their personal visions of what Buddhist monasticism *can* and *should* be in the twenty-first century.

Concluding Remarks

I have discussed some of the changes introduced by Hạnh in his revised monastic code, both in light of previous modes of *vinaya* adaptation and in light of some issues that have been emphasized in secondary literature as particularly trouble-some for modern-day Buddhist monastics. In both cases, what is most unconven-tional about Hạnh's code is the *form* in which he has chosen to adapt monastic law. For while similar adaptations are attested in other monastic communities in

Thích Nhất Hạnh's Monastic Code 271

different parts of the world, these are achieved through the more traditional "local ordinances", leaving the ideal of the *Prātimokṣa* intact. Other monastic communities, on the other hand, uphold the rules by making use of "legalizers". As noted by Numrich, what is adapted, and to what extent, depends on what is considered acceptable, on practical concerns, as well as on the laity. This, one can argue, has always been the case, since several of the issues examined here and identified as particularly challenging for present-day Buddhist monks have in fact been the subject of adaptation and negotiation for a long time.

One could argue that Hạnh's redaction of the *Prātimokṣa*, and the relaxation of the rules that it in many cases entails, represents a diminution of Buddhist monastic discipline. However, I would argue that, unconventional as it may be in some respects, it also shows a pragmatic attitude and a willingness to take monastic discipline seriously. Although many of Hạnh's choices are surely debatable, his revised code should be seen, as Hạnh himself states, as an attempt to make sure that Buddhist monasticism can survive, and perhaps even flourish in the West by presenting Buddhist monastics with clear rules that correspond to the realities they today face. Most likely, it will not be the last such attempt. Since Hạnh's monastic code was published in 2004, it is already in some respects out-dated. For example, the dominance of Facebook since the publication of the revised monastic code could hardly have been foreseen.[74] Consequently, while monks are not allowed to have a private email account except with the permission of the monastic community,[75] Hạnh's monastic code does not include any rules concerning monks having Facebook accounts, which it seems very many monks, for instance in present-day Sri Lanka, do in fact have.[76] This, and other developments surely are, and will continue to be, the object of much discussion and compromise in monastic communities all over the world.[77]

Hạnh himself addresses such concerns in the conclusion to the revised code, stating that further revisions of the precepts must be made every ten or twenty years, in order to make sure that they are up to date (2004: 155). He further elaborates on some of the principles that should underlie these future revisions. Instead of being a collection of prohibitions (like the "Classical" and, for the most part, the revised *Prātimokṣa*), the future *Prātimokṣa* will incorporate the bodhisattva ideal of helping others and performing good deeds (2004: 159–160). The revised *Prātimokṣa* published in 2004 is thus just the beginning, and the next revision, if Hạnh's recent health problems do not put a stop to it, promises to be far less conventional than the present one.

Abbreviations

BD IV Horner ([1951] 1971)

D *The Sde-dge Mtshal-par Bka'-'gyur: A Facsimile Edition of the 18th Century Redaction of Si-tu Chos-kyi-'byun -gnas Prepared under the Direction of H.H. the 16th Rgyal -dban 'Karma-pa.* 103 vols. Delhi: Delhi Karmapae Chodhey Gyalwae Sungrab Partun Khang, 1976–1979.

272 *Jens W. Borgland*

Sp   Available online through the Tibetan Buddhist Resource Center (www. tbrc.org).

Sp   Takakusu and Nagai ([1924] 1975)

T   *Taishō shinshū daizōkyō* 大正新脩大藏經. Edited by Takakusu Junjirō 高楠順次郎 and Watanabe Kaikyoku 渡邊海旭. 100 vols. Tokyo: Taishō issaikyō kankō kai 大正一切經刊行會, 1924–1935. Available online through the SAT Daizōkyō Text Database (http://21dzk.l.u-tokyo.ac.jp/SAT/ddb-bdk-sat2.php?lang=en).

Vin I   Oldenberg (1879)

Vin III   Oldenberg (1881)

Notes

1. This is, naturally, somewhat of a simplification. Note, for example, that Buddhism was introduced into China in the first century CE, but that "no Chinese version of the monastic rules (*vinaya*) was produced before the 3rd century. The most basic rules were probably transmitted orally" (Zürcher [1984] 2002: 197; cf. also Yifa [2002] 2009: 3–4; Heirman 2007). And while the monastic precepts were transmitted to Japan, they were for the most part abandoned a long time ago (cf. Bodiford 2005: 185, 2010: 127).
2. Pāli: *Pātimokkha*. For a discussion of the etymology, see von Hinüber (1985: 60–62). I will primarily employ Sanskrit terminology throughout this chapter.
3. See Numrich (1998). On the variety of attitudes towards monasticism among Western Buddhists, see Schedneck (2009).
4. The only mention of this code that I know of occurs in a footnote (see Clarke 2009: 28, n. 97). See also n. 69.
5. Considering Hạnh's background in the Vietnamese Zen tradition, this is what is to be expected. Moreover, Hạnh explicitly states that his revised *Prātimokṣa* has kept the traditional number of rules (Hạnh 2004: 17). The number given is 250 rules for monks, which is the total number of rules only in the *Prātimokṣa* of the Dharmaguptaka school (Pachow 1955: 11). However, interestingly, the one time Hạnh does make a direct reference to one of the extant *vinayas* it is not the *Dharmaguptaka vinaya* but the so-called *Vinaya* in five parts (Hạnh 2004: 24). This can only refer to the *vinaya* of the Mahīśāsakas, the *wufenlu* (五分律), i.e. the "Five-Part *vinaya*". The *Dharmaguptaka vinaya* is referred to as *sifenlu* (四分律), i.e. the "Four-Part *vinaya*". Hạnh also quotes (or rather paraphrases) a passage from the *Mahīśāsaka vinaya* (see below and n. 34).
6. This section is known as the *Khandhaka* in the *Theravāda vinaya*. The term *Skandhaka*, a Sanskritized form of the Pāli term *Khandhaka*, is conventionally used by scholars to refer to these sections across *vinaya* traditions. However, this Sanskritized form is, to my knowledge, not attested in any of the extant *vinayas* or compendia. In the *Mūlasarvāstivāda vinaya* this section, of which about four-fifths are extant in Sanskrit (Wille 1990: 16), is known as the *Vinayavastu*. The Chinese translations of these sections of the *Sarvāstivāda vinaya* (T 1435) and the *Mahīśāsaka vinaya* (T 1421) use the term *fa* (法), which usually translates Skt. *dharma*. In the *Dharmaguptaka vinaya* (T 1428) the term *quiandu* (揵度), seemingly a transliteration of *Khandha(ka)*, is found (Clarke 2015: 99). Because of the seeming variety of terms used to denote these sections in the various *vinayas*, I will refer to these sections collectively as "Chapters", which is the English translation of both Skt. *vastu* and Pāli *khandhaka*.
7. All of these texts are available almost only in Chinese. Beal's translation of the Dharmaguptaka *Prātimokṣa* (1871: 206–239) is not reliable. The content of the Dharmaguptaka *Prātimokṣa* can be accessed through Pachow's excellent comparative study of

Thích Nhất Hạnh's Monastic Code 273

the *Prātimokṣa* (1955). Despite the recent efforts of the Bodhi Foundation for Culture and Education towards translating the *Dharmaguptaka vinaya* into English, some of which has already been published at https://dharmaguptakavinaya.wordpress.com, it will take considerable time for this work to be completed.

8. The *Bhikṣuṇīvibhaṅga* of the Dharmaguptaka school has been translated into English (Heirman 2002). Cf. also the translation of the *Bhikṣuṇīvibhaṅga* of the Theravādins (Hüsken 1997), and the comparative study by Kabilsingh (1984), although the latter must be used with due caution.

9. While first published in 2004, the revised code is reported to first have been "released" already a year earlier at the Choong Ang Sangha University in Seoul (Hạnh 2004: ix).

10. Cf. also Expression of Regret Offence (*pāyattika*) 110 in the revised code. The Plum Village website (Plum Village 2014a, 2014b) does not say anything about the *Prātimokṣa*.

11. Pāli *uposatha*. For the performance of the *poṣadha* ceremony cf. the MSV *Poṣadhavastu* (Poṣ-v 59–60) (Hu-von Hinüber 1994: 344–346). See also Pachow (1955: 60), Chung (1998: 38), and Gombrich ([1984] 2002: 81–82). However, note that the *Prātimokṣa's* legal and ceremonial functions are tightly interwoven. The purity (*pariśuddhi*) of all the monks, i.e. being free from any unredressed offence (*āpatti*), is an essential precondition for the performance of the *poṣadha* ceremony.

12. Six *vinaya*s, each identified as belonging to a different *vinaya* school and different with regard to the exact content, are said to be extant in their entirety, although the difficulty of knowing what constitutes a "complete vinaya" has been pointed out (Clarke 2002). Three of the *vinaya*s are today in use. The *Theravāda vinaya* is used in South and Southeast Asia, the *Mūlasarvāstivāda vinaya* in the Tibetan tradition, and the *Dharmaguptaka vinaya* in East Asian Buddhism. However, the use of the *Vinayasaṃgraha* among Buddhist nuns in China noted by Chiu (2014: 39) indicates that the regional distribution of monastic legal traditions is less watertight than is perhaps often assumed. Cf. also Clarke (2006).

13. For convenience, see Yuyama (1979) and Pachow (1955), but note von Simson (1986, 2000) as well as the *Prātimokṣa* ascribed to the Kāśyapīyas (cf. T 1460) and Mahāsāṃghika-Lokottaravādins (Pachow and Mishra 1956).

14. "Oddly enough, the most basic of all *vinaya* texts [i.e. the *Pātimokkha*] is not, as it stands, a part of the Canon, though *it has canonical status*" (Gombrich 1988: 92, emphasis added). Cf. also von Hinüber (1996: 9). Prebish, however, considers the *Prātimokṣa* as being "paracanonical" (2003: 49, 69, n. 14).

15. In addition to the *Prātimokṣa* prescriptions (*paññatti*) or rules themselves, and in some cases also secondary prescriptions (*anupaññatti*) where the original rule was either loosened or tightened, the *Vibhaṅga*s contain "introductory stories" (*vatthu*) to each of the *Prātimokṣa*s prescriptions and secondary prescriptions, a word analysis (*padabhājaniya*) explaining the words of the rule, and a casuistry (Kieffer-Pülz 2014: 49, n. 23–26). On the casuistries of the Pāli *Suttavibhaṅga*, cf. Derrett (2003).

16. Cf. n. 6. The *Mahāsāṃghika vinaya*, however, stands out (Frauwallner 1956: 198–207; but note the more recent critique of some of Frauwallner's conclusions in Clarke 2004). The *vinaya*s also contain other texts or sections, which shall not concern us here.

17. Cf. Vin I 191,21–23 (BD IV 255). The exception for monks who are ill is given immediately afterwards (Vin I 191,24–35; BD IV 255), followed by specifications of what kinds of vehicles that may then be used (Vin I 191,36ff.; BD IV 255ff.). Note, however, that most of the *vinaya*s do contain a rule prohibiting nuns from riding vehicles in the *Prātimokṣa* for nuns (Kabilsingh 1984: 118; for the rule in the Dharmaguptaka *Bhikṣuṇī Prātimokṣa*, see Heirman 2002: 919–921).

18. It is difficult, if not impossible, to give even an approximate date. The *Samantapāsādikā*, admittedly not an early text, declares that "it is impossible to reverse the (Pātimokkha) sutta" (*suttaṃ hi appaṭivattiyaṃ*, Sp 231,27 quoted and translated in von Hinüber 1995: 14).

274 *Jens W. Borgland*

19. Schopen problematizes the common translations "accept" and "have" for the Skt. verb *ud*+√*grah*, since these are rather the meanings of *prati*+√*grah* (2000: 102). As he points out, its more literal meaning is rather "pick up", and it is elsewhere clearly distinguished from *prati*+√*grah* (2000: 102, n. 28). It could perhaps be argued that what is in fact forbidden by the *Prātimokṣa* is "picking up gold and silver" (from the ground?), and not "accepting" or "having" it. Whatever the original intention of the rule, this does not seem to be how the rule was understood. The Tibetan and Chinese translations of the MSV *Prātimokṣa* render the verb *len* and *zhuo* (捉) respectively (cf. D Ca 10a5 and T 1454 503b6), both of which mean simply "take" or "grasp". Moreover, in the MSV version of the incidents leading to the council of 700 arhats (*Kṣudrakavastu*, D Da 323b4–332a2), the tenth and last of the objectionable practices that the monks of Vaiśālī engaged in involved accepting (*thob*) treasure (*dbyig*), gold (*gser*), and jewels (*rin po che*) in their alms bowls (*lhuṅ bzed*) (D Da 325a2–4), which is later identified as a *naiḥsargika pāyattika* (*spaṅ ba'i ltuṅ byed*, D Da 327b5).
20. Tib. *gser daṅ dṅul* (D Ca 10a5), which in the *Vibhaṅga* is explained as "riches and gold" (*gser daṅ dṅul źes bya ba ni dbyig daṅ gser*, D Cha 146b4; Tib. *dbyig* translates Skt. *dhana, vasu*, etc., although it may also translate *hiraṇya*, "gold"; see Negi 1993: 4007) The Chinese translation reads *jin yin* (金銀), "gold and silver", and even adds "money" (*qian* 錢) (T 1454 503b6). The Chinese *Vibhaṅga* extends "gold and silver" to include also *kārṣāpaṇas* (*bei chi* 貝齒), while "money" is explained as being made of gold and so forth (錢者金等錢) (T 1442 470c7–8).
21. Note, however, the Chinese translation of the MSV *Prātimokṣa* and *Vibhaṅga* in n. 20.
22. The Chinese translation, which mentions money in the *Prātimokṣa* (see n. 20; although note that it is not unique in doing so, see n. 52) and *kārṣāpaṇas* in the *Vibhaṅga* commentary complicates this picture, as do different chronological layers in the *Vibhaṅga* (see von Hinüber 1996: 13–14). Another possibility explored by Schopen is that the authors and redactors of the MSV may have simply chosen to ignore the *Prātimokṣa* rule (2000: 100).
23. Pāli: *katikā, katikāvatta, katikasaṇṭhāna* (Ratnapala 1971: 6–13; Kieffer-Pülz 2014: 59, n. 79).
24. This is at least the case with the *Theravāda, Mahāsāṃghika* and *Mūlasarvāstivāda vinaya*s (Kieffer-Pülz 2014: 59–61).
25. According to Blackburn, these local ordinances seem—together with commentaries, compendia and certain *sutta*s—to have played a more important role in monastic education in Sri Lankan monastic orders than the canonical *vinaya* (1999: 289).
26. I here follow Jansen (2013: 112–113, 2014: 598, n. 8) in translating *bca'yig* as "monastic guidelines" rather than "monastic constitution" (Ellingson 1990).
27. Although the *qinggui* literature is associated with Chan Buddhism, nearly identical rules were compiled in Tiantai monasteries (Heirman 2012: 441, n. 31). These texts did not replace the *vinaya*s, but rather offered additional practical guidelines (Heirman 2012: 441).
28. Pāli *kappiyakāraka*. For the *kappiyakāraka* and the monastery servant or slave (*ārāmika*) in Pāli sources cf. Kieffer-Pülz (2007: 15–21).
29. For references to the *Theravāda vinaya* cf. Kieffer-Pülz (2007: 20, n. 66). As explained by Gombrich, the *function* of the *kappiyakāraka* is acknowledged in the *Prātimokṣa*, although the term *kappiyakāraka* is not there used (1988: 92).
30. Note, however, that Jansen's statement is not made with reference to the *Prātimokṣa*.
31. However, Rahula was very vague regarding what, exactly, this should entail (see 1978: 65), with the exception that the rule prohibiting the use of shoes should not be observed (1978: 66).
32. Although Hạnh does recognize the importance of the *saṃgha's* reputation (2004: 25–27), he makes few references to lay opinion. The importance of laypeople and

Thích Nhất Hạnh's Monastic Code 275

their sensibilities is repeatedly recognized throughout the monastic codes (see e.g. Horner [1938] 1949: xiv, ff.; Schopen 2007: esp. 61–62), as it is in modern discussions on *vinaya* adaptation (see below).

33. Hạnh offers the example of buying and selling drugs (2004: 17), which strangely enough does not seem to be prohibited per se in the revised code.

34. 復告諸比丘。雖是我所制。而於餘方不以爲清淨者。皆不應用。雖非我所制。而於餘方必應行者。皆不得不行 (T 1421 153a14–17). I owe my knowledge of this passage to an unpublished paper by Jeffrey Kotyk uploaded on http://academia.edu. The translation above is my own, although I benefited from Kotyk's translation. The passage here cited appears to be found in one of (?) the chapters on medicine (Frauwallner 1956: 183; Clarke 2015: 66). It is found at the very end of this section following a longer exposition concerning food, but appears to be phrased in rather general terms. Note also that this is not the only time Hạnh quotes the *Mahīśāsaka vinaya* (see n. 5).

35. But note the context of the passage (n. 34).

36. The first two of these issues are highlighted by Numrich (1994: 26–27, 1996: 46–50), who also adds issues concerning chastity and relations with women, as well as rules concerning food (see also Numrich 1996, 1998). The use of money is primarily discussed by Chiu (2014). Some of these issues are also addressed by Harris (1998), Bell (2000), Buddharakkhita (2006), Cheng (2007), and Borchert (2011).

37. The three allowed robes are the "upper robe" (*uttarāsaṅga*), the "inner robe" (*antarvāsa*), and the "outer robe" (*saṃghāṭi*). The *saṃghāṭi* is meant for outside use (Kieschnick 1999: 12–14; Heirman 2014: 471). In addition to these, several kinds of special robes, such as a "toilet robe" (Heirman 2014: 471) are allowed (Upasak 1975: 88–91).

38. Cf. Numrich (1996: 47), Harris (1998: 10), and Buddharakkhita (2006: 28–29, 39–40, 43–50, 2012) for ridicule and other problems caused by this "exotic" appearance.

39. Cf. Vin I 197,31–198,10 (BD IV 266–267). The Buddha allowed sandals with additional layers in the soles, and the use of certain kinds of animal skins as covers.

40. Cf. Release and Expression of Regret Offence (*naiḥsargika-pāyattika*) 16, which in addition to the usual three robes states that a monk may not own more than three long robes (the *ao trang and ao nhat binh*), and more than three suits (*vat ho*) worn under the long robe.

41. Cf. Release and Expression of Regret Offence (*naiḥsargika-pāyattika*) 16.

42. Expression of Regret Offence (*pāyattika*) 93.

43. Expression of Regret Offence (*pāyattika*) 95.

44. Release and Expression of Regret Offence (*naiḥsargika-pāyattika*) 17 and 18.

45. *bhagavato etam atthaṃ ārocesuṃ. na bhikkhave yānena yāyitabbaṃ. yo yāyeyya, āpatti dukkaṭassā 'ti* (Vin I 191,21–23; for English cf. BD IV 255). See n. 17. Although I have not been able to find a general prohibition against monks driving vehicles in the *Dharmaguptaka vinaya*, the chapter on leather does contain a short passage in which an old and frail monk that was not able to walk is allowed to ride a vehicle (T 1428 848c1–3), suggesting that young and healthy monks are not to do so. I am grateful to Ann Heirman for providing me with this reference.

46. This, one may add, is not a problem only in the urban Western setting, nor is it restricted to Buddhist monastics, as evidenced by the death of the eighty-seven-year-old Jain scholar-monk Muni Jambu Vijayji in 2009. Travelling on foot together with other Jain monks from the town of Balotra (Rajasthan), the group of monks was hit by a truck. Two monks died, and several were severely injured (Institute of Jainology 2009).

47. Release and Expression of Regret Offence (*naiḥsargika-pāyattika*) 6.

48. Expression of Regret Offence (*pāyattika*) 86.

49. Fine Manners Offences (*śaikṣa*) 59.

50. Fine Manners Offences (*śaikṣa*) 60.

51. Fine Manners Offences (*śaikṣa*) 61.

276   Jens W. Borgland

52. Although the reference to money is not found in the Sarvāstivāda or Theravāda *Prātimokṣa*s themselves (only gold and silver are mentioned there), several of the schools, including the Dharmaguptaka, include "or money" here (Pachow 1955: 112). Moreover, the canonical commentary on this rule in the Theravāda *Suttavibhaṅga* adds "or whatever is used" (*ye vohāraṃ gacchanti*) (Vin III 237,36 quoted and translated in von Hinüber 1995: 11), on the basis of which von Hinüber states: "thus including even paper money, if not credit cards" (1995: 11).

53. However, Cheng suggests that modern pilgrimage may be unintentionally changing the practice of Sri Lankan monastics on this matter, since East Asian pilgrims are unaware that Sri Lankan monks are not to be given cash offerings (2007: 125)

54. Borchert's fieldwork among Theravāda communities in southwest China shows that there too monks use money, either donated by the laity or earned through "commercial labor" (Borchert 2011: 184) or a government salary (Borchert 2011: 180). Concerning some of the issues on which Borchert's discussion of monastic labour touches upon the *vinaya*, it is worth pointing out that activity such as sweeping the monastery, as well as employing such activity as a punishment (Borchert 2011: 178), is attested in *vinaya* sources (cf. Schopen 1998). Concerning some of the duties and activities that Borchert calls "administrative labor" (Borchert 2011: 180, 183–184), see Silk (2008).

55. Note, however, the *paṇḍupalāsa*s mentioned in the *Samantapāsādikā* (Yifa [2002] 2009: 62). Numrich too mentions the *anagārika*s in the American context (1998: 158). The use of a legalizer is also reported by Buddharakkhita in Uganda, although he does not use the term (Buddharakkhita 2012: 57). Note also the example from a Theravāda monastery in Chiang Mai mentioned by Borchert, who reports that monks merely *having* money was viewed as less problematic than their using it to buy something. As a consequence, Borchert himself or a novice would be sent to buy soda for the abbot of the temple in which Borchert did fieldwork (2011: 170).

56. Sangha Restoration Offence (*saṃghāvaśeṣa*) 11.

57. Sangha Restoration Offence (*saṃghāvaśeṣa*) 18, Expression of Regret Offence (*pāyattika*) 70.

58. Release and Expression of Regret Offence (*naiḥsargika-pāyattika*) 29.

59. Release and Expression of Regret Offence (*naiḥsargika-pāyattika*) 7.

60. Release and Expression of Regret Offence (*naiḥsargika-pāyattika*) 28. This rule, and the absence of any rule prohibiting digging, indicates that monks not only can, but may even be expected to, take part in some kinds of farming activities. See also Expression of Regret Offence (*pāyattika*) 57 and 66.

61. Expression of Regret Offence (*pāyattika*) 69.

62. Release and Expression of Regret Offence (*naiḥsargika-pāyattika*) 8. An exception is here made if one has the permission of the *saṃgha* to study Buddhism abroad.

63. Release and Expression of Regret Offence (*naiḥsargika-pāyattika*) 13.

64. Release and Expression of Regret Offence (*naiḥsargika-pāyattika*) 19.

65. Fine Manners Offences (*śaikṣa*) 21.

66. Fine Manners Offences (*śaikṣa*) 63.

67. Release and Expression of Regret Offence (*naiḥsargika-pāyattika*) 4.

68. Release and Expression of Regret Offence (*naiḥsargika-pāyattika*) 1.

69. As pointed out by Shayne Clarke (2009), cf. n. 4. For the *vinaya* regulations on masturbation, see Derrett (2006). Another such example pointed out by Clarke is the removal of the reference to bestiality in the first *pārājika* rule of the revised code.

70. Cf. Pachow (1955), although meat and fish are classified as delicacies that monks may not specifically ask to be served unless they are sick (Pachow 1955: 142, *pāyattika* 40).

71. For the *Theravāda vinaya*, cf. Vin I 238,5–9 (BD IV 325). The same rule is found in the *Dharmaguptaka vinaya* (Faure 1998: 151; Yifa [2002] 2009: 56). For an overview of the rules concerning food, many of which have been highlighted as particularly problematic for modern-day monks, see Frauwallner (1956: 94–95).

Thích Nhất Hạnh's Monastic Code 277

72. For the Dharmaguptaka version of Devadatta's five points, see T 1428 594b2ff. (translated in Deeg 1999: 209, n. 54).
73. Cf. Yifa ([2002] 2009: 56–57), who mentions the *Brahma Net Sūtra*, the *Laṅkāvatāta Sūtra*, and the *Aṅgulimālika Sūtra* as examples.
74. Facebook was launched in 2004, although at first only among students at Harvard, and became facebook.com in 2005 (Philips 2007).
75. Release and Expression of Regret Offence (*naiḥsargika-pāyattika*) 5.
76. Iselin Frydenlund, personal communication, December 2014. See also n. 77. Note, however, that the revised code does contain several rules limiting monks' access to and use of the Internet which would potentially impact their access to social media. For instance, a monk may not go "on to the Internet alone without another monk next to him as a protection against getting lost in toxic Websites" (Expression of Regret Offence [*pāyattika*] 81), and is not allowed to have a private email account, except with the permission of the monastic community (Release and Expression of Regret Offence [(*naiḥsargika-pāyattika*)] 5).
77. Note Borchert's (2011: 187) comments while discussing the *vinaya* in the modern context: "Sanghas thus have to engage in interpretation of the *vinaya* to decide if social networking sites, for example, are useful tools for monks or against the spirit of being a monk."

References

Beal, Samuel. 1871. *A Catena of Buddhist Scriptures*. London: Trübner.

Bell, Sandra. 2000. "Being Creative with Tradition: Rooting Theravāda Buddhism in Britain." *Journal of Global Buddhism* 1: 1–23.

Birnbaum, Raoul. 2003. "Buddhist China at the Century's Turn." *China Quarterly* 174 (1): 428–450.

Blackburn, Anne M. 1999. "Looking for the Vinaya: Monastic Discipline in the Practical Canons of the Theravāda." *Journal of the International Association of Buddhist Studies* 22 (2): 281–310.

Bodiford, William M. 2005. "Bodhidharma's Precepts in Japan." In *Going Forth: Visions of Buddhist Vinaya: Essays Presented in Honour of Professor Stanley Weinstein* [Kuroda Institute Studies in East Asian Buddhism], edited by William M. Bodiford, 185–209. Honolulu: University of Hawai'i Press.

———. 2010. "The Monastic Institution in Medieval Japan: The Insider's View." In *Buddhist Monasticism in East Asia: Places of Practice* [Routledge Critical Studies in Buddhism], edited by James A. Benn, Lori Meeks, and James Robson, 125–147. London: Routledge.

Borchert, Thomas. 2011. "Monastic Labor: Thinking about the Work of Monks in Contemporary Theravāda Communities." *Journal of the American Academy of Religion* 79 (1): 162–192.

Buddharakkhita, Bhante. 2006. *Planting Dhamma Seeds: The Emergence of Buddhism in Africa*. Kuala Lumpur: Sasana Abhiwurdhi Wardhana Society.

———. 2012. "Tales, Trials and Tribulations of Teaching Dhamma in Uganda." In *Teaching Dhamma in New Lands: Academic Papers Presented at the 2nd IABU Conference Mahachulalongkorn-Rajavidyalaya University, Main Campus Wang Noi, Ayutthaya, Thailand*, edited by Khammai Dhammasami, Padmasiri de Silva, Sara Shaw, Dion Peoples, and Jamie Cresswell, 56–68. Accessed 4 January 2015. http://www.undv.org/vesak2012/book/teaching_dhamma_in_new_lands.pdf.

Cheng, Wei-Yi. 2007. *Buddhist Nuns in Taiwan and Sri Lanka: A Critique of the Feminist Perspective* [Routledge Critical Studies in Buddhism]. New York: Routledge.

278   *Jens W. Borgland*

Chiu, Tzu-Lung. 2014. "Rethinking the Precept of Not Taking Money in Contemporary Taiwanese and Mainland Chinese Buddhist Nunneries." *Journal of Buddhist Ethics* 21: 9–56.

Chung, Jin-Il. 1998. *Die Pravāraṇā in den kanonischen Vinaya-Texten der Mūlasarvāstivādin und der Sarvāstivādin*. Göttingen: Vanderhoeck & Ruprecht.

Clarke, Shayne. 2002. "The Mūlasarvāstivādin Vinaya: A Brief Reconnaissance Report." In *Sakurabe Hajime hakushi kiju kinen ronshū: shoki bukkyō kara abidaruma e* 櫻部建博士喜寿記念論集 初期仏教からアビダルマへ / *Early Buddhism and Abhidharma Thought: In Honour of Doctor Hajime Sakurabe on His Seventy-Seventh Birthday*, edited by Sakurabe Hajime Hakushi Kiju Kinen Ronshū Kankōkai 櫻部建博士喜寿記念論集刊行会, 45–63. Kyoto: Heirakuji shoten 平樂寺書店.

———. 2004. "Vinaya Mātṛkā: Mother of the Monastic Codes, or Just Another Set of Lists? A Response to Frauwallner's Handling of the Mahāsāṃghika Vinaya." *Indo-Iranian Journal* 47 (2): 77–120.

———. 2006. "Miscellaneous Musings on Mūlasarvāstivāda Monks: The Mūlasarvāstivāda Vinaya Revival in Tokugawa Japan." *Japanese Journal of Religious Studies* 33 (1): 1–49.

———. 2009. "Monks Who Have Sex: Pārājika Penance in Indian Buddhist Monasticisms." *Journal of Indian Philosophy* 37 (1): 1–43.

———. 2015. "Vinayas." In *Brill's Encyclopedia of Buddhism*. Vol. 1, edited by Jonathan Silk, 60–87. Leiden: Brill.

Deeg, Max. 1999. "The Saṅgha of Devadatta: Fiction and History of a Heresy in the Buddhist Tradition." *Journal of the International College for Advanced Buddhist Studies* 2: 183–218.

Derrett, J. Duncan M. 2003. "Buddhist Casuistry: The Ultimate in Purity: A Study in the Vinaya." *Adyar Library Bulletin* 67: 35–46.

———. 2006. "Monastic Masturbation in Pāli Buddhist Texts." *Journal of the History of Sexuality* 15 (1): 1–13.

Dreyfus, Georges B. J. 2003. *The Sound of Two Hands Clapping: The Education of a Tibetan Buddhist Monk*. Los Angeles: University of California Press.

Ellingson, Ter. 1990. "Tibetan Monastic Constitutions: The bca'-yig." In *Reflections on Tibetan Culture: Essays in Memory of Turrell V. Wylie* [Studies in Asian Thought and Religion], edited by Lawrence Epstein and Richard F. Sherburne, 205–229. Lewiston: Edwin Mellen Press.

Faure, Bernard. 1998. *The Read Thread: Buddhist Approaches to Sexuality*. Princeton, NJ: Princeton University Press.

Frauwallner, E. 1956. *The Earliest Vinaya and the Beginnings of Buddhist Literature* [Serie Orientale Roma 8]. Rome: Istituto Italiano per il Medio ed Estremo Oriente.

Gombrich, R. F. 1988. *Theravāda Buddhism: A Social History from Ancient Benares to Modern Colombo*. London: Routledge and Kegan Paul.

———. (1984) 2002. "The Evolution of the Sangha." In *The World of Buddhism*, edited by H. Bechert and R. F. Gombrich, 77–89. London: Thames & Hudson.

Hạnh, Thích Nhất. 2004. *Freedom Wherever We Go: A Buddhist Monastic Code for the Twenty-First Century*. Berkeley: Parallax Press.

Harris, Elizabeth J. 1998. *Ānanda Metteyya: The First British Emissary of Buddhism* [Wheel Publication 420/422]. Kandy: Buddhist Publication Society. Accessed 10 December 2014. http://www.bps.lk/olib/wh/wh420.pdf.

Heirman, Ann. 2002. *"The Discipline in Four Parts": Rules for Nuns According to the Dharmaguptakavinaya*. 3 vols. New Delhi: Motilal Banarsidass.

———. 2007. "Vinaya: From India to China." In *The Spread of Buddhism* [Handbook of Oriental Studies Volume 16], edited by Ann Heirman and Stephan Peter Bumbacher, 167–202. Leiden: Brill.

Thích Nhất Hạnh's Monastic Code 279

————. 2008. "Becoming a Nun in the Dharmaguptaka Tradition." *Buddhist Studies Review* 25 (2): 174–193.

————. 2012. "Sleep Well! Sleeping Practices in Buddhist Disciplinary Rules." *Acta Orientalia Academiae Scientiarum Hungaricae* 65 (4): 427–444.

————. 2014. "Washing and Dyeing Buddhist Monastic Robes." *Acta Orientalia Academiae Scientiarum Hungaricae* 67 (4): 467–488.

Horner, I. B. (1938) 1949. *The Book of the Discipline (Vinaya Piṭaka)*. Vol. 1, *Suttavibhaṅga*. London: Luzac.

————. (1951) 1971. *The Book of the Discipline (Vinaya-Piṭaka)*. Vol. 4, *Mahāvagga*. London: Luzac.

Hume, Lynne. 2013. *The Religious Life of Dress: Global Fashion and Faith*. London: Bloomsbury.

Hüsken, Ute. 1997. *Die Vorschriften für die buddhistische Nonnengemeinde im Vinaya-Piṭaka der Theravādin*. Berlin: Dietrich Reimer Verlag.

Hu-von Hinüber, Haiyan. 1994. *Das Poṣadhavastu: Vorschriften für die buddhistische Beichtfeier im Vinaya der Mūlasarvāstivādins* [Studien zur Indologie und Iranistik 13]. Reinbek: Verlag für Orientalistische Fachpublikationen.

Institute of Jainology. 2009. "An Eminent Jain Saint Dies in Road Accident." 13 November. Accessed 19 December 2014. http://www.jainology.org/666/an-eminent-jain-saint-dies-in-road-accident/.

Jansen, Berthe. 2013. "How to Tame a Wild Monastic Elephant: Drepung Monastery According to the Great Fifth." In *Tibetans Who Escaped the Historian's Net: Studies in the Social History of Tibetan Societies*, edited by Charles Ramble, Peter Schwieger, and Alica Travers, 111–139. Kathmandu: Vajra Books.

————. 2014. "The Monastic Guidelines (bCa' yig) by Sidkeong Tulku: Monasteries, Sex and Reform in Sikkim." *Journal of the Royal Asiatic Society*, 3rd ser., 24 (4): 597–622.

Kabilsingh, Chatsumarn. 1984. *A Comparative Study of Bhikkhunī Pāṭimokkha* [Chaukambha Oriental Research Studies 28]. Varanasi: Chaukhambha Orientalia.

Kay, David N. 2004. *Tibetan and Zen Buddhism in Britain: Transplantation, Development and Adaptation* [Routledge Critical Studies in Buddhism]. New York: Routledge.

Kieffer-Pülz, Petra. 2007. "Stretching the Vinaya Rules and Getting Away with It." *Journal of the Pali Text Society* 29: 1–49.

————. 2014. "What the Vinayas Can Tell Us about Law." In *Buddhism and Law: An Introduction*, edited by Rebecca Redwood French and Mark A. Nathan, 46–62. New York: Cambridge University Press.

Kieschnick, John. 1999. "The Symbolism of the Monk's Robe in China." *Asia Major* 12 (1): 9–32.

Kondinya, Bhikshu. 1986. *Monastic Buddhism among the Khamtis of Arunachal*. New Delhi: National Publishing House.

Negi, J. S. 1993–2005. *Bod skad daṅ legs sbyar gyi tshig mdzod chen mo: Tibetan-Sanskrit Dictionary*. 16 vols. Varanasi: Dictionary Unit, Central Institute of Higher Tibetan Studies.

Nguyen, Cuong Tu, and A. W. Barber. 1998. "Vietnamese Buddhism in North America: Tradition and Acculturation." In *Faces of Buddhism in America*, edited by Charles S. Prebish and Kenneth K. Tanaka, 129–146. Berkeley, CA: University of California Press.

Numrich, Paul David. 1994. "Vinaya in Theravāda Temples in the United States." *Journal of Buddhist Ethics* 1: 23–32.

————. 1996. *Old Wisdom in the New World: Americanization in Two Immigrant Theravada Buddhist Temples*. Knoxville: University of Tennessee Press.

280   *Jens W. Borgland*

———. 1998. "Theravāda Buddhism in America: Prospects for the Sangha." In *Faces of Buddhism in America*, edited by Charles S. Prebish and Kenneth K. Tanaka, 147–162. Berkeley, CA: University of California Press.

Oldenberg, Hermann. 1879. *Vinaya Piṭakaṃ: One of the Principal Buddhist Holy Scriptures in the Pāli Language*. Vol. 1, *The Mahāvagga*. London: Williams and Norgate.

———. 1881. *The Vinaya Piṭakaṃ: One of the Principal Buddhist Holy Scriptures in the Pāli Language*. Vol. 3, *The Suttavibhaṅga*, First Part. London: Williams and Norgate.

Pachow, W. 1955. *A Comparative Study of the Prātimokṣa on the Basis of Its Chinese, Tibetan, Sanskrit and Pali Versions*. Santineketan: Santiniketan Press.

Pachow, W., and R. Mishra. 1956. *Pratimokṣa-Sūtra of the Mahāsāṃghikas: Critically Edited for the First Time from the Palm-Leaf Manuscripts Found in Tibet*. Allahabad: Ganganatha Jha Research Institute.

Philips, Sarah. 2007. "A Brief History of Facebook." *Guardian*, 25 July. Accessed 15 December 2014. http://www.theguardian.com/technology/2007/jul/25/media.newmedia.

Plum Village. 2014a. "Becoming a Monastic." Accessed 3 December. http://plumvillage. org/about/becoming-a-monastic/.

———. 2014b. "Five-Year Monastic Training." Accessed 3 December. http://plumvillage. org/about/five-year-monastic-training/.

———. 2014c. "Plum Village." Accessed 3 December. http://plumvillage.org/about/ plum-village/.

Prebish, Charles S. 2003. "Varying the Vinaya: Creative Responses to Modernity." In *Buddhism in the Modern World: Adaptations of an Ancient Tradition*, edited by Steven Heine and Charles S. Prebish, 45–73. New York: Oxford University Press.

Rahula, Walpola. 1978. "The Problem of the Prospect of the Saṅgha in the West." In *Zen and the Taming of the Bull: Towards a Definition of Buddhist Thought: Essays by Walpola Rahula*, 55–67. London: Gordon Fraser.

Ratnapala, Nandasena. 1971. *The Katikāvatas: Laws of the Buddhist Order of Ceylon from the 12th Century to the 18th Century (Critically Edited, Translated and Annotated)* [Münchener Studien zur Sprachwissenschaft]. Munich: Kitzinger.

Schedneck, Brooke. 2009. "Western Buddhist Perceptions of Monasticism." *Buddhist Studies Review* 26 (2): 229–246.

Schopen, Gregory. 1992. "On Avoiding Ghosts and Social Censure: Monastic Funerals in the Mūlasarvāstivāda Vinaya." *Journal of Indian Philosophy* 20 (1): 1–39.

———. 1998. "Marking Time in Buddhist Monasteries: On Calendars, Clocks, and Some Liturgical Practices." In *Sūryacandrāya: Essays in Honour of Akira Yuyama On the Occasion of His 65th Birthday*, edited by Paul Harrison and Gregory Schopen, 157–179. Swisttal-Odendorf: Indica et Tibetica Verlag.

———. 2000. "The Good Monk and His Money in a Buddhist Monasticism of 'The Mahāyāna Period.'" *Eastern Buddhist* 32 (1): 85–105.

———. 2001. "Dead Monks and Bad Debts: Some Provisions of a Buddhist Monastic Inheritance Law." *Indo-Iranian Journal* 44: 99–148.

———. 2007. "Cross-Dressing with the Dead: Asceticism, Ambivalence, and Institutional Values in an Indian Monastic Code." In *The Buddhist Dead: Practices, Discourses, Representations* [Studies in East Asian Buddhism 20], edited by Bryan J. Cuevas and Jacqueline I. Stone, 60–104. Honolulu: University of Hawai'i Press.

Silk, Jonathan. 2008. *Managing Monks: Administrators and Administrative Roles in Indian Buddhist Monasticism*. New York: Oxford University Press.

Takakusu, J., and M. Nagai. (1924) 1975. *Samantapāsādikā: Buddhaghosa's Commentary on the Vinaya Piṭaka*. Vol. 1. London: Pali Text Society.

Thích Nhất Hạnh's Monastic Code 281

Upasak, C. S. 1975. *Dictionary of Early Buddhist Monastic Terms*. Varanasi: Bharati Prakashan.

Von Hinüber, Oskar. 1985. "Die Bestimmung der Schulgehörigkeit buddhistischer Texte nach sprachlichen Kriterien." In *Zur Schulzugehörigkeit von Werken der Hīnayāna-Literatur.* Vol. 1 [Abhandlungen der Akademie der Wissenschaften in Göttingen 149], edited by Heinz Bechert, 57–75. Göttingen: Vandenhoeck & Ruprecht.

———. 1995. "Buddhist Law According to the Theravāda-Vinaya: A Survey of Theory and Practice." *Journal of the International Association of Buddhist Studies* 18 (1): 7–46.

———. 1996. *A Handbook of Pāli Literature* [Indian Philology and South Asian Studies]. Berlin: De Gruyter.

Von Simson, Georg. 1986. *Prātimokṣasūtra der Sarvāstivādins*. Vol. 1. Göttingen: Vandenhoeck & Ruprecht.

———. 2000. *Prātimokṣasūtra der Sarvāstivādins*. Vol. 2, *Kritische Textausgabe, Übersetzung, Wortindex sowie Nachträge zu Teil I.* Göttingen: Vandenhoeck & Ruprecht.

Walters, Jonathan S. 2014. "Flanked by Images of Our Buddha: Community, Law, and Religion in a Premodern Buddhist Context." In *Buddhism and Law: An Introduction,* edited by Rebecca Redwood French and Mark A. Nathan, 135–149. New York: Cambridge University Press.

Wille, Klaus. 1990. *Die Handschriftliche Überlieferung des Vinayavastu der Mūlasarvāstivādin* [Verszeichnis der orientalistischen Handschriften in Deutschland]. Stuttgart: Franz Steiner Verlag.

Yifa. (2002) 2009. *The Origins of Buddhist Monastic Codes in China: An Annotated Translation and Study of the Chanyuan Qinggui* [Kuroda Institute Classics in East Asian Buddhism]. Honolulu: University of Hawai'i Press.

Yuyama, Akira. 1979. *Systematische Übersicht über die buddhistische Sanskrit-literatur.* Vol. 1, *Vinaya Texte*. Wiesbaden: Franz Steiner Verlag.

Zürcher, Erik. (1984) 2002. " 'Beyond the Jade Gate': Buddhism in China, Vietnam and Korea." In *The World of Buddhism*, edited by Heinz Bechert and Richard F. Gombrich, 193–211. London: Thames & Hudson.

16 Modernizing American Zen through Scandal

Is "The Way" Really the Way?

Stuart Lachs

Introduction

When Joshu Sasaki Roshi[1] (1 April 1907–27 July 2014) died at age 107, he was perhaps the oldest Zen master in the world. He was sanctioned as a Zen master, or *roshi*, by the prestigious Myōshin-ji lineage in Japan, and many saw him as the most authentic old-style tough Rinzai[2] *roshi*. In spite of his limited English and solid but short five-foot frame, Sasaki was by most accounts a charismatic teacher. One Western monk, a long-time student of his, described him as "a living relic" and "literally the last of his kind" (Haubner 2013: 205). Sasaki spent most of his adult life in Europe and America, where he attracted thousands of students, among them celebrities such as the Canadian singer and songwriter Leonard Cohen.[3] When Sasaki died, his organization Rinzai-ji had over twenty-five affiliated centres across the United States, and also had groups in Austria, Canada, Germany, the Netherlands, and Norway. Sasaki also ran retreats in Spain, New Zealand, Belgium, and Poland.

I shall show how Sasaki's Zen encompassed a mixture of features from traditional Japanese Zen and features often attributed to so-called modern Buddhism. In the long run, however, some of these features are mutually exclusive. This incompatibility of features becomes especially clear when looking at the crisis that hit Sasaki's organization in 2012, following reports that Sasaki had sexually abused many of his female Zen students over a period spanning fifty years.

Sasaki was among the first group of post-World War II Japanese Zen teachers who came to Europe and America as missionaries in order to establish practice centres. From the beginning, these Japanese *roshi* were highly successful: through their monastic training and experience in temples, they were well schooled to deliver convincing public performances; they were well trained in the technical language of Zen and familiar with the language of the popular genres of *koan* and *mondo*[4] literature that attracted Westerners; they were adept at performing rituals; and last but not least, their comportment and outwards appearance (robes, shaved heads, sitting posture, ways of bowing, etc.) perfectly matched their American students' expectations of an authentic, iconoclastic, mysterious, and fully enlightened Zen *roshi* from Japan. These expectations, however, were shaped mainly by literature that presented to Westerners idealized Zen masters of bygone times

Modernizing American Zen through Scandal   283

(Berger 1963: 127). These factors established the Zen *roshi*'s charisma and success, and as we will see below, many of these factors for a long time also prevented internal criticism and processes of change within the Zen organizations.[5] Yet in the long run a number of these Zen centres had to change when trouble with their *roshi* surfaced, and as American students slowly matured in their view of Zen. After going through difficult periods, these reorganized Zen groups became more open organizations, less hierarchical, with more stress on gender equality, and importantly, the new leaders/*roshi* are not invested with the unquestionable authority their Japanese predecessors had.

Sasaki's Zen Buddhism at the time of writing constitutes a transitional phase in this process of Zen's reformulation in the contemporary American context. Sasaki and the organization he built up follows a pattern similar to that of other groups of Japanese Zen teachers who came to America after World War II.

Outline of Sasaki's Life

Sasaki was born in April 1907 into a farming family near Sendai in Miyagi prefecture, Japan.[6] At the age of fourteen he became one of the first disciples of Joten Sōko Miura Rōshi, who would later become head of Myōshin-ji,[7] one of the preeminent Rinzai temple complexes in Japan. Sasaki was ordained as *osho* (priest) at the age of twenty-one. From the ages of twenty-eight to thirty-seven, he trained as an *unsui* (Zen monk in training) at Myōshin-ji Sodo and then Zuigan-ji Sodo (training monastery), when Miura Rōshi became abbot there. In 1944, Sasaki was appointed to a temple office called *fusu* (in charge of financial affairs) at Zuigan-ji and in 1947, at the age of forty, he received his authority as *rōshi* and became abbot of Yotoku-in at Zuigan-ji. In 1953, Sasaki Roshi was assigned to become the abbot of the abandoned temple Shoju-an, which had been founded by the teacher of Hakuin (1686–1768), the famous reviver of Rinzai Zen in Japan, who stressed strenuous training and the integration of meditation and *koan* practice. The temple was in disrepair, and Sasaki set about restoring it while still teaching Zen, until he was sent to the United States in 1962.

Robert Harmon and Gladys Weisbart, two members of the Joshu Zen Temple in Little Tokyo, Los Angeles, aimed at bringing a Japanese Rinzai Zen monk to Los Angeles to lead their group. Their desire was to have an authorized Zen master to teach "authentic" Rinzai Zen. In Sasaki, they found an interested candidate, and the abbot of Myōshin-ji, Daiko Furukawa Roshi, formally requested Sasaki to begin teaching Zen in the United States. In departure, Sasaki is said to have taken the traditional ceremony of permanent departure from Japan, implying that he would be buried in America (Fields 1992: 245).

Further, according to the Rinzai-ji website, Sasaki arrived in Los Angeles on 21 July 1962. Initially he lived in a garage at his sponsor Harmon's house. Later Harmon rented a small house as residence for Sasaki and as the group's *zendo* (meditation hall). There Sasaki conducted daily Zen meetings. He also arranged weekly meetings at the homes of some of his students and gave *sanzen*,[8] private

284 *Stuart Lachs*

meetings of the *roshi* with individual students. In November 1963, Sasaki and his Zen students founded the Rinzai Zen Dojo Association. Over the next few years, as Sasaki's reputation spread throughout Southern California, he led group *zazen* (Zen meditations) in homes in the Hollywood Hills, Laguna Beach, and Beverly Hills. Already by 1966 the group outgrew its quarters and started holding *zazen* in office space donated by Harmon. In 1968, the Rinzai Zen Dojo Association changed its name to Rinzai-ji and bought its first property, a complex of buildings surrounded by high walls, named Cimarron Zen Center after its location on Cimarron Street in Los Angeles. Three years later, with Zen attracting many followers across America, Mt. Baldy Zen Center was opened as Rinzai-ji's main training centre, high in the San Gabriel Mountains east of Los Angeles. Mt. Baldy Zen Center gained a reputation in American Zen circles for its rigorous if not severe practice. Most of Rinzai-ji's monks and nuns have received some or all of their training at Mt. Baldy Zen Center. The organization continued to expand. In 1974 Rinzai-ji bought an old Catholic monastery in Jemez Springs, New Mexico, which is now known as Bodhi Manda Zen Center. It became Sasaki's second non-urban training centre, offering daily *zazen* and communal work practice.

By 1974, Sasaki had a well-established reputation in the United States as an authentic and demanding Rinzai *roshi* with three major properties in America under his control and with many fully ordained disciples (*osho*). But as early as the 1970s there had been rumours in the American Zen community of Sasaki fondling women students in *sanzen*, the private interview with the *roshi*, which is an integral part of *koan* meditation practice. These first rumours coincided with the tearing apart of major Zen centres in America, starting in 1975,[9] because of sexual and financial scandals involving their spiritual leaders, the Zen masters. Yet for the longest time Sasaki remained under the radar. Rather, in contrast to scandals elsewhere, he stood out as an authentic, demanding "real deal" master. In fact, even as rumours were circulating, his reputation increased for decades, since his assumed purity was highlighted as more of his fellow Zen teachers "fell".

The Disclosures

But all this was to take a dramatic turn on 16 November 2012, when Eshu Martin, a former monk of Sasaki's organization Rinzai-ji, posted an open letter on the Sweeping Zen website, which immediately went viral. Martin's letter "Everybody Knows" spoke openly about what until then were tightly kept secrets regarding Sasaki Roshi, but also disclosing his organization's complicit role in these processes. Martin's letter begins:

> Joshu Sasaki Roshi, the founder and Abbot of Rinzai-ji is now 105 years old, and he has engaged in many forms of inappropriate sexual relationship with those who have come to him as students since his arrival here more than 50 years ago. His career of misconduct has run the gamut from frequent and repeated non-consensual groping of female students during interview [*sanzen*], to sexually coercive after hours "tea" meetings, to affairs and sexual

Modernizing American Zen through Scandal   285

interference in the marriages and relationships of his students. Many individuals that have confronted Sasaki and Rinzai-ji about this behavior have been alienated and eventually excommunicated, or have resigned in frustration when nothing changed; or worst of all, have simply fallen silent and capitulated. For decades, Joshu Roshi's behavior has been ignored, hushed up, downplayed, justified, and defended by the [board of directors], monks, nuns and students that remained loyal to him. . . . Certainly, as an organization, Rinzai-ji has never accepted the responsibility of putting a stop to this abuse, and has never taken any kind of remedial action.[10]

The publication of this letter initiated a torrent of further disclosures. Stories accumulated, often with great detail, while ex-insiders with close knowledge of the organization now felt free to talk openly. With this new flow of information, it was also revealed that Sasaki, while still in Japan in the late 1940s and early 1950s, was at the centre of a number of sexual scandals and financial affairs, such as the so-called Zuiganji Affair. This affair involved the embezzlement of several million yen of temple funds allocated for temple renovation, and Sasaki's spending of the embezzled funds for "a pleasure/spending spree in a way inappropriate for a religious figure/man of the cloth", as the High Court judge phrased it. When questioned by a reporter about his involvement with women, Sasaki replied, "With regard to the matter of women, this is my distress as a human being." Sasaki was found guilty and sentenced to serve eight months in prison.[11]

When Sasaki went to America in the early 1960s, neither the abbot, Furukawa Roshi of Myōshin-ji, nor anyone else ever mentioned Sasaki's chequered history in Japan. While Sasaki's sexual transgressions may not have been considered out of the ordinary for a Zen monk,[12] it is hard to imagine that embezzling monastery funds would have been taken lightly. It might therefore well be that sending Sasaki to the United States was a way for Myōshin-ji to get rid of a troublesome monk who had embarrassed the monastery and his teacher Miura Roshi, who had to resign as abbot of Myōshin-ji in 1952, when Sasaki was prosecuted. Remember, too, that Sasaki is said to have taken the traditional ceremony of permanent departure from Japan—this was a one-way trip.

With these disclosures, a number of women in America on the receiving end of Sasaki's transgressions reported how they felt vindicated for leaving, how they felt abused and used, and how they never realized that they were only one of perhaps hundreds. As one former *inji*, or personal attendant, wrote, "I was given what I thought was a special position (because of my deep dedication) but I was a disposable sex object."[13] A poem by another victim, Chizuko Karen Tasaka, shall be given in full here, since it vividly describes not only Sasaki's transgressions,[14] but also his disdain for his female and male disciples alike, and the non-responsiveness of the *osho*s to women asking for support. It also shows how Sasaki declared his forceful demands for sex as Zen teaching, ignoring at least one woman's resistance, anger, and confusion:

Roshi, you are a sexual abuser
"Come" you say as you pull me from a handshake onto your lap

286 *Stuart Lachs*

"Open" you say as you push your hands between my knees, up my thighs
fondle my breasts
rub my genitals
french kiss me

you put my hand on your genitals
stroke your penis
jack you off?
this is sanzen?

my friend—she was inji
sex with roshi

she tried to say no
you demanded, demanded, demanded
demon demand the force of a tornado

sex with roshi
for whose best interest?

I told you I don't like it.
I asked you why you do this?
You said, "nonattachment, nonattachment, you nonattachment"

I told you as shoji,[15] "women very angry, very upset"
I asked you why you do this.
You said: "Be good daughter to roshi, and good wife to G. [her husband]."
Roshi, that is incest. So many women trying to shake the shame from their
voices of
Sex with roshi

We came to you with the trust of a student
You were our teacher
You betrayed us
You violated our bodies
You rape our souls

You betrayed our previous student-teacher relationship
You abuse us as women
You emasculate our husbands and boyfriends

Roshi, you are a sexual abuser
Your nuns you make your sexual servants
Your monks and Oshos are crippled with denial
Roshi, Sexual Abuser.[16]

This poem, as disturbing as it is, gives us a few clues to understanding mechanisms that contributed to the long silence about Sasaki's transgressive behaviour
towards his female students.

Problematic Aspects of Sasaki's Zen

Already in Japan, Sasaki's sexual and financial misbehaviours were swept under the carpet by Myōshin-ji officials—thus saving face and avoiding shame for the institution and its leaders. While Sasaki's "distress with women" continued to persist in the United States, it also continued to be covered up by the board of directors of Rinzai-ji and by many of Sasaki's older male disciples. When Rinzai-ji was finally forced to reply, they first dismissed the disclosures as "allegations", and later the board of directors falsely claimed that these allegations were all new to them. Sasaki's earlier problems with women in Japan underlines that his problems in the West were neither new nor caused by cultural misunderstandings, as some of his loyalists maintained.

Yet there exist a number of reports that show that women tried to address these issues with Sasaki and with older male students. One woman hired a Japanese translator to "confront Sasaki with her pain because he refused to acknowledge her when she confronted him in English. Sasaki refused to acknowledge the translator."[17] There were also a few attempts by some of his *osho*s and long-term lay students to change his behaviour towards women or get him to understand the harm it caused them, their boyfriends, husbands, and friends and family. All this fell on Sasaki's deaf ears. Sasaki's own response to concerns presented to him by his students amounted to him threatening to stop teaching and leave should he be forced to change his behaviour.[18] He also expressed the view that having sex with young women kept him young. Sasaki clearly viewed his own position as Zen master as beyond criticism, being the very top of an absolute hierarchy. His position was based not only on the fact that he was an authorized Rinzai *roshi*,[19] but also that he was the oldest living *roshi* from Japan residing in America, who had brought authentic Zen practice to the United States and his lineage from the famous Myōshin-ji monastery. This made him an authorized spokesman for the Rinzai tradition and imputed him to be a person of guaranteed belief and trust, an absolute presence. This situation can fittingly be explained with Bourdieu (1991: 125): "One of the privileges of consecration consists in conferring an undeniable and indelible essence on the consecrated individual [so that] it authorizes transgressions that would otherwise be forbidden. The person who is sure of his cultural identity can play with the rules of the cultural game."

Also Sasaki's senior *osho* and loyalists left no room to question his behaviour. When women complained to monks, students who were older in the practice and higher in the hierarchy, they rarely met with sympathy. As a senior *osho* declared, "If you do not like it, leave."[20] One woman confronted Sasaki in the 1980s and reports that she found herself an outcast afterwards. She said that afterwards "hardly anyone in the *sangha* (group of practitioners), whom I had grown up with for 20 years, would have anything to do with us" (Oppenheimer and Lovett 2013).[21] Sasaki's belief in, and practice of, an unquestionable hierarchy was absorbed by his older disciples. Sasaki's students' acceptance of his unquestionable authority and legitimacy was inculcated through a long and slow process of their own acceptance in the group and their gaining a place in Sasaki's hierarchy.

288 *Stuart Lachs*

His close students understood that sacrificing women to Sasaki's sexual desires was part of the price of being an intimate and advanced student, of bowing to Sasaki's position of absolute authority.

Sasaki's loyal *osho*s were a group close to him, and who were more committed than ordinary lay students. They held positions of importance, were dressed in robes, and interpreted and explained Sasaki's teaching to lay practitioners.[22] In the process, they made clear that if someone had a problem with Sasaki's behaviour, it was a sign of their own lack of understanding Zen.[23]

Similar views were commonly held in many Zen centres.[24] The Rinzai-ji *osho*s thus—with the exception of very few—remained silent to protect their years of practice along with their elevated positions in the hierarchy. This attitude is closely connected to the severity of Sasaki's retreats and practice periods, functioning also as rites of initiation. Numerous psychological experiments have shown that people's adherence to an institution is directly proportional to the severity and painfulness of the rites of initiation (Bourdieu 1991: 123–124). The severity of Sasaki's retreats, especially in winter, led long-term practitioners to believe they were becoming extraordinary people—a status they were not willing to sacrifice. After many retreats and long periods at their monastery, they incorporated the Rinzai way of walking, standing, and speaking, displaying their "distinctive differences" (Bourdieu 1991: 124). Sure enough, some *osho*s certainly felt they needed more spiritual training, and others no doubt wanted to receive Dharma transmission and so become Zen masters themselves. Some also might have hoped for a promotion to have a centre of their own or to maintain some perks, such as positions of authority. Other *osho*s, after decades in the organization, had attained such positions of authority and privilege and may well have wondered how they could function in "ordinary" life.

The claim that whatever Sasaki (or any other *roshi*) did was in fact Zen teaching even amounted to declaring that what for the women constituted sexual abuse was really a teaching method. When a young woman who was Sasaki's *inji* at the time complained about Sasaki's constant sexual advances, one monk replied that "sexualizing is teaching for particular women".[25] The monk's theory, widespread in Sasaki's circle, was that such physicality could check a "woman's overly strong ego" (Oppenheimer and Lovett 2013). Sasaki claimed that his sexual advances were in fact teaching non-attachment and emptiness, core Zen values. Sasaki and his loyalists thus in effect claimed that these acts, which seemed self-serving and abusive to the unenlightened, were really examples of Mahāyāna Buddhist *upāya*—skilful means that teach the Dharma in a way that the students need, whether they recognize it or not.

Zen's ideological underpinnings base all its authority and legitimacy on the idea of an unbroken lineage of enlightened Zen *roshi* going back to the historical Buddha Śākyamuni.[26] According to this mythology, each *roshi* has realized his Buddha mind or Buddha nature, and has the same insight as Śākyamuni Buddha. Each *roshi* is viewed as a person who has transcended his ego, hence has no selfish motives. A *roshi* is concerned only with the welfare of all sentient beings. Like a mirror, the enlightened *roshi* reflects back what the student needs. Commonly, a Zen student who dared to criticize the master's action, or even questioned it, would be stamped by senior disciples as not understanding Zen.[27] It was common around Western Zen centres, especially so with Asian masters, to believe that whatever the master did was for selfless reasons to help their students and to spread the Dharma. Accordingly, if a female student receives sexual advances by the *roshi*, this is exactly what she needs—only that she, as an unenlightened being, cannot understand this.

It is important to realize that the women, who remained silent for such a long time, became accomplices in their own abuse. They themselves had bought into Zen's idealized ideology. This is not surprising, as the ideology is repeated constantly in Zen literature and in stories, *koan*s, and talks, which juxtapose the enlightened Zen master in contrast to the mass of unenlightened people who cannot understand the enlightened master. Even when some women left the organization or were forced to leave by Sasaki loyalists, they were hesitant to speak out publicly for fear of giving Zen or the master a bad name or of exposing how they accepted and submitted to their own abuse.

This power of Zen ideology, embodied by the Japanese Zen *roshi*, is hard to understand without considering the power of investiture by the Zen institution. All rites of institutions are "acts of social magic" that legitimate a boundary, while obscuring the arbitrary nature of this boundary (Bourdieu 1991: 105–126). Zen Dharma transmission, the basis of its lineage construction, creates this divide between the supposedly enlightened master and everyone else. This is especially so with Asian teachers, who are naively considered to be more authentic by their Western students and who learned to perform their role through years of monastic training. In this context, the extreme hierarchy of Sasaki and his cohort of Asian Zen teachers/missionaries functioned well and for long.

The Democratization of Access to Information

Interestingly, a feature often mentioned in connection with modern Buddhism, namely democratization, has contributed substantially to ending the secrecy and subsequently modernizing contemporary Zen in America.

Access to modern mass communication served Sasaki's reputation and helped spur his organization's growth in the competitive international religious market place. At the same time, the World Wide Web, and especially its character as a relatively democratic venue to spread and to collect information, also backfired on Sasaki by circumventing the internal hierarchies that had prevented troubling news from spreading from within his organization. The Sasaki scandal was opened to the world on the website Sweeping Zen with Eshu Martin's open letter, which was then posted on websites around the globe and later picked up by radio, TV, and newspapers, including the *Los Angeles Times* and the *New York Times*. The Sasaki Archive website played an important role in the further disclosure and spread of the reports of former Zen students. The website is run by Kobutsu Malone, an ordained Rinzai Zen monk, who also runs the Shimano Archive website with material related to the years of scandal around Eido Shimano. The power

290   *Stuart Lachs*

of the World Wide Web exposed the scale of the events and provided the venue for more people to speak out. These women and men had in the past seen themselves as isolated and individual cases, often looking for shortcomings in themselves rather than with Sasaki or Rinzai-ji. This is a common response if someone leaves a Zen centre: failure is usually attributed to their shortcomings and weaknesses, and not to the centre or the *roshi*. Yet the dissemination of information over the World Wide Web circumvented traditional Zen's control of information, thereby weakening people's belief and trust in the fully enlightened Zen master and the related absolute hierarchy. This process of democratization of sharing information thus dragged Western Zen into the realm of Buddhist modernity.

Conclusion: The Beginnings of a Renewal of Zen in America

We have now looked at Joshu Sasaki Roshi as an example of the early phase of Zen in America. I argue that Sasaki's Zen Buddhism was a transitional form of Zen in the West, combining both modern and traditional characteristics: Sasaki's Zen was a form of modern Buddhism by virtue of its distinct break with tradition, in that it addressed mostly laypeople of both sexes and concentrated on lay meditation practice, foregrounding internal experience rather than ritual practice. Sasaki, like other Zen teachers from Asia, attracted many lay followers.[28] In his teachings and retreats, he stressed meditation and the experiences that flow from it as the main practice. He offered to his lay followers the intense and demanding schedule of monastic life—meditation, *sanzen*, and *teisho*[29]—that he experienced in Japan.[30] He was perhaps the most active Zen master in the West, running on average twenty week-long retreats (*sesshin*) a year for forty years (Sasaki 2014: inside cover). This fits nicely with several of the characteristics of modern Buddhism listed by Lopez (2002; cf. Baumann 2004) and McMahan (2008), most strikingly the emphasis on meditation, including the unprecedented widespread practice of meditation among the laity.[31]

Yet Lopez also shows that the beginnings of what he calls modern Buddhism can be traced back to the late nineteenth century, being a result of the dialogue between leading Buddhist monks and Protestant intellectuals. In contrast, the absolute lack of interest and willingness of Sasaki to engage in a dialogue concerning his behaviour or attitude points to his very traditional or conservative stance. Moreover, Sasaki was a traditionalist in terms of his insistence on hierarchy rather than equality, his explicit rejection of democratic ideas,[32] the secrecy in terms of the organization and its financial dealings, and his clear acceptance and underlining of strong gender hierarchies.

Sasaki's case is especially interesting because it is an extreme example of cultural confrontation. He was, after all, a Japanese man raised in early twentieth-century rural Japan. His ideas on women, democracy, and psychology, of which he was extremely critical,[33] hardly matched the views of his Western followers. His ideas on marriage in Japan seemed idealized and nationalistic, while his ideas of Western marriage seemed just naïve and uninformed (Sasaki 1984). As the most traditional among the Zen masters/teachers that came from Japan in the 1960s,

Sasaki was also most demanding in obedience to absolute hierarchy. Although he spent more than half his adult life in Europe and America, he saw himself above questioning by his disciples. The organization that developed around him fully endorsed his traditionalist ways, hiding his transgressive sexual and financial life from most ordinary members.[34]

Sasaki's authority and his Zen Buddhist institution began to collapse in late 2012 through the major scandal surrounding Sasaki and senior clergy (*oshos*) and board of directors, who assisted in keeping Sasaki's behaviour secret. Because of his failing health and no doubt the rising scandal, Rinzai-ji announced on 1 April 2013 that Sasaki would step down as abbot on 21 July. Sasaki named an abbot designate and two vice-abbot designates for Rinzai-ji,[35] while underlining that these were administrative, not spiritual appointments.[36] Meanwhile, senior members of Rinzai-ji have become more open to admitting Sasaki's misdeeds and their own failure to confront abuse. And while it is clear that things will change, and that Sasaki's Zen Buddhism was therefore only a phase in a longer process of modernization of Zen in America, at the time of writing it is not yet clear what these changes will exactly look like.

Other Zen groups in America that had formed around this first group of Zen masters from Japan or Korea had gone through similar trajectories: American students looking for "authentic" experience embraced these foreign missionaries/ Zen masters as living examples of the masters they had read about in Zen hagiographic and idealized Zen literature. The Asian Zen masters on their part brought along their culturally inherited value system, including strong emphasis on hierarchy and on knowing one's place in society, on unquestioned obedience to authority, and very little sense of gender equality—all aspects almost directly opposite of characteristics of modern Buddhism. Eventually, the mismatch of practices and expectations surfaced in scandals involving the idealized Zen master abusing sex and alcohol and engaging in shady financial dealings.

After going through often difficult periods of self-examination, discussion, and meetings with outside facilitators, usually with psychology backgrounds, American Zen groups reorganized as institutions that more closely match forms of modern Buddhism, with more open and more democratic ways of functioning, a stronger emphasis on gender equality, a weakening of hierarchical power relations, and with a more ecumenical attitude towards other religions and groups, and importantly, not presupposing that the Zen master/teacher is a fully enlightened being above any questioning.

Judging from the development of other Zen groups in America that had to face similar problems, it is likely that Rinzai-ji will adopt structures and ideas that are closer to modern forms of Buddhism than to continue mimicking traditionalist Japanese Zen culture. There is no question that gender hierarchy has weakened in many Zen centres in America, opening up leadership positions for women. For instance, Roshi Wendy Egyoku Nakao is the abbess of the Zen Center of Los Angeles since 1999, and the lineage chart of Shunryu Suzuki of the San Francisco Zen Center[37] and that of the Sanbokyodan Zen sect[38] contain many women *roshi* leading groups around the Western world. The same goes for the White Plum

292   *Stuart Lachs*

Asanga, an organization of teachers in the Maezumi lineage of Los Angeles. With regard to Rinzai-ji, we have yet to see how authority will be redistributed among the senior *osho*s, perhaps shared with senior laypeople, how the board of directors will be chosen and function, and how Rinzai-ji, at present without an authorized Zen master to attract new students and to lead *koan* study, will compete in the international religious marketplace.

Notes

1. *Roshi* is a Japanese honorific title used in Zen, which can be translated as "old teacher" or "old master". In Zen groups connected to Japan, so-and-so *roshi* is most of the time abbreviated to *roshi*. In America, the titles "Zen master" and *roshi* are used interchangeably.
2. There are two major sects of Zen in Japan, Rinzai and Sōtō. Sōtō has many more members, while Rinzai is somewhat associated with the upper classes. Rinzai stresses *koan* meditation, and Sōtō stresses *shikantaza*—just sitting. There is also the Sanbokyodan sect (The Three Treasures), a mixture of Rinzai and Sōtō founded by Yasutani Roshi in 1954 and popular in the West.
3. "Leonard Cohen on Mt. Baldy", YouTube video, 45:41, posted by "ALB123Videos", 14 June 2011, http://www.youtube.com/watch?v=HJuJQI0RMiw.
4. *Mondo* are short dialogues, really questions and answers between a teacher and student wherein the teacher displays a truth directly. It is not a method of logical argument.
5. Charisma is related to "what has happened before" and "to the social context of its appearance". Interestingly, Weber (1978) points out that charisma becomes "routinized" in following generations, which is exactly what happened in Zen groups in America.
6. The following summary is mainly based on Sasaki's biography as given on the Rinzai-ji website ("Denkyo Kyōzan Jōshū Sasaki, Rōshi (1907–2014)", accessed 2 November 2014, http://www.rinzaiji.org/joshu-sasaki-roshi/).
7. Myōshin-ji is *both* a single temple complex in Kyoto *and* the administrative head of the Myōshin-ji *branch* (or sub-sect) of the Rinzai Zen sect. It is by far the largest sect of Rinzai Zen, approximately as large as the other thirteen sects of Rinzai Zen combined. It owns about 3,500 temples spread across Japan and nineteen associated monasteries.
8. *Sanzen* is considered the heart of Rinzai Zen practice. The student meets the *roshi* in private, often many times a day during week-long *sesshin*s (meditation retreats). In these meetings, the student is to present her/his understanding of the *koan* s/he is working on to the *roshi*, through words, gestures, or other means (see Heine and Wright 2000 for a discussion of *koan*s).
9. In 1975, the Zen Studies Society and Eido Shimano were the first to be affected by scandal. They were followed by Richard Baker of the San Francisco Zen Center, Maezumi of the L.A. Zen Center, Katagitri of the Minneapolis Zen Center, Seung Sahn of the Providence Rhode Island Zen Center, and Dennis Merzel of the Bar Harbor Maine Zen Center. Later pretty much the same type of scandal happened again with Merzel at the Kanzeon Zen Center in Salt Lake City, Utah, and with Walter Nowick of Moonspring Hermitage Zen Center in Surry, Maine. I mention only the most prominent Zen centres across America; some less prominent Zen centres had similar trouble.
10. "Everybody Knows—Kyozan Joshu Sasaki Roshi and Rinzai-ji", accessed 27.11.2012, http://sweepingzen.com/everybody-knows-by-eshu-martin/.
11. "Zuiganji Affair Translations", accessed 14 November 2014, https://sites.google.com/site/zuiganjiaffair/home. These newspaper reports were translated by Jundo Cohen, an American lawyer and Zen priest living in Japan for twenty years.

12. In Japan, monks are not necessarily celibate. They marry, have children, and often "go over the wall (of the monastery)", that is, go to pleasure areas.
13. "Sex with Roshi", accessed 14 November 2014, http://sasakiarchive.com/PDFs/20130106_Sex_with_Sasaki.pdf. The woman was in her early twenties at the time, while Sasaki was in his seventies. She was appointed personal attendant of the *roshi*. As *inji* the woman woke Sasaki in the morning and helped put him to bed at night. She reports about daily sexual encounters with Sasaki over months. In Japan the *inji* is usually an older monk, but Sasaki consistently picked young women. Sasaki also had sex with some of his nuns, including the abbess of Mt Baldy, Gesshin Myoko ("Zen and the Emotional/Sexual Contraction", accessed 12 October 2014, http://sasakiarchive.com/PDFs/20121123_O'Hearn_Conscious.pdf). Sasaki and Gesshin Myoko had a fall-out when she was jealous of Sasaki having sexual meetings with another woman student. Later, Sasaki erased Gesshin from the list of people he ordained.
14. Sasaki seemed to have a particular focus on women's breasts. Many women relate how in *sanzen* he told them to show their breasts, and he often attempted to fondle them, but also many mentioned his viewing and fondling their genitalia and being asked to view and touch his genitalia. With some women it advanced to oral sex and intercourse. The Independent Witness Council estimated that he initiated sexual advances with as many as 300 women.
15. The "zendo mother figure" (Haubner 2013: 14).
16. "To Joshu Sasaki Roshi: Roshi You Are a Sexual Abuser", accessed 14 November 2014, http://sasakiarchive.com/PDFs/20130221_Chizuko_Tasaka.pdf. The poem was written by Chizuko Karen Tasaka (1951–2010) and was sent to Sasaki in 1988. Chizuko died in 2010. Her family and friends felt that she would want her story to be known.
17. "Sasaki's Misconduct", accessed 12 January 2015, http://sasakiarchive.com/PDFs/20121206_Anka_Spencer.pdf.
18. Among traditional Japanese Zen practitioners, Sasaki's interest in sex would not in itself be a cause for concern, but rather his letting it take too big a part in his life and interfering with his role of Zen master (Benedict 1946: 183–184).
19. Sasaki was hardly the only Rinzai *roshi* who felt he did not have to answer to people beneath him in the hierarchy.
20. "Sexual Allegations about Joshu Roshi", accessed 29 September 2014, http://sasakiarchive.com/PDFs/19971208_To_Sasaki.pdf.
21. The woman asked to remain anonymous to protect her privacy.
22. This group of loyal *oshos* may thus be characterized as "a charismatic aristocracy, an inner circle that developed around the charismatic leader within his growing flock" (Bell 2002: 238); see also Weber (1978: 1119).
23. "Zen and the Emotional/Sexual Contraction", accessed 12 October 2014, http://sasakiarchive.com/PDFs/20121123_O'Hearn_Conscious.pdf.
24. These words were repeated almost verbatim by older students of Richard Baker Roshi of the San Francisco Zen Center when newer students, not quite fully socialized into the Zen centre's ideology, complained over different aspects of Baker's high living. See Lachs (2002).
25. "As It Happens" podcast, accessed 15 November 2014, http://sasakiarchive.com/Audio/20130219_asithappens.mp4. This is from a podcast from CBC Radio of an interview with Nikki Stubbs, who as a young woman was a student of Sasaki for three years.
26. For a fuller discussion of Zen's legitimating story, see Lachs (2002: esp. "The Zen Institution"). Other sects of Buddhism in China and Japan based their authority on particular texts as opposed to Zen, which at least ideologically separated itself from texts and based its legitimacy on Dharma transmission between teacher and student.
27. We have seen exactly these words expressed by senior disciples of Sasaki, Eido Shimano, Richard Baker, and other masters when some students raised questions about their behaviour.

294 *Stuart Lachs*

28. It needs to be said, though, that some of his followers ordained and became monks or nuns.
29. In general, a *teisho* is a Dharma talk given by a Buddhist teacher. In Zen, however, it is a talk given by a teacher on a *koan* or a Zen text. Sasaki (1973: 12) described a *teisho* as a talk about the experiences or manifestations of old Zen masters. "It doesn't matter if you understand it or not, I just talk. You don't need to understand *teisho* at all."
30. He offered intense seven-day meditation retreats (*sesshins*). Sasaki's retreats had a reputation of being severe, especially the ones held at his home monastery.
31. Other characteristics of modern Buddhism, according to Lopez (2002), are, for example, a focus on social engagement, an ethic of compassion, an ecumenical attitude towards other sects, and deemphasizing religious orthodoxy, ritual, and mythology. McMahan (2008) defines Buddhist modernity in very similar terms.
32. Sasaki was openly critical of Western democratic ideas, marriage, and above all psychology.
33. "To: Rinzai-ji Board of Directors", accessed 27.5.2013, http://sasakiarchive.com/PDFs/20130527_Gregory_Campbell.pdf. The letter was posted by Gregory Campbell, who claims he was Sasaki's most frequent translator for twenty years from the early 1970s on: "I bitterly recall how often 'Roshi' would rant and rave in public talks about how his most 'stupid' students were therapists."
34. The board of directors of Rinzai-ji covering for Sasaki was repeated in other Zen groups and in the Tibetan group Vajradhatu founded by Chogyam Trungpa. Trungpa's Dharma heir Tom Rich/Osel Tendzin was HIV-positive while being openly sexually active, yet the board of directors kept this hidden for four years (Bell 1998: 64).
35. "Announcement of New Abbot- and Vice-Abbots-designate of Rinzai-ji", accessed 28 September 2014, http://sasakiarchive.com/PDFs/20130401_Paul_Humphreys.pdf.
36. Throughout the scandal, Sasaki never let go of his complete control, including the financial control, of his institution. The finances were never independently audited, and there was no accountability for funds being moved among several corporate accounts, with money from non-profit accounts being used to buy gifts for Sasaki's sexual partners ("Summary of the Findings of the Witness Council Concerning Allegations of Sexual Behaviors by Joshu Sasaki", accessed 13 October 2014, http://sasakiarchive.com/PDFs/20130111_Summary_Findings.pdf). Interestingly, these findings mirror much of the Zuigan-ji Affair in Japan that sent Sasaki to jail.
37. Shunryu Suzuki Roshi was the founder of the San Francisco Zen Center. The Center's website lists twelve people in his lineage, four being women. To see how quickly the number of women teachers has grown, see Martin (2012: Appendix). Katagiri was one of the twelve people listed in Suzuki's lineage, though his lineage chart lists over fifty people with slightly less than half being women.
38. See http://www.ciolek.com/wwwvlpages/zenpages/haradayasutani.html.

References

Baumann, Martin. 2004. Review of *A Modern Buddhist Bible: Essential Readings from East and West*, edited by Donald S. Lopez, Jr. *Journal of Global Buddhism* 5: 15–18. Accessed 20 October 2014. http://www.globalbuddhism.org/5/baumann04.htm.

Bell, Sandra. 1998. "'Crazy Wisdom', Charisma, and the Transmission of Buddhism in the United States." *Nova Religio: The Journal of Alternative and Emergent Religions* 2 (1): 55–75.

———. 2002. "Scandals in Emerging Western Buddhism." In *Westward Dharma: Buddhism Beyond Asia*, edited by Charles S. Prebish and Martin Baumann, 230–244. Berkeley, CA: University of California Press.

Benedict, Ruth. 1946. *The Chrysanthemum and the Sword: Patterns of Japanese Culture*. New York: Meridian.

Berger, Peter L. 1963. *Invitation to Sociology*. New York: Doubleday.

Bourdieu, Pierre. 1991. *Language and Symbolic Power*. Cambridge, MA: Harvard University Press.

Fields, Rick. 1992. *How the Swans Came to the Lake: A Narrative History of Buddhism in America*. Boston: Shambala.

Haubner, Jack Shozan. 2013. *Zen Confidential: Confessions of a Wayward Monk*. Boston: Shambhala.

Heine, Steven, and Dale S. Wright, eds. 2000. *The Koan: Texts and Contexts in Zen Buddhism*. Oxford: Oxford University Press.

Lachs, Stuart. 2002. "Richard Baker and the Myth of the Zen Roshi." Accessed 5 October 2014. http://www.thezensite.com/ZenEssays/CriticalZen/RichardBaker_and_the_Myth.htm.

Lopez, Donald S., Jr., ed. 2002. *A Modern Buddhist Bible: Essential Readings from East and West*. Boston: Beacon Press.

Martin, Andrea. 2012. *Ceaseless Effort: The Life of Dainin Katagiri*. Minneapolis: Minnesota Zen Meditation Center.

McMahan, David L. 2008. *The Making of Buddhist Modernism*. Oxford: Oxford University Press.

Oppenheimer, Mark, and Ian Lovett. 2013. "Zen Groups Distressed by Accusations against Teacher." *New York Times*, Asia Pacific Section, 11 February. Accessed 5 November 2014. http://sasakiarchive.com/PDFs/20130211_NYTimes.pdf.

Sasaki, Joshu Roshi. 1973. *Buddha Is the Center of Gravity*. Taos, NM: Lama Foundation.

———. 1984. "Joshu Sasaki Roshi Says on Married Zen." *Zen Notes* 31 (10): n.p. Accessed 10 October 2014. http://www.firstzen.org/ZenNotes/1984/1984–10_Vol_31_No_10_October_1984.pdf.

———. 2014. *About Tathagata Zen*. Edited by Kendo Hal Roth. Translated by Michel Mohr. Los Angeles: Rinzai-ji Press.

Weber, Max. 1978. *Economy and Society*. Edited by Guenther Roth and Claus Wittich. Berkeley,CA: University of California Press.

Index

Abe Mitsuie: introduction to 67, 68; Paek's meeting with 72–4, 78–80; Yi's and Kang's approach to 76–7
acquisition of consciousness 42, 43
anarchist communism 6, 33, 41–2
anti-clericalism 55, 59
Asian Buddhists 20, 67, 84, 246, 250

Bát Nhã Monastery 195–7, 198
Bat-Ochir, Sarandavaa 126, 128
Bhikkhunīsangha 243, 245–8, 250–1
bonreki (Indic calendrical sciences) 38–9; see also Sada Kaiseki
British colonialism 213–15
Buddhism/Buddhists: anarchist society and 40–3; borderland of 133–4; campaigning for official recognition 2; capitalist transformation and 36; Chinese nationalism and 155–8; Chogye order 167, 168; economics and 38, 46; European constructions of 209–10; governmentality and 158–61; Kalmyk community 95; lay identity of 58–9; Limbu community 134–5; marginalization of 2, 66; masculine self-disciplining issues 173–7; meditation utilization by 175; Mongol Empire and 93; nationalism and internationalism and 56–8; non-celibate 103; nonviolence and 204–8, 213; as pacifist 204–7, 209–10; pluralism 3–4, 102, 106, 122; "political" 207–9; in post-Mao China 151–61; reformers 21, 67, 69, 84, 120; revival of 128; romantic vision of 216; Seoul as a contentious site for 68–9; socialism and 47; in Sri Lanka 204–17; support of 19; Theravāda 206–7; Vietnamese 183–96; violence issues in 205, 212–13; as a "world religion" 56, 57, 62; see also temples

Buddhismus, Staat und Gesellschaft (Bechert) 16
Buddhist chaplains see chaplaincy/ chaplains
Buddhist doctrine 1, 174, 205, 208, 210
Buddhist Enlightenment 16, 17, 18, 20, 27
Buddhist ethics 204, 209, 210
Buddhist modernism: access to information and 289–90; canonical texts and 249–50, 260; contradictions related to 3; defined 13–14; establishment and upstart 52–4; increased involvement of women in 123–5; influence of 4; introduction to 1; in Kalmykia 91–111; in Mongolia 115–29; multiple 105–10; nationalism and internationalism and 56–8; origins of 1–2; Ōtani-ha Feminist movement and 228–31; religion and superstition and 54–6; renewal of Zen and 282, 290–2; in Republican China 51–62; rethinking about 13–17; Theravāda nuns and 243–52; this worldly and other-worldly and 60–1; Unitarianism and 24–5; Watanabe Kaikyoku's role in 21–4, 27
Buddhist monastic law: adaptation of 261–4; canonical texts and 249–50, 260; conclusion about 270–1; description of 259; getting around rules in 263; modern world and 264–70; *Prātimoksa* 259–61, 265, 271; Thích Nhất Hạnh and 261
Buddhist nationalism 62, 192, 208
Buddhists see Buddhism/Buddhists
Buddhist thought 3, 33
bunmei kaika ("civilization and development") 40
Buraku Liberation League 225, 228, 230, 235
business temples by females 126–7

298 *Index*

California, Bhikkhunīsangha in 247–8
canonical texts 249–50, 260
capitalist transformation: Buddhism's
stance towards 36; considerations
related to 34–8, 46–8; introduction to
33–4; Itō Shōshin and 43–6; of modern
Japan 33–48; Sada Kaiseki and 38–40;
Uchiyama Gudō and 40–3
celibacy issues 101, 104, 109, 124
Central Kalmyk Buddhist Monastery 91,
97–101, 103–4, 107–10
Central Khurul: Internet site of 100; for
laity 98; monastic community 99; source
of income for 99–100
Central Preaching Hall 74–7
chaplaincy/chaplains: conclusion about
177–9; denominations 167, 177;
foremost task of 172; introduction to
165–9; masculine self-disciplining and
173–7; reasons for choosing career as
169–73; as uniformed officers 168
"character tutoring" 173, 174
charitable work 22, 23, 58, 160, 161
China Dream 156, 158
Chinese Buddhism 52, 60, 61, 154, 158–9
Chinese Buddhist Association 53, 55, 59
Chinese Communist Party (CCP) 151,
153–5, 157–61
Chinese nationalism 155–8
Chinggis Khan 92, 93, 126, 128
Chogye order 167, 168
Chosŏn era 68, 80
Christianity: in Kalmykia 96–7; Orthodox
96, 153, 154; socialist movement by
42–3; Yumaism and 137–8
Christian missionaries 25, 59, 84, 105,
213
Chùa Linh Ứng 186–7, 197
colonial Seoul 68–9
communist revolution 53, 62
Confucianism 152, 154, 156, 158, 161
conservatives and reformers 52, 59
Constitution Order of 1978 135
cross-cultural ethics 206, 207
Cultural Revolution 62, 152, 154, 155

Dalai Lama 53, 93, 95–7
Da Nang city 185–7
debt and gratitude concept 20–1
degeneration theory 207–9
Deng Xiaoping 151, 152
de-traditionalization 109, 137, 139
Dharma Centers 96, 103, 109, 118–20
Dharmapala, Anagarika 67, 71–2, 213–15

Dōbōkai movement 225–6, 228–9, 232–3,
235, 238
Dual Sect arrangement 69, 71, 74–7
Dulumjav temple 124–5
Dutthagāmani, King 215

"engaged Buddhism" 191, 192
Enkhsaikhan 126, 128
Eshu Martin's open letter 284–5, 289
establishment institutions 52–4
ethnic identity 5, 91, 134, 137
European Enlightenment 16, 116, 134
"evil cults" 159, 161

Federation of Bōmori Associations 227,
230–1, 234
female temples 123–7
foreign religions 8, 159, 160
Freedom of Consciousness and Religious
Associations 94, 107
freedom of religion: in China 54; in Japan
233–4; in Vietnam 183, 185, 190,
193–6, 198

Gandan Darjaalin 126
Gandan Monastery 118, 120, 121, 122
Gandhian influence 215–17
Gelugpa institutions 100, 102, 110
Gelugpa monasteries 98, 108–9, 121–2,
128
Gelugpa order 91, 93, 98, 102, 103
Gelugpa tradition 6, 117–20
gender equality 128, 226, 230, 232, 291
globalization 39, 117, 198, 259
Gospel of Buddhism (Carus) 13
Gotō Zuigan 77, 78, 80–1
governmentality, Buddhism and 158–61
Great Enlightenment Teaching 82, 83

Han Yong'un 66–7, 70–5, 81
Heibon no jikaku (Uchiyama) 41, 42
heterodoxy 54, 110
High Treason Incident 27, 41
Hinduism 135, 210, 212, 213
History of British India, The (Mill) 210
humanist morality pillars 27
Human Life Buddhism 61
Human Rights Watch 183, 184

Imje Sŏn-centered Buddhism/movement
67–80
industrial capitalism 17, 36
internationalism, nationalism and 56–8
Itō Shōshin 33, 35, 37, 43–6

Japanese Buddhism: Abe's views about 79–80; introduction to 3, 18; *see also* capitalist transformation; Korean Buddhism

Japan's modernization: cosmic mission of 43–6; innovative alternatives to 38–40; in Meiji period 34

Jebtsundampa Khutugtu Center 118–19

Jōdo sect 21, 22, 23

Jōdo Shinshū 225, 228, 229

Joshu Sasaki Roshi: early life of 283–4; introduction to 282–3; poem about transgressions 285–6; problematic aspects of 287–9; sexual scandals about 284–6, 289

Kagyu traditions 121–2

Kalachakra Culture Center 119–20

Kalmyk Buddhist Union 95, 96, 107, 108

Kalmykia: as autonomous region 94; Buddhist institutions in 107, 109, 110; Buddhist modernities and 105–10; Central Monastery 97–101; Christianity in 96–7; conclusion about 110–11; deportation event 94; historical background 92–4; introduction to 91–2; monastic life rejection in 101–5; population decline in 104; religious revival in 94–7

Kalmyk lamas 101, 102

Kang Taeryŏn 68, 74–7

Karmapa's teachings 138, 142

King Dutthagāmani 215

Kiyozawa Manshi 43, 229, 237, 239, 242

Knapp, Arthur May 24

kokutai (Japanese national essence) 21, 45

Korean Buddhism: Abe's concept about 79–80; as "Buddhism in dilemma" 66; Central Preaching Hall and 74–6; colonial Seoul issues 68–9; conclusion about 83–4, 178–9; Imje Movement and 76–80; introduction to 66–8; marginalization of 66, 80; masculine self-disciplining issues 175–6; Myōshinji temple and 80–1; Paek Yongsŏng and 69–74

Kōtoku Shūsui 25, 27, 40, 48, 49

laity: Central Khurul for 98; monastic community and 58–60; Yinguang and 53

lamas: Kalmyk 101, 102; non-celibate 101, 103, 104

legalizers, use of 263–4, 266–7, 269, 271

Limbu community: close ties to Buddhism 134–5; Hinduism and 135; introduction

to 133–4; political considerations for 140–2; religious affiliation of 135–6; rise of 136–7; ritual specialists and 138–9, 142; traditional authority issues 139–40

Mahāyāna Buddhism 22, 23, 158–9, 161, 188

Making of Buddhist Modernism, The (McMahan) 3

masculine self-disciplining 173–7

masturbation issues 269

meat consumption 269–70

meditation, utilization of 175–6

Meiji period 19, 24, 34, 35, 226

Meiji state/government 33, 38, 40

military chaplaincy *see* chaplaincy/chaplains

military service 166, 169–71, 177–8

"mindfulness" Buddhism 192, 194

mindfulness meditation 8, 174, 175, 261, 264

modernism *see* Buddhist modernism

modern nation-state 2, 47, 151, 199

modern networks 226–8, 231

monastic community: Central Khurul 99; "community of resistance" 189–90; dress code for 266; incompatibility of 60; introduction to 54, 59; laity and 58–60; masturbation issues 269; meat consumption by 269–70; money and trade issues 267–8; transportation issues 266–7; use of legalizers for 263–4, 266–7, 269, 271; *Vinaya* rules for 100; *see also* Buddhist monastic law

monasticism: celibate 101, 104, 109; of Gelugpa order 91; revival of 92, 98–9, 103

monastic regulations 249, 251, 263, 266

money and trade issues 267–8

Mongol Aura and Energy Center 126–7

Mongolia: conclusion about 127–9; Gelugpa tradition and 117–20; historical background 116–17; increase in temples in 120–7; introduction to 115–16

mugaai ("selfless love") 43–5, 49

Mugaen organization 43, 44

multiple modernities 34, 106

Museifu kyōsan kakumei (Uchiyama Gudō) 41

mutual aid 21–4, 33, 43, 44, 47

Myōshinji temple 78–81

nationalism 56–8, 187

national networks 226–8, 231

300 *Index*

national salvation 6, 56, 57, 62
nation state 2–4, 47, 56, 84, 197–8
neo-Confucianism 18, 19, 66, 68, 171
neo-traditionalism 109, 111
New Age healing/spirituality 126, 127, 128, 129
New Buddhism/Buddhists: birth of 17–20; principles of 19; Saji Jitsunen 25–6; Unitarianism and 24–5; Watanabe Kaikyoku 21–4, 27; *see also* Buddhist modernism
New Buddhism magazine 18, 20
New Buddhist Fellowship 16, 17, 21, 26–7
Ninth Jebtsundampa 122
non-celibate lamas 101, 103, 104
non-Gelugpa Buddhism 120–2
non-killing precept 208
nonviolence: Buddhism and 204–8, 213; puzzlements about 210–12; as a strategic tool 213–15
Nyamsambuu 118
Nyingma traditions 121–2

Oirats 92–3, 100
Ōkuni Takamasa 37, 48
old Buddhism 5, 17, 18, 19, 23
oracular tradition 125
Orthodox Christianity 96, 153, 154
orthodoxy 16, 54, 55, 155, 159
Ōtani-ha Feminist movement: Buraku Liberation League and 230; individual choice in a family religion and 231–5; language of 228–31; modern networks and 226–8; Shin Buddhism and 226–31
Ouyang Jingwu 53–4, 59

pacifism: absolute and universalist 208; Buddhism and 204–7, 209–10; conclusion about 217; degeneration theory and 207–9; Gandhian influence and 215–17; introduction to 204; nonviolence and 210–12; puzzle of 206–7; violence and 212–15
Paek, Yongsŏng: Anagarika Dharmapala and 71–2; as a Buddhist propagator 69–71; Central Preaching Hall and 74–6; conclusion about 83–4; foray into mining 80–1; Gotō Zuigan and 81; Imje Movement and 76–80; introduction to 66–8; Korean Buddhism and 69–74; meeting with Abe 72–4, 78–80; new religion and 81–3
pagodas *see* temples
peace and conflict studies 215–17

Peace by Peaceful Means: Peace and Conflict, Development and Civilization (Galtung) 217
People's Republic of China (PRC) 152, 166
Plum Village community 191–2, 194–7, 261, 269–70
pluralism 102, 106, 108, 122, 154
"political" Buddhism 207–9
"positive orientalism" 204, 211, 217
post-Mao China: Buddhism and governmentality and 158–61; Chinese nationalism and 155–8; conclusion about 161; introduction to 151; secularization issues 151–5
Prātimoksa: different versions of 261–4; introduction to 259–61; revised 260, 265, 268, 269, 271
progressive modernism 16, 225
"Protestant Buddhism" 105, 116, 133, 137, 143
"proxy resident priests" 227
"pseudo-religions" 82, 83
"pure" Buddhism 98, 100, 105, 106, 210
Pure Karma Society 55, 57, 58, 59, 61
Pure Land: other-worldly 60–1; Uchiyama Gudō and 42, 43; Vietnamese Buddhism and 189, 197, 198; Watanabe Kaikyoku and 21, 22; Yinguang and 53, 61

Qing dynasty 51, 58, 151
Quan Âm statue 186–7

Red Tradition temples 121–2, 124, 128
"re-enchanted" society 183, 184, 187–9, 193–6
Reform and Opening Up policies 151, 154
reformers and conservatives 19, 52, 59, 152, 229
reform movements 235–7
religion: attitudes towards 187–8; nationalism and 187; superstition and 54–6; violence and 207–8
religious affiliations 68, 135, 165
religious communities 107, 141, 185
"religious fever" 153, 154, 159
religious market: introduction to 3, 5, 8, 9; in Kalmykia 108; in Mongolia 118, 129; in South Korea 165, 166; strategies for 173–7
religious modernism 16, 58, 134, 142, 143
religious organizations 94–5, 107, 151, 160, 195
religious pluralism 106, 108, 154

religious repression 7, 94, 153, 184, 198
religious revival: in Kalmykia 94–7; in Mongolia 120; in Russia 154; in Vietnam 185, 186, 187
"repaying debts" 20, 23, 27
Republican China: conclusion about 62; establishment and upstart 52–4; introduction to 51–2; lay and monastic and 58–60; nationalism and internationalism and 56–8; religion and superstition and 54–6; *see also* post-Mao China
re-traditionalization 109
Return to the True Teachings, The (Paek) 70
Rinzai *roshi* 284, 287
Rinzai temple 77–8, 283
Rinzai Zen Dojo Association 284
ritual actions/specialists 138–40, 142
Russia: Oirats and 92–3; policies towards *sangha* 94; religious revival in 154; *see also* Kalmykia

Sada Kaiseki 33, 35, 37–40, 47
Saibai keizairon (Sada Kaiseki) 39, 49
Saji Jitsunen 25–6
sangha: corruption issues 59–60; introduction to 24; non-celibate Buddhists and 103; Russia's policies towards 94; state of crisis 59
Sarandavaa Bat-Ochir 126, 128
Sarvōdaya movement 215, 216
Scheduled Tribes (ST) 135, 140, 141
secular Buddhism: debt and gratitude concept and 20–1; introduction to 13–17; New Buddhism and 17–20; Watanabe Kaikyoku and 21–4
secularization: description of 153; failure of 151–5; introduction to 54; in Mongolia 127–8; theory 106, 153
self-adjustment capabilities 174–5
selfless love 43–6
sexual scandals 284–6, 289
Shajin Lama 95, 96, 98, 107
Shimaji Mokurai 35–6
Shin Buddhism: conclusion about 237–8; individual choice in a family religion and 231–5; introduction to 225–6; Ōtani-ha Feminist movement and 226–31; reform movements and 235–7
Shinto 45
Sikkim: borderland of Buddhism in 134–6; introduction to 133–4; *see also* Limbu community; Yumaism
social activism 20–3, 26–7, 198

social Darwinism 33, 36, 170
socialist movement 24–5, 40, 42–4, 46–7
South Korean army: chaplaincy and 165–9; chaplains and 169–73; conclusion about 177–9; masculine self-disciplining issues 173–7
Soviet Union 94, 99, 103, 106–8, 154
Sri Lanka, Buddhism in 204–17
State Agency of Religious Affairs (SARA) 157, 159
state religion 8, 93, 152, 158, 165–9
Subba, J. R. 136–43
superstition, religion and 54–6
syncretic religion *see* Yumaism

Taixu (monk) 53, 57–61, 67, 192
Taoism 152, 154, 156, 159
Telo Tulku Rinpoche 91, 95–8, 100–1, 107
temples: business 126–7; Chùa Linh Ứng 186–7; founded by female leaders 123–5; increase in 120–2; Yumaism and 138; Zen-style 78
Temples-Turn-to-Schools movement 151
temple wives: conclusion about 237–8; individual choice in a family religion and 231–5; introduction to 226; Ōtani-ha Feminist movement and 226–31; reform movements and 235–7
tenant farmers 41, 42
Thailand, Bhikkhunīsangha in 247–8
Theravāda Buddhism 206–7, 209–10, 248, 252
Theravāda nuns: Bhikkhunīsangha and 245–8; conclusion about 252; historical background 243–4; monastic law and 249–50; ordination of 244; practices of 248; *Vinaya* norms and 250–2
Thích Nhất Hạnh: historical background 189–93; introduction to 185; monastic code 261, 264–70; return of 193–6
"this-worldly" soteriology 60–1
Tibetan Buddhism: Buddhism in Mongolia and 116; Gelugpa school of 91, 102, 106, 117; introduction to 7, 21; Yumaism and 138–9
traditionalization 243, 248
transportation issues 266–7
true Buddhism 55, 84, 105, 143, 209

Uchiyama Gudō 33, 35, 37, 40–3
Unified Buddhist Church of Vietnam (UBCV) 189–91, 194, 197
Unitarianism 24–5

302 *Index*

United Nations Day of Vesak Celebrations 195–6
upstart institutions 52–4

Vajrapāni oracle 125
vernacular modernity 34–5
Vietnam: conclusion about 196–9; Da Nang city in 185–7; freedom of religion in 183, 185, 190, 193–6, 198; introduction to 183–5; "re-enchanted" society 183, 184, 187–9; Thích Nhất Hạnh and 189–96
Vietnam Buddhist Sangha 190, 196, 198
vinaya adaptation 260, 266, 268, 270
Vinaya norms 250–2
violence, Buddhism and 205, 207–8, 212–15

war, justifications for 211, 215
Warp and Woof Society 17
Watanabe Kaikyoku 21–4, 27
Western astronomy 38
Western Buddhism/Buddhists 16, 36, 99, 124, 246–7
Wise Words of Master Yinguang, The (Yinguang) 53

women, increased involvement of 123–5
Women's Group to Consider Sexual Discrimination in the Ōtani-ha 227
Wŏnjong Sect 68, 69, 70
World Buddhist Householder Grove 54, 55, 57, 58
World Parliament of Religions 214
Writings of Master Yinguang, The (Yinguang) 53

Xi Jinping 155, 157

Yi Hoegwang 68, 71, 72, 74
Yinguang 52, 53, 59, 61
Yoshida Kyūichi 36–7, 50, 242
Yumaism: conclusion about 142–3; influences on 137–9; introduction to 133–4; propagation of 141–2; "scientific" rationale for 139; traditional authority issues 139–40; *see also* Limbu community

Zen Buddhism 72, 187–9, 283, 290, 291
Zen *roshi* 282, 288, 289
Zizek, Slavoj 50

Printed in Great Britain
by Amazon